D0752302

Readings in Cognitive Psychology

Readings in
Cognitive Psychology

Applications, Connections, and
Individual Differences

Bridget Robinson-Riegler

Augsburg College

Gregory Robinson-Riegler

University of St. Thomas

PEARSON

Boston • New York • San Francisco
Mexico City • Montreal • Toronto • London • Madrid • Munich • Paris
Hong Kong • Singapore • Tokyo • Cape Town • Sydney

Executive Editor: *Karon Bowers*
Editorial Assistant: *Carolyn Mulloy*
Marketing Manager: *Taryn Wahlquist*
Editorial Production Service: *Chestnut Hill Enterprises, Inc.*
Manufacturing Buyer: *JoAnne Sweeney*
Cover Administrator: *Kristina Mose-Libon*
Electronic Composition: *Omegatype Typography, Inc.*

For related titles and support materials, visit our online catalog at www.ablongman.com.

Copyright © 2004, Pearson Education, Inc.
All rights reserved. No part of the material protected by this copyright notice may be reproduced or utilized in any form or by any means, electronic or mechanical, including photocopying, recording, or by any information storage and retrieval system, without written permission from the copyright owner.

To obtain permission(s) to use material from this work, please submit a written request to Allyn and Bacon, Permissions Department, 75 Arlington Street, Boston, MA 02116, or fax your request to 617-848-7320.

Between the time website information is gathered and then published, some sites may have closed. Also, the transcription of URLs can result in typographical errors. The publisher would appreciate being notified of any problems with URLs so that they may be corrected in subsequent editions.

Library of Congress Cataloging-in-Publication Data was not available at the time of publication.

ISBN: 0-205-35867-5

Printed in the United States of America

10   9   8   7   6   5   4   3   2   1   08   07   06   05   04   03

Contents

Preface

Students are not as excited about cognitive psychology as they could be. They also aren't as excited about research as they could be. In spite of its obvious relevance to daily life, students often perceive cognition research as an esoteric exercise. Perhaps this is because the emphasis on abstract theory and rigorous research methodology that characterizes cognition research makes the field seem rather abstract, abstruse, obtuse...fill in the adjective.

This perception of cognition research is unfortunate because in reality, cognitive psychology research is (sometimes astonishingly) elegant, interesting, applicable, and obviously relevant. We figured there needed to be a research reader that made this more apparent to students. To this end, we've chosen articles that will pique student interest, while still capturing the rigor, elegance, and importance of cognitive psychology research. Specifically, the articles included in this reader accomplish at least one (usually more) of the following:

- discuss individual differences in cognition
- have an applied emphasis
- address a particularly interesting question, or feature particularly interesting materials or manipulations
- can be related easily to several different facets of cognition (e.g., working memory and reading) rather than just one.
- are intersubdisciplinary (e.g., relating cognitive psychology to social psychology) or interdisciplinary (e.g., relating cognitive psychology to marketing)

The emphasis on applied and unique research reports that lie a bit off the beaten path of cognitive psychology research is certainly not to underestimate the significance or intrigue of the more venerable "classic" topics that continue to drive research in the field. The reports chosen for this volume relate to fundamental topics such as the distinction between top-down and bottom-up processing, divided attention, proactive interference, language learnability, and expertise. Hence, students will get a good deal of exposure to fundamental concepts that have helped define the study of cognition. They will also be exposed to a range of research methods; the studies herein run the methodological gamut from descriptive to experimental. Finally, they will receive exposure to a range of scientific journals in the field; the articles in this reader come from eight different scholarly publications.

We had a second goal in producing the reader. Our own experience in teaching reveals that students are quite challenged in reading primary research sources, to the point that many of them "don't like research." Many of these same students, after being faced with the task of critically analyzing primary research sources, come back to us and express appreciation for the exercise, and give testament as to its value. Therefore, we didn't want this reader to be simply a collection of articles. We wanted to bring the articles alive (or rather, the students alive) by posing critical thinking questions along with each article.

Reader features:

The research articles are grouped into three broad areas that follow the traditional information-processing flow of cognition: Perception and working memory, long-term memory, and higher-level cognitive processing (i.e., language, problem solving, and decision making). Before each article, we present a brief listing of the major **conceptual issues and theoretical questions** addressed by the research. Each article is also accompanied by a **de-jargonizing** section, in which unfamiliar terms and concepts are defined. At the end of each article are three sets of critical thinking questions directed at students, to aid them in their analysis and understanding of the research. The **Introduction: Critical Thinking Questions** focus on the background and motivation for the study in question, and can be answered with a close and critical read of the report's introduction. The **Method: Critical Thinking Questions** require students to get a feel for what happened in the experiment (i.e., what they would have done as participants or experimenters) and also give students practice in identifying important elements of the research design (i.e., identifying variables, levels of independent variables, and control procedures). Finally, the **Results/Discussion: Critical Thinking Questions** require students to consider the major features of the results, and how they fit with (or fail to fit with) the authors' background story and hypotheses.

There are a number of ways this reader might be employed. It's probably most appropriately used for a cognitive research methods course. The articles included address a wide range of conceptual issues and use many research methodologies, both standard and not-so-standard. So an excursion through the articles presented herein would be an excellent introduction to cognitive psychology research. This reader might even be considered for use as a supplement in a general research methods course that emphasizes critical analysis of primary research sources. It might also serve as a supplement for a survey course in cognition. As noted above, we have attempted to include a range of concepts that loosely follow the information-processing sequence that characterizes most cognition texts.

It should be noted that the articles are presented in their entirety, so some of the more involved discussions of methodology and data analysis make for some pretty tough sledding. The critical thinking questions posed attempt to keep students focused on the broader issues and questions addressed by the research, lest they miss the forest for the trees.

Contributors

Elizabeth Allen, Psychology Department, University of California, Santa Cruz, CA

Terry Kit-Fong Au, Department of Psychology, University of California, Los Angeles, CA 90095-1563

Anna Bradley, Department of Psychology, University College London, 26 Bedford Way, London WC1E 6BT

Kathryn A. Braun, Harvard Business School

Michael F. Bunting, University of Illinois, Department of Psychology (M/C 285), 1007 West Harrison Street, Chicago, IL 60607-7137

Maureen A. Callanan, Psychology Department, University of California, Santa Cruz, CA

Penny Chiappe, California State University, Fullerton, CA

A. R. A. Conway, University of Illinois, Department of Psychology, (M/C 285), 1007 West Harrison Street, Chicago, IL 60607-7137

Nelson Cowan, University of Missouri, Columbia, MO

Kevin Crowley, Learning Research Development Center, Room 727, 3939 O'Hara St., Pittsburgh, PA 15260

Mary T. Curren, School of Business Administration and Economics, California State University, Northridge, CA

Rhiannon Ellis, University of Pittsburgh

Julie Foertsch, LEAD Center, 1402 University Ave., University of Wisconsin-Madison, WI 53706

Jean E. Fox Tree, Psychology Department, University of California, Santa Cruz, CA 95063

Adrian Furnham, Department of Psychology, University College London, 26 Belford Way, London WC1E 6BT

Morton Ann Gernsbacher, Department of Psychology, University of Wisconsin-Madison, WI 53706

Katrin R. Harich, School of Business Administration and Economics, California State University, Fullerton

Lynn Hasher, Department of Psychology, University of Toronto

William A. Johnston, University of Utah, Salt Lake City, UT 84112-0215

Sun-Ah Jun, Department of Linguistics, University of California, Los Angeles, CA 90095-1563

Simon Kemp, Psychology Department, University of Canterbury, Christchurch, New Zealand

Leah M. Knightly, Department of Psychology, University of California, Los Angeles, CA 90095-1563

Elizabeth Loftus, University of Washington

Therese A. Louie, School of Business Administration, University of Washington, Seattle, WA

Sara Matteson, Department of Psychiatry, University of Rochester Medical Center, and Rochester Psychiatric Center, Rochester, NY

Matthiew S. McGlone, Department of Psychology, Lafayette College, Easton, PA 18042-1781.

Helga Noice, Elmhurst College, Elmhurst, IL

Janet S. Oh, Department of Psychology, University of California, Los Angeles, CA 90095-1563

Kathy Pezdek, Department of Psychology, Claremont Graduate University, Claremont, CA 91711

Dennis L. Rosen, School of Business, University of Kansas, Lawrence KS 66045

David Rubin, Duke University, Durham, NC

S. R. Schmidt, Psychology Department, Middle Tennessee State University, Murfreesboro, TN 37132

Mercedes Sheen, Psychology Department, University of Canterbury, Christchurch, New Zealand

Linda S. Siegel, University of British Columbia, Vancouver, British Columbia, Canada

Steven M. Silverstein, Department of Psychiatry, Weill Medical College of Cornell University, White Plains, NY

Surendra N. Singh, Associate Professor, School of Business, University of Kansas, Lawrence KS 66045

David Strayer, Department of Psychology, 380 S. 1530 E., Room 502, University of Utah, Salt Lake City, UT 84112-0251

Harriet R. Tenenbaum, Harvard University, Graduate School of Education, Cambridge, MA

Jessica Tofighbakhsh, Department of Psychology, Lafayette College, Easton, Pa 18042-1781

Joe Underwood, Department of Psychology, Claremont Graduate University, Claremont, CA 91711

Suzanne K. Vosburg, New York State Psychiatric Institute, New York, NY

Sharlene D. Walbaum, Box 219, Department of Psychology, Quinnipiac College, Mount Carmel, Hamden, CT 06418

Alan R. Williams, Middle Tennessee State University, Murfreesboro, TN 37132

Readings in Cognitive Psychology

1

Perception, Attention, and Working Memory

An Investigation of Subliminal Embed Effect on Multiple Measures of Advertising Effectiveness

Dennis L. Rosen and Surendra N. Singh

Abstract

The effect of subliminal sex and death embeds on attention to advertising, change in attitude, behavioral intention, and day-after recall of advertising were investigated for two products. Contrary to findings in some previous research, no significant effects were indicated in the current study at any level. A review and comparison to previous research is provided, along with a possible explanation for conflicting research findings in the area.

Conceptual Issues and Theoretical Questions

- Can messages of which we are unaware (more specifically, embedded images) affect consumer attitudes and/or behavior?
- Would more consistent effects of subliminal embeds be revealed with a wider range of measures?
- Would more consistent effects of subliminal embeds be revealed if the embeds related to the Freudian motives of sex and death?

De-Jargonizing

subliminal perception: the purported tendency to be influenced by stimuli presented below the level of conscious awareness

threshold: the level of stimulus energy at which a person would report the presence of a stimulus 50% of the time

Rosen, D. L., & Singh, S. N. (1992). An investigation of the subliminal embed effect on multiple measures of advertising effectiveness. *Psychology and Marketing*, 9, 157–173. Copyright © 1992 John Wiley & Sons, Inc. This material is used by permission of the publisher.

hierarchy-of-effects model: model of advertising effectiveness which proposes that ad processing occurs in a sequence of stages, from ad perception to ad-influenced action

affective responses: the (often automatic) positive or negative reactions we have to people, places, and things

semantic differential: a scale anchored by semantic opposites (e.g., easy–difficult), along which a person makes some sort of rating

covariate: a variable that is thought to change predictably along with another variable

effect size: a measure of the difference between two experimental groups or conditions, in terms of standard deviation units; reliable differences tend to be associated with bigger effect sizes

internal validity: the degree of control imposed within a research investigation

The topic of **subliminal perception** has long represented an emotionally charged area of research with practical and ethical implications. The premise of subliminal perception has been that the unconscious mind can receive information presented below the **threshold** for conscious perception (Dixon, 1971). The result may be attitude and even behavioral change based on information that the individual is not consciously aware of receiving.

Some psychology studies have shown the effects of subliminal perceptions on the affective responses (e.g., Bach & Klein, 1957; Kunst-Wilson & Zajonc, 1980; Zajonc, 1980). However, in the marketing/advertising literature, results have been generally negative, though there have been reports that subliminal presentations can affect subject self-perception of thirst (Hawkins, 1970) and subject rankings of a competitive set of product brands (Cuperfain & Clarke, 1985). (See Moore, 1982, for a comprehensive review.)

Subliminal Embeds

Most studies cited above have used subliminal presentations below the threshold for perception generally through the flashing of material on a screen. Over the years, however, the definition of a subliminal presentation has expanded to include the hiding of pictures and/or words within other visual material (e.g., Bagley & Dunlap, 1979; Kelly, 1979). These subliminal embeds are usually clearly visible once pointed out, but otherwise remain unnoticed by those who view the presented material. Again it is assumed that attitude and behavior are affected via nonconscious perception of the material.

The writings of Key on subliminal perception (1973, 1976, 1980) have emphasized the supposed use of embeds in advertising. His allegations, though devoid of scientific evidence, have done much to stir the public's imagination and tendency to believe that embeds are being used at least sometimes in advertising (Zanot et al., 1983). The public's concern has reached the point that several states have considered laws to control the supposed use of embeds in advertising (Psarras, 1986). Academic research on embed effects has produced mixed findings. A weakness of much of this research has been the use of only one or two effectiveness measures (e.g., attitude change, change in behavioral intent) and the limited embed variations involved (i.e., use of only one form of embedded word or picture).

The purpose of this study is to demonstrate the effects, or lack thereof, for sex- and death-related embed material on print advertising effectiveness as measured at four different levels of advertising effectiveness. The effectiveness levels will follow the **hierarchy-of-effects model,** the most dominant model of advertising effectiveness to date (Barry, 1987). First we will review some theory underlying the supposed effects of embeds and the results of previous research.

Theory and Practice

Types of Subliminal Presentation

It might be helpful to think of information presentation taking place at several levels of consumer awareness. At the uppermost level would be information presentation of which the consumer has full conscious awareness. The material is not hidden and, assuming the consumer is paying attention, she or he should be able to remember and state the nature of the information.

At the opposite end would be subliminal information for which the consumer is assumed to have no conscious awareness. The common way of presenting this subliminal information is by flashing it on a screen so quickly that it cannot be consciously noticed (as it is below the sensory perception threshold), or through the incorporation of low-volume presentations masked by music or sounds. Note that these presentation methods preclude individuals from consciously being aware of the information even if they want to because it is actually below the threshold for conscious perception.

Embeds, of course, fall into this no-awareness category, but with an important difference. Embeds are actually consciously perceivable if pointed out to those observing the presentation. Their subliminal aspect comes not from presentation below the threshold for possible perception but rather from the fact that they are not recognized at the conscious level for what they are. They are presented visually and are often interpreted by viewers as part of a shadow, reflection, or other image common to the pictorial presentation.

In this sense, embeds are part of the background or setting in an ad with one important difference. Other background information is clearly discernable to any attentive viewer, and embeds are deliberately hidden such that they can be spotted only when pointed out.

Theoretical Support

Low-Involvement Information Processing.
Theoretical support for embed effects is offered by the theory of low-involvement information processing. The theory of low-involvement processing is recognized as having had significant effect on theoretical development and research in advertising and consumer behavior (Engel, Blackwell, & Miniard, 1986). Low-involvement processing, as stated by Krugman (1965), involves the consumer's passive acquisition of information. It is implied in this process that the consumer may not be consciously aware of all material presented. Yet, ultimately, the effect on behavior is expected. Krugman (1977) refers to the process as involving consumer use of "...peripheral seeing—i.e., seeing without 'looking at' and without being aware that seeing has occurred" (p. 10).

Although this acquisition of information usually occurs without the individual being consciously aware of it (hence, a lack of recall of the information), the information nonetheless may have an impact on his or her attitudes and purchase behavior. Although it may, on the face of it, seem implausible that people's attitudes and behaviors could be affected by the unconscious acquisition of information, there is evidence showing that under certain conditions, attitudes may be formed even before one becomes consciously aware of the stimulus object.

Zajonc and his associates have shown that the "overt **affective responses** may be unrelated to prior cognitive outcomes which result from stimulus exposure" (Wilson & Zajonc, 1980, p. 557). For example, subjects reveal clear preferences for exposed stimuli over novel stimuli even though in recognition tests they could not discriminate between exposed stimuli and novel stimuli. (See Wilson, 1979; Zajonc, 1980, and studies cited therein.) Embed effects may operate in a similar fashion.

Sex and Death Motives.   Frequently, the embed material claimed by popular writers to be present in advertising is either of a sexual nature or refers to death. The supposed emphasis on such material comes from Freudian theory. Freud emphasized the individual's repressed sexual desires as well as the subconscious death wish as important aspects of human personality and motivation. Sex and death presentations would supposedly appeal subconsciously to the id, that aspect of the personality that strives for gratification and is the reservoir of life and death instincts (Hall & Lindzey, 1957).

The importance of the sexual symbolism of some products for marketing and advertising has also been noted by motivational theorists like Ernest Dichter. His *Handbook of Consumer Motivations* (Dichter, 1964) provides sexually related explanations for motivation toward use and behavior related to such common items as asparagus, rice, and women's gloves. Thus, through the use of embeds, the advertiser could supposedly address at a low-awareness level a motivation for purchase that could not be addressed (or not as directly addressed) at a high-awareness level.

The emphasis on sexual symbolism and deep-seated motivations for the use of common products has lost favor over the years. However, there is no denying the importance of sex in advertising. Despite its application across a wide variety of products, the association between sex and use of some products would appear to be much stronger than for others. For example, a stronger association would be expected between sex and cologne than between sex and soft drinks. Thus, even without deep subconscious references to sex, embed presentations that refer to sex may be able to enhance the thought processes already associated with some products.

The motivating nature of an embedded death symbol may seem obscure. Whether or not we actually do possess some subconscious death wish as Freud suggested, it is clear that we are intrigued by death and danger (if only striving to avoid them) and that they are more strongly associated with some products than others. This suggests that death-related embeds might be able to produce some attitudinal response, perhaps positive, perhaps negative.

Of course, writers like Key contend that the effect on sales of such sex or death embed presentations is positive. However, if such presentations are able to have an effect in the first place, it would appear intuitively likely that effect on attitude or behavior could also be negative (i.e., such presentations might provide negative connotations to the subconscious). Thus, the initial question to address is whether any effects, positive or negative, can be had through embeds.

Research on Embeds

The distinct nature of the embed presentation suggests that research on its effects is needed separate from research on the effects of other presentation methods. Although interest in the area of embeds has increased, research efforts have still been limited and results mixed. Bagley and Dunlap (1979) asked subjects to describe their feelings after viewing a set of print ads. Those exposed to ads with sexually oriented embeds used words to describe their feelings that were classified as more "turned on" than did those in the control group for two of the four products involved. Unfortunately, the question of relevance for the dependent measure as well and its unclear definition leaves one with findings that are difficult to interpret.

Kelly (1979) found no significant difference in unaided recall of brand name or illustrations between subjects exposed to embed ads versus nonembed ads. However, Kelly's experimental group saw actual product advertisements that had been previously defined by Key as possessing embeds, and the control ads were other real advertisements chosen because of their similarity to the embed ads in terms of product type and creative elements. Because Key has never provided any proof of his assertion of embed presence in advertising, one can not know if Kelly's negative findings were due to the lack of embed effects or the lack of any embeds in the test advertising.

Some positive effects were found by Kilbourne, Painton, and Ridley (1985). The researchers also started with actual print ads, this time for liquor and cigarettes, which they and a group of colleagues and students identified as containing sex embeds. Nonembed versions of these same ads were then professionally developed. Subjects exposed to the embed or nonembed versions of both ads completed attitude and behavioral intention scales. A significant interaction was found with more positive ratings only occurring for the embed ad for liquor. Analysis of galvanic skin response on a separately run and smaller sample found a marginally significant effect for embeds but no interaction with product. Again, one can question whether embeds were actually present in the test ads. And it is possible that through removal of the assumed embeds in the control ads, the authors inadvertently changed the visible portions of the ad in some manner that could have made them less appealing.

Caccavale, Wanty, and Edell (1981) improved on the process by exposing test subjects to specially made sex-embed print advertising and comparing attitude-toward-the-ad measures and behavioral-intention measures for these subjects to those for a control group. The test was conducted for five snack foods. Results were mixed. with some support for embed effect on both measures.

More recently, Gable, Wilkens, Harris, and Feinberg (1987) made their own embed and nonembed versions of ad illustrations for four products. Subjects presented with paired (unlabeled embed and nonembed) versions were asked to indicate the photo of the pair they preferred for each of four products involved. Significant differences were found for three of the products, with the nonembed version preferred for the food and beer photos and the embed version preferred for the pen photo. Given the negative results for two products, the authors concluded that embeds do not have an effect and that the only positive result was due to chance. Their conclusion ignores the possibility that embeds might produce negative effects in some cases or that the effects may be a function of the type of embed used and type of product involved. Further, a measure of preference for the picture may not be directly related to other measures of effect on purchase behavior or attitude toward the product advertised.

Issues in Research

Measurement of Effects.   A major concern when researching the area of embed effect is selection of the appropriate dependent measures. Advertisers commonly use one or more of a variety of techniques to determine the effectiveness of an advertisement. These techniques are based on the ability of the ad to attract and hold attention; its ability to change attitudes toward the product, the person using the product, and the ad itself; the ability of the consumer to remember the ad or product 24 hours later (known as DAR or day-after recall); and the impact of the ad on behavioral intention (Klein & Tainiter, 1983; Leckenby & Plummer, 1983).

Although change in behavior may be the ultimate goal, it is generally recognized that such change is unlikely to occur from the single exposure that is often involved in ad testing (Sissors, 1983). Logically, however, a lower-level change (such as the ability to hold attention) during a single exposure may signal the ability of the presentation to facilitate behavioral change over the multiple exposures that will occur in the ad campaign. Past studies of embed effects have tended to be limited in the number of measures used. Lack of support for embed effects in studies such as Kelly (1979) and Gable et al. (1987) may have, therefore, resulted from lack of measurement for lower-level effects.

Given the debate in the advertising profession concerning the appropriateness of the various measures and the subtle effects that embeds are likely to have, it seems very important that measures at several levels of potential effects be taken. The lack of significant findings in some studies or for some products may reflect this lack of measurement at multiple levels of potential effects.

The Stimuli.   Further, any research in the area must address problems with selection of the embed stimulus. As noted earlier, the embeds supposedly used by advertisers are frequently related to sex and death. Thus obscene words, pictures of naked figures, skulls, or other allusions to death might be appropriate stimuli. The appropriateness of these stimuli may vary, however. The word *sex,* for example, might be considered much more appropriate and positive than pictures of parts of the body which might, in fact, produce a negative reaction. However, research at this point has only dealt with the effects of sexual embeds (at least in those studies that describe the nature of the embeds used). And here, studies have employed mainly words (Caccavale et al., 1981) or pictures (Kilbourne et al., 1985), but have not simultaneously studied the effects of both forms of presentation. Because there are differences in the manner in which words and pictures are represented in memory (Kosslyn & Shwartz, 1977; Nelson, Reed, & Walling, 1976), it is possible that the effects of each type of embed presentation may differ.

If embed material does impact on advertising effectiveness, it seems logical that the effects may differ not only by product, which has been a major area of research emphasis, but also by type of embed. An interaction between product and embed type may also exist. For example, the embedded word "sex" might produce positive effects in an ad for cologne and no effects in an ad for liquor. Differences in embed effects by type, and the interaction of type of embed with product category have thus far not been studied. Caccavale et al. (1981) point out the need for such research in their discussion of the area.

Research Objective and Hypotheses

Although Key asserts that embeds help to sell products, the purpose here was to determine if embeds can have any effect, positive or negative, as measured at the various levels of advertising effectiveness. Further, since Key's emphasis, and the public's fascination, has been with sex and death embeds, their impact was specifically addressed. The study was also designed to investigate the manner in which any effects vary across product categories and types of embed used. Based on the above discussion, the following hypotheses were derived for testing:

H1: The inclusion of embed material, either words or pictures, referring to sex or death in print advertising will have significant impact on one or more measures of the advertisement's effectiveness.

H2: The impact of sex or death embed material on print advertising effectiveness will vary by the type of embed and type of product.

More specifically:

H2a: Sex-related embeds will produce more positive effects for cologne advertising than will death-related embeds.

H2b: Death-related embeds will produce more positive effects for liquor advertising than will sex-related embeds.

Method

Stimuli

Stimuli were developed representing three embed types: sex (the word *sex*), body (naked figure of a woman and phallic symbols, no words present), and death (a combination of the word *death* with pictures of skulls) as well as a control (no embeds) presentation. Thus the embed stimuli provided the sex and death emphasis most commonly referred to by Key as well as a picture/word presentation comparison. The materials were professionally embedded in black-and-white print ads for two products, liquor and cologne. Liquor has been frequently cited in the writings of Key as using embeds and has also been used in previous research in the area. Cologne represented a product whose romance association would more closely relate it to some of the embed stimuli. Due to differences in packaging between the two product categories and the need to hide the embed material, stimuli for the three embed-type conditions could not be identical between the product categories.

Actual print ads for lesser-known brand name products were used in constructing the stimuli. The stimuli consisted of the treatment ads (involving embeds or control) for each product category and three "filler" ads involving no embeds which were used to help disguise the purpose of the study. Pretesting indicated students were generally unfamiliar with the brand names used (though the name of one familiar brand of liquor used as a filler ad was replaced with a fictitious name). The treatment ads each presented only the container of product on a gray background with limited copy. The ads were adjusted through cropping so the containers were presented at approximately the same size and position in each ad. The filler ads also tended to emphasize the container of product with nondescript backgrounds. Pretesting was conducted with approximately 70 students similar to the respondents to insure that the embeds in the test ads were not noticeable when first presented via slide projector but were clearly visible when pointed out to these same subjects, thus meeting the definition of embeds.

Experimental Design and Procedure

Given that the embed material could not be identical between product conditions, the experimental design developed as a set of one-way ANOVAs. Four treatment levels were involved: sex, death, body, and control. One-way ANOVAs were conducted for each of the advertising effectiveness measures (described below) across treatment levels separately for each product category. Subjects were 150 college students (juniors and seniors, both males and females). Subjects were randomly assigned to one of the two product conditions (exposure to either liquor or cologne print ads) and one of the four treatments (exposure to a test ad containing either sex, death, or body embeds, or no embeds). Thus each subject was exposed to one kind of embed (except for no-embed control groups) for one product category. This was done under the guise of an advertising analysis study which, subjects were told, was "concerned with the effectiveness of various types of advertising."

Subjects, appearing individually for the study, were seated in front of a screen on which slides of the four products in the category were presented one at a time. Subjects were told to look at the first ad for as long as they desired and then to say "ok." At this signal, the assistant removed the ad from the screen and presented a set of questions to answer. The procedure was then repeated for the three remaining filler ads in the product category. To prevent the subjects from becoming overly analytical due to familiarity with the dependent measures, the treatment ad was shown first in each condition, followed by the three nontreatment filler ads.

Dependent Measures

Measures were developed for each of four levels of advertising effectiveness: attention to the ad, attitude (toward the ad, brand, and purchaser), behavioral intention change, and 24-hour recall. Before the slide presentation, subjects were asked to assume they were making a purchase in the category and to allocate 10 points (constant sum) among the competitive set of brands listed in alphabetical order indicating the likelihood that they would purchase the brands for themselves or a friend. This represented a premeasure for effect of presentation on behavioral intention. The amount of time the subject spent viewing the test ad was recorded by the experimenter without subject awareness as a measure of attention attraction.

Following slide presentation exposure to each individual ad, subjects first completed a questionnaire that asked them to write down any thoughts they had while viewing the ad. These statements were later checked to see if subjects made reference to the embeds indicating that they were, in fact, visible. Subjects then completed measures of attitude toward the ad, the brand of product, and the person who uses the brand. All scales were in **semantic-differential format**. The bipolar adjectives used for attitude toward person included items related to both sex (e.g., sexy-repulsive, attractive-ugly) and death (e.g., fearless-fearful, brave-timid). The brand scales were different for each product category, reflecting attributes of the product involved. Attitude scores for each scale were the sum of ratings on each scale item. Scale items are shown in Table 1.1. Items with an asterisk were later removed from analysis as subsequently explained.

Following the viewing of all four slides, subjects were again asked to assume they were in a purchase situation and to indicate likelihood of purchase for the brands through a

TABLE 1   *Scale Items*

Attitude toward the Ad		Attitude toward the Person
Interesting/Dull	Sexy/Repulsive	Good/Bad
Arousing/Unarousing	Fearless/Fearful	Happy/Unhappy
Pleasing/Annoying	Aroused/Unaroused	Successful/Unsuccessful*
Believable/Not Believable	Influential/Influenced*	Daring/Cowardly
Convincing/Unconvincing	Brave/Timid	Sensual/Frigid
Good/Bad	Attractive/Ugly	Hopeful/Despairing*
Informative/Uninformative	Controlling/Controlled	Excited/Calm
I Liked It/I Disliked it	Frenzied/Sluggish*	In Control/Cared For

Attitude toward the Brand	
Cologne	*Liquor*
Sweet Smelling/Harsh Smelling	Smooth/Harsh
Unromantic/Romantic	Strong Tasting/Weak Tasting
Inexpensive/Expensive	Refreshing/Oppressive
Masculine/Feminine*	Expensive/Inexpensive
Lower Class/Upper Class	Good Tasting/Bad Tasting
Fashionable/Everyday	Relaxing/Agitating
Young/Old	High Quality/Low Quality
Good Smelling/Bad Smelling	Impressive/Unimpressive
Restrained/Daring	Good Value/Poor Value
Sexy/Sexless	Good for Me/Bad For Me
Good For Me/Bad For Me	High Alcohol/Low Alcohol

*Scale items later dropped from analysis.

10-point, constant sum allocation among the competitive set listed in alphabetical order. This postmeasure, with the premeasure used as a **covariate,** provided an indication of ad effect on behavioral intention. Subjects then completed a questionnaire in which they stated what they believed the purpose of the study to be and any difficulties experienced in instructions or scale completion. Finally, subjects were informed that they had to appear the next day for debriefing. An appointment was set for approximately 24 hours later. At that time, a day-after recall measure was administered which asked subjects to provide the name and/or description of each of the ads they had seen. Subjects then received additional information on the purpose of the study and were informed of the importance of not discussing the study with other students.

Analysis and Results

Cognitive response statements were reviewed to determine any subject awareness of embed material. Data for six subjects were removed from analysis based on possible indication of embed awareness. Data for four more subjects were dropped because of problems with instructions as indicated in their questionnaires. All subjects indicated that they believed the ad-testing story presented as the purpose of the study. Reliability analysis was performed on each of the four scale measures using coefficient alpha for the remaining subjects. Reliabilities were 0.89 for attitude toward ad, 0.83 for product attitude (liquor), and 0.89 for product attitude (cologne) with one of the original scale items removed due to a negative item-total correlation.

As noted previously, the attitude-toward-person scale included items related to both sex and death. As a check of the scale's ability to measure these components, the 16 items of the scale were subjected to a principal components analysis with varimax rotation. Three significant factors emerged. These factors, interpreted as "boldness" (Factor 1), "attractiveness" (Factor 2), and "arousal" (Factor 3) are shown on Table 1.2. Four adjective items (influential, successful, frenzied, and hopeful) were judged to not as clearly load on a factor and, therefore, were not used in formation of the attitude-toward-person composite score (a simple sum of item ratings). The 12 items used in the composite score had a coefficient alpha of 0.89 indicating high reliability. Reliabilities for the individual subscales were 0.87, 0.79, and 0.75, respectively.

Test of Hypotheses

The hypotheses were tested through the use of a series of one-way ANOVAs for each of the dependent measures, except recall, for each product category. Recall was measured as a categorical variable and was therefore analyzed through the use of chi-square tests. Table 1.3 shows the cell means and cell sizes for the various treatment conditions. Table 1.4 presents results for each of the dependent measures tested through one-way ANOVAs including overall attitudes toward the user and the measure's component subscales. As indicated in the table, none of the results were significant at the 0.05 level.

Part of the reason for the lack of significant findings may be the small **effect sizes** involved. We calculated the effect sizes from the data published in a number of embed

TABLE 2 *Factor Loading for Attitude-Toward-Person Scale Items[a]*

Scale Items	Factor 1	Factor 2	Factor 3
Brave/Timid	0.80	—	—
Fearless/Fearful	0.76	—	—
Daring/Cowardly	0.75	—	0.37
Controlling/Controlled	0.74	0.44	—
In Control/Cared For	0.71	0.47	—
Good/Bad	—	0.78	—
Sexy/Repulsive	—	0.74	—
Successful/Unsuccessful	0.54	0.68	—
Attractive/Ugly	0.39	0.66	—
Influential/Influenced	0.53	0.58	—
Hopeful/Despairing	—	0.57	0.41
Happy/Unhappy	—	0.51	—
Excited/Calm	—	—	0.79
Aroused/Unaroused	—	—	0.75
Sensual/Frigid	—	0.42	0.61
Frenzied/Sluggish	—	0.40	0.53

[a]Only factor loading of 0.35 or above are shown.

studies. The effect-size estimates ranged from 0.0 for one condition in a study by Caccavale et al. (1981) to 0.18 for one condition in a study by Kelly (1979). In our study, the power of the F test to detect such a small effect size varied from 0.08 to 0.09. Hence, the a priori probability of the F test rejecting the null hypothesis is rather low—about 9% under the given circumstances.

The only measure to approach significance was time watching ad for liquor. The longest time was indicated under the "body" condition, and the shortest time was indicated under the "death" condition. This finding is the opposite condition effect hypothesized for liquor. None of the embed effects were significantly different from the control group. Nor was this measure found to even approach significance for cologne. Thus, our results did not indicate a significant effect for embeds on any of these measures.

To test results on recall, subjects' responses were classified as indicating no recall, recall of brand or ad, and recall of both brand and ad. Given the categorical nature of the data, we prepared a contingency table as shown in Table 1.5. The small cell sizes involved (some subjects did not return for the recall measure) required collapsing of the table. Because most subjects indicated some recall, those subjects indicating no recall were combined with those indicating recall of only the ad *or* brand and compared to those indicating recall of *both* ad and brand. Differences were not found to be significant across embed condition. Nor were results significant when the three embed conditions were combined and tested versus the control.

TABLE 3   *Means and Cell Sizes by Condition**

Cologne				
Dependent Variable	*Condition*			
	Body	Death	Sex	Control
Time Watching	19.45	35.41	22.27	30.39
	(13)	(17)	(21)	(17)
Attitude toward Ad	27.15	23.95	28.96	25.21
	(13)	(19)	(24)	(19)
Attitude toward Brand	37.23	32.63	37.92	34.79
	(13)	(19)	(24)	(19)
Attitude toward User	53.00	48.00	54.24	47.47
	(13)	(17)	(21)	(17)
Bold Component	22.85	21.16	23.25	19.58
	(13)	(19)	(24)	(19)
Attractive Component	16.69	15.58	17.54	15.16
	(13)	(19)	(24)	(19)
Arousal Component	13.46	12.79	13.25	12.21
	(13)	(17)	(21)	(17)
Preference Allocation	.92	3.37	2.08	1.47
	(13)	(19)	(24)	(19)
Liquor				
	Body	Death	Sex	Control
Time Watching	32.86	14.58	18.56	20.18
	(18)	(17)	(13)	(17)
Attitude toward Ad	34.00	36.64	31.91	36.56
	(16)	(11)	(11)	(16)
Attitude toward Brand	52.39	54.82	51.69	54.47
	(18)	(17)	(13)	(17)
Attitude toward User	57.94	54.09	55.27	57.63
	(16)	(11)	(11)	(16)
Bold Component	26.89	23.88	24.69	25.82
	(18)	(17)	(13)	(17)
Attractive Component	18.44	17.35	17.92	18.35
	(18)	(17)	(13)	(17)
Arousal Component	13.06	12.82	13.38	13.47
	(18)	(17)	(13)	(17)
Preference Allocation	2.53	2.24	2.23	1.94
	(17)	(17)	(13)	(17)

[a]Cell sizes are in parentheses.

TABLE 4 *One-Way Analysis of Variance for each Dependent Measure by Product[a]*

Dependent Variable	Effect Mean Square (Residual Mean Square)	DF	F	Probability[b]
Cologne				
Time Watching	870.06 (840.10)	3 (64)	1.04	0.38
Attitude toward Ad	101.86 (55.70)	3 (71	1.83	0.15
Attitude Brand	114.32 (120.36)	3 (71)	0.95	0.42
Attitude toward User	210.90 (113.47)	3 (64)	1.86	0.15
Bold Component	55.26 (25.51)	3 (71)	2.17	0.10
Attractive Component	24.55 (14.84)	3 (71)	1.65	0.19
Arousal Component	5.43 (13.94)	3 (71)	0.39	0.76
Preference Allocation				
Covariate (premeasure)	1.94	1	0.15	0.70
Main Effect	20.01 (12.94)	3 (70)	1.55	0.21
Liquor				
Time Watching	1088.71 (448.32)	3 (61)	2.43	0.07
Attitude toward Ad	62.96 (67.99)	3 (50)	0.30	0.83
Attitude Brand	36.73 (87.41)	3 (61)	0.42	0.74
Attitude toward User	44.57 (77.88)	3 (50)	0.57	0.64
Bold Component	29.53 (19.46)	3 (61)	1.52	0.22
Attractive Component	4.27 (11.82)	3 (61)	0.36	0.78
Active Component	1.41 (7.06)	3 (61)	0.21	0.89
Preference Allocation				
Covariate (premeasure)	13.96	1	6.81	0.01
Main Effect	2.18 (2.05)	3 (59)	1.07	0.37

[a]$V = 75$ for cologne and 65 for liquor.
[b]Power of the F test was 0.09 in all cases except for the attitude.

TABLE 5   *Contingency Table for Recall by Embed Condition and Product Category*

| | Cologne | | | | | |
| | Embed Condition | | | | Row | |
Recall	Body	Death	Sex	Control	Total	Precent
None	1	4	2	2	9	13.2
Ad or Brand Only	4	5	6	3	18	26.5
Both Ad and Brand	8	8	13	12	41	60.3
Column Total	13	17	21	17		
Percent	19.1	25.0	30.9	25.0		
	Liquor					
None	3	2	2	4	11	20.4
Ad or Brand Only	7	7	4	4	22	40.7
Both Ad and Brand	6	2	5	8	21	38.9
Column Total	16	11	11	16		
Percent	29.6	20.4	20.4	29.6		

Discussion

Our findings indicated no statistically significant effects for embeds at any level of advertising effectiveness that we measured. Naturally, there are limitations to our study, such as the single exposure involved, the lack of a realistic advertising presentation environment, and the limited product categories covered. These limitations reflect the practical limitations of laboratory research and the need to maintain **internal validity** of the findings. Within these limitations, however, our study does show that simply embedding sex- or death-related words or pictures in advertising is not likely to create the substantial positive attitude and behavior change professed by Key (or a negative effect, for that matter).

Critics might contend that negative findings were to be expected all along and that our results support the obvious (Saegert, 1987). Such a view, however, ignores notable theoretical support for the possible existence of embed effects as discussed previously, as well as a number of positive findings reported in previous studies. Further, the broader topic of subliminal presentation receives continued study by psychologists and is an area of considerable debate (Holender, 1986). Thus, contained research in the area is justified.

One interpretation of our findings would be that embeds do not work. However, we feel that such an interpretation would be premature. In fact, as noted in our detailed review of the area, studies taken as a whole have produced a mixture of conflicting results. Assuming that this mix of findings is not due to errors in experimental design, the results may indicate that the effectiveness of an embed is much more dependent on the kind of embed used and the product involved than is generally recognized. Perhaps if additional embed types and/or product categories had been employed in our study, positive (or negative) effects might have been noted. Other researchers may have found embed effects in past studies as a function of accidentally producing a better match between the embed type (e.g., sex, death, ad pitch), form (e.g., words, pictures), and even representation (e.g., particular word and/or graphic presentation) involved and the product or message that the ad was trying to communicate.

The question then becomes which embeds to use with which product categories. Unfortunately, Freudian theory does not suggest what pairings of embeds and products should produce results. For example, it could be argued that both sex and death embeds could have a positive effect on sales of a variety of products like cigarettes. The use of a Freudian-based analysis method like free association or projective techniques like word association might help develop pairings of embeds and products for testing of embed effects.

However, a logical test of embed effects in future research may be to simply ignore sex and death embeds and concentrate on those words, symbols, and pictures that have been shown to be of value at the conscious level. For example, would the embedded presentation of a well-known corporate symbol, advertising character, or advertising slogan produce more positive attitude change when viewing editorial material or even an ad for the product? If results from past studies are any indication, the effects of such elements are going to be rather small. Hence, future researchers should use repeated exposures to the stimuli and relatively large sample sizes to detect these effects.

If future research suggests an interaction between embeds and product type, this would imply that processing of information is more sophisticated at the subconscious level than is generally recognized by researchers. If this is true, it would have significant implications for advertisers in their implementation of subtleties in creative execution. In fact, it is perhaps time for researchers to move up a step from researching the effects of "hidden words or pictures" to researching the effects of less hidden but still "unnoticed" elements of advertising. Does placement, expression, dress, etc., of extras, positioning of props, and other elements have as much potential effect in advertising as the attention paid by advertisers might suggest? Research in this area could prove helpful in providing further insights.

References

Bach, S., & Klein, G. S. (1957). Conscious effect of prolonged subliminal exposures of words. *American Psychologist, 12,* 397.

Bagley, G. S., & Dunlap, B. J. (1979). Subliminally embedded ads: A "turn on?" In *Proceedings of the Southern Marketing Association.*

Barry, T. E. (1987). The development of the hierarchy of effects: An historical perspective. *Current Issues & Research in Advertising, 2,* 251–295.

Caccavale, J. G., Wanty, T. C. III, & Edell, J. A. (1981). Subliminal implants in advertisements: An experiment. In *Advances in consumer research* (Vol. 9, pp. 418–423). Association for Consumer Research.

Cuperfain, R., & Clarke, T. K. (1985). A new perspective of subliminal perception. *Journal of Advertising, 14,* 36–41.

Dichter, E. (1964). *Handbook of consumer motivations.* New York: McGraw-Hill.

Dixon, N. F. (1971). *Subliminal perception: The nature of a controversy.* London: McGraw-Hill.

Engel, J. F., Blackwell, R. D., & Miniard, P. W. (1986). *Consumer behavior* (5th ed.). Chicago: The Dryden Press.

Gable, M., Wilkens, H. T., Harris, L., & Feinberg, R. (1987). An evaluation of subliminally embedded sexual stimuli in graphics. *Journal of Advertising, 16*, 26–31.

Hall, C. S., & Lindrey, G. (1957). *Theories of personality.* New York: Wiley.

Hawkins, D. (1970). The effects of subliminal stimulation on drive level and brand preference. *Journal of Marketing Research, 8*, 322–326.

Holender, D. (1986). Semantic activation without conscious identification in dichotic listening, parafoveal vision, and visual masking: A survey and appraisal. *The Behavioral and Brain Sciences, 9*, 1–64.

Kelly, J. S. (19791. Subliminal embeds in print advertising: A challenge to advertising ethics. *Journal of Advertising, 8*, 20–24.

Key, W. B. (1973). *Subliminal seduction,* Englewood Cliffs, NJ: Signet.

Key, W. B. (1976). *Media sexploitation.* Englewood Cliffs, NJ: Prentice-Hall.

Key, W. B. (1980). *The clamplate orgy.* Englewood Cliffs, NJ: Prentice-Hall.

Kilbourne, W. E., Painton, S., & Ridley, D. (1985). The effect of sexual embedding on responses to magazine advertisements. *Journal of Advertising, 14*, 48–55.

Klein, P. R., & Tainiter, M. (1983). Copy research validation: The advertiser's perspective. *Journal of Advertising Research, 23*, 9–18.

Kosslyn, S. M., & Shwartz, S. P. (1977). A simulation of visual imagery. *Cognitive Science, 1*, 265–295.

Krugman, H. E. (1965). The impact of television advertising: Learning without involvement. *Public Opinion Quarterly, 29*, 349–356.

Krugman, H. E. (1977). Memory without recall, exposure without perception. *Journal of Advertising Research, 17*, 7–12.

Kunst-Wilson, W., & Zajonc, R. (1980). Affective discrimination of stimuli that cannot be recognized. *Science, 207*(1), 557–558.

Leckenby, J. D., & Plummer, J. T. (1983). Advertising stimulus measurement and assessment research: A review of advertising testing methods. *Current Issues & Research in Advertising, 2*, 135–165.

Moore, T. E. (1982). Subliminal advertising: What you see is what you get. *Journal of Marketing, 46*, 38–47.

Nelson, D. L., Reed, V. S., & Walling, J. R. (1976). Pictorial superiority effect. *Journal of Experimental Psychology: Human Learning and Memory, 2*, 523–528.

Psarras, C. (1986). Before you rush into the article, relax and enjoy the nice headline. *The Wall Street Journal,* Sec 2.

Saegert, J. (1987). Why marketing should quit giving subliminal advertising the benefit of the doubt. *Psychology and Marketing, 4*, 107–120.

Sissors, J. Z. (1983), Confusions about effective frequency. *Journal of Advertising Research, 22*, 33–37.

Wilson, W. R. (1979). Feeling more than we can know: Exposure effects without learning. *Journal of Personality and Social Psychology, 37*, 811–821.

Wilson, W. R., & Zajonc, R. B. (1980). Affective discrimination of stimuli that cannot be recognized. *Science, 207* (1), 557–558.

Zajonc, R. B. (1980). Feeling and thinking: preferences need no inferences. *American Psychologist, 35*(2), 151–175.

Zanot, E. J., Pincus, J. D., & Lamp, E. J. (1983). Public perceptions of subliminal advertising. *Journal of Advertising, 12*, 39–45.

Introduction: Critical Thinking Questions _____

? Do subliminal embeds involve a complete lack of awareness? Explain. In spite of this, in what sense might embeds still be considered "subliminal"?

? What is low-involvement information processing, and how do the authors think its effects might be revealed?

? Explain the logic behind the predictions of (a) sex-related embeds having greater facilitatory effects on cologne advertising than death embeds and (b) death-related embeds having greater facilitatory effects on liquor advertising than sex-related embeds.

? Identify the problems that have made previous research on embeds difficult to interpret. How does the present study attempt to remedy the problem?

? Describe the authors' hypotheses.

Method: Critical Thinking Questions _____

? Describe what you would have been asked to do, had you been a participant in this experiment.

? Name the independent variables in the experiment, and their levels. Describe how each of these variables was operationalized. For each variable, state whether it was manipulated in a between-subjects or within-subjects fashion. How many conditions were there in the experiment?

? What was (were) the dependent variable(s) in the experiment?

? What aspects of the methodology were implemented to deal with possible confounds?

Results/Discussion: Critical Thinking Questions _____

? Did any of the measures of advertising effectiveness yield positive effects of subliminal embeds? Were there any evident trends or hints of possible effects?

? Where do the authors stand on the question of possible effectiveness/ineffectiveness of subliminal embeds? Should embeds be used?

? After reading this study, you may feel there are other issues or questions that would be worthwhile or intriguing to address. Pose one of these questions (other than those suggested by the authors) that could be investigated empirically.

Reduced Top-Down Influence in Auditory Perceptual Organization in Schizophrenia

Steven M. Silverstein, Sara Matteson, and Raymond A. Knight

Abstract

Perceptual organization of auditory information is influenced by both the physical characteristics and the categorization of irrelevant information. This study sought to determine the degree to which schizophrenia patients could utilize acoustic properties and contextual cues (top-down factors) to segregate relevant from irrelevant material in an auditory stream. On a modification of I. Neath, A. M. Surprenant, and R. G. Crowder's (1993) auditory suffix task, both schizophrenia and control participants demonstrated better recall of relevant information when irrelevant information had different physical characteristics, compared with when both arose from the same source. In contrast, schizophrenia patients were unaffected by a contextual manipulation that allowed controls to reduce the interfering effect of an irrelevant stimulus. These data suggest that a reduced ability to utilize contextual information plays a role in the perceptual organization dysfunction in schizophrenia.

Conceptual Issues and Theoretical Questions

- What factors underlie schizophrenics' poor performance on tasks requiring perceptual organization?
- To what degree does the schizophrenics' deficit in perceptual organization reflect bottom-up factors (e.g., processing of perceptual "data")?

Silverstein, S. M., Matteson, S., and Knight, R. A. (1996). Reduced top-down influence in auditory perceptual organization in schizophrenia. *Journal of Abnormal Psychology, 105,* 663–667. Copyright © 1996 by the American Psychological Association. Reprinted with permission.

- To what degree does the schizophrenics' deficit in perceptual organization reflect top-down factors (e.g., expectations or contextual information)?

De-Jargonizing

gestalt laws: proposed by the Gestalt psychologists; principles that allow for organization of incoming sensory information

bottom-up processing: perceptual processes driven by features of the stimulus

top-down processing: perceptual processes driven by context, expectations, or previous knowledge

precategorical acoustic store: proposed by Crowder and Morton (1969); a sensory storage system capable of holding a few pieces of auditory information for a few seconds following presentation

uncategorized form/precategorical: stage of processing in which incoming sensory information has not yet been identified or classified; thought to characterize early perceptual processes

perseveration: continued preoccupation with something that is no longer relevant

In several studies, schizophrenia patients have demonstrated a visual perceptual organization deficit: a reduced ability to rapidly group stimulus components into object representations according to the **gestalt "laws"** (Cox & Leventhal, 1978; Place & Gilmore, 1980; Silverstein et al., 1996). The causes of schizophrenia patients' poor performance in visual perceptual organization tasks, however, remain unclear. An unresolved issue in this literature concerns the extent to which this deficit reflects impaired bottom-up visual processing, as opposed to a higher order failure in representing contextual information about the test situation and then in using this information to allocate attentional resources to the processing of relevant stimulus characteristics (Knight, 1992).

Studies of auditory perceptual organization in nonclinical populations have used the auditory suffix paradigm (Ayres, Jonides, Reitman, Egan, & Howard, 1979; Neath, Surprenant, & Crowder, 1993) to clarify the role of **bottom-up** versus **top-down** contributions to perceptual organization, making auditory suffix tasks useful for the study of schizophrenia. In this paradigm, participants listen to lists of elements (typically numbers) and are told to ignore the suffix, usually a zero, that follows the last item in each list. Despite the knowledge that a suffix will occur, recall performance, especially for the last item in the list, declines significantly relative to a baseline, no-suffix condition. The traditional interpretation of this finding held that the to-be-remembered items are stored briefly in **uncategorized form** in **precategorical acoustic storage** (PAS; Crowder & Morton, 1969). This model further posited that new material (e.g., the suffix) would interfere with material stored in PAS only if it was included in the same perceptual stream as the list items, which could only occur when the new material was acoustically similar to those items. Because PAS was assumed to be precategorical, top-down factors such as expectations or the meaning of the new information were hypothesized not to affect the degree of interference with recall from PAS. Recent evidence has challenged this view, however: For example, investigators have found that the potency of a stimulus's ability to interfere in the suffix paradigm depends on the context in which it is interpreted, rather than on the acoustic properties of the stimulus (Ayres et al., 1979; Neath et al., 1993).

For example, in Neath et al's (1993) Study 1, participants heard recorded lists of nine numbers, each one followed by one of five suffixes: the experimenter speaking "moo"; the experimenter speaking "woof" (i.e., a dog bark); the sound of a real cow, the sound of a real dog barking; and the experimenter speaking the onomatopoetic word "braa." Half of the participants were told that the "braa" sound was produced by a real sheep, and half were told that it was the experimenter. When the "braa" suffix was defined as an animal, it had little effect on recall. For the participants told it was the experimenter making the "baa" sound, however, interference with recall was high and was equivalent to that in the experimenter-spoken "moo" and "woof" conditions.

In their second experiment, which used a within-subjects design, Neath et al. (1993) told half of the participants that they would be hearing lists followed by suffixes that would be the experimenter speaking the sounds "moo," "woof," or "baa" Halfway through the experiment, these participants were told that the "baa" sound was actually a real sheep. For the remainder of the session, these participants then heard the real cow and real dog suffixes in addition to the "baa" suffix. After reframing, the "baa" sound as an animal and presenting it in the context of other animal sounds, Neath et al. found that the "baa" suffix interfered little with performance and to a degree equivalent to that of the other real animal sounds. These data indicated that the same physical stimulus can produce varying degrees of interference with recall depending on the context in which it is interpreted by the research participant. When the participant categorizes the suffix as originating from a different source than the previous material, it is not included in the same perceptual stream as that material and has little effect on recall.

To our knowledge, there have been no previous studies of auditory perceptual organization in schizophrenia. Therefore, our goal in this study was to compare the performance of schizophrenia and control participants on a version of Neath et al.'s (1993) Study 2 task. If schizophrenia patients can render the "baa" suffix ineffective in the second half of the experiment, this would indicate that they are able to use contextual information to produce top-down feedback to auditory perceptual organization processes. On the other hand, if the "baa" suffix continues, to function as if spoken by the experimenter in the second half of the session, while the real animal suffixes produce less interference than the experimenter-spoken suffixes, this would indicate an intact ability to group stimuli based on physical characteristics but an impairment in generating contextually driven feedback to perceptual organization processes.

Method

Participants

Eighteen schizophrenia patients (13 men and 5 women, mean age = 38.78 years) and 18 nonpatient controls (5 men and 13 women, mean age = 36.33 years) volunteered to participate. The schizophrenia patients were all inpatients at the Rochester Psychiatric Center, a state hospital. Patients had means of 9.33 total hospitalizations and 102.77 total months of hospitalization in their lifetimes. All patients were on stable doses of antipsychotic medications. In addition, 47% of the patients were taking anticholinergic medications, 29% were taking antidepressants, and 18% were taking benzodiazepines. All participants were screened for histories of traumatic brain injury, seizure disorder or other neurologic disorders, mental retardation, ongoing substance abuse, or auditory impairment. Research diagnoses were made using the Structured Clinical Interview for the revised third edition *Diagnostic and statistical manual of mental disorders* (American Psychiatric Association, 1987) (*DSM-III-R*) Diagnosis—Patient version (SCID–P; Spider, Williams, Gibbon, & First, 1990) and chart information. SCID–P interviews were conducted by S. Silverstein, who had previously established a high degree of reliability on SCID interviews with the Diagnostic and Psychopathology Unit of the UCLA Clinical Research Center for Schizophrenia and Psychiatric Rehabilitation (mean k = .82, mean sensitivity = .77, mean specificity = .88). Nonpatient controls were hospital staff. All participants were paid $5.

Materials

Stimuli were identical to those used in Neath et al's (1993) Study 2, with the exemption that 60 rather than 120 trials were used. The nine-item lists were composed of the digits 1–9 in random order, spoken in a male voice. Each digit was presented within a 500-ms envelope, with an offset-to-onset delay of 500 ms between envelopes. One suffix was presented after each nine-item list. The suffixes consisted of the same male voice speaking the sounds "moo" or "woof," the sound of a real cow "moo," the sound of a real dog bark, or the male voice speaking the sound "baa" in a manner that was ambiguous as to whether it originated from the experimenter or a real sheep. The real cow suffix lasted 1,500 ms, the experimenter-spoken "moo" lasted 1,000 ms, the real dog bark lasted 500 ms, the experimenter-spoken "woof" lasted 1,000 ms, and the "baa" suffix lasted 1,000 ms. The numbers and the "baa," "moo," and "woof" suffixes were digitized on a Macintosh Plus computer. The real cow and dog suffixes were digitized recordings of genuine animals.

Design and Procedure

After obtaining informed consent, we gave participants the following instructions:

> You are going to listen, through these headphones, to a man saying lists of nine numbers. After each list of nine numbers, he will say an animal sound, either moo, woof, or baa. After the animal sound, please tell me the nine numbers you just heard. They can be given in any order you like, as long as you show me, on this form, which number goes in which space. For example, you can give me the last three, then the first three, then the middle three if you like. In many cases, you may not remember all the numbers. If this happens, try to guess for those spaces you are not sure about so that you always tell me nine numbers.

During the first 30 trials, the suffixes used were the experimenter-spoken "moo" and "woof" sounds and the experimenter-spoken ambiguous "baa." Each suffix was used on 10 trials. The order of suffix presentation was randomized with the constraint that the first trial use a cow suffix, the second use a dog suffix, and the third use the sheep suffix. This constraint was imposed in order to establish a context prior to the initial occurrence of the ambiguous sheep suffix.

> After the 30th trial, participants were informed as follows: Now I want to tell you a few more things about this task. The sheep sound you have been hearing was not the same man that was saying the cow and dog sounds. It was actually a real sheep. So, for the rest of the session, when you hear the sheep sound, you'll know it is a real sheep. Also, the cow and dog sounds you will hear for the rest of the session will be a real cow and a real dog.

For the rest of the session, the suffixes used were the real cow and dog stimuli and the experimenter-spoken "baa," which participants were told originated from a sheep. The order of suffix presentation during the second half of the session followed the same randomization procedure used during the first half of the session.

Participants spoke their responses to the experimenter and observed the experimenter recording their responses on a specially prepared answer sheet. They were encouraged to make corrections, prior to the next trial, if they wished to change the order of any digits or add a digit to a list position for which they were previously unable to recall a digit.

All participants heard the same 60 lists in the same order. A tone preceded each list by 2 s to prepare participants for the following list. Approximately 20 s elapsed between the offset of the suffix and the tone indicating the onset of the next trial. The test stimuli were recorded directly from a Macintosh Plus computer onto a standard audio cassette tape and played to participants through a Radio Shack CTR-69 cassette recorder. Participants listened to test stimuli through Realistic Nova 55 headphones. The stimuli was also played aloud through an Archer mini amplifier for the experimenter.

Results

Participants

The schizophrenia and nonpatient control groups did not differ in age, $t(34) = -0.67, p > .5$. The nonpatient control group had more years of education ($M = 15.17$) than the schizophrenia group ($M = 12.17$), $U = 253, p < .005$. To determine the relationship between years of education and recall, we computed a combined score averaging performance in the real cow and real dog conditions for each participant. Because little interference with recall was predicted with these genuine animal suffixes, they represented the closest conditions to a base-line. There was no relationship between education and recall for controls, $r(15) = .16, ns$, whereas a strong relationship emerged for schizophrenia patients, $r(15) = .76, p < .001$. This finding is likely to reflect an earlier onset of illness being associated with poorer overall recall. The relationship between years of education and the difference between the animal-sheep and human-sheep suffixes was not significant for the patients, $r(15) = .36, p > .15$.

Recall Performance

The critical test of the hypothesis involved recall performance of the final item in the list.[1] For the following analyses, data from the real cow and real dog suffixes were combined to form an "animal" condition (20 trials total), and data from the experimenter-spoken cow and dog sounds were combined to form a "human" condition (20 trials total). Data from the experimenter-spoken "baa" trials in the first half of the session formed a separate "human-sheep" condition (10 trials total), and data from the "baa" trials in the second half of the session, after participants were told it was a real sheep, formed the "animal-sheep" condition (10 trials total).

Data are graphically displayed in Figure 2.1. The groups differed in overall recall from Position 9, collapsed across suffix conditions, $F(1, 34) = 39.25$, $p < .0001$. There was also a significant main effect of suffix condition, $F(3, 102) = 11.76$, $p < .0001$. The critical test of the study's hypothesis involved the Group × Suffix Condition interaction, which was significant, $F(3, 102) = 3.34$, $p < .03$.

To examine more specifically evidence of an auditory perceptual organization deficit, we performed four planned contrasts. These involved the following comparisons: (a) "animal–sheep" versus "human–sheep," a test of the extent to which context can change the effectiveness of a single stimulus; (b) "animal–sheep" versus "human," a second test of the extent to which contextual factors can alter the potency of a previously interfering stimulus; (c) "animal-sheep" versus "animal," a test of the effectiveness of the context manipulation in the second half of the session; and (d) "human" versus "animal," a test of sensitivity to purely acoustic factors in auditory perceptual organization.

---

[1]In the interest of brevity, full descriptions of recall at all serial positions are not reported. Auditory suffix effects are typically greatest in the final serial position, and it is common for data from only the final position to be analyzed (e.g., Neath et al., 1993, Study 2).

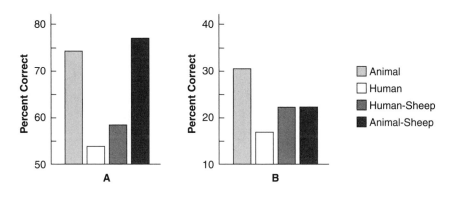

FIGURE 1   *Percent correct recall from Serial Position 9, by suffix condition, for (A) control group and (B) schizophrenia group.*

The contrast comparing the "human" and "animal" conditions reached statistical significance, $F(1, 34) = 30.52, p < .0001$. Most important, however, the Contrast × Group interaction test was not significant, $F(1, 34) = 1.18, p > .28$. Better recall in the "animal" suffix condition compared with the "human" condition was demonstrated by both the control (20% superiority), $F(1, 17) = 19.29, p < .0005$, and schizophrenia (14% superiority), $F(1, 17) = 11.36, p < .005$ groups. These data indicate that schizophrenia participants were able to exclude the suffix from the auditory stream when acoustic factor, alone clearly defined it as originating from a different source than the list items. The remaining three contrasts and Group × Contrast interaction tests examined whether the groups differed in their ability to use contextual factors (i.e., the information that the "baa" suffix originated from a real sheep and not a human) to effectively organize the auditory stream.

The contrast comparing the "animal–sheep" versus "human-sheep" conditions reached statistical significance, $F(1, 34) = 4.35, p < .05$. More important, the Group × Contrast interaction test was significant, $F(1, 34) = 4.35, p < .05$. For the control group, accuracy from the ninth position was over 18% easier when the "baa" suffix was defined as originating from a sheep compared to when it was understood to be spoken by the experimenter. In contrast, the schizophrenia group obtained identical scores in these two conditions, signifying their inability to exclude the "baa" suffix from the perceptual stream of digits after being told it was from a real sheep.

The contrast comparing the "animal–sheep" versus "human" conditions reached statistical significance, $F(1, 34) = 19.64, p = .0001$. More important, the Group × Contrast interaction test was significant, $F(1, 34) = 7.26, p = .01$. The control group demonstrated a large (23%) difference in accuracy between these conditions, indicating that the "baa" suffix no longer functioned as if spoken by the experimenter after participants were told it originated from a sheep, $F(1, 17) = 24.57, p < .0001$. In contrast, the schizophrenia group demonstrated only a 6% difference between these conditions, again indicating that the "baa" suffix continued to function as if spoken by a human even after patients were told it originated from a sheep, $F(1, 17) = 1.56, p > .22$.

The overall contrast comparing the "animal–sheep" and "animal" conditions did not reach statistical significance, $F(1, 34) = 1.96, p > .17$. There was, however, a significant interaction between the difference between conditions and group, $F(1, 34) = 7.07, p < .02$. To the extent that the context manipulation was successful, these conditions should produce nearly equivalent performance. This was the case for the control group, who demonstrated only a 2.5% difference in accuracy, $F(1, 17)$—0.65, $p > .43$. For controls, being told that the "baa" suffix originated from a real sheep, even though it actually did not, was enough to make it function as if it did. In contrast, the schizophrenia group demonstrated over an 8% difference in favor of the real animal condition, $F(1, 17) = 10.69, p < .005$.

Discussion

The performance of the control group in this study replicated the findings in Neath et al.'s (1993) Study 2. The performance of the schizophrenia group, however, clearly revealed their inability to exclude the "baa" suffix from the perceptual stream after being told that it originated from a real sheep and not the same person speaking the list items. In contrast to these group differences regarding the contextual manipulation, both groups were clearly able to exclude genuine animal sounds from the auditory stream. The latter suggests that selective attention processes that involve little or no top-down influence (i.e., early selection processes based mainly on physical characteristics of stimuli) are intact in schizophrenia. Taken together, these findings support the hypothesis that an impairment in the ability to utilize contextual information (Cohen & Servan-Schreiber, 1992) is a major factor in schizophrenia patients' perceptual organization difficulties.

Although the present results are being interpreted within the framework of an auditory perceptual organization deficit, they are also consistent with findings from other areas. Schizophrenia patients' inability to alter the potency of the sheep suffix after the contextual manipulation may be seen as an example of **perseveration,** also observed in studies that have used the Wisconsin Card Sorting Test (WCST; Heaton, 1981; Lysaker & Bell, 1994). In contrast to studies that used the WCST, however, the present data demonstrate schizophrenia patients' inability to utilize explicit contextual information, as well as subsequent effects on earlier cognitive processes. The present study also shares similarities with studies of cross-modal reaction time (Zubin, 1975). In these studies, schizophrenia patients, unlike controls, obtained slower reaction times to signals that were of a different sensory modality than the previous signal (e.g., a visual stimulus trial following an auditory stimulus trial) compared with reaction times to a signal that was of the same sensory modality as the prior one (Sutton, Hakarem, Zubin, & Portnoy, 1961). Moreover, Waldbaum, Sutton, and Kerr (1975) demonstrated that even after they eliminated uncertainty by informing participants what the sensory modality of the next signal would be, schizophrenia patients still showed significant reaction time slowing on cross-modal trials. The extent to which the apparent failures of context processing in this study and the reaction time data in the studies just cited reflect excessive facilitation of similar stimuli and inhibition of novel stimuli (e.g., animal-sheep), as Zubin (1975) hypothesized, remains untested. Finally, although it is not possible to definitively generalize the present findings of top-down impairment to past studies of visual perceptual organization dysfunction, schizophrenia patients have performed abnormally on an analogous visual task, the visual suffix paradigm (Cox & Leventhal, 1978). Moreover, studies using other visual perceptual organization paradigms support the influence of top-down impairment in the abnormal performance of schizophrenia patients on these tasks (Silverstein et al., 1996).

The present findings need replication with these and other stimulus sets before the role of top-down impairment in auditory perceptual organization dysfunction in schizophrenia can be comprehensively understood. The use of nonschizophrenia patient control groups in these studies would aid in determining if an auditory perceptual organization deficit is as specific to schizophrenia as its visual counterpart appears to be. In addition, although studies of putatively psychosis-prone persons indicate normal perceptual organization, including normal performance in the visual suffix paradigm (Silverstein, Raulin, Pristach, & Pomerantz, 1992), the auditory perceptual organization abilities of this important group are unknown.

Finally, the relationship of auditory perceptual impairments to specific symptoms and symptom clusters in schizophrenia is an issue worthy of further study. It can be argued that schizophrenia patients' difficulties in auditory tasks are more closely related to the clinical phenomena of distractibility, confusion, and overstimulation than are performance deficiencies in the visual information processing tasks that are more commonly studied. For example, an auditory perceptual organization deficit involving impaired top-down feedback could lead to a failure to attenuate information that is not highly relevant at a particular moment and to a subsequent equal weighting of auditory inputs (e.g., several voices in a crowded room). This would reduce the degree to which any one stream of information is followed and comprehended and reduce the amount of attentional resources available to process the significance of, or behavioral expectations associated with, any one stream. Efforts to understand the sequelae of auditory attentional impairments may further our understanding of the way in which certain symptoms of schizophrenia are produced, in addition to facilitating the development of novel rehabilitative interventions.

References

American Psychiatric Association. (1987). *Diagnostic and statistical manual of mental disorders* (3rd ed., revised). Washington, DC: Author.

Ayres, T. J., Jonides, J., Reitman, J. S., Egan, J. C., & Howard, D. A. (1979). Differing suffix effects for the same physical stimulus. *Journal of Experimental Psychology: Human Learning and Memory, 5,* 315–321.

Cohen, J. D., & Servan-Schreiber, D. (1992). Context, cortex, and dopamine: A connectionist approach to behavior and biology in schizophrenia. *Psychological Review, 99,* 45–77.

Cox, M. D., & Leventhal, D. N. (1978). A multivariate analysis and modification of a preattentive perceptual dysfunction in schizophrenia. *Journal of Nervous and Mental Disease, 166,* 709–718.

Crowder, R. G., & Morton, J. (1969). Precategorical acoustic storage (PAS). *Perception & Psychophysics, 5,* 365–373.

Heaton, R. (1981). *Wisconsin Card Sorting Test manual.* Odessa, FL: Psychological Assessment Resources, Inc.

Knight, R. A. (1992). Specifying cognitive deficiencies in poor premorbid schizophrenics. In E. F. Walker, R. H. Dworkin, & B. A. Comblatt (Eds.), *Progress in experimental personality and psychopathology research* (Vol. 15, pp. 253–289). New York: Springer.

Lysaker, P., & Bell, M. (1994). Insight and cognitive impairment in schizophrenia: Performance on repeated administrations of the Wisconsin Card Sorting Test. *Journal of Nervous and Mental Disease, 182,* 656–660.

Neath, I., Surprenant, A. M., & Crowder, R. G. (1993). The context-dependent stimulus suffix effect. *Journal of Experimental Psychology: Learning, Memory, and Cognition, 19,* 698–703.

Place, E. J. S., & Gilmore, G. C. (1980). Perceptual organization in schizophrenia. *Journal of Abnormal Psychology, 89,* 409–418.

Silverstein, S. M., Knight, R. A., Schwarzkopf, S. B., West, L. L., Osborn, L. M., & Kamin, D. (1996). Stimulus configuration and context effects in perceptual organization in schizophrenia. *Journal of Abnormal Psychology, 105,* 410–420.

Silverstein, S. M., Raulin, M. L., Pristack., E. A., & Pomerantz, J. R. (1992). Perceptual organization and schizotypy. *Journal of Abnormal Psychology, 101,* 265–270.

Spitzer, R. L., Williams, J. B. W., Gibbon, M., & First, M. B. (1990). *Structured Clinical Interview for DSM—III-R Patient Edition (SCID–P, Version 1.0).* Washington, DC: American Psychiatric Press.

Sutton, S., Hakarem, G., Zubin, J., & Portnoy, M. (1961). The effect of shift of sensory modality on serial reaction time: A comparison of schizophrenics and normals. *American Journal of Psychology, 74,* 224–232.

Waldbaum, J. K., Sutton, S., & Kerr, J. (1975). Shifts of sensory modality and reaction time in schizophrenia. In M. L: Kietzman, S. Sutton, & J. Zubin (Eds.), *Experimental approaches to psychopathology* (pp. 167–176). New York: Academic Press.

Zubin, J. (1975). Problem of attention in schizophrenia. In M. L. Kietzman, S. Sutton, & J. Zubin (Eds.), *Experimental approaches to psychopathology* (pp. 139–166). New York: Academic Press.

Introduction: Critical Thinking Questions _____

? Describe the basic suffix paradigm. Why does the addition of a suffix seem to interfere with list recall, and how might this be attributed to a precategorical acoustic store?

? At first, the interference from a suffix was thought to be purely perceptual in nature (i.e., an auditory signal interfering with another auditory signal). Describe how recent research has challenged this conclusion.

? How did the Neath et al. (1993) study demonstrate that the same physical stimulus can lead to different degrees of interference, based solely on subject expectation? What is the relationship between how a participant categorizes a suffix, and whether it has an interfering effect?

? Outline what should happen in the researchers' replication of the Neath et al. procedure if schizophrenics have deficits in top-down perceptual organization processes.

Method: Critical Thinking Questions _____

? Describe what you would have been asked to do, had you been a participant in the experiment.

? Name the independent variables in the experiment, and their levels. Describe how each of these variables was operationalized. For each variable, state whether it was manipulated in a between-subjects or within-subjects fashion. How many conditions were there in the experiment?

? What was (were) the dependent variable(s) in the experiment?

? What aspects of the methodology were implemented to deal with possible confounds?

Results/Discussion: Critical Thinking Questions _____

? Explain the pattern of results found in the "human" vs. "animal" conditions, for the schizophrenia group and the nonschizophrenia group (control group). What does this indicate about the ability of the schizophrenia group to exclude a suffix from the perceptual stream?

? Explain the pattern of results found in the "human-sheep" vs. "animal-sheep" conditions, for the schizophrenia group and the nonschizophrenia group (control group). What does this indicate about the ability of the schizophrenia group to exclude a suffix from the perceptual stream?

? The authors contend that "…selective processes that involve little or no top-down influence (i.e., early-selection processes based mainly on physical characteristics of stimuli) are intact in schizophrenia. Taken together, these findings support the hypothesis that an impairment in the ability to utilize contextual information is a major factor in schizophrenia patients' perceptual organization difficulties." Explain how their results support this claim.

? The authors offer some speculation regarding how the perceptual organization deficits seen in schizophrenia might relate to some of the symptom clusters that characterize the disorder. Briefly describe their view.

? After reading this study, you may feel there are other issues or questions that would be worthwhile or intriguing to address. Pose one of these questions (other than those suggested by the authors) that could be investigated empirically.

Driven to Distraction

Dual-Task Studies of Simulated Driving and Conversing on a Cellular Telephone

David L. Strayer and William A. Johnston

Abstract

Dual-task studies assessed the effects of cellular-phone conversations on performance of a simulated driving task. Performance was not disrupted by listening to radio broadcasts or listening to a book on tape. Nor was it disrupted by a continuous shadowing task using a handheld phone, ruling out, in this case, dual-task interpretations associated with holding the phone, listening, or speaking. However, significant interference was observed in a word-generation variant of the shadowing task, and this deficit increased with the difficulty of driving. Moreover, unconstrained conversations using either a handheld or a hands-free cell phone resulted in a twofold increase in the failure to detect simulated traffic signals and slower reactions to those signals that were detected We suggest that cellular-phone use disrupts performance by diverting attention to an engaging cognitive context other than the one immediately associated with driving.

Conceptual Issues and Theoretical Questions

- Is the perceived link between cellular-telephone usage and increased danger of motor vehicle accidents a causal one?
- Is the observed interference between cell-phone usage and driving ability the result of attentional or physical limitations?
- How does cell-phone usage impact the ability to react quickly to signal changes?
- How does the pattern of observed interference between cell-phone usage and driving ability change as the driving task becomes more difficult?

Strayer, D. L., & Johnston, W. A. (2001). Driven to distraction: Dual-task studies of simulated driving and conversing on a cellular telephone. *Psychological Science, 12,* 462–466. Copyright © 2001 Blackwell Publishing. Reprinted by permission. David Strayer, Department of Psychology, 380 S. 1530 E., Room 502, University of Utah, Salt Lake City, UT 84112-0251; e-mail:strayer@psych.utah.edu.

De-Jargonizing

working memory: the set of processes used to manipulate the information that occupies conscious awareness

mental arithmetic: computations performed without the aid of any external calculating aid

dual-task: situation requiring participants to engage in two different tasks concurrently

pursuit tracking: task requiring participants to keep a stylus in contact with a continuously moving target

shadowing: task that requires participants to repeat (i.e., shadow) one source of input.

multiple resource models: models of attention that proposed several pools of capacity that are differentiated in terms of modality of input (e.g., visual vs. auditory)

The use of cellular telephones has skyrocketed in recent years, with 116 million subscribers in the United States as of June 1, 2001 (Cellular Telecommunications Industry Association, 2001). This increase in cell-phone users has been accompanied by an increase in the number of individuals concurrently driving and talking on the cell phone. For example, recent surveys indicate that 85% of cell-phone owners use their phone at least occasionally while driving, and 27% report using their phones on half of their trips (Goodman, Bents, et al., 1999; Goodman, Tijerina, Bents, & Wierwille, 1999). The precise effects of cell-phone use on public safety are unknown; however, driver inattention and other human error have been linked to as much as 50% of the motor-vehicle accidents on U.S. highways (U.S. Department of Transportation, 1998). Because of the possible increase in risks associated with the use of cell phones while driving, several legislative efforts have been made to restrict cell-phone use on the road. In fact, the use of cellular phones while driving is currently restricted in at least nine countries (Goodman, Bents, et. al., 1999; Goodman, Tijerina, et al., 1999). In most cases, the legislation regarding cell phones and driving makes the tacit assumption that the source of any interference from cell-phone use is due to peripheral factors such as dialing and holding the phone while conversing. Among other things, this report evaluates the validity of this assumption.

One source of evidence concerning the association between cell-phone use and motor-vehicle accidents comes from a report by Redelmeier and Tibshirani (1997). In this study, the cellular-phone records of 699 individuals involved in motor-vehicle accidents were evaluated. It was found that 24% of these individuals were using their cell phone within the 10-min period preceding the accident. The authors claimed that cell-phone use was associated with a fourfold increase in the likelihood of getting into an accident, and that this increased risk was comparable to that found for driving with a blood alcohol level above the legal limit. In addition, these authors found no reliable safety advantages for those individuals who used a hands-free cellular device. The authors concluded that the interference associated with cell-phone use was due to attentional factors rather than to peripheral factors such as holding the phone.

The field studies of Redelmeier and Tibshirani (1997) establish a correlation between all-phone use and motor-vehicle accidents, but they do not necessarily imply that use of cell phones causes an increase in accident rates. There may be self-selection factors creating an association between cell-phone use and accidents. For example, people who drive and use their cell phone may be more likely to engage in risky behavior, and this increase in risk taking may underlie the correlation. Similarly, being in a highly emotional state may increase one's likelihood of driving erratically and may also increase one's likelihood of talking on the cell phone. In order to assess the possible causal relationship between cell-phone use and automobile accidents, carefully controlled experiments, such as the ones described m this report, are needed.

Prior research has established that the manual manipulation of equipment (e.g., dialing the phone, answering the phone, adjusting the radio) has a negative impact on driving (e.g., Briem & Hedman, 1995; Brookhuis, De Vries, & De Waard, 1991). However, the effects of a prone conversation itself on driving are not as well understood, despite the fact that the duration of a typical phone conversation may be up to two orders of magnitude greater than the time required to dial or answer the phone (Goodman, Bents, et al., 1999; Goodman, Tijerina, et al., 1999). Briem and Hedman (1995) found that simple phone conversations did not adversely affect the ability to maintain road position. However, several studies using cell phones have found that **working memory tasks** (Alm & Nilsson, 1995; Briem & Hedman, 1995), **mental arithmetic tasks** (McKnight & McKnight, 1993), and reasoning tasks (Brown, Tickner, & Simmonds, 1969) disrupt simulated-driving performance. Although these earlier studies provide an important piece of the puzzle, the nature of many of these phone tasks differs considerably from the typical cell-phone conversation.[1]

In the current research, we focused on the cell-phone conversation, because it comprises the bulk of the time engaged in this **dual-task** pairing. We sought to determine the extent to which cell-phone conversations might interfere with driving and, if they do interfere with driving, to determine the precise nature of the interference. In particular, the *peripheral-interference* hypothesis, tacitly endorsed by the majority of legislative initiatives on the topic, attributes any interference from cell phones to peripheral factors such as holding the phone while conversing. By contrast, the *attentional* hypothesis attributes any interference to the diversion of attention from driving to the phone conversation itself.

Experiment 1

Our first study was designed to contrast the effects of handheld and hands-free cell-phone conversations on a simulated-driving task (viz., **pursuit tracking**). We also included a control group who listened to the radio while performing the simulated-driving task. As participants performed the simulated-driving task, occasional red and green lights flashed on the computer display. If participants saw a green light, they were instructed to continue. However, if a red light was presented, they were to make a braking response as quickly as possible. The red-light/green-light manipulation was included to determine how quickly participants could react to the red light, as well as to determine the probability of failing to detect these simulated traffic signals, under the assumption that slowed reaction time to

---

[1]Interestingly, Radeborg, Briem, and Hedman (1999) provided evidence that suggests driving is also likely to disrupt the cell-phone conversation, implying that the dual-task interference is bi-directional.

traffic signals and failure to notice them would contribute significantly to any increase in the risks associated with driving and using a cell phone.

Method

Participants

Forty-eight undergraduates (24 male, 24 female) from the University of Utah participated in the experiment. They ranged in age from 18 to 30, with an average age of 21.3. All had normal or corrected-to-normal vision and received a perfect score on the Ishihara color blindness test (Ishihara, 1993). Participants were randomly assigned to the three groups: radio control, handheld phone, and hands-free phone.

Stimuli and Apparatus

Participants performed a pursuit tracking task in which they used a joystick to maneuver the cursor on a computer display to keep it aligned as closely as possible to a moving target. The target position was updated every 33 ms and was determined by the sum of three sine waves (0.07 Hz, 0.15 Hz, and 0.23 Hz). The target movement was smooth and continuous, yet essentially unpredictable. At intervals ranging from 10 to 20 s ($M = 15$ s), the target flashed red or greets, and participants were instructed to press a "brake button" located in the thumb position on top of the joystick as rapidly as possible when they detected the red light. Red and green lights were equiprobable and were presented in an unpredictable order.

Procedure

The study consisted of three phases. The first phase was a warm-up interval that lasted 7 min and was used to acquaint participants with the tracking task. The second phase was the single-task portion of the study and comprised the 7.5-min segments immediately preceding and immediately following the dual-task portion of the study. During the single-task phase, participants performed the tracking task by itself. The third phase was the dual-task portion of the study, lasting 15 min. The dual-task condition required the participants to engage in a conversation with a confederate (or listen to a radio broadcast of their choosing) while concurrently performing the tracking task.

Participants in the phone-conversation groups were asked to discuss either the then-ongoing Clinton presidential impeachment or the Salt Lake City Olympic Committee bribery scandal (conversations were counterbalanced across participants). The confederate was seated in a different room than the participant and did not know whether the participant was using a handheld or hands-free phone. The confederate's task was to facilitate the conversation and also to ensure that the participant listened and spoke in approximately equal proportions during the dual-task phase. Throughout the phone conversation, the computer recorded when the participant was talking and when the participant was listening to the confederate. Participants in the radio control group listened to a radio broadcast of their choosing during the dual-task portion of the experiment.

Results and Discussion

Figure 3.1a presents the probability of missing simulated traffic signals. Overall, miss rates were low; however, the probability of a miss more than doubled when participants were engaged in conversations on the cell phone. In the figure, the data for the two cell-phone groups (hands-free and handheld) are collapsed because a preliminary analysis indicated that there were no reliable differences between these groups, $F(1, 30) = 0.06$, $p > .80$. A one-way analysis of variance (ANOVA) indicated that the probability of missing red lights increased from single- to dual-task conditions for the combined cell-phone group, $F(1, 30) = 8.8$, $p < .01$. By contrast, the difference between single- and dual-task conditions was not reliable for the radio control group, $F(1, 15) = 0.64$, $p > .44$.

The reaction time to the simulated traffic signals is presented in Figure 3.1b. As with the miss data, the data for the two cell-phone groups (handheld and hands-free) were collapsed because preliminary analyses indicated that there were no reliable differences between these groups, $F(1, 30) = 0.01$, $p > .90$. A one-way ANOVA revealed that participants in the combined cell-phone group responded more slowly in the dual-task condition than in the single-task condition, $F(1, 30) = 28.9$, $p < .01$.[2] A subsidiary analysis of this combined group found that the disruptive effects of the phone conversation were greater when participants were talking than when they were listening to the confederate, although both dual-task deficits were reliable, $F(2, 60) = 19.8$, $p < .01$. There again was no indication of a dual-task decrement for the radio control group. Indeed, there was a tendency for reaction time to decrease in the dual-task condition for this group, $F(1, 15) = 3.2$, $p > .09$.

These data are important because they demonstrate that the phone conversation itself resulted in significant slowing in response to simulated traffic signals, as well as an increase

---

[2]Miss rates were also greater when participants were speaking than when they were listening; however, this trend was not reliable.

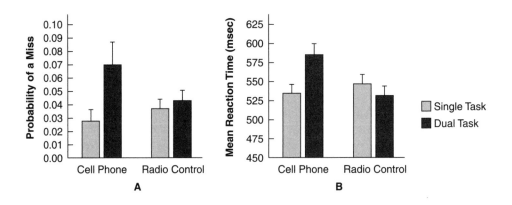

FIGURE 1   *Probability of missing the simulated traffic signals (a) and mean reaction time to the simulated traffic signals (b) in single- and dual-task conditions in Experiment 1.*

in the probability of missing these signals. Moreover, the fact that handheld and hands-free cell phones resulted in equivalent dual-task deficits indicates that the interference was not due to peripheral factors such as holding the phone while conversing. These data are also consistent with the studies reporting no reliable performance differences between participants using handheld and hands-free cell phones (Redelmeier & Tibshirani, 1997).

Additional Control Condition

There were no dual-task decrements associated with listening to radio broadcasts in Experiment 1. Although this control condition mimicked real-world situations, the broadcasts involved a mixture of music and speech, and we did not assess how well participants attended to this material. Therefore, we ran an additional control condition in which participants listened to a selected passage from a book on tape during the dual-task portion of the study. Participants were informed that at the completion of the study they would be asked a series of questions about the book on tape. Only participants who received scores of at least 90% on this posttest were included in the subsequent analyses. Thus, the book-on-tape control condition was specifically designed to ensure that participants attended to the verbal material in the dual-task portion of the study.

Method

Twenty undergraduates (10 male and 10 female) from the University of Utah participated. They ranged in age from 18 to 30, with a mean age of 20.8. All had normal or corrected-to-normal vision and received a perfect score on the Ishihara color blindness test (Ishihara, 1993).

The procedure was identical to that used for the radio control condition, with the exception that participants listened to selected portions from a book on tape (Brokaw, 1998) during the dual-task phase of the experiment. At the end of the study, participants completed a 10-item multiple-choice questionnaire to assess the degree to which they had attended to the verbal material from the book on tape. Four participants who failed to score at least 90% on the posttest were omitted from subsequent analyses, resulting in a sample of 16 participants who clearly attended to the book on tape.

Results and Discussion

Results were similar to those for the radio control condition: There was no difference between the single- and dual-task conditions either in the rate of missing simulated traffic signals (.017 vs. .026, respectively), $F(1, 15) = 0.77$, $p > .39$, or in the reaction time to these signals (541 ms vs. 537 ms, respectively), $F(1, 15) = 0.12$, $p > .73$. Thus, listening to a book on tape did not result in significant impairment on the simulated-driving task. These findings are important because they rule out interpretations that attribute the dual-task deficits associated with a cell-phone conversation to simply attending to verbal material. Active engagement in the cellphone conversation appears to be necessary to produce the dual-task interference observed in Experiment 1.

Subsidiary analyses were also performed on the dual-task/single-task difference scores for the cell-phone and control groups. In these analyses, the radio and book-on-tape control groups were combined, because preliminary analyses revealed that these groups did not differ significantly from each other (all $ps > .30$). Indeed, the planned comparisons reported earlier indicated that neither control group exhibited reliable dual-task decrements. The aggregated data were analyzed using a 2 (group: cell phone vs. control) × 2 (task: single vs. dual) split-plot ANOVA. Analysis of the difference scores revealed that the increase in miss rates from single- to dual-task conditions was greater for the cell-phone group than for the control group, $F(1, 62) = 4.97$, $p < .05$, and that the increase in reaction time from single- to dual-task conditions was greater for the cell-phone group than for the control group, $F(1, 62) = 29.9$, $p < .01$. Finally, an analysis of covariance indicated that neither gender nor age contributed to the group differences reported in this experiment (all $ps > .30$).

Experiment 2

In our second study, we attempted to more specifically localize the source of cell-phone interference on driving. Participants performed the simulated-driving task on both an easy, predictable course and a difficult, unpredictable course. After a warm-up phase acquainting participants with the simulator, they performed each course in single-task mode as well as in two dual-task conditions involving the use of a cell phone. One of the dual-task conditions was a **shadowing** task in which the participants performed the simulated-driving task while they repeated words that the experimenter read to them over a hand-held cell phone. Thus, the shadowing dual-task condition assessed the contribution of holding the phone, listening, and speaking to the dual-task performance deficits. The other dual-task condition was a word-generation task that was identical to the shadowing task with the exception that the participant was required to generate a new word that began with the last letter of the word read by the experimenter. For example, if the experimenter read the word "molar," the participant was required to generate a word that began with the letter r (e.g., "robot"). Note that the only difference between the two dual-task conditions was the attentional demands imposed by the word-generation process. In this study, we measured the deviations from the ideal tracking position under the assumption that deviations in tracking would contribute significantly to any increase in the risks associated with driving while using a cell phone.

Method

Participants

Twenty-four undergraduates (12 male and 12 female) from the University of Utah participated in the experiment. They ranged in age from 18 to 26, with an average age of 20.5. All had normal or corrected-to-normal vision and received a perfect score on the Ishihara color blindness test (Ishihara, 1993).

Stimuli and Apparatus

In the easy course, the position of the target was determined by a 0.035-Hz sine wave. In the difficult course, the target position was determined using the same algorithm as in Experiment 1; however, the red-light/green-light manipulation from the first study was not included in this variant of the tracking task, because we found that responding to the simulated traffic signals added substantial noise to the tracking data.

Procedure

Participants performed a pursuit tracking task similar to that used in the first study. The easy and difficult conditions were blocked in counterbalanced order, and the order of single- and dual-task conditions was counterbalanced within each level of course difficulty. In both dual-task conditions, the experimenter read four- and five-letter words to the participant at a rate of one word every 3 s. The word lists used in the experiment were counterbalanced across participants and conditions.

Results and Discussion

Figure 2 presents the root mean squared (RMS) tracking error as a function of experimental condition. The data were analyzed using a 2 (tracking difficulty: easy vs. difficult) × 3 (task: single, shadowing, and word generation) repeated measures ANOVA. The analysis revealed that RMS error increased as a function of tracking difficulty, $F(1, 23) = 49.8$, $p < .01$, and task, $F(2, 46) = 13.4$, $p < .01$, and that these two effects interacted, $F(2, 46) = 7.7$, $p < .01$. A series of planned comparisons clarified the nature of this interaction. Single-task tracking error increased from the easy to the difficult condition, $F(1, 23) = 48.8$, $p < .01$. The shadowing dual-task condition did not reliably differ from the single-task control condition, $F(1, 23) = 3.7$, $p > .07$. However, the word-generation task produced significant increases in

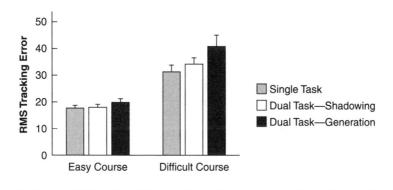

FIGURE 2 *Root mean squared (RMS) tracking error for the easy and difficult courses in single- and dual-task conditions in Experiment 2.*

tracking error, $F(1, 23) = 17.6$, $p < .01$, and this effect was especially pronounced in the difficult driving condition, $F(1, 23) = 10.0$, $p < .01$. The fact that the shadowing task did not reliably elevate tracking error further discredits interpretations that attribute dual-task cell-phone deficits to peripheral factors such as holding the phone while conversing. In addition, these data indicate that the peripheral processes of speaking and listening do not appear to be major sources of interference. However, it is important to caution that our studies do not rule out all peripheral sources of interference. Indeed, there was a trend toward interference in the shadowing task that may have important implications in the real world (cf. Loftus, 1996). Moreover, there is clear evidence that manipulation of a phone while dialing is associated with significant dual-task interference (e.g., Briem & Hedman, 1995; Brookhuis et al., 1991).

General Discussion

The principal findings are that (a) when participants were engaged in cell-phone conversations, they missed twice as many simulated traffic signals as when they were not talking on the cell phone and took longer to react to those signals that they did detect; (b) these deficits were equivalent for handheld and hands-free cell-phone users; and (c) tracking error increased when participants used the cell phone to perform an active, attention-demanding word-generation task but not when they performed a shadowing task.

These data are consistent with an attention-based interpretation in which the disruptive effects of cell-phone conversations on driving are due primarily to the diversion of attention from driving to the phone conversation itself. The largest dual-task performance deficits were obtained in the generative portions of the cell-phone conversations; however, even the listening components were associated with dual-task decrements. Thus, the simulator studies described in this report and the field studies of Redelmeier and Tibshirani (1997) provide converging evidence on the locus of interference. We note that these results are problematic for **multiple-resource models** of divided attention (e.g., Wickens, 1992). Such models suggest that an auditory-verbal-vocal cell-phone conversation should not interfere substantially with a visual-spatial-manual driving task (see also Briem & Hedman, 1995; Moray, 1999). Indeed, attending to auditory inputs in the radio and book-on-tape control conditions of Experiment 1 and in the shadowing task of Experiment 2 did not lead to dual-task interference; however, conversing using either a handheld or a hands-free cell phone in Experiment 1 and word generation in Experiment 2 resulted in significant interference. Wickens (1999) has suggested that multiple-resource models might be able to account for the interference between cell-phone conversations and driving because there may be an overlap in the stages of processing between the two tasks. But given the similarity of the stages of processing in the shadowing and generation conditions of Experiment 2, this interpretation would seem to erroneously predict similar patterns of dual-task interference for these two conditions.[3]

---

[3]Because performance was not measured in single-task shadowing and generation conditions, it is possible that the differences in dual-task interference are due to differences in the difficulty of the two tasks. Even so, the differences in difficulty would be associated with attention-demanding generative components of processing, rather than with peripheral processes associated with holding the phone, listening, and speaking.

We suggest that cellular-phone use disrupts performance by diverting attention to an engaging cognitive context other than the one immediately associated with driving. Some aspects of driving are inherently unpredictable (e.g., reacting to a child who darts across the street), and when attention is diverted from the driving context, the appropriate reactions to these unpredictable events will be impaired. Thus, the dual-task decrements described in this article appear to be consistent with the literatures on task and attention switching (e.g., Allport, Styles, & Hsieh, 1994; Gopher, Greenshpan, & Armony, 1996; Rogers & Monsell, 1995).

It is also interesting to consider the potential differences between cell-phone conversations and in-person conversations with other occupants of the vehicle. Although there need not be differences between these two modes of communication, there is evidence that in-person conversations are modulated by driving difficulty, so that as the demands of driving increase, participation by all participants in a conversation decreases (Parks, 1991). By contrast, at least one of the participants in a cellular-phone conversation is unaware of the current driving conditions (and may even be unaware that the cell-phone user is driving). Under such circumstances, it is less likely that the conversation will be modulated as a function of the real-time variations in driving difficulty. Moreover, although other in-car dual-task activities (e.g., dialing the phone, eating a sandwich) are under the direct control of the driver, when the driver engages in a cell-phone conversation, he or she is no longer solely in control of the dynamics of the conversation (i.e., a cell-phone conversation is jointly controlled by the participants).

In sum, we found that conversing on either a handheld or a hands-free cell phone led to significant decrements in simulated-driving performance. Thus, the available evidence indicates that there are at least two sources of interference with driving associated with concurrent cell-phone use: one due to peripheral factors such as manipulating the phone while dialing (e.g., Briem & Hedman, 1995; Brookhuis et al., 1991) and one due to the phone conversation itself. Our data imply that legislative initiatives that restrict handheld devices but permit hands-free devices are not likely to reduce interference from the phone conversation, because the interference is, in this case, due to central attentional processes.

References

Allport, A., Styles, E. A., & Hsieh, S. (1994). Shifting intentional set: Exploring the dynamic control of tasks. In C. Umilta & M. Moscovitch (Eds.), *Attention and performance IV* (pp. 421–452). Cambridge, MA: MIT Press.

Alm, H., & Nilsson, L. (1995). The effects of a mobile telephone task on driver behaviour in a car following situation. *Accident Analysis and Prevention, 27,* 707–715.

Briem, V, & Hedman, L. R. (1995). Behavioral effects of mobile telephone use during simulated driving. *Ergonomics, 38,* 2536–2562.

Brokaw, T. (1998). *The greatest generation (sound recording: abridged)* [Cassette]. New York: Random House Audio Books.

Brookhuis, K. A., De Vries, G., & De Waard, D. (1991). The effects of mobile telephoning on driving performance. *Accident Analysis and Prevention, 23,* 309–316.

Brown, I. D., Tickner, A. H., & Simmonds, D. C. V. (1969). Interference between concurrent tasks of driving and telephoning. *Journal of Applied Psychology, 53,* 419–424.

Cellular Telecommunications Industry Association. (2001). *CTIA's world of wireless communications* [On-line]. Available: http://www.wow-com.com/

Goodman, M. J., Bents, F. D., Tijerina, L., Wierwille, W., Lener, N., & Benel, D. (1999). *An investigation of the safety implications of wireless communication in vehicles: Report summary* (On-line). Available: http://www.nhtsa.dot.gov/people/injury/research/wireless/#rep

Goodman, M. J., Tijerina, L., Bents, F. D., & Wierwille, W. W. (1999). Using cellular telephones in vehicles: Safe a unsafe? *Transportation Human Factors, 1,* 3–42.

Gopher, D., Greenshpan, Y., & Armony, L. (1996). Switching attention between tasks: Exploration of the components of executive control and their development with training. In *Proceedings of the Human Factors and Ergonomics Society 40th annual meeting* (pp. 1060–1064). Philadelphia: Human Factors and Ergonomics Society.

Ishihara, S. (1993). *Ishihara's tests for colour-blindness.* Tokyo, Japan: Kanehara & Co.

Loftus, G. R. (1996). Psychology will be a much better science when we change the way we analyze data. *Current Directions in Psychological Science, 5,* 161–171,

McKnight, A., & McKnight, A. (1993). The effect of cellular phone use upon driver attention. *Accident Analysis and Prevention, 25,* 259–265.

Moray, N. (1999). Commentary on Goodman, Tijerina, Bents, and Wierwille, "Using Cellular Telephones in Vehicles: Safe or Unsafe?" *Transportation Human Factors, 1,* 43–46.

Parks, A. M. (1991). Drivers business decision making ability whilst using carphones. In E. Lovessey (Ed.), *Contemporary ergonomics: Proceedings of the Ergonomic Society annual conference* (pp. 427–432). London: Taylor & Francis.

Radeborg, K., Briem, V., & Hedman. L. R. (1999). The effect of concurrent task difficulty on working memory during simulated driving. *Ergonomics, 42,* 767–777.

Redelmeier, D. A., & Tibshirani, R. J. (1997). Association between cellular-telephone calls and motor vehicle collisions. *The New England Journal of Medicine, 336,* 453–459.

Rogers, R. D., & Monsell, S. (1995). Costs of a predictable switch between simple cognitive tasks. *Journal of Experimental Psychology: General, 124,* 207–231.

U.S. Department of Transportation. (1998). *Transportation Statistics Annual Report, 1998: Long-distance travel and freight, chapter 3* [On-line]. Available: http://www.bts.gov/programs/transtu/tsar/tsar98/chap3.pdf

Wickens, C. D. (1992). *Engineering psychology and human performance.* New York: HarperCollins.

Wickens, C. D. (1999). [Letter to the editor]. *Transportation Human Factors, 1,* 205–206.

Introduction: Critical Thinking Questions _____

? What descriptive statistics and field studies exist to suggest a link between cell-phone usage and driving accidents, and what steps have lawmakers taken to address the link?

? Why can't a causal link between cell-phone usage and driving be assumed, based on the results of these descriptive/field studies?

? What does previous experimental research suggest about the link between cell-phone usage and driving ability?

? What does previous research suggest about working memory tasks and driving ability? How are these studies limited in their ability to generalize to cell-phone usage?

? Compare and contrast the peripheral-interference hypothesis and the attentional hypothesis.

? How does Experiment 2 attempt to extend the findings of Experiment 1, and how did the experimental tasks employed allow for this extension?

Method: Critical Thinking Questions _____

? For each experiment, describe what you would have been asked to do, had you been a participant.

? Name the independent variables in each experiment, and their levels. Describe how each of these variables was operationalized. For each variable, state whether it was manipulated in a between-subjects or within-subjects fashion. How many conditions were there in each experiment?

? What was (were) the dependent variable(s) in each experiment?

? What aspects of the methodology were implemented to deal with possible confounds?

Results/Discussion: Critical Thinking Questions _____

? Describe the results of Experiment 1, as pictured in Figure 1. Where were dual-task decrements observed? Where weren't they observed? Be sure to describe if any of these effects were impacted by particular aspects of the conversation. What are the implications of these differences?

? Describe the interaction between task difficulty and single- vs. dual-task conditions pictured in Figure 2.

? Describe the attention-based interpretation of the results offered by the authors, and how it fits with their findings (as well as those of previous studies).

? Given the attention-based interpretation of the results, which findings seem to be consistent with "multiple resource" views of attention? Which findings make multiple resource views untenable? Why?

? Some question whether a cellular phone conversation while driving is really any different from talking to another occupant of the car while driving. What do the researchers have to say about this distinction?

? After reading this study, you may feel there are other issues or questions that would be worthwhile or intriguing to address. Pose one of these questions (other than those suggested by the authors) that could be investigated empirically.

The Cocktail Party Phenomenon Revisited: The Importance of Working Memory Capacity

Andrew R. A. Conway, Nelson Cowan, and Michael F. Bunting

Abstract

Wood and Cowan (1995) replicated and extended Moray's (1959) investigation of the cocktail party phenomenon, which refers to a situation in which one can attend to only part of a noisy environment, yet highly pertinent stimuli such as one's own name can suddenly capture attention. Both of these previous investigations have shown that approximately 33% of subjects report hearing their own name in an unattended, irrelevant message. Here we show that subjects who detect their name in the irrelevant message have relatively low working-memory capacities, suggesting that they have difficulty blocking out, or inhibiting, distracting information.

Conceptual Issues and Theoretical Questions

- What underlies individual differences in the cocktail party phenomenon—why are some people more likely than others to detect their name in an unattended channel?
- What role do inhibitory processes play in producing the cocktail party phenomenon?
- Can individual differences in experiencing the cocktail party phenomenon be explained via individual differences in the efficiency of working memory?

De-Jargonizing

divided attention task: a task that requires one to attend to multiple messages concurrently, and respond appropriately to each

Conway, A. R., Cowan, N. A., & Bunting, M. F. (2001). The cocktail party phenomenon revisited: The importance of working memory capacity. *Psychonomic Bulletin and Review, 8,* 331–335. Reprinted by permission of Psychomic Society, Inc.

selective attention task: a task that requires one to attend to one message while ignoring others

retrieval inhibition: phenomenon in which the retrieval of some concepts renders other concepts *less* retrievable.

proactive interference: occurs when information already encoded in memory impairs the encoding of new information

negative priming effect: an inhibitory effect whereby responses are slowed to stimuli that have been previously presented, but ignored

A fundamental question in cognitive science is how humans selectively attend to certain aspects of their environment, enabling detailed processing of those aspects, while of necessity ignoring other aspects. Beginning in England during World War II, psychologists developed laboratory tasks to identify individuals skilled in attending within a busy environment (Lachman, Lachman, & Butterfield, 1979). Cherry (1953) developed the dichotic listening procedure in which the task is to repeat aloud or "shadow" the message presented to one ear and ignore a different message presented to the other ear. Subjects were very successful in this task, but when asked to recall the content of an ignored message, they were able to report only physical features such as gender of the voice or whether the message was speech or tone; little or no semantic content was reported. Partly on the basis of this work, Broadbent (1958) developed a theoretical model of selective attention, according to which environmental stimulation is filtered out of awareness if it is identified as irrelevant to the subject's current concerns on the basis of its superficial physical features (e.g., voice, color, or location).

Broadbent's (1958) model has been seriously challenged, however, by demonstrations of *semantic* processing of unattended information. For example, Moray (1959) found that some subjects detect their own name when it is presented in an unattended auditory channel. Contrary to popular belief, not all subjects demonstrate this "cocktail party effect." In fact, Moray found that only 33% of subjects reported hearing their own name when it is inserted into the irrelevant message. Using more sophisticated technology, Wood and Cowan (1995) replicated Moray's experiment and found 34.6% of subjects reported hearing their own name presented in the irrelevant message.

The purpose of the present experiment is to explain why some, but not all, subjects demonstrate the cocktail party effect. An examination of individual differences in the cocktail party effect raises some interesting possibilities. On the one hand, it is possible that the most capable subjects notice their names because they are able to monitor the irrelevant message with no damage to shadowing performance. On the other hand, it is possible that only the least capable subjects notice their names because they are poor at maintaining attention on the relevant message in the presence of distraction.

We measured subjects' capability using the construct of working memory, which is considered to be a cognitive system consisting of storage buffers as well as a central executive control mechanism. The function of working memory is to actively maintain goal-relevant information in the service of complex cognition (Baddeley & Hitch, 1974; Miyake & Shah, 1999). The limited capacity of working memory presumably constrains cognitive performance. We measured this capacity with the *operation span* task (Turner & Engle, 1989), in which series of displays were presented, each containing a simple mathematical problem and an unrelated word. The span was based on the length of the series that could be processed with the subject still able to recall all of the words. Various investigations have demonstrated that individuals with high working-memory capacity out-perform individuals with low working-memory capacity on a range of tasks (Daneman & Carpenter, 1980; Daneman & Merikle, 1996; Engle, Tuholski, Laughlin, & Conway, 1999; Gilhooly, Logie, Wetherick, & Wynn, 1993; Toms, Morris, & Ward, 1993) and that individuals who score high on tests of working-memory capacity are better at blocking out, or inhibiting, distracting information (Conway & Engle, 1994; Conway, Tuholski, Shisler, & Engle, 1999; Gernsbacher, 1993; Hasher & Zacks, 1988; Rosen & Engle, 1997). We used the operation span task to identify high and low working-memory capacity individuals and had subjects perform a dichotic listening task in which their own name was presented in the irrelevant message, following as closely as possible the procedure reported by Wood and Cowan (1995).

Method

Subject Selection

The sample comprised 40 (17 male, 23 female) native English-speaking undergraduates from the University of Illinois at Chicago with normal hearing, who received course credit for participation. Informed consent, approved by the local internal review board, was obtained from all subjects. Half were categorized as having a high working-memory span and half a low working-memory span on the basis of scores that fell in the upper or lower quartile of a larger sample of subjects who carried out the operation span task. All subjects repeated the same relevant message, but half of each span group was randomly assigned to an experimental condition in which the subject's first name occurred after 4 min of shadowing and the other half, after 5 min of shadowing. Any subject who received his or her name at 4 (or 5) min also received a yoked subject's name at 5 (or 4) min.

Operation Span Task Procedure

The procedure was adapted from a previous study (Turner & Engle, 1989) to measure working-memory capacity. The subject was presented with a series of displays on a computer screen. Each display contained a mathematical operation and an unrelated word (e.g., IS (6+4)/2 = 5? DOG). The subject's task for each display was to say the equation aloud, answer "yes" or "no" as to whether the equation was true, and then say each word. When the series of displays ended, the task was to write all of the words on a response sheet. The number of displays in a series varied from 2 to 6. Three series of each length were presented for a total of 15 series, with series length randomized and not predictable by the subject. The subject's span score was the cumulative number of words recalled from series that was perfectly recalled in the correct serial order, with no points awarded for imperfect recall of a series. The average score was 24.85 (range of 17–44) for high-span subjects and

8.22 (range of 6–12) for low-span subjects. Subjects in the middle two quartiles of the range of span scores were omitted from the study. Performance levels on various versions of verbal working-memory tasks like this one are highly correlated with one another (Daneman & Merikle, 1996; Engle et al., 1999).

Selective Listening Procedure

Subjects were tested individually in a well illuminated, sound-insulated room. The auditory stimuli, obtained from Wood and Cowan (1995), were recorded onto a normal-bias audio cassette and then digitized onto a computer at a sampling rate of 22 kHz and dynamic range of 16 bits. They were presented through stereo head-phones at a constant volume for all subjects. The relevant message contained 330 monosyllabic words recorded in a monotone female voice at the rate of 60 words per minute and lasted 5.5 min. The irrelevant message contained 300 monosyllabic words recorded in a monotone male voice. The onset of the irrelevant message began 30 sec after the attended message, allowing for a brief practice period without distraction. The onsets of the words were synchronized across messages. The order of the words was identical across subjects except for the names, which were digitally inserted into the irrelevant message in place of a word after 4 and 5 min of shadowing. Each subject's first name was inserted into the irrelevant message. The experimenter was aware of each subject's name because each had previously been in the lab to perform the operation span task.

Subjects were instructed to listen to the message presented to the right ear and to repeat (shadow) each word as soon as it was presented, making as few errors as possible and to ignore the distractions coming to the left ear. Subjects shadowed until all sounds in the attended message stopped. During shadowing, the experimenter was seated at a separate table in the same room and recorded shadowing errors. After shadowing, the subject completed a questionnaire regarding the irrelevant message, identical to one used by Wood and Cowan (1995). Subjects stating that they detected something unusual in the irrelevant message when queried all went on to specify that it was their own name.

Results and Discussion

Using retrospective report immediately after the shadowing task, we found that 20% of high-span subjects and 65% of low-span subjects reported hearing their name in the irrelevant message (see Figure 4.1). Fisher's exact test indicated that the probability of obtaining these proportions by chance alone (under the assumption that high-and low-span subjects actually are equally prone to detecting their name in the irrelevant message) is only $p = .005$. No subject reported hearing a yoked control subject's name that also was presented. Clearly, the low-span subjects detected their own names more often.

Low-span subjects also encountered more difficulty performing the shadowing task. This is reflected in the finding that low-span subjects committed significantly more shadowing errors ($M = 20.88$) than did high-span subjects ($M = 10.00$) [$t(32) = 2.18, p = .04$]. Given this finding, we wanted to ensure that the name-detection difference between high- and low-span subjects was not simply a result of more attention shifts on the part of the low-span

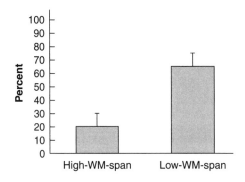

FIGURE 1 *The proportion of high- and low-span subjects who reported hearing their name in the irrelevant message.*

subjects. Therefore, we examined shadowing errors for the two words in the relevant message preceding the name. There were no group differences in shadowing two words before the name [$t(32) = 1.0, p > .10$] or one word before the name [$t(32) = 1.0, p > .10$], ruling out the possibility that the low span subjects detected their names more often than did the high-span subjects, simply because their attention wandered to the irrelevant message at the opportune time (in fact, only one person committed a shadowing error on either word). There was a difference between high- and low-span subjects in shadowing errors committed concurrently with the presentation of the name [$t(32) = 2.59, p = .01$], suggesting that the presentation of the name resulted in distraction much more so for low-span subjects.

We also examined shadowing errors after the presentation of the name. Presumably, detecting one's own name in the irrelevant message would result in a decrement to performance of the shadowing task. As shown in Figure 2, a much higher proportion of subjects who noticed their name made shadowing errors on the two words following the name (marked "name+1" and "name+2"). On the two words to be shadowed immediately after presentation of their own name, high-span subjects who reported hearing their name made significantly more shadowing errors than those who did not [$t(15) = 3.04, p = .01$]. Similarly, on these two words, low-span subjects who reported hearing their name made more shadowing errors than those who did not [$t(15) = 2.50, p = .03$]. Thus, the pertinence of the subject's own name sometimes served as a distraction and resulted in a reallocation of attention to the name, significantly more frequently in low-span subjects. However, this distraction did not persist for more than two words. High-span subjects who reported hearing their own name were no more likely to commit a showing error three words after the name than were high-span subjects who did not report hearing their own name [$t(15) = 0.75, p > .10$]. Similarly, low-span subjects who reported hearing their own name were no more likely to commit a shadowing error three words after the name than were low-span subjects who did not report hearing their own name [$t(15) = 1.74, p > .10$].

The higher incidence of name detection in low-span subjects is particularly striking because the opposite result was possible. It could have been that high-span subjects, be-

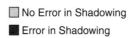

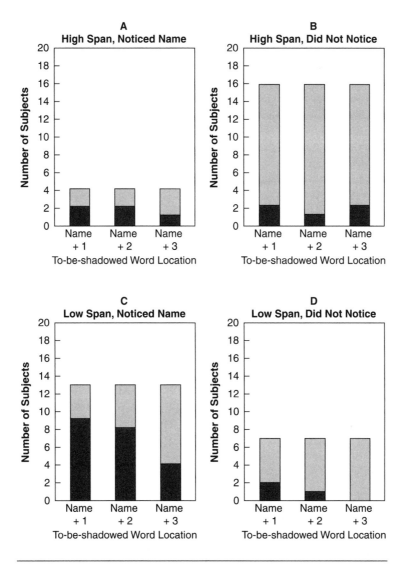

FIGURE 2 *The number of high- and low-span subjects who did and did not notice their own names in the irrelevant message in a selective listening task (heights of frequency bars), and the proportion of those subjects who made errors in shadowing words in the relevant message (dark portion of bars) that occurred 1, 2, or 3 words after the subject's name (abscissa parameter). Panel A: High-span subjects who noticed their names. Panel B: High-span subjects who did not notice their names. Panel C: Low-span subjects who noticed their names. Panel D: Low-span subjects who did not notice their names. Many more low-span subjects noticed their names, and subjects who noticed their names made proportionally many more shadowing errors in the name +1 and name +2 positions.*

cause of their greater capacity, have the ability to monitor the irrelevant message so as to hear their names. This certainly was not the case. The critical factor seems to be the ability to block information from the irrelevant message. High-span subjects are more capable of this and were therefore less likely to hear their names, and they also were less susceptible to a consequential disruption of relevant task performance.

Also striking is that the operation span task is essentially a **divided attention task,** whereas the dichotic listening task is clearly a **selective attention task,** yet subjects who performed well on one task also performed well on the other. Therefore, it is clearly not the case that some subjects habitually or spontaneously divide their attention when performing cognitive tasks. Rather, it appears that there is a general cognitive ability that allows subjects to perform well on both tasks. We argue that this ability is intimately linked to working memory capacity.

Working memory capacity is a critical cognitive characteristic, and one's capacity has a major impact on the quality of cognitive performance. Some researchers even suggest that working memory capacity is the most important factor in general fluid intelligence (Conway, Cowan, Bunting, Therriault, & Minkoff, in press; Engle et al., 1999; Kyllonen, 1996). A fundamental aspect of intelligent behavior, linked to working memory, is the ability to inhibit distracting information (Dempster, 1991). Although the present experiment does not provide direct evidence of inhibition of information presented in the irrelevant channel, the interpretation that high-span subjects are better at inhibiting distracting information than are low-span subjects is consistent with previous research. For example, in the context of memory retrieval, several experiments have demonstrated that high-span subjects are more likely to reveal **retrieval inhibition** effects and subsequently less **proactive interference** than are low-span subjects (Conway & Engle, 1994; Kane & Engle, 2000; Rosen & Engle, 1997, 1998). Also, high-span subjects reliably reveal the **negative priming effect,** whereas low-span subjects do not (Conway et al., 1999). Whether or not an inhibitory mechanism is necessary to account for these findings, it is clear that the ability to handle cognitive interference is a dimension on which high- and low-working memory span individuals differ.

Finally, the present result does not answer the question of whether working-memory capacity drives inhibitory ability or vice versa. One interpretation is that working-memory capacity is a "resource" that fuels the central executive, which is responsible for maintaining activation to relevant information and suppressing distracting information (Conway & Engle, 1994). Another interpretation is that working-memory capacity refers to the "contents" of working memory, and as such, inhibitory ability regulates the contents and therefore the capacity of working memory (Hasher & Zacks, 1988). The present results are compatible with either view. Our goal here is not to resolve this issue but to demonstrate the importance of working memory for classic selective attention tasks such as dichotic listening and to possibly extend the range of tasks of working memory that will be investigated, which will ultimately lead to a better understanding of the working-memory system, selective attention, and inhibition.

References _____

Baddeley, A. D., & Hitch, G. (1974). Working memory. In G. H. Bower (Ed.), *The psychology of learning and motivation* (Vol. 8, pp. 47–89). New York: Academic Press.

Broadbent, D. E. (1958). *Perception and communication.* New York: Pergamon.

Cherry, E. C. (1953). Some experiments on the recognition of speech, with one and with two ears. *Journal of the Acoustical Society of America, 25,* 975–979.

Conway, A. R. A., (Cowan, N., Bunting, M. F., Therriault, D. J., & Minkoff, S. R. B. (in press). A latent variable analysis of working memory capacity, short-term memory capacity, processing speed, and general fluid intelligence. *Intelligence.*

Conway, A. R. A., & Engle, R. W. (1994). Working memory and retrieval: A resource-dependent inhibition model. *Journal of Experimental Psychology: General, 123,* 354–373.

Conway, A. R. A., Tuholski, S. W., Shisler, R. J., & Engle, R. W. (1999). The effect of memory load on negative priming: An individual differences investigation. *Memory & Cognition, 27,* 1042–1050.

Daneman, M., & Carpenter, P. A. (1980). Individual differences in working memory and reading. *Journal of Verbal Learning & Verbal Behavior, 19,* 450–466.

Daneman, M., & Merikle, P. M. (1996). Working memory and language comprehension: A meta-analysis. *Psychonomic Bulletin & Review, 3,* 422–433.

Dempster F. N. (1991). Inhibitory processes: A neglected dimension of intelligence. *Intelligence, 15,* 157–173.

Engle, R. W., Tuholski, S. W., Laughlin, J. E., & Conway, A. R. A. (1999). Working memory, short-term memory and general fluid intelligence: A latent variable approach. *Journal of Experimental Psychology: General, 128,* 309–331.

Gernsbacher, M. A. (1993). Less skilled readers have less efficient suppression mechanisms. *Psychological Science, 4,* 294–298.

Gilhooly K. J., Logie R. H., Wetherick N. E., & Wynn V. (1993). Working memory and strategies in syllogistic-reasoning tasks. *Memory & Cognition, 21,* 115–124.

Hasher, L., & Zacks, R. T. (1988). Working memory, comprehension, and aging: A review and a new view. In G. H. Bower (Ed.), *The psychology of learning and motivation* (Vol. 22, pp. 193–225). San Diego: Academic Press.

Kane, M. J., & Engle, R. W. (2000). Working-memory capacity, proactive interference, and divided attention: Limits on long-term memory retrieval. *Journal of Experimental Psychology: Learning, Memory, & Cognition, 26,* 336–358.

Kyllonen, P. G. (1996). Is working memory capacity Spearman's *g?* In I. Dennis & E. Tapsfield (Eds.), *Human abilities. Their nature and measurement* (pp. 49–75). Mahwah, NJ: Erlbaum.

Lachman, R., Lachman, J. L., & Butterfield, E. C. (1979). *Cognitive psychology and information processing: An introduction.* Mahwah, NJ: Erlbaum.

Miyake, A., & Shah, P. (1999). *Models of working memory: Mechanisms of active maintenance and executive control.* New York: Cambridge University Press.

Moray, N. (1959). Attention in dichotic listening: Affective cues and the influence of instructions. *Quarterly Journal of Experimental Psychology, 11,* 56–60.

Rosen, V. M., & Engle, R. W. (1997). The role of working memory capacity in retrieval. *Journal of Experimental Psychology: General, 126,* 211–227.

Rosen, V. M., & Engle, R. W. (1998). Working memory capacity and suppression. *Journal of Memory & Language, 39,* 418–436.

Toms, M., Morris, N., & Ward, D. (1993). Working memory and conditional reasoning. *Quarterly Journal of Experimental Psychology, 46A,* 679–699.

Turner, M. L., & Engle, R. W. (1989). Is working memory capacity task dependent? *Journal of Memory & Language, 28,* 127–154.

Wood, N. L., & Cowan, N. (1995). The cocktail party phenomenon revisited: Attention and memory in the classic selective listening procedure of Cherry (1953). *Journal of Experimental Psychology: Learning, Memory, & Cognition, 21,* 255–260.

Introduction: Critical Thinking Questions

? Describe the classic speech shadowing paradigm that has been used to investigate the processes of selective attention.

? How did Broadbent's theory attempt to account for the initial findings from studies of selective attention? Why does semantic processing of unattended material challenge the model?

? The authors present two possibilities regarding individual differences in the cocktail party phenomenon, characterizing it either as a success or as a failure. Describe each of these alternatives.

? How does an operation-span task assess the capacity of working memory? How should performance of this task (i.e., working-memory capacity) relate to the cocktail party phenomenon?

Method: Critical Thinking Questions

? Describe what you would have been asked to do, had you been a participant in the experiment.

? Name the independent variables in the experiment, and their levels. Describe how each of these variables was operationalized. For each variable, state whether it was manipulated in a between-or within-subjects fashion. How many conditions were there in the experiment?

? What was (were) the dependent variable(s) in the experiment?

? What aspects of the methodology were implemented to deal with possible confounds?

Results/Discussion: Critical Thinking Questions

? Describe the major result—how did the incidence of the cocktail party phenomenon relate to working-memory capacity?

? What happened to shadowing performance before, at the same time, and after the participant's name was presented? Did these effects occur for all participants? If not, what accounted for the differences?

? Relate the major finding of the study to the notion of inhibitory processing; how might the failure of inhibitory processing lead to the incidence of the cocktail party phenomenon?

? After reading this study, you may feel there are other issues or questions that would be worthwhile or intriguing to address. Pose one of these questions (other than those suggested by the authors) that could be investigated empirically.

2

Memory Processes and Distortions

Marking Time

The Effect of Timing on Appointment Keeping

Sharlene D. Walbaum

*Abstract*_____

The retrospective memory literature suggests that people develop internal representations of time based on the stable occurrence of events in time. Two experiments were conducted to investigate whether the temporal structure of daily life affects prospective remembering. Fifty-six subjects in Experiment 1 were randomly assigned to an appointment time scheduled either during the 'work' week (assumed to be more routine-filled or structured) or the weekend (assumed to be less structured). Results, while non-significant, indicated that the number of reminders may have mediated performance. There was an attempt to control this in Experiment 2. The results indicate that appointments imbedded within more structured days are more easily recalled. © 1997 by John Wiley & Sons, Ltd.

Conceptual Issues and Theoretical Questions _____

- What factors affect prospective remembering—remembering to carry out future actions?
- What is the impact of concurrent activity on prospective memory success?
- What role do temporal (time-based) factors play in prospective remembering, more specifically, appointment keeping?

De-Jargonizing _____

retention interval: the amount of time that intervenes between the encoding and retrieval of some event

Walbaum, S. D. (1997). Marking time: The effect of timing on appointment keeping. *Applied Cognitive Psychology, 11,* 361–368. Copyright © 1997 by John Wiley & Sons, Ltd. Reproduced by permission of John Wiley & Sons Limited.

Most memory research focuses on retrieving images, words, or feelings from the past—hence the term 'retro-spective' memory. In the last decade, researchers have begun to study 'pro-spective' memory or the way cognitive representations and processes are involved in remembering to carry out planned actions. Prospective memory (PM) researchers use a variety of techniques to understand what it is, how it functions, and what factors affect it (Harris, 1984). Researchers have used interviews and questionnaires to explore perceived PM problems, PM abilities, and PM strategies (Beal, 1985; Herrmann, 1984; Lovelace and Twohig, 1990). PM researchers also conduct analog or quasi-experimental studies in which subjects carry out an assigned action in a context that is somewhat naturalistic, but over which the researcher exerts a degree of control. Such designs are used to study the effect of variables like incentive (c.f., Meacham and Singer, 1977), **retention interval** (c.f., Wilkins, as cited in Harris, 1984), type of cue (c.f., Meacham and Leiman, 1982), and context (c.f., Ceci and Bronfenbrenner, 1985) on PM.

The design of the research being reported here fits in the latter category. It is a systematic attempt to examine the impact of concurrent activities on prospective recall, an effort recommended by Martin (1986). It concerns appointment keeping, one type of prospective remembering. Appointments involve non-routine actions that must be carried out within very strict time constraints—this distinguishes appointment keeping from many other prospective memory tasks like remembering to take vitamins or buy groceries. Because precise timing is a necessary component of appointment keeping, the temporal structure of daily life might affect how well we carry out this task. Specifically, the periods of time within a day that are committed to routine activities could be used as reference points or anchors for the timing of an appointment.

The research being reported here parallels the efforts of other researchers who think that memory may operate differently depending on whether it is being tested in a naturalistic or a laboratory setting (c.f., Ceci and Bronfenbrenner, 1985). Prospective memory strategies used during an interval measured in days or weeks are likely to differ from those used during an interval measured in minutes or even hours. For example, assume that a subject's task is to remind the researcher of something at a particular time. If the time frame is an hour, a strategy like mental rehearsal is likely to be used and to be effective. In contrast, if the time frame is a week, rehearsal is unlikely to be tried or to be effective. Subjects in the latter case would be much more likely to use external strategies.

The literature on temporal factors in retrospective remembering suggests that people develop internal representations of time to orient themselves. They retrieve the timing of a past event by using knowledge about the timing of either routine or notable events. For example, Loftus and Marburger (1983) found that retrospective recall was more successful when subjects were given a well-known event to refer to as a sort of landmark in time. When subjects were told that the to-be-recalled event happened either before or after the eruption of Mt. St. Helens, their retrieval was more accurate. After reviewing survey research on retrospective memory, Jobe, Tourangeau, and Smith (1993) made the point that subjects apparently date target events by comparing them to the timing of well-known events. The order of past events in memory forms a structure in past time that can be used to facilitate retrospective recall. Similarly, knowledge about the order of planned, routine events can form a structure in future time that could be used to facilitate prospective recall.

It seems reasonable to assume that temporal orientation would be most likely to affect prospective remembering when timing is crucial, as it is in appointment keeping. Two experiments were conducted to investigate whether an appointment that is imbedded within a routine-filled day is easier to keep than one imbedded within a less scheduled day. Based on the retrospective memory work, it was hypothesized that more routines have the effect of lending structure to internal representations of time and can, therefore, provide internal cues for accurate timing in the service of appointment keeping.

Experiment 1

Method

Subjects

Fifty-nine residential Mount Holyoke College students were randomly assigned to either the 'weekend' condition or the 'weekday' condition. Their task was to keep an appointment scheduled between 10 a.m. and 2 p.m.

Materials

A Panasonic answering machine, Model No. KX-Tl720, 'stamped' each call with the appropriate time and date. The machine's time was used as the standard for measuring the difference between a subject's assigned call-in time and the time of her actual call.

The 'Prospective Memory Questionnaire for Students' was used to gauge subjects' perceptions of their prospective memory functioning and skills. It was based on the 'Metamemory Questionnaire' (Zelinski, Gilewski & Thompson, 1980), but with a more narrow focus. Subjects rated how frequently they used 14 prospective memory strategies, including 8 from the MMQ and 6 strategies that were identified during an earlier survey study.

Design and Procedure

Subjects attended a group meeting during which they filled out a schedule indicating the timing and type of their usual activities on Tuesdays, Wednesdays, Saturdays, and Sundays, between the hours of 10 a.m. and 2 p.m. They also made note of open or 'free' intervals that were 'at least 5 minutes long or long enough to find a phone and make a call'.

Subjects were told that they would be notified of their appointments one week in advance, both by campus mail and by phone (all students have answering machines). The appointment was to be kept by making a phone call, during which subjects were to describe everything they had done to keep the appointment. They were urged to call even if they missed their appointed time and to do so as soon as they remembered.

During the ensuing week, each subject was randomly assigned to a weekday (Tuesday or Wednesday) or a weekend (Saturday or Sunday) appointment time. Once a subject was assigned to a time slot, her schedule was checked to make sure there were no conflicts. When a conflict arose, the subject was randomly assigned to one of the time slots within the same condition.

The appointment phone line was used only for scheduled calls during this study. Twenty-four hour access made it possible for late subjects to call in as soon as they remembered. All subjects completed the Prospective Memory Questionnaire last because self-report about memory tends to be more accurate after engaging in a related task.

Results

The minutes that elapsed between a subject's appointment time and the time of her call was termed 'call-in latency'. The data for three subjects were omitted from the analysis of latency (two from the weekend condition and one from the weekday) because their latencies exceeded 24 hours. Of those subjects who were included in the analysis ($N = 56$), 27 were in the weekend condition and 29 in the weekday condition. An alpha level of 0.05 was used for all tests. A non-parametric test was used to analyse group differences because of negative skew in the distribution of latencies. The median call-in latencies for the two groups were similar (i.e. weekend $Mdn = 4$ minutes, weekday $Mdn = 3$ minutes), but the range of latencies was much larger for weekend subjects (681 minutes) than weekday subjects (346). A Mann–Whitney U analysis of the call-in latencies revealed no significant effect of time condition, Z corrected for ties ($N = 56$) = –0.33.

The tapes of the call-in reports were transcribed and coded using a coding system based on the strategies included in the PMQ (see Table 1). The inter-rater reliability for the coding system was significant, $r = 0.88$, $p < 0.001$.

The overall mean number of strategies reported to have been used was 2.36. A Spearman's correlational analysis revealed that the number of strategies was significantly negatively correlated with latency ($r_s = -0.27$, $p < 0.05$). As the number of reminders increased, call-in latencies decreased. The two most frequently mentioned strategies were

TABLE 1   *Frequency of strategy use in Experiment 1 contrasted with mean strategy use-ratings reported on the Prospective Memory Questionnaire (N = 56)*

Strategy	N	Use-rating
Mentally associated with other events	12	5.87
Review mental schedule	15	5.85
Put appointment on list of things to do	2	5.67
Use related object as cue	0	5.31
Leave verbal message in obvious place	34	5.26
Write message in appointment book	4	4.96
Write message in desk or wall calendar	30	4.96
Mentally rehearse appointment details	13	4.24
Ask someone to remind you	13	3.59
Put message on self (e.g., on hand)	5	3.59
Set clock to remind you	3	2.35
Use neutral object as environmental cue	0	2.02
Put nonspecific cue on self	0	1.28
Set a watch to remind you	0	1.22

writing a message on a desk or wall calendar ($n = 30$) and writing a message on a note (rather than a calendar) and leaving it in an obvious location ($n = 34$). Many subjects reported using both.

These data were compared to their ratings for strategies on the PMQ (see Table 1). The two strategies used most frequently in the experiment were not the two with the highest use-ratings. Leaving a note in an obvious place and making an entry in a calendar were given the fifth- and seventh-highest use-ratings, respectively. 'Mental association' was the top-ranked strategy on the PMQ, but only 21% of the subjects reported using it in the experiment. Likewise, only 27% said that they used the second-highest ranked strategy, 'review mental schedule'. Less than 4% reported using two other strategies rated in the top five, relying on a list or a related object to cue recall.

Discussion

The results of the Mann–Whitney U test were not significant; however, the range of latencies for subjects in the weekend condition was twice that of weekday subjects. Also, the number of reported reminders was negatively related to latency. These outcomes indicate the need for another test of the main hypothesis—that routinely scheduled activities provide fixed points or 'time-marks' for an internal time-frame and that these time-marks facilitate the encoding and subsequent recall of appointment information.

The significant (although small) negative correlation between the number of reported strategies and the call-in latencies may reflect either a tendency for the more punctual subjects to use more reminders, or a tendency for them to remember having used more strategies, or a tendency for them to just report having used more strategies. If the former is the case, the results of Experiment 1 can only support the assertion that reminders help people remember. A second experiment was designed to test the time-marking hypothesis under more carefully controlled circumstances.

Experiment 2

Method

Subjects

Twenty-nine residential Mount Holyoke College students were randomly assigned to either the weekday ($N = 14$) or the weekend ($N = 15$) condition.

Materials

The same materials were used as in Experiment 1. In addition to these, each subject received an unlined index card with the following information printed on it: appointment time, date, and the phone number she was to call.

Design and Procedure

The design and procedure were the same as before, with one exception. Subjects were instructed to only use one external reminder. They received note cards to use as reminders when they received their appointment notices. Each subject was instructed to attach the notecard to the door frame of her dormitory room at eye level, so the note would be seen when leaving. They were carefully reminded not to use any other external cue.

Results

The median latency for the weekend subjects (N = 15) was 61 minutes and for weekday subjects (N = 14) it was 3.5 minutes. A Mann–Whitney U test was used to analyse the call-in latencies for the two groups. There was significant effect of condition, Z corrected for ties (N = 29) = –2.06. The range for the weekend latencies was 590 minutes, while it was 77 minutes for weekday latencies.

   In addition, the schedule entries submitted by subjects at the start of both Experiments 1 and 2 were analysed using a chi-square test. The schedule entries were coded using the following coding categories: *chore* (e.g., 'clean room'), *externally schedule* (e.g. 'go to class'), *leisure* (e.g. 'listen to music in room') or *mixed* (e.g., as a single entry, 'hang out with friends *or* go to post office'). Then, frequencies within each category were tallied. Weekend entries were compared to weekday entries using a 2 × 4 chi-square analysis and the results were significant, χ^2 (8, N = 288) = 10.66, π < 0.01. The post-hoc analysis indicated that significantly more of the weekday entries (56%) consisted of externally scheduled activities when compared to the weekend entries (38%). In contrast, leisure activities were significantly more likely to be entered on weekend schedules (17%) than on weekday schedules (8%).

General Discussion

Results from Experiment 2 indicate that it was easier to keep an appointment when it was scheduled during the week. This effect emerged when subjects were restricted to one reminder; latencies for weekend subjects were much shorter in Experiment 1 (*Mdn* = 4 minutes) than they were in Experiment 2 (*Mdn* = 61). In both experiments, the variation in response latencies was much larger for weekend than weekday subjects.

   The experimental manipulation, which minimized available external support for remembering, prompted subjects to rely more heavily on their internal time frames. Weekend time frames, being less structured, offered weekend subjects less internal support (i.e., provided them with fewer internal reminders). Consequently, they were much more likely to be late for their appointments and more time passed before they finally remembered. On the other hand, weekday subjects could rely on a more structured internal time frame. Response latencies for weekday subjects remained about the same across experiments (*Mdn* = 3 vs. *Mdn* = 3.5), despite the relative absence of external cues in the second study. There was also a drop in the range of their latencies (from 346 to 77 minutes); less variation in Experiment 2 may indicate that internal time cues (when available) can be quite effective reminders.

These results run counter to what one might expect, given work by researchers such as Koriat, Fischhoff, and Razel (1976) and Shanon (1979). Their research indicates that subjects use the weekend days as mental landmarks when engaging in retrospective recall. As Friedman (1986) pointed out, weekends are probably more memorable because people spend more time thinking about them, whether in anticipation, during them, or through recollection. However, in the research being reported here, weekend appointments were not easier to remember. It appears that what makes a weekend day memorable in retrospect is different from what we would use to carry out prospective remembering. Retrospective and prospective remembering may involve different temporal frameworks. The former may depend on a more global frame of reference, like the structure of a week, while the latter may depend more on local or daily time structure, such as is provided by routine activities.

The significant relationship between number of reminders and call-in latency suggests that more punctual subjects were using more reminders. They tended to use external strategies like notes and calendars, a result that is in accordance with other studies of actual strategy use. Children and adults generally prefer to use external strategies because they are reliable and are less effortful than mental strategies such as rehearsal (e.g. Intons-Peterson and Fournier, 1986; Kreutzer, Leonard and Flavell, 1975). In an interesting contrast, subjects' PMQ use-ratings indicated that they favoured internal strategies like mental association and mental review. These ratings were probably a reflection of what subjects know about effective strategies, and not what they actually do. The contrast here between self-report and behaviour underscores the importance of studying prospective remembering directly.

The post-hoc analysis of subjects' schedules supports the decision to operationalize 'time structure' in terms of segments of the week. The schedule entries differ in their potential to structure a day. Externally scheduled activities are most likely to provide structure because of their routine and stable timing. There were significantly more of these activities on weekdays. Chores and leisure activities are less likely to provide stable structure, because their timing can vary. Chores were listed as frequently on weekdays as on weekends, but leisure activities were listed significantly less often on weekdays. In summary, subjects described their weekdays as involving more activities with potential for structuring time while their weekends involved fewer.

Variation in 'time structure', as operationalized in the study being reported here, could have been confounded by other aspects of weekend/weekday variation. For example, the greater number of leisure activities on the weekend could affect motivation, making subjects less attentive to the appointment-keeping task. This explanation accounts for the results of Experiment 2, but for an alternative explanation like this one to be adequate, it would need to address the no-group-difference finding from Experiment 1. The pattern of results from the latency and correlational analyses taken together suggests that the different time contexts impacted on prospective recall. Future attempts to expand on these results should employ a different operational definition of the time structure concept.

In conclusion, the experiments reported here offer at least preliminary evidence that time periods marked by routinely occurring events support recall of a novel event. Attempts should be made to replicate these results. Many other factors are likely to affect one's success on such a task, factors such as the number and type of reminders, the degree to which routine events are truly habitual, familiarity with the task of appointment keeping, and the person's motivation. Future research should extend the current results through a systematic examination of these factors.

References

Beal, C. R. (1985). Development of knowledge about the use of cues to aid prospective retrieval. *Child Development, 56,* 631–642.

Ceci, S. J. and Bronfenbrenner, U. (1985). 'Don't forget to take the cupcakes out of the oven': Prospective memory, strategic time-monitoring, and context. *Child Development, 56*(1), 152–164.

Friedman, W. J. (1986). The development of children's knowledge of temporal structure. *Child Development, 57,* 1385–1400.

Harris, J. E. (1984). Remembering to do things: A forgotten topic. In J. E. Harris and P. E. Morris (Eds.), *Everyday memory, actions, and absent-mindedness* (pp. 71–92). London: Academic Press.

Herrmann, D. J. (1984). Questionnaires about memory. In J. E. Harris and P. E. Morris (Eds.), *Everyday memory, actions, and absent-mindedness* (pp. 153–172). London: Harcourt, Brace, Jovanovich.

Intons-Peterson, M. J. and Fournier, J. (1986). External and internal memory aids: When and how to use them. *Journal of Experimental Psychology: General, 115,* 267–280

Jobe, J. B., Tourangeau, R. and Smith, A. F. (1993). Contributions of survey research to the understanding of memory. *Applied Cognitive Psychology 7,* 567–584.

Koriat, A., Fischhoff, B. and Razel, O. (1976). An inquiry into the process of temporal orientation. *Acta Psychologica, 40,* 57–73.

Kreutzer, M. A., Leonard, C. and Flavell, J. H. (1975). An interview study of children's knowledge about memory. *Monographs of the Society for Research in Child Development, 40*(1, Serial No. 159).

Loftus, E. F. and Marburger, W. (1983). Since the eruption of Mt. St. Helens, has anyone beaten you up? Improving the accuracy of retrospective reports with landmark events. *Memory and Cognition, 11,* 114–120.

Lovelace, E. A. and Twohig, P. T. (1990). Healthy older adults' perceptions of their memory functioning and use of mnemonics. *Bulletin of the Psychonomic Society, 28*(2), 115–118.

Martin, M. (1986). Ageing and patterns of change in everyday memory and cognition. *Human Learning, 5,* 63–74.

Meacham, J. A. and Leiman, B. (1982). Remembering to perform future actions. In U. Neisser (Ed.), *Memory observed Remembering in natural contexts* (pp. 327–336). San Francisco: Freeman.

Meacham, J. A. and Singer, J. (1977). Incentive in prospective remembering. *Journal of Psychology, 97,* 191–197.

Shanon, B. (1979). Yesterday, today, and tomorrow. *Acta Psychologica, 43,* 469–476.

Zelinski, E. M., Gilewski, M. J. and Thompson, L. W. (1980). Do laboratory tests relate to self assessment of memory ability in the young and old? In L. W. Poon, J. L. Fozard, L. S. Cermak, D. Arenberg and L. W. Thompson (Eds.), *New directions in memory and aging* (pp. 519–544). Hillsdale, New Jersey: Lawrence Erlbaum.

Introduction: Critical Thinking Questions

? What are the two general ways in which prospective memory has been investigated?

? What is the difference between appointment keeping and other prospective memory tasks, and how might the temporal structure of day-to-day life influence it?

? What is the main difference between prospective memory as tested in a laboratory setting and a real-world setting? How might this difference affect the strategies used by people in these respective situations?

? What do previous findings suggest regarding the role of temporal factors in retrospective remembering? How might such factors operate in prospective remembering?

? The author hypothesizes a relationship between routine and prospective memory success. Describe her hypothesis.

? How did Experiment 2 differ from Experiment 1, and what was the purpose of the change?

Method: Critical Thinking Questions

? For each experiment, describe what you would have been asked to do, had you been a participant.

? Name the independent variables in each experiment, and their levels. Describe how each of these variables was operationalized. For each variable, state whether it was manipulated in a between-subjects or within-subjects fashion. How many conditions were there in the experiment?

? What was (were) the dependent variable(s) in each experiment?

? What aspects of the methodology were implemented to deal with possible confounds?

Results/Discussion: Critical Thinking Questions

? What did Experiment 1 reveal about prospective memory strategies? In general, were strategies helpful? Which strategies were most commonly used?

? Did the strategies actually used by the participants in Experiment 1 match with the strategies they listed on the pre-experiment questionnaire? Explain.

? Although no difference in prospective memory success was found in Experiment 1, what findings suggested some sort of difference between the routine and non-routine was likely the case?

? In Experiment 2 was there any difference in prospective memory success between the routine and non-routine groups?

? The present findings seem to conflict with those obtained for retrospective memory for events that occurred on weekends vs. weekdays. Describe this difference. The author proposes that retrospective and prospective memory may involve "different temporal frameworks." Explain her argument.

? What interesting discrepancy was found between self-reported prospective memory behavior and actual behavior? What does this indicate about how prospective memory should be studied? Why?

? The author offers several ideas for future research. Choose one and explain why you think it should be investigated, and how you might go about investigating it.

? After reading this study, you may feel there are other issues or questions that would be worthwhile or intriguing to address. Pose one of these questions (other than those suggested by the authors) that could be investigated empirically.

Memory for Humorous Cartoons

Stephen R. Schmidt and Alan R. Williams

Abstract

Incidental memory for three types of cartoons was compared: original cartoons, literal transla-tions of the originals, and weird *cartoons created by inserting incongruous material into the lit-eral translations. In Experiment 1, the three types of cartoons were mixed together in lists. In Experiment 2, each list contained only two cartoon types. In both experiments, original cartoons were remembered better than the literal and the weird cartoons, whereas the literal and the weird cartoons were equally well remembered. The detection of incongruities, or attempts to resolve those incongruities, cannot adequately explain the observed humor effects. The results were also inconsistent with both rehearsal and distinctiveness interpretations. Rather, humor per se appears to support good memory performance. Perhaps participants elaborated or gave sustained atten-tion to humorous material at the expense of less humorous material.*

Conceptual Issues and Theoretical Questions

- Does humor make an event more memorable?
- What are the possible mechanisms through which humor might produce better memory for an event?
- Is humor beneficial to memory in and of itself, or does its beneficial effect derive from some other (conflated) factor (e.g., increased attention, distinctiveness, etc.)?

De-Jargonizing

incidental instructions: study conditions in which participants are not informed of a forthcom-ing memory test

intentional instructions: study conditions in which participants are told to prepare for a forth-coming memory test

Schmidt, S. R., & Williams, A. R. (2001). Memory for humorous cartoons. *Memory and Cognition, 29,* 305–311. Reprinted by permission of Psychonomic Society, Inc.

von Restorff effect: phenomenon whereby items that are physically different in some way (i.e., a word printed in red ink presented among other words presented in black) are better remembered

isolation effect: phenomenon whereby list items are better remembered if isolated from other items in some manner

bizarre imagery effect: the finding that forming a bizarre image of some set of concepts leads to better memory for those concepts, relative to conditions in which a non-bizarre image is formed

within-list design: design in which different item types (e.g., funny and unfunny cartoons) are combined in the same list

interrater reliability: the degree of consistency in rating observed in a set of raters

orthographic distinctiveness: the degree to which a word's lettering looks unique, or distinct from other words (*lynx* is orthographically distinct; *house* is not)

One of the major goals of memory research is to determine why some events are more memorable than others. This goal can be achieved by studying how variations in the learning materials influence memory. Thus, numerous researchers have investigated the effects of word frequency, word concreteness, imagery value, pleasantness, sentence complexity, sentence bizarreness, and emotional stimuli on memory. However, very little attention has been paid to how humor influences memory. Humor is often employed by educators, advertisers, entertainers, and even politicians to gain our attention and sustain our interest. It is important that we determine how this potent and pervasive stimulus variable influences memory performance.

Previous research has established that humor enhances memory. For example, Kaplan and Pascoe (1977) demonstrated that humorous examples from a lecture were remembered better than serious examples. Similarly, humor can enhance memory for advertisements (Duncan, Nelson, & Frontzak, 1984; Gelb & Zinkhan, 1986). However, much of this earlier research provided only anecdotal or quasi-experimental support for the positive effect of humor on memory. When relevant mnemonic variables are controlled, conditions leading to a humor effect are clearly limited. Schmidt (1994) found that humorous sentences were recalled better than nonhumorous sentences in lists containing both sentence types. However, a homogeneous list of humorous sentences was not remembered better than a homogeneous list of nonhumorous sentences. In fact, enhanced recall of humorous sentences was found at the expense of the nonhumorous sentences in the same list. The humor effect was found with **intentional** but not **incidental instructions.** Finally, the effects of humor were observed with measures of sentence recall and not with measures of memory for sentence details. These limitations to the impact of humor on memory are of great practical and theoretical interest. The goals of the research presented below were to further delineate the conditions leading to positive effects of humor on memory and to evaluate several explanations for those effects.

One important empirical issue concerning the impact of humor on memory is the potential confound between humor and incongruity. Incongruity results when material is presented out of context, or when unusual combinations of material are presented. Investigations concerning the **von Restorff effect,** the **isolation effect,** and the **bizarre imagery effect** can be viewed as attempts to understand the impacts of incongruity on memory (Schmidt, 1991). Several theorists have argued that incongruity is a source of humor (Deckers & Devine, 1981; Suls, 1972). In text comprehension, humor may result from violations of readers' predictions concerning upcoming text (Suls, 1972). Readers are "surprised" when their predictions are thwarted, and they search for a rule that allows the ending of the sentence to match the beginning. Consider the following sample sentence from Schmidt (1994): "There are three ways a man can wear his hair: parted, unparted, and departed" (p. 966). The reader does not expect the word *departed,* which creates an incongruity. The reader then searches for a rule that allows the sentence to make sense. If a rule is found, the incongruity is resolved, and the reader perceives humor. Failure to find an appropriate rule leads to puzzlement with no perception of humor.

Although it is clear that humor often contains incongruities, the role that incongruity plays in determining the effects of humor on memory is unclear. Researchers have argued that incongruity may lead to increased attention to stimuli (Green, 1958; Karis, Fabiani, & Donchin, 1984; Schmidt, 1991). The putative effects of humor on memory may result from the perception of the inherent incongruities and the resultant increased attention. Alternatively, the attempt to resolve the incongruities contained in humorous material may involve cognitive processes that lead to good memory performance. That is, readers may engage in elaborative processes while searching for a rule to make a humorous sentence comprehensible. This elaboration may lead to increased memory for the humorous material. Finally, the resolution of the incongruity and/or the resultant perception of humor may lead to increased memory for the humorous material. It is important that we disentangle how detecting an incongruity, attempting to resolve that incongruity, resolving the incongruity, and perceiving humor all individually influence memory performance.

A second important issue is determining whether the humor effect is limited to intentional learning conditions. Perhaps the sentences employed in the Schmidt (1994) experiment were simply not funny enough, or perhaps the experiment lacked sufficient statistical power. If the humor effect does occur only in intentional learning, certain explanations of the effect can be easily eliminated. For example, increased attention to incongruity is thought to be an automatic process (Ohman, 1979). If the humor effect is limited to intentional learning, it cannot be the result of an automated attention response to incongruous material.

The fact that the humor effect was limited to intentional learning led Schmidt (1994) to favor a rehearsal explanation of his results. He argued that humorous material received increased rehearsal at the expense of nonhumorous material. Several additional findings supported this conclusion. Recall of humorous sentences had a negative impact on the recall of nonhumorous sentences, suggesting a tradeoff between processing humorous and processing nonhumorous material. Furthermore, the humor effect was limited to **within-lists designs.** Such designs are necessary before humorous items can be rehearsed at the expense of nonhumorous items.

Despite this early support, recent research has tended to undermine the differential rehearsal hypothesis. Vella-Brodrick, Jory and Whelan (1996) compared memory for humorous and nonhumorous sentences under experimenter-paced and self-paced conditions. Contrary to the differential rehearsal hypothesis, the humor effect occurred in both the experimenter-paced and the self-paced conditions. A rehearsal explanation would be further undermined if the humor effect were to be found in incidental learning.

In summary, the research presented below had two primary motivations. First, we attempted to separate the potential effects of incongruity and humor on memory. Second, we provided further tests for the humor effect under incidental learning conditions. Our research team selected from Gary Larson's published collections cartoons that we judged to be extremely funny. With a stronger manipulation of humor, we hoped to find a humor effect with incidental instructions. Three versions of selected cartoons were created to aid in the separation of humor and incongruity. The first type of cartoon was the original and unaltered version. The originals contained incongruities between the captions and the pictures and were intended to be humorous. In one cartoon, for example, a woman is standing at a window calling her dog. The dog is pictured running full speed down the front walk toward the front door of the house. The door contains a small dog door that is clearly nailed shut, with the hammer and nails displayed in the foreground of the cartoon. The caption reads: "Here Fifi! C'mon!… Faster, Fifi!" A second type of cartoon depicted a "literal" translation of the cartoon caption. In this version, we eliminated the humor of the cartoon by removing the incongruent pictorial material. In the example above, all evidence that the door was nailed shut was removed from the picture, including the hammer and nails. A third type of cartoon (weird) was created by adding incongruent information to the literal versions. In the weird cartoons, the incongruity could not be resolved, and consequently these cartoons ought not to have been humorous. In the weird version of our example, the dog was removed from the literal version and replaced by a large snake. The three versions of each cartoon enabled us to contrast the effects of (1) incongruity plus humor (original cartoon), (2) neither incongruity nor humor (literal version), and (3) incongruity with no humor (weird version). Thus, the effects of incongruity and humor on memory could be separated.

Experiment 1

In Experiment 1, all three types of cartoons were mixed together in a within-lists design. In addition, incidental learning instructions were employed to determine whether the humor effect could be found under conditions that minimize intentional verbal rehearsal processes.

Method

Participants

Eighty-four participants from the Psychology participant pool were randomly assigned to three experimental conditions. The participant pool consists primarily of students earning course credit for General Psychology. Students in other psychology courses participated for extra credit.

Materials and Design

Twenty-four cartoons were selected from Larson (1985, 1987, 1988). Three versions of each cartoon were prepared: original, literal, and weird. The literal versions were created by whiting out incongruous information and adding literal interpretations by cutting and pasting elements from other cartoons. Similarly, the weird versions were creating by pasting incongruent elements from unrelated cartoons into the literal cartoons. All cartoons contained picture elements drawn only by the original artist. In addition, each version of a cartoon contained the same caption. The cartoons were photographed on slide film. The slides were then used to present the material on a screen in front of the students, using a Kodak Ektagraphic slide projector controlled by an electronic timing device. Three experimental conditions were tested that represented the counterbalancing of cartoons across cartoon types. These three arbitrary conditions contained 28, 30, and 26 participants. Each cartoon was presented in its original, literal, and weird forms across participants. Cartoon type was manipulated within subjects.

In a pilot study, 24 participants were asked to use a 5-point scale to rate each slide on four dimensions: familiarity, humor, bizarreness, and comprehensibility. A summary of the rating data is presented in Table 1. Significant differences were observed across cartoon types in the humor ratings [$F(2,40) = 33.68$, $MS_e = 0.7774$], bizarreness ratings [$F(2,40) = 4.69$, $MS_e = 1.3082$], and comprehension ratings [$F(2,40) = 13.55$, $MS_e = 0.7422$]. Newman-Keuls tests revealed that the original cartoons were rated as more humorous ($M = 5.10$) than the literal ($M = 3.08$) and weird ($M = 3.25$) cartoons, but the literal and weird cartoons were not significantly different from one another. The humorous and weird cartoons were rated as more bizarre than the literal cartoons, with means equal to 3.92, 4.27, and 3.21, respectively. The difference in bizarreness ratings between the humorous and the weird cartoons was not significant. The comprehension ratings revealed that the humorous cartoons ($M = 1.56$) were easier to understand than the literal ($M = 2.61$) and weird ($M = 2.87$) cartoons. The difference between the literal and the weird cartoons was not significant.

Procedure

The participants were told that the experiment concerned the relationship between the perception of humor and mathematical abilities. The instructions described the slide presentation of the cartoons and a subsequent arithmetic task. Each slide was presented for 15 sec, followed by a 15-sec rating period. During the rating period, the participants were asked to rate the humor of the cartoons and rate "how difficult is it to get the humor in the cartoon." Following the slide presentation, the students were asked to perform arithmetic for 5 min.

TABLE 1 *Ratings of the Three Cartoon Types on Four Scales*

	Rating Scale			
Cartoon Version	*Humor*	*Bizarreness*	*Familiarity*	*Comprehension*
Original	5.10	3.92	2.67	1.56
Literal	3.08	3.21	2.55	2.61
Weird	3.25	4.27	2.22	2.87
$F(2,40) =$	33.68*	4.69*	0.86	13.55*

*$p < .05$.

They were then allotted 10 min to recall the cartoons. On the memory test, they were asked to write a brief description of each slide that they remembered and to recall the captions of those slides. The memory test was unexpected.

Results and Discussion

The probabilities of picture recall, caption recall, and word recall served as measures of cartoon memory. A picture was scored as recalled if the experimenter could uniquely identify the cartoon from a participant's description. Caption recall was scored by a lenient criterion. If the experimenter could identify the cartoon from the recalled caption and at least one word was correctly recalled, the participant was given credit for that cartoon caption. For the probability of word recall, we computed the proportion of words that were accurately recalled; changes in number and tense were allowed, and synonyms were accepted. Two researchers independently scored each of these variables, and discrepancies were resolved. **Interrater reliabilities** were determined for a subset of the participants ($n = 30$). There were three disagreements in the 720 judgments of picture and caption recall, yielding reliabilities in excess of 99% for these two measures. Reliability for word recall was 94%. Two additional measures of cartoon memory were derived from the original three. A strict measure of caption recall was defined as the recall of 50% or more of the words from a caption. We also calculated the probability of word recall, given lenient caption recall (words/caption). This conditional probability provided a measure of memory for detailed caption information. In order to isolate the effects of cartoon type from a potential primacy effect, data from the first three cartoons (one of each type) were excluded from the analyses. The results for each of the memory measures are discussed below and summarized in Table 2. The level of significance for all tests was set at $p < .05$.

A main effect of cartoon type was observed for three of the memory measures: picture recall [$F_1(2,162) = 7.45$, $MS_e = 0.2421$; $F_2(2,12) = 15.35$, $MS_e = 0.1175$], word recall [$F_1 (2,162) = 5.09$, $MS_e = 0.0527$; $F_2(2,12) = 6.00$, $MS_e = 0.0447$], and lenient caption recall [$F_1(2,162) = 9.16$, $MS_e = 0.2120$, $F_2(2,12) = 13.89$, $MS_e = 0.1398$]. With each of these measures, Newman-Keuls tests indicated that original cartoons were remembered better than the literal and weird cartoons. Recall of literal and weird cartoons did not differ significantly. Cartoon type did not significantly affect recall as measured by strict caption recall [$F_1 (2,162) = 1.22$, $MS_e = 0.1129$; $F_2(2,12) = 1.01$, $MS_e = 0.1364$] or words recalled

TABLE 2 *Probability of Picture Recall, Caption Recall, Word Recall, and Word Recall from Recalled Captions as a Function of Cartoon Type From Experiment 1*

Cartoon Version	Pictures Recalled	Words Recalled	Captions Lenient	Captions Strict	Words/ Caption
Original	.45	.16	.40	.14	.38
Literal	.35	.12	.29	.11	.40
Weird	.37	.13	.31	.12	.40

per caption recalled [F_1 (2,100) = 0.5 8, MS_e = 0.0106; F_2 cannot be calculated when word recall is conditionalized on caption recall].

The different memory measures converge on a common pattern of results. On memory measures sensitive to cartoon access (picture, word, and lenient sentence recall), humorous cartoons were remembered better than literal and weird cartoons. On measures that focus on recall of detailed cartoon information, cartoon type had no effect on memory. These results conform to the pattern reported by Schmidt (1994), who demonstrated that humor affected recall of sentences but not of sentence detail. The results also are consistent with results reported by McDaniel and Einstein (1986), who found that bizarre imagery aided sentence access but not recall of words from accessed sentences.

The present pattern of results helped to distinguish among the effects of detecting an incongruity, processes aimed at resolving the incongruity, and the resolution of the incongruity and perception of humor. The humorous and the weird cartoons were rated equally bizarre; however, the participants remembered more humorous cartoons than weird cartoons. Thus, humor is apparently the potent mnemonic variable with these materials rather than incongruity or bizarreness. Perhaps the humorous cartoons were processed more extensively than the nonhumorous cartoons. The literal cartoons were easy to understand; thus, their processing could have been quickly completed. The humorous cartoons required increased processing as the participants attempted to "get" the cartoons. However, the participants ought to have processed weird cartoons at least as extensively as the original cartoons, because the weird cartoons were mixed in the humorous cartoons and the participants had every reason to try to "get" the humor in the weird cartoons. The humor effect must be attributed to the actual resolution of the incongruity and/or the resultant perception of humor, rather than to increased processing in search of humor.

Humor clearly enhanced memory under conditions that minimized the influence of intentional verbal rehearsal. The participants did not expect a memory test. Unless there is some intrinsic reason to rehearse humorous material, there was little reason for participants to rehearse in this task. In addition, the complex visual and verbal composition of the cartoons should have made verbal rehearsal difficult. Thus, the results weaken the rehearsal explanation of the humor effect.

Perhaps the humorous cartoons were distinctive within the context of a set containing humorous, weird, and literal cartoons. The distinctive qualities of the humorous cartoons might have led the participants to give those cartoons increased attention or elaboration during encoding. Alternatively, distinctive material might benefit from a special status at retrieval (DeLosh & McDaniel, 1996), being recalled first and subjected to less output interference than common material. Some support for a distinctiveness interpretation was obtained in an analysis of output order. The output percentiles for original, literal, and weird cartoons were 52.89, 58.25, and 63.24, respectively, revealing a significant main effect [F_1(2,122) = 4.15]. Additional evidence concerning the role of distinctiveness is presented below.

Experiment 2

The purpose of Experiment 2 was to explore the role that list structure plays in producing the humor effect, and to further examine the impacts of incongruity and distinctiveness on memory. In Experiment 1, the lists contained all three types of cartoons, limiting the generality of the results. In Experiment 2, sets of cartoons were created that contained only two types of cartoons. One set contained original and literal cartoons, a second set contained original and weird cartoons, and a third set contained weird and literal cartoons.

Given the results already reported, original cartoons should be remembered better than literal cartoons in the original/literal lists. This result can be explained by any number of hypotheses, including increased attention to incongruous material, increased elaboration in search of humor, distinctiveness, and sustained attention due to humor per se. However, the theoretical options would be narrowed if the humor effect was also obtained in a set composed of half original cartoons and half weird cartoons. According to the incongruity hypothesis, such a set would be equivalent to an all-bizarre list. Original cartoons should not be retained better than the weird cartoons, because both are equally incongruous. This pattern of results would also challenge the notion that the humor effect can be attributed to the increased elaboration aimed at resolving incongruities. Participants should attempt to "get" the humor in both the original and the weird cartoons. However, a distinctiveness explanation might still be viable: The original cartoons were both humorous and unusual, whereas the weird cartoons were simply unusual. Humorous material may "stand out" in the context of the nonhumorous weird cartoons, in manner analogous to the effects of bizarreness (McDaniel, Einstein, DeLosh, May, & Brady, 1995) and **orthographic distinctiveness** (Hunt & Elliott, 1980) found in 50/50 lists. The distinctiveness interpretation does not require, a priori, that the humorous cartoons be remembered better than the weird cartoons, but such a finding would not contradict the distinctiveness interpretation. Observation of the humor effect in the original/weird list would be most consistent with the hypothesis that humor, rather than incongruity or distinctiveness, supports good memory for cartoons.

Experiment 2 also provided a way to test the distinctiveness interpretation of the humor effect. Perhaps in Experiment 1 the literal and weird cartoons were perceived as a homogeneous set of "unfunny cartoons." Because the original cartoons were funny, they stood out as a group from these background cartoons. Thus, the original cartoons were remembered best, and no difference was observed between the memory of the literal and that of the weird cartoons. However, if a list contains only weird and literal cartoons, the incongruity in the weird cartoons should make them distinctive and thus they should be recalled better than the literal cartoons. The fact that the weird cartoons were rated as more bizarre than the literal cartoons adds weight to this argument. Alternatively, if the perception of humor produces the memory effects, then literal and weird cartoons should be retained equally well because they were judged as equally humorous.

In summary, four potential explanations of the humor effect were tested in this experiment: incongruity, elaboration in search of humor, distinctiveness, and humor per se. Each explanation makes a different prediction concerning the paired comparisons of the three cartoon types. These predictions are presented in Table 3.

Method

Participants

One hundred and twenty-eight students were selected from the same source as in Experiment 1.

TABLE 3   *Memory Predictions of Four Hypotheses for Each List Structure in Experiment 2*

	List Structure		
Hypothesis	*Orignal/Literal*	*Original/Weird*	*Weird/Literal*
Incongruity	O > L	O = W	W > L
Elaboration in search of humor	O > L	O = W	W > L
Distinctiveness	O > L	O ≥ W	W > L
Humor per se	O > L	O > W	W = L

Note: O, Original; L, Literal; W, Weird. See text for an explanation of each hypothesis.

Materials and Design

The set of cartoons was the same as that employed in the first experiment. The order of the cartoons remained constant across experiments, but the particular versions of the cartoons were rearranged to create the six experimental conditions. These conditions were created by crossing three list structures with two counterbalancing groups of cartoons. Type of cartoon was manipulated within subjects, but each participant viewed only two types of cartoons. One list structure contained original and weird cartoons ($n = 44$); another list structure contained original and literal cartoons ($n = 41$); and a third list structure contained weird and literal cartoons ($n = 43$). Across participants, each cartoon appeared in each form within a given list structure. That is, one group of participants viewed the weird form of Cartoon 1 and the original form of Cartoon 2, whereas a second group viewed the original form of Cartoon 1 and the weird form of Cartoon 2.

Procedure

The procedure was nearly identical to that employed in Experiment 1. Participants viewed each cartoon for 15 sec, followed by a 15-sec rating task. They then performed 5 min of arithmetic and were given 10 min to recall the cartoons. As in Experiment 1, the memory test was unexpected. The only procedural difference was that participants were asked simply to rate the humor of the cartoons.

Results and Discussion

In Experiment 1, data from the first three cartoons were discarded prior to the analyses. These three cartoons represented one cartoon of each type. In this experiment, each list contained only two types of cartoons. In order to be as consistent as possible with the previous study, we discarded data from the first two cartoons in Experiment 2. A summary of the memory data is presented in Table 4.

The effects of cartoon type varied as a function of the particular combinations of cartoons contained in the list, with the interactions between list structure and type of cartoon

TABLE 4 *Probability of Picture Recall, Caption Recall, Word Recall, and Words/Caption Recall as a Function of Type of Cartoon and List Structure in Experiment 2*

Cartoon Version	Pictures Recalled	Words Recalled	Captions Lenient	Captions Strict	Words/ Caption
List Containing Original and Weird Cartoons					
Original	.36	.18	.35	.21	.52
Weird	.31	.15	.30	.16	.49
List Containing Original and Literal Cartoons					
Original	.45	.23	.45	.25	.50
Literal	.32	.16	.31	.17	.49
Lists Containing Weird and Literal Cartoons					
Weird	.35	.15	.32	.18	.49
Literal	.35	.14	.31	.15	.43

Note: Cartoon type was manipulated within subjects.

significant for picture recall [$F_1(2,122) = 5.00$, $MS_e = 0.1337$; $F_2(2,20) = 4.46$, $MS_e = 0.2107$], word recall [$F_1(2,122) = 3.61$, $MS_e = 0.0518$; $F_2(2,20) = 5.21$, $MS_e = 0.0359$], and lenient caption recall [$F_1(2,122) = 5.45$, $MS_e = 0.1772$, $F_2(2,20) = 6.37$, $MS_e = 0.1516$]. This interaction was not significant with strict recall of captions [$F(2,122) = 1.18$, $MS_e = 0.0940$] or with the conditional probability of word recall given caption recall [$F(2,119) = 1.03$, $MS_e = 0.0105$].

The LSD tests revealed essentially the same pattern of results when memory for pictures, words, and captions (scored leniently and strictly) was compared across conditions. In each case, original cartoons were recalled better than literal and weird cartoons, and the literal and weird cartoons were retained equally well. A different pattern of results emerged in the analysis of the conditional probability of word recall, given caption recall. Only the difference between the weird ($M = .49$) and the literal cartoons ($M = .43$) proved reliable [$F(1,119) = 5.98$]. These results replicated those of Experiment 1 and are consistent with the results of Schmidt (1994). In addition, the present results support the position that humor, rather than the incongruity contained in humorous cartoons, leads to good memory. Furthermore, any elaboration of humorous cartoons can be attributed to their humor rather than to the fact that they stand out as different from the rest of the cartoons.

In Experiment 1, the memorial consequences of resolving incongruities could not be clearly differentiated from the effects of the perception of humor. The design of Experiment 2 provided an opportunity to separate these effects by assessing recall as a function of rated humor in lists that contained unresolvable incongruities (i.e., the weird cartoons). The recall data were sorted into two groups based on each participant's rating of the individual cartoons to determine whether rated humor alone had a significant effect on recall performance. Cartoons in the upper half of rated humor were recalled significantly better than cartoons in the lower half as measured by picture recall [$F(1,122) = 10.15$, $MS_e =$

0.2337], word recall [$F(1,122) = 8.99$, $MS_e = 0.0670$], lenient caption recall [$F(1,122) = 11.87$, $MS_e = 0.2232$], and strict caption recall [$F(1,122) = 5.09$, $MS_e = 0.1504$]. None of the interactions with list structure approached significance ($Fs < 1.0$), suggesting that the most humorous cartoons were remembered better in every combination of cartoon types. We were particularly interested in whether this finding was reliable within the lists containing a combination of literal and weird cartoons. A priori tests revealed that cartoons in the upper half of rated humor were recalled better than those in the lower half even in the literal/weird lists as measured by picture recall [$F(1,122) = 3.72$, $MS_e = 0.2337$, $p = .056$], word recall [$F(1,122) = 4.41$, $MS_e = 0.0670$], lenient caption recall [$F(1,122) = 4.69$, $MS_e = 0.2232$], and strict caption recall [$F(1,122) = 4.07$, $MS_e = 0.1504$]. These findings further support the claim that humor, rather than bizarreness, distinctiveness, incongruity, or the resolution of incongruities, supports good memory for cartoons.

As in Experiment 1, output percentiles for recalled cartoons were calculated for each cartoon type. There was a marginally significant interaction between cartoon type and list structure [$F(2,120) = 2.88$, $MS_e = .0278$, $p = .06$], indicating that output order was a function of the particular pairing of cartoon types. Newman-Keuls tests revealed that original cartoons were recalled earlier (mean output percentile = 52.21) than weird cartoons ($M = 63.73$) in the lists containing original and weird cartoons. Original cartoons were also recalled earlier ($M = 54.75$) than literal cartoons ($M = 57.24$) in that list pairing, but this difference was not reliable. No difference in mean output percentile was found in the literal ($M = 57.48$)/weird ($M = 57.24$) pairing.

General Discussion

The major findings of this research can be summarized as follows. First, humorous original cartoons were recalled better than literal or weird cartoons. Second, the humor effect occurs under incidental learning instructions, as well as under intentional learning instructions (Schmidt, 1994). Third, cartoon humor led to enhanced recall of cartoon gist, but not increased recall of detailed wording of the cartoon captions. Each of these conclusions, along with its implications, is discussed below.

Researchers have argued that humor arises as a result of incongruity (e.g., Deckers & Devine, 1981; Suls, 1972). In many studies of bizarre imagery, incongruous sentences have led to better recall than have common sentences (e.g., McDaniel & Einstein, 1986). Thus, a reasonable hypothesis was that good memory for humorous materials resulted from the incongruities contained in those materials. The cartoons employed in the experiments reported above tested specifically whether incongruity or humor enhanced memory. Both the weird and the original cartoons contained incongruent material, and the weird cartoons were rated as nominally more bizarre than the original cartoons. Nonetheless, the humorous original cartoons were recalled better than the weird cartoons.

In addition, incongruity failed to have an effect on memory even in a contrast between weird cartoons and literal cartoons. Instead, the weird and literal cartoons rated as more humorous in this list structure were recalled better than those rated as less humorous. The incongruities in the weird cartoons could not be resolved easily, suggesting that participants may have perceived humor in these cartoons without fully comprehending them. Furthermore, the literal cartoons did not contain incongruous elements; thus, incongruity resolution could not explain their humorous content either. The memory effects in the re-analysis of the weird/literal condition are therefore more likely due to perception of humor rather than the resolution of incongruities. Of course, some research participants might have found idiosyncratic means of resolving the incongruities in the weird cartoons, and they might have found and resolved incongruities in some of the literal cartoons. These idiosyncratic resolutions could then have been responsible for both the perception of humor and the good recall of the cartoons rated as humorous. It may not be possible to disentangle these two variables. In fact, theories of humor are built on the assumption that the resolution of incongruities causes the perception of humor (e.g., Deckers & Devine, 1981; Suls, 1972). However, the most direct interpretation of the results of Experiments 1 and 2 is that the perception of humor is more closely related to memory performance than is the putative resolution of cartoons that by definition do not contain incongruities (the literal cartoons) or do contain incongruities that are not easily resolved (the weird cartoons).

The results reported above also provided a test of the distinctiveness interpretation of the humor effect. Two factors initially supported this interpretation: The humor effect appears limited to mixed list designs (Schmidt, 1994), and humorous material is recalled prior to nonhumorous material in the same list. However, the distinctiveness interpretation erroneously predicted better recall of weird cartoons than of literal cartoons. In addition, it does not explain why cartoons rated as humorous were recalled better than those rated as nonhumorous in the weird/literal list.

Schmidt (1994, Experiment 4) failed to find significant differences in the recall of humorous and nonhumorous sentence versions in an incidental memory task. Some of the individual measures of sentence recall (e.g., proportion of words recalled) did reveal reliable effects, but the F_2 ratios were generally below critical value across the various memory measures. Considering the experiments reported above, we can conclude that the failure to find a significant effect of humor in incidental memory in Schmidt (1994) was a Type II error. Even in the incidental memory conditions reported by Schmidt (1994), rated humor was significantly related to sentence recall. This finding was replicated in Experiment 2, reported above. Clearly, humor enhances memory in both intentional and incidental learning tasks, a finding that requires a modification or extension of the selective rehearsal hypothesis. Differential rehearsal of humorous cartoons was first suggested (Schmidt, 1994) because the humor effect was limited to intentional learning. In addition, simple verbal rehearsal is not possible with the complex visual and verbal nature of the cartoons employed in this series of experiments. In order for the selective rehearsal hypothesis to remain tenable, it must explain why participants rehearsed the humorous cartoons, how that rehearsal took place, and why such rehearsal is not responsive to variations in presentation rate (Vella-Brodrick et al., 1996).

The cartoons employed in the present series of studies allowed us to test memory for captions that remained constant across experimental conditions. On memory measures that reflected access to the gist of the captions (i.e., lenient caption recall), humor enhanced memory. On measures that reflected detailed memory for the captions (the conditional recall of words from captions recalled), no effect of humor on memory was observed. Schmidt (1994) compared memory for humorous sentences written by famous authors such as Mark Twain with memory for nonhumorous sentences written by the experimenters. The sentences created by famous authors were more memorable, a finding that could be attributed to the humor effect or to other differences between the sentences. The results reported above were not compromised by such differences in the wordings of the materials. Thus, we can now be more confident that humor does not improve memory for the detailed wording of the humorous material. This finding provides an answer to an interesting puzzle. If humor aids memory, why is it so difficult to retell a joke? Humor helps you remember the gist of the joke, but successfully telling the joke may require memory for its exact wording.

These results provide strong evidence for the mnemonic benefit of humor. In addition, the humor effect was obtained under conditions in which an effect of incongruity or bizarreness was not obtained, suggesting that the humor effect is stronger than the bizarreness effect. Perhaps the many self-help books suggesting the use of bizarre imagery as a memory aid (e.g., Lorayne & Lucas, 1974) should also include humor as a mnemonic device. In addition, a reevaluation of the many studies demonstrating that bizarreness aids memory may be warranted. Some of the bizarre materials employed in those studies may also have been humorous. Confidence in the bizarreness effect should be weakened until it is demonstrated that the bizarreness effect can be obtained when materials are equated for humor.

Perhaps the best explanation of the humor effect is that humorous material may lead to sustained attention and subsequent elaborative processes. This sustained attention is not simply verbal rehearsal, nor does it require an intention to learn the material. However, Schmidt (1994) found that sustained attention to humorous material is often at the expense of nonhumorous material presented at about the same time. The eventual success or failure of the sustained attention hypothesis will depend on its ability to explain why people pay attention to humorous material at the expense of nonhumorous material.

References

Deckers, L., & Devine J. (1981). Humor by violating an existing expectancy. *Journal of Psychology,* **108,** 107–110.

DeLosh, E. L., & McDaniel, M. A. (1996). The role of order information in free recall: Application to the word-frequency effect. *Journal of Experimental Psychology: Learning, Memory, & Cognition,* **22,** 1136–1146,

Duncan, C. E. P., Nelson, J. E. P., & Frontzak, N. L. (1984). The effect of humor on advertising comprehension. In T. C. Kinnear (Ed.), *Advances in consumer research* (Vol. 1, pp. 432–437). Valdosta, GA: Association for Consumer Research.

Gelb, B. D., & Zinkhan, G. M. (1986). Humor and advertising effectiveness after repeated exposures to a radio commercial. *Journal of Advertising,* **15,** 15–20.

Green, R. T. (1958). The attention-getting value of structural change. *British Journal of Psychology,* **49,** 311–314.

Hunt, R. R., & Elliott, J. M. (1980). The role of nonsemantic information in memory: Orthographic distinctiveness effects on retention. *Journal of Experimental Psychology: General,* **109,** 49–74.

Kaplan, R. M., & Pascoe, G. C. (1977). Humorous lectures and humorous examples: Some effects upon comprehension and retention. *Journal of Educational Psychology,* **69,** 61–65.

Karis, D., Fabiani, M., & Donchin, E. (1984). "P300" and memory: Individual differences in the von Restorff effect. *Cognitive Psychology,* **16,** 177–216.

Larson, G. (1985). *Valley of the far side.* Kansas City, MO: Universal Press.

Larson, G. (1987). *The far side observer.* Kansas City, MO: Universal Press.

Larson, G. (1988). *Night of the crash-test dummies.* Kansas City, MO: Universal Press.

Lorayne, H., & Lucas, J. (1974). *The memory book.* New York: Ballantine.

McDaniel, M. A., & Einstein, G. O. (1986). Bizarre imagery as an effective memory: The importance of distinctiveness. *Journal of Experimental Psychology: Learning, Memory, & Cognition, 12,* 54–65.

McDaniel, M. A., Einstein, G. O., DeLosh, E., May, C., & Brady, P. (1995). The bizarreness effect: It's not surprising, it's complex. *Journal of Experimental Psychology: Learning, Memory, & Cognition, 21,* 422–435.

Ohman, A (1979). The orienting response, attention, and learning: An information-processing perspective. In H. D. Kimmell, E. H. van Olst, & J. E. Orlebeke (Eds.), *The orienting reflex in humans* (pp. 443–471). Hillsdale, NJ: Erlbaum.

Schmidt, S. R. (1991). Can we have a distinctive theory of memory? *Memory & Cognition, 19,* 523–542.

Schmidt, S. R (1994). Effects of humor on sentence memory. *Journal of Experimental Psychology: Learning, Memory, & Cognition, 20,* 953–967.

Suls, J. M. (1972). A two-stage model for the appreciation of jokes and cartoons: An information-processing analysis. In J. H. Goldstein & P. E. McGhee (Eds.), *The psychology of humor* (pp. 81–100). New York: Academic Press.

Vella-Brodrick, D. A., Dory, M. K., & Whelan, T. A. (1996). *Effects of humor on sentence recall: A test of the rehearsal and attention hypotheses.* Unpublished manuscript.

Introduction: Critical Thinking Questions _____

? Schmidt (1994) found that humorous sentences were recalled better than nonhumorous sentences, but only under certain conditions. Describe these conditions.

? The researcher notes that the effects of humor are unclear because humor is often confounded with incongruity. Explain the nature of this confound.

? If incongruity does benefit memory, there are a number of mechanisms that may be responsible. Describe these factors.

? Earlier results seemed to indicate that enhanced memory for humorous materials occurred more readily under intentional learning condition. Describe why this led Schmidt (1994) to propose a rehearsal view of the benefit. What evidence undermines or would undermine this rehearsal account, and why?

? What manipulation did the researchers use to increase the chances of finding a humor effect under incidental memory conditions? Why do you think this manipulation was proposed to have an effect?

? Describe each of the cartoon variations used by the researchers, and how each of the conditions in Experiment 1 allowed them to tease apart the possible beneficial effects of (a) humor and (b) incongruity.

? Describe the three list conditions tested in Experiment 2. Refer to Table 3 and explain the predictions made by the humor per se hypothesis plus one of the other three hypotheses.

Method: Critical Thinking Questions _____

? For each experiment, describe what you would have been asked to do, had you been a participant.

? For each experiment, name the independent variables, and their levels. Describe how each of these variables was operationalized. For each variable, state whether it was manipulated in a between-subjects or within-subjects fashion. How many conditions were there in the experiment?

? What was (were) the dependent variable(s) in each experiment?

? What aspects of the methodology were implemented to deal with possible confounds?

Results/Discussion: Critical Thinking Questions _____

? Memory performance in Experiment 1 seemed to indicate that cartoon access was aided by humor, but recall of detailed cartoon information was not. Describe this in more detail.

? Given the results of Experiment 1, the researchers conclude that "…humor is apparently the potent mnemonic variable…rather than incongruity or bizarreness." How did they arrive at that conclusion?

? How do the results of the experiments seem to rule out incongruity and distinctiveness as explanations for the beneficial effects of humor?

? Why are the results of these experiments problematic for the differential rehearsal hypothesis?

? The results of the study seem to provide an explanation of why a joke is so hard to retell, even if we found it to be very funny. How might this anomaly be explained?

? After reading this study, you may feel there are other issues or questions that would be worthwhile or intriguing to address. Pose one of these questions (other than those suggested by the authors) that could be investigated empirically.

Music While You Work

The Differential Distraction of Background Music on the Cognitive Test Performance of Introverts and Extraverts

Adrian Furnham and Anna Bradley

Abstract

The current study looked at the distracting effects of 'pop music' on introverts' and extraverts' performance on various cognitive tasks. It was predicted that there would be a main effect for music and an interaction effect with introverts performing less well in the presence of music than extraverts. Ten introverts and ten extraverts were given two tests (a memory test with immediate and delayed recall and a reading comprehension test), which were completed, either while being exposed to pop music, or in silence. The results showed that there was a detrimental effect on immediate recall on the memory test for both groups when music was played, and two of the three interactions were significant. After a 6-minute interval the introverts who had memorized the objects in the presence of the pop music had a significantly lower recall than the extraverts in the same condition and the introverts who had observed them in silence. The introverts who completed a reading comprehension task when music was being played also performed significantly less well than these two groups. These findings have implications for the study habits of introverts when needing to retain or process complex information.

Conceptual Issues and Theoretical Questions

- What is the effect of background music on people's performance of various cognitive tasks?
- Are different personality types impacted differently by the presence of background music?
- Do specific characteristics of the background music (e.g., the style of music) play a role in the effect?

Furnham, A., & Bradley, A. (1997). Music while you work: The differential distraction of background music on the cognitive test performance of introverts and extraverts. *Applied Cognitive Psychology, 11,* 445–455. Copyright © 1997 by John Wiley & Sons, Ltd. Reproduced by permission of John Wiley & Sons Limited.

De-Jargonizing _____

optimum level of arousal: the level of alertness that is associated with optimum performance
introvert: person who tends to be shy and withdrawn from interactions with others
extravert: person who is outgoing and seeks interactions with others
electrodermally: measurement of sweat; also known as galvanic skin response

Introduction

'Music is a friend of labour for it lightens the task by refreshing the nerves and spirit of the worker.' William Green (quoted in Clark, 1929)

The effects of background music on task performance have been of interest to three groups of researchers: applied psychologists concerned with whether productivity may be increased by playing music at work; cognitive psychologists in studying how music affects attention and processing in various specific tasks; and personality theorists who are primarily interested in how individual differences in arousal affect cognitive task performance in the presence of musical distraction.

Since the turn of the century researchers have been interested in the possible benefits of music at work. During the 1940s and 1950s there was a flurry of interest as to whether music affected either morale (satisfaction) or productivity at work (Newman, Hunt and Rhodes, 1966) or both. Results showed that much depended on the type of music, as well as the particular task performed. In a review of the extensive work up to that point, Uhrbrock (1961) noted the following:

1. Unqualified claims that increased production results from the introduction of music into the work situation are not proven.
2. The social implications of music in industry as an incentive system ultimately should be faced. A question may be asked, 'Is this a legitimate device that gives pleasure to workers and profit to employers?'
3. Feelings of euphoria during periods of music stimulation have a physiological basis, which is evidenced by changes in blood pressure that occur in some participants while listening to music.
4. Factory employees prefer working where music is played rather than where it is not played.
5. Not all workers like music while they work. From 1 to 10 percent are annoyed by it.
6. Quality of work can be adversely affected by the use of music in the work situation.
7. Instrumental, rather than vocal, music is preferred during working hours by the majority of workers.
8. There is a negative correlation between age and preference for work music.

9. At least three investigators have reported that young, inexperienced employees, engaged in doing simple, repetitive, monotonous tasks, increased their output when stimulated by music.
10. Evidence has been presented that demonstrates that experienced factory operators, whose work patterns were stabilized and who were performing complex tasks did not increase their production when music was played while they worked.
11. At times music has had an adverse effect on the output of individual employees, even though they reported that music was 'quite pleasant' (p. 36).

There has, however, been a significant resurgence in the area partly because of the cost and availability of relatively new technology, namely the personal stereo headset. For instance, Oldham, Cummings, Mischel, Schmidthe and Zhan (1995) found that for those who preferred to work with music, its relaxing qualities had significant effects on performance, organizational satisfaction and ratings of fatigue.

The research in this area has concentrated primarily on the effects of different types or styles of music (Sogin, 1988) or loudness of music (Wolfe, 1983) on the performance on various cognitive tasks. This study focuses on the role of individual differences, namely introversion-extraversion, on task performance in the presence of music versus silence.

There remain, however, a large number of contradictory findings about the effects of music on task performance and satisfaction. It has been shown that playing music whilst carrying out a repetitive task can raise performance levels, particularly when this music is played just after the arousal level has peaked (Fox and Embrey, 1972). However, they also found that when music was played consistently throughout the duration of a task, there was no resultant difference in the level of performance to when the task was completed in silence.

Etaugh and Ptasnik (1982) found their participants, who seldom studied with background music, showed better comprehension in a laboratory study when they learned in silence, while those who frequently studied with music performed better when in the presence of music. Kiger (1989) required 54 high-school students to read a passage of literature in silence, or with low or high 'information-load' music based on criteria of loudness, variety, complexity and tonal range. Reading comprehension scores were significantly higher in the low information-load condition than in either silence or the high information-load condition. He argued slow, soft, repetitive low-information music provides optimally arousing conditions.

Mayfield and Moss (1989) examined the effect of music tempo on task performance in two studies. The task was collecting and choosing stock prices and calculating the percentage of change in price from week to week. One group performed the task in silence, one listened to fast-paced music and one to slow-paced music. They found no difference in the quality or quantity of the work produced by the groups. A second replicative study, however, did yield significant differences: the (student) subjects' performances were higher in the fast-paced (rock music) condition than with the slow music, although the subjective level of distraction was higher. They could not fully explain the inconsistent findings but argued that complex managerial tasks are probably best performed in silence.

The introduction of music into the workplace has been found to increase employee morale, resulting in fewer absentees and a decrease in employee turnover (Roberts, 1959), but Kellaris and Kent (1992) suggested that music that is pleasing to the ear, such as major key music, actually makes time seem to pass more slowly.

Some of the contradictory findings in the area may be due to differences in the task being measured, as well as not measuring the fundamental personality trait differences of the participants. For instance, Konz (1962) studied the effects of music on college students while they completed two different tasks. One was a manual assembly task and the other was a letter-matching task. The results showed an improvement of 17% and 18% respectively. The mental task was, however, performed significantly better in the presence of music. Yet, whilst Freeburne and Fleischer (1952) claimed that music makes no difference to performance on complex mental tasks (equally true for people of high and low intelligence), Dannenbaum (1945) found that people are less able to detect geometric faults in the presence of music and Kirkpatrick (1943) found that music hinders work demanding mental concentration.

Smith (1961) hypothesized that music reduces the tension and boredom that are highly correlated with routine work but acts as a distracter for complex mental work. He found music played in the break periods between complex mental activities had no effect on performance. Similarly, Perrewe and Mizerski (1987) found music had no effect on how subjects perceived tasks, be they complex or simple.

The question of whether it is better to perform complex mental tasks in the presence of noise stimulation or silence is an important one, with numerous practical implications for industry and education. An early report conducted by Cantril and Allport (1935) found that, at that time, 68% of students worked with the radio on. Now that students have access to personal stereos, CD players and many other forms of audio entertainment the question would seem to be more important than ever. It is also relevant to office workers and factory workers, some of whom are allowed 'the luxury' of personal or shared music while they work (Furnham, Richardson and Miller, 1996).

Oldham et al. (1995) found a significant, positive effect on performance, organization satisfaction and mood states when personal headsets playing music were used in an office situation. However, their participants were self-selected, as the treatment group were those who expressed that they would like to work with the music on. The participants were also allowed to choose the duration, type of music and when it was presented. The headsets also served the dual purpose of blocking out any background noise. Personal preference and use may thus have confounded results. In the current study, all participants experienced music of a set length and type with no background distraction.

Another of the main problems in reviewing the above experiments is their inconsistent definition of a mentally taxing task. In the present study, tasks were chosen that may reflect the sort of task a school-aged child would be set as a homework assignment, that is, a learning and recall task and a reading and question-answering task.

More importantly, none of the above studies have taken into account the personality trait differences of the participants, which have been shown to be relevant in learning (Eysenck, 1981). If it is assumed that music improves performance on repetitive tasks because it is stimulating, then the effect of music on participants in such studies should relate to their individual differences in **optimum levels of arousal.** Eysenck (1967) argued that **introverts** and **extraverts** differ in terms of their cortical arousal. Those who are classified as introverts have been shown to have a lower optimum arousal threshold and therefore do not need much stimulation before passing their optimum functioning level. Those who are extraverts have higher optimum arousal thresholds and therefore tend to seek arousal or stimulating situations. Stelmach (1981) reviewed the extensive psychophysiology evidence that supports this hypothesis. Gray (1964) linked these categories with the Russian ideas of strong (extravert) and weak (introvert) nervous systems. In fact, Gray's (1981) theory suggests that anxiety (neuroticism) may act as a mediating factor between extraversion and task performance. Vermonlayeva-Tomina (1964) found that those with a strong nervous system tended to learn more in distracting situations than those with a weak nervous system.

This study, therefore, hypothesized that introverts would be more negatively, and extraverts more positively, affected by the introduction of extra stimulation, for example music, into their work environment. However, it could be argued that because of the complexity of the music and/or the task performance, the musical stimulation might be too great even for extraverts, and hence lead to an overall negative effect on their performance. Indeed, Konĕcni (1982) argued that all music processing inevitably takes up cognitive capacity and, therefore, potentially any music may be detrimental to all performance. Indeed, the existing literature does suggest that background music is more likely to lower performance in particular individuals than raise it above base-rate levels in silence.

It has been demonstrated that when studying in a library, introverts were significantly more likely to choose a place to work away from the bustle of certain areas, while the extraverts were more attracted to the latter as a work place (Campbell and Hawley, 1982). This provides further evidence of the regulation of arousal differences between introverts and extraverts. Careful experimental work measuring critical arousal **electrodermally** and manipulating arousal by caffeine dosages has also shown that playing simple tunes can significantly alter the cognitive-task performance of extraverts and introverts (Smith, Wilson and Davidson, 1984). The results showed very clearly that base-rate or manipulated arousal difference leads to attentional variables between introverts and extraverts.

Morgenstern, Hodgson and Law (1974) found that extraverts actually performed better in the presence of distractions than they did in silence, while introverts showed a deficit in performance. Their participants were asked to attend to, and remember, a number of words out of a long list that was read to them, whilst they were being read a passage by the same voice. They were given a means of controlling the balance of sound between the word list and the passage, but the greater this difference, the more the words to be remembered were distorted. Their study posed three questions: Is the preference for distortion or distraction related to the personality dimension of introversion/extraversion? Do the two groups of participants differ in their performance on the task? How did the subject arrive at their preferred balance? They found that extraverts make extravagant sweeping movements in their efforts to find a balance, while introverts make fewer, smaller adjustments. This finding was consistent with Eysenck's theory that the introvert's nervous system is overdamped. There was a trend for introverts to avoid distraction when the personality dimension was compared with choice of distortion/distraction, and they did not perform the task as well although the effect was not statistically significant.

In an early experiment in this area, Daoussis and McKelvie (1986) found that, although extravert subjects reported working with music twice as much as introverts (50% versus 25% of the time), both groups reported playing background music very softly. Both groups were given a reading recall test in which they were instructed to spend 10 minutes reading 2 passages (of about 900 words) with a view to answering specific questions immediately afterwards. Half of each group did the task in silence and half in the presence of rock and roll music played at low volume. While there was no difference in the scores of extraverts, introverts' performances were, as predicted, significantly poorer in the presence than in the absence of music. They concluded that this supported the arousal and performance hypothesis of Eysenck (1967).

Various studies have examined the distracting effects of television on cognitive processing. Recent research on television distraction effects (Armstrong and Greenberg, 1990; Armstrong, Boiarsky and Mares, 1991) reported significant performance decrements for several measures, i.e. spatial problem solving, mental flexibility, and reading comprehension as a function of television. These results were consistent with the idea that background television influences performance by causing cognitive processing limits to be exceeded on complex tasks. While indicative of a television distraction influence on parallel cognitive activities, Armstrong's research did not investigate the possibility of individual differences among children in their parallel processing capabilities. This point is particularly pertinent in the light of psychological research showing that personality factors such as introversion-extraversion are important mediators of individual cognitive performance in the process of distraction (Morgenstern *et al.*, 1974). More recently, Furnham, Gunter and Peterson (1994) conducted a study into the effects of the presence of an operating television on introverts and extraverts, while they completed reading comprehension tasks. They found, as predicted, a significant interaction, $F(1, 39) = 7.41$, $p<0.01$, between the personality dimension and the treatment effect. In other words, the introverts and extraverts performed equally well with the television off, but the extraverts performed better than the introverts when the television was on.

The current study looks at the effects of (pop) music on introverts' and extraverts' performance on two cognitive tests. It further tests the arousal-performance hypothesis on three different tasks: specifically, that extraverts with low levels of arousal would perform better on various cognitive tasks in the presence of radio programmes (mainly music), since their arousal would be raised towards the optimum level. The hypothesis tested was that introverts and extraverts will perform equally well on tasks that are completed in silence; however in the presence of distracting music the introverts will not perform as well as the extraverts. It is predicted that there will be a main effect for music because of the complexity of the task (with music, performance will decline) and also a music × personality interaction.

Method

Participants

Eighty-eight undergraduate students completed the Eysenck Personality Questionnaire (Eysenck and Eysenck, 1975). The semi-interquartile range was used to select those participants who had high and low extraversion scores. These twenty-two participants were then given a Sentence Verification Intelligence test (Baddeley, 1968), to ascertain their verbal intelligence so that results could not be attributed to the possible moderation of intelligence. Two participants were dropped from the experiment because of their low scores on this test. There were then no differences in the cognitive ability of the two groups; the mean of the introverts on this test was well within the 80% confidence interval of that of the extraverts. The selection thus resulted in 20 participants, 10 introverts (mean EPQ score = 7.00, mean age = 20.4) and 10 extraverts (mean EPQ score = 19.8, mean age = 23.3). Participants were paid a small amount in return for their participation. The male to female ratio was 3:4. All participants reported their first language to be English.

Materials

The participants were given two tests. One was a reading comprehension test taken from the GMAT (Graduate Admission Tests) (Martison, 1992) range of tests. This reading comprehension consisted of a 400-word passage and 6 multiple-choice questions. The participants were allowed a maximum of 10 minutes to complete the test, but all finished well within this time limit. The participants scored two points for each correct answer. The other test was a memory test from the British Ability Scales range of tests. The test was similar to Kim's Game where participants look at a number (say 30) of objects for a period of time, attempting to memorize them for later free recall. Participants were shown a piece of paper that had 20 pictures of everyday objects on it. They were allowed to look at the sheet for 2 minutes, during which time they had to memorize as many of the objects as they could. They were then required to name the objects they had been shown. Participants scored one point for each correct answer. The participants were then tested again on the objects shown after a period of 6 minutes. During this interval, to divert their attention, they were given a simple math quiz, taken from Eysenck's (1981) *Know your own intelligence* paperback book. Their performance on this test was not included in the analysis. The music was taken from a mid-morning radio programme on Virgin 105.8 FM and consisted of three major key, upbeat pop songs (Sowing the Seeds of Love, Tears for Fears; A New Sensation, INXS; and Strange Girl, Cream). These songs were separated by a male disc jockey talking. The total time of chat amounted to just over 2 minutes. The duration of the extract was 10 minutes and all participants finished the relevant test within this time. The tape recording of the same music was used throughout.

Procedure

Participants were given a pre-test questionnaire to complete, which consisted of personal details, and were asked about their level of fatigue. They were told that the experiment was confidential and that they could cease participation at any time. The participants were then given the tasks to do, one at a time. The memory test, reading comprehension and treatment and control conditions were all counter balanced, so that no effect of fatigue or residual distraction could confound the results. One task was performed in silence, and the other with the radio extract played at quiet volume on a personal stereo with in-built speakers. The extract was the same for each subject and was kept on until the subject had finished the task. Completing both these tests took no longer than 20 minutes. When both tasks had been completed the participants were than given a post-test questionnaire enquiring about levels of motivation, and how distracting they found the radio, rated on a 7-point Likert scale. It also enquired into how often they usually worked with the radio on. The participants were then debriefed, paid and thanked for their participation.

Results

The results of the tests were analysed using a 2 × 2 between-participants analysis of variance. For the immediate recall of the pictures on the page (memory 1), there was no main effect of introversion/extraversion $F(1, 19) = 0.26$ ns), or interaction effect ($F(1, 18) = 0.13$ ns), but there was a main effect of whether the music was on or off ($F(2, 18) = 4.85$, $p < 0.05$). For the delayed recall of the pictures, after an interval of 6 minutes (memory 2) there were no main effects of introversion/extraversion ($F(1, 19) = 0.26$ (ns) or music on/off ($F(2, 18) = 0.62$ ns). There was an interaction between the personality dimensions and the treatment condition ($F(1, 18) = 7.61$, $p < 0.025$). For the reading comprehension, there were no main effects of music on/off ($F(1, 18) = 3.75$ ns) or introversion/extraversion ($F(1, 18) = 3.75$ ns) but there was an interaction between the two ($F(1, 18) = 8.82$, $p < 0.01$). There was thus one (out of three) significant main effect for music and two significant interactions. The personality dimension resulted in no significant main effect under any condition.

Concerning the questions on the post-test questionnaire, only four Pearson's correlations showed significance ($N = 20$ throughout). They were the subject's self-rating of how distracting they found the radio with their EPQ score, $r = -0.76$, $p<0.005$. Extraverts said they were less distracted than introverts. How often they said they worked with the radio on was correlated with EPQ score, $r = 0.51$, $p<0.025$. Extraverts said they worked more often with the radio on than the introverts. How often they listened to the radio in general was correlated with EPQ, $r = 0.39$, $p<0.05$. Extraverts said that they listened to the radio more often than introverts. The distraction self rating and the frequency of study in the presence of radio were also correlated, $r = -0.56$, $p<0.01$, showing that those who found the radio more distracting while they were working were those who were least likely to choose to work with it playing.

TABLE 1   *The Means and Standard Deviations for Introverts and Extraverts for Each of the Tests under Each Condition*

Treatment condition	Introvert			Extravert		
	Mem. 1	Mem. 2	RC	Mem. 1	Mem. 2	RC
Music						
Mean	14.4	10.8	6.2	15.6	15.6	9.2
SD	2.61	2.39	1.48	2.19	2.19	1.10
Music off						
Mean	14.8	14.4	9.0	13.6	13.6	9.6
SD	3.03	2.70	2.00	2.70	1.79	1.67

Note: Mem. 1 is the short-term memory recall score; Mem. 2 is the recall score after 6 minutes; RC is the reading comprehension multiple-choice answer score.

Discussion

The results indicate that although the level of immediate recall is no different between the introverts and the extraverts, performance is marginally lowered in the presence of music, though it should be pointed out that only one of the three analyses produced a significant effect. The recall of the pictures after 6 minutes was worse for the introverts who observed them with the music on. This finding implies that the short-term memory effects are small, but the introverts who worked with the music on were less able to store the information for later recall than extraverts. Introverts were also less able to complete the reading comprehension as successfully in the presence of music. It appears that some mental processes, for example those of attention and recall, are more affected by the presence of a distraction than others. The interval of 6 minutes between the immediate recall and the delayed recall was not very great and simply the recommended time taken to complete the distracter task. It may be that if this time were increased, then the results would show greater difference. The study, however, could not throw light on which particular cognitive processes are affected by background music.

The focus of this study was on individual difference in the distracting effect of background music. The correlations obtained from the post-test questionnaire would seem to suggest that those people whose EPQ scores showed them to be introverts, did have different study habits to those classified as extraverts. As in the experiment by Campbell and Hawley (1982), where the different personality types positioned themselves at different places in the library, the participants' reports of their choice of radio listening were explored in the current study. They indicated the noise levels they usually worked with and how frequently they listened to the radio while working. The overall listening frequency in their day-to-day life was also obtained for analysis. Introverts were less likely to work with the radio on, listened to the radio less in general and found it more distracting in the test situation. There was also a negative correlation between how often the participants normally worked with the radio on and how distracting they found it on this occasion.

The results show that the extraverts in this study were more likely to work with the radio on when at home. The introverts were not used to working with the radio on and found it distracting; it also affected their test scores. It could be that when music is first introduced into a work situation, when the subject is not used to working in the presence of music, there is a drop in quality and quantity of work completed. However, when the music has been played for a long period of time, these effects could disappear. Perhaps if the music were played to the introverts for a reasonably long period of time, they would adapt to it and their cognitive performance would begin to improve. Yet the Eysenckian hypothesis would still maintain that the morale/satisfaction of the introverts would be lower than that of the extraverts even though their performance were not different.

In order to investigate the processes that are affected most by the presence of a distraction, further studies using tasks that test many different mental processes would be required. Certainly one could categorize tasks by type (verbal, spatial, numerical) but also by complexity/difficulty or the amount of cognitive processing required. Although there may well be minor differences in terms of the type of task (memory, comprehension), it is most likely to be the complexity of the task that music, or any other stimulus, is likely to affect.

The type of music that was played could also be an important factor in the results obtained. Freeburne and Fleischer (1952) varied the type of music in their experiment between classical, jazz and modern. In the present experiment the music was popular music that was frequently played on the commercial radio. It is possible that different distraction effects may be found depending on the subjects' liking of the music or its complexity (North and Hargreaves, 1996). Music may be in major or minor key as well as atonal. Whereas major keys tend to evoke positive feeling, minor keys evoke melancholy and atonal music is generally conceived of as less pleasant (Kellaris and Kent, 1992). Further, the speed and tempo may make a difference to distraction, as well as whether the music is simply orchestral or has lyrics. The music component in this study is, in effect, simply testing the influence of some additional stimulation versus no stimulation on performance, and does not tell us about the effects of music as such. To explain why music should have the particular effect that it does, further research might investigate two or more different types of music, depending on tempo, complexity or familiarity, all of which relate to processing requirements.

The findings of this study are relevant to all those who work in a communal area, be it an open-plan office or a student workroom. The tasks used in this case were designed to bear resemblance to the tasks a school child or adolescent may be set as school homework, namely learning and comprehension. Because of the nature of the memory task, the participants were not told that they were going to have to recall the objects on the page a second time. It would be more comparable to a piece of learning school work if they had been told that they would be required to do this. This study is also relevant to all those who will work in an open-plan office at some point in their career. Some people may thrive with music on while others, the extreme introverts, will find it immensely debilitating. This consideration is important for management who wish to optimize the output of their workforce.

This study replicated the study by Furnham *et al.* (1994) with a different medium (music from the radio rather than television); similar findings were obtained. The introverts performed significantly less well in the presence of a distracting stimulus on two of the three personality and music interactions. It should, however, be pointed out that for the reading completion task, the performance of the extraverts was also marginally hampered, but not to the same extent as the introverts. The implications of this finding are important for those who want to maximize their work potential. Certainly there seems little evidence that the presence of background distraction (television, music, talk) actually facilitates performance in complex cognitive tasks, even for extraverts, though it seems clear that it nearly always impairs the performance of introverts.

References

Armstrong, C. and Greenberg, B. (1990). Background television as an inhibitor of cognitive processing. *Human Communication Research,* **16,** 355–386.

Armstrong, C., Boiarsky, G. and Mares, M. (1991). Background television and reading performance. *Communication Monographs,* **58,** 235–253.

Baddeley, A. (1968). A three-minute reasoning test based on grammatical transformations. *Psychonomic Science,* **10,** 341–342.

Campbell, J. B. and Hawley, C. W. (1982). Study habits and Eysenck's Theory of Extraversion-Introversion. *Journal of Research in Personality,* **16,** 139–146.

Cantril, H. and Allport, G. W. (1935). *The Psychology of Radio,* 1st Edn. New York: Harper and Brothers.

Dannenbaum, A. (1945). The effect of music on visual acuity. *Sarah Lawrence Studies,* **4,** 18–26.

Daoussis, I. and McKelvie, S. (1986). Musical preferences and effects of music on a reading comprehension test for extraverts and introverts. *Perceptual and Motor Skills,* **62,** 283–289.

Etaugh, C. and Ptasnik, P. (1982). Effects of studying to music and post-study relaxation on reading comprehension. *Perceptual and Motor Skills,* **55,** 141–142.

Eysenck, H. (1967). *The biological basis of personality.* Springfield, IL: Thomas.

Eysenck, H. (1981). *Know your own IQ.* Harmondsworth: Penguin.

Eysenck, H. and Eysenck, S. (1975). *The Eysenck Personality Questionnaire.* London: Hodder & Stoughton.

Eysenck, M. (1981). Learning, memory and personality. In H. Eysenck (Ed.), *A Model for Personality* (pp. 169–207). Heidelberg: Springer Verlag.

Fox, J. G. (1971). Background music and industrial efficiency—A review. *Applied Ergonomics,* **2,** 70–73.

Freeburne, C. M. and Fleischer, M. S. (1952). The effect of music distraction upon reading rate and comprehension. *Journal of Educational Psychology,* **43,** 101–110.

Furnham, A., Gunter, B. and Peterson, E. (1994). Television distraction and the performance of introverts and extraverts. *Applied Cognitive Psychology,* **8,** 705–711.

Furnham, A., Richardson, S. and Miller, T. (1996). Ear dominance and telephone sales Laterality. Paper under review.

Gray, J. (1964). Strength of the nervous system and levels of arousal: A reinterpretation. In J. Gray (Ed.), *Pavlov's typology* (pp. 289–366). Oxford: Pergamon.

Gray, J. (1981). A critique of Eysenck's theory of personality. In H. Eysenck (Ed.), *A model for personality.* Berlin: Springer-Verlag.

Kellaris, J. J. and Kent, R. J. (1992). The influence of music on customer's temporal perception. *Journal of Consumer Psychology,* **4,** 365–376.

Kiger, D. (1989). Effects of music information load on a reading-comprehension task. *Perceptual and Motor Skills,* **69,** 531–534.

Kirkpatrick, F. H. (1943). Music takes the mind away. *Personnel Journal,* **22,** 225–228.

Konečni, V. (1982). Social interaction and musical preference. In D. Deutsch (Ed.), *The psychology of music.* New York: Academic Press.

Konz, S. A. (1962). *The effect of background music on productivity of two different monotonous tasks.* Paper to Human Factors Society, New York.

Martison, T. H. (Ed.) (1992). *Graduate admission tests, Practice papers for applicants.* Arco Academic Test Preparation Series.

Mayfield, C. and Moss, S. (1989). Effect of music tempo on task performance. *Psychological Reports,* **65,** 1283–1290.

Morgenstern, S., Hodgson, R. J. and Law, L. (1974). Work efficiency and personality. *Ergonomics,* **17,** 211–220.

Newman, R., Hunt, D. and Rhodes, F. (1966). Effect of music on employee attitude and productivity in a skateboard factory. *Journal of Applied Psychology,* **50,** 493–496.

North, A. and Hargreaves, D. (1996). Response to music in aerobic exercise and yogic relaxation classes. *British Journal of Psychology,* **89,** 535–547.

Oldham, G., Cummings, A., Mischel, L., Schmidthe, J. and Zhan, J. (1995). Listen while you work? Quasi-experimental relations between personal-stereo headset use and employee work responses. *Journal of Applied Psychology,* **80,** 547–564.

Perrewe, P. and Mizerski, R. (1987). Effect of music on perceptions of task characteristics. *Perceptual and Motor Skills,* **65,** 165–166.

Roberts, J. W. (1959). Sound approach to efficiency. *Personnel Journal,* **38,** 6–8.

Smith, B., Wilson, R. and Davidson, R. (1984). Extrodermal activity and extraversion. *Personality and Individual Differences,* **5,** 59–65.

Smith, W. A. (1961). Effects of industrial music in a work situation requiring complex mental activity. *Psychological Reports,* **8,** 159–162.

Sogin, D. (1988). Effect of three different musical styles of background music on coding by college-age students. *Perceptual and Motor Skills,* **67,** 275–280.

Stelmach, R. (1981). The psychophysiology of extraversion and neuroticism. In H. Eysenck (Ed.), *A model for personality.* Berlin: Springer-Verlag.

Uhrbrock, R. (1961). Music on the job: its influences on worker morale and productivity. *Personnel Psychology,* **14,** 9–38.

Vermonlayeva-Tomina, L. B. (1964). In J. Gray (Ed.), *Pavlov's typology.* Oxford: Pergamon.

Wolfe, D. (1983). Effects of music loudness on task performance and self-report of college-aged students. *Journal of Research in Music Education,* **31,** 191–201.

Introduction: Critical Thinking Questions

? Consider the early finding regarding the effect of background music on performance in a work environment. How do individual differences mediate the effects of background music on performance.

? Based on the literature reviewed by the researchers, summarize the effects of background music with respect to (a) the time at which the music is played; (b) the type of music; (c) playing music habitually during studying; (d) the effects on morale.

? How do introverts and extroverts differ in their optimal level of arousal, and how might this difference relate to the effects of background music on cognitive performance?

? What does the evidence indicate regarding the distracting effects of television?

? What predictions do the researchers make regarding the effects of background music on the cognitive performance of introverts and extraverts?

Method: Critical Thinking Questions

? Describe what you would have been asked to do, had you been a participant in the experiment.

? Name the independent variables in the experiment, and their levels. Describe how each of these variables was operationalized. For each variable, state whether it was manipulated in a between-subjects or within-subjects fashion. How many conditions were there in the experiment?

? What was (were) the dependent variable(s) in the experiment?

? What aspects of the methodology were implemented to deal with possible confounds?

Results/Discussion: Critical Thinking Questions

? Explain the results of the study—the effects of background music on performance in each of the tasks used and the interaction. What do these results indicate about the effects of background music on STM and the storage of information in LTM (look in the discussion for the answer to this question).

? Describe the correlational analysis—which measures were associated with one another? Describe the relationship reflected in each significant correlation.

? Were the experimental findings consistent with the reported behavior of extroverts and introverts in their daily lives? Explain.

? Introverts appear to be detrimentally affected by the presence of music. However, the authors suggest an alternative interpretation of this finding. Describe this alternative.

? The authors suggest two additional factors that may mediate the effect of background music on the performance of extraverts and introverts. Describe these factors.

? Interview some acquaintances and friends of both the extraverted and introverted type about their work habits, and whether or not they listen to background music. Do you find any discernible pattern regarding the presence of music, the type of music, etc?

? After reading this study, you may feel there are other issues or questions that would be worthwhile or intriguing to address. Pose one of these questions (other than those suggested by the authors) that could be investigated empirically.

Make My Memory

How Advertising Can Change Our Memories of the Past

**Kathryn A. Braun, Rhiannon Ellis,
and Elizabeth F. Loftus**

Abstract

Marketers use autobiographical advertising as a means to create nostalgia for their products. This research explores whether such referencing can cause people to believe that they had experiences as children that are mentioned in the ads. In Experiment 1, participants viewed an ad for Disney that suggested that they shook hands with Mickey Mouse as a child. Relative to controls, the ad increased their confidence that they personally had shaken hands with Mickey as a child at a Disney resort. The increased confidence could be due to a revival of a true memory or the creation of a new, false one. In Experiment 2, participants viewed an ad for Disney that suggested that they shook hands with an impossible character (e.g., Bugs Bunny). Again, relative to controls, the ad increased confidence that they personally had shaken hands with the impossible character as a child at a Disney resort. The increased confidence is consistent with the notion that autobiographical referencing can lead to the creation of false or distorted memory.

Conceptual Issues and Theoretical Questions

- Can imagining an event increase one's conviction that the event actually did occur?
- Can imagining childhood events change the memory for those events?
- Can such imagination inflation effects be induced by advertisements?
- What are the mechanisms whereby imagining leads to memory distortion or false memory creation?
- Can autobiographical advertising lead participants to create memories for events that did not happen?

Braun, K. A., Ellis, R., & Loftus, E. F. (2002). Make my memory: How advertising can change our memories of the past. *Psychology and Marketing, 19*, 1–23. Copyright © (2002) John Wiley & Sons, Inc. This material is used by permission of the publisher.

De-Jargonizing

autobiographical referencing: in advertising, the relating of a product to one's personal past

counterfactual thinking: imagining scenarios that conflict with reality

source attribution: processes involved in identifying the source of the memory for some event.

interrater reliability: the degree of consistency in rating observed among a set of raters

Advertisers play off consumers' memories and emotions through the use of **autobiographical referencing.** The use of such referencing can cause consumers to focus less on rational product information and more on the feelings evoked by their recollected memories (Sujan, Bettman, & Baumgartner, 1993). Increasingly, marketers are using this technique to appeal to Baby Boomers where these past images represent lasting expressions of freedom and youth (Marconi, 1996). For example, Walt Disney celebrated the 25th anniversary of Disney World in Orlando with an advertising campaign entitled "Remember the Magic." The ads resembled vintage home movies and featured scenes of people swimming, meeting Mickey Mouse, and enjoying themselves on the theme park's exciting rides. The campaign's aim may have been to remind consumers of their own past happy childhood memories of the park in order to get them to revisit.

But what if such referencing could change what consumers remember about their childhood memories of visiting the park? Not all consumers have had happy experiences at Disney nor do they all have the ability to accurately conjure up those childhood images at will. Because consumers may use the advertising as a cue to recollect their past experience, there is the possibility that these recently generated advertising images may alter what consumers ultimately remember about their own childhood. After all, there is evidence that cues that get people to think over and over again about manufactured childhood events can be a relatively easy way to create false memories or beliefs about childhood (Loftus, 1997). Such findings have raised concerns about the accuracy of memories surfaced in hypnosis, guided imagery, or other prompts in psychotherapy (Lindsay & Read, 1994; Loftus & Ketcham, 1994).

Marketers have found that autobiographical memories may be spontaneously activated within the context of an advertising message (Baumgartner, Sujan, & Bettman, 1992; Krugman, 1967). Marketers have further shown that they can increase the likelihood consumers will activate their memories by focusing on experiential information (Wells, 1986) or using dramatic narratives in their advertising campaigns (Boller, 1990). Autobiographical ads may cause consumers to imagine themselves in the advertised event, and this vicarious experience may alter how consumers remember their own past.

What if Disney's "Remember the Magic" campaign implanted memories into consumers of things that never happened? The possibility that marketing stimuli can direct, guide, or change consumers' autobiographical memories has gone largely untested. This research investigates whether the use of autobiographical referencing can cause imaginings of experiences (even impossible ones) that lead consumers to become more confident that certain events had happened to them as children. This possibility holds both managerial opportunities and ethical ramifications.

Autobiographical Memory

Autobiographical memory can be defined as memory of past personal experiences. There has been much attention toward finding ways of accessing this type of knowledge because it is an important foundation of one's self-concept (Hyman, Husband, & Billings, 1994). Sigmund Freud, for instance, believed his patients had repressed traumatic childhood memories in their subconscious and believed it was necessary to understand his patients' original childhood experiences in order to understand their adult problems.

Psychoanalysts believe childhood is important for understanding relationships because this is when attachment occurs, and those early relationships are thought to be prototypical of later relationships (Ainsworth, 1985). As applied to the consumer setting, early childhood brand relationships may set the emotional stage for later adult brand relationships. Consumers' memories of brands or brand experiences from childhood thus may have a great consequence in their decision making, as they conjure up those past emotional attachments: "These trails of autobiographical memories—they are perceived as veridical records accompanied by strong visual and, hence, vivid reliving of the original experience—are not only important in themselves, but especially because they suggest that the *original* emotions are also likely to be important components of autobiographical memories" (Baumgartner et al., 1992, p. 55, italics added).

Both psychoanalysts and marketers use cues to prod people to remember their past. In his work Freud eventually came to the conclusion that his patients were fantasizing much of their childhood experiences based on his own suggestions. The marketing-research paradigms have focused on how brands might associate themselves with *actual* past consumer experiences. Virtually no research has examined memories of brand experiences, in particular childhood ones, and the manner in which the advertising influences those recollections. In light of previous findings on autobiographical referencing an important and yet unexplored question arises: Might exposure to an autobiographical ad alter consumer's recollection of a past childhood experience or even create a memory of an experience that never happened? For instance, some childhood memories may be based more on recurring ads consumers are exposed to rather than on recollection of actual childhood events. Similarly, some consumers may come to believe that they had taken part in an experience when in fact they had only viewed an ad of the event.

This alteration is possible because of the reconstructive nature of memory (see Schacter, 1995 for a full review; Braun, 1999, for its application in marketing). A consumer's past is constantly being updated to fit one's changing self-knowledge and social contexts (Bruner, 1986; Neisser & Fivush, 1994; Spence, 1982). The process of rewriting one's history is natural and allows one to adapt to possibilities in the future (Hyman & Pentland, 1996). As time passes there lies a greater likelihood that temporally available information will be used to reconstruct, and perhaps distort, how the experience is remembered (Thompson, Skowronski, Larsen, & Betz, 1996).

False Memories and Imagination Inflation

Memories that have had time to fade are particularly subject to distortion. For example, Loftus and Pickrell (1995) suggested to adult participants that at age five they had been lost in a shopping mall and rescued by an elderly person. About a quarter of the adults fell sway to this suggestion. Using a similar procedure, Hyman and Pentland (1996) suggested and had participants imagine having spilled a bowl of punch at a wedding as a child. About a quarter of adults fell sway to this suggestion, and even more did so when imagination of the experience was encouraged. The false memories typically incorporated the punch-bowl incident into a broader account based on accurate personal knowledge. These studies show that with suggestion and imagination a significant minority of people can be led to believe that they had experiences that were manufactured, and many of them elaborated upon those false experiences with idiosyncratically produced details.

The act of imagining oneself having a childhood experience forces people to create alternatives to reality (if the experience never happened; Roese, 2000 discusses other effects of **counterfactual thinking**). The ease with which these vividly pictured figments of the imagination come to mind may promote their acceptance as real regardless of their actual veridicality (Schwarz, 1996). Such imagining might induce **source attribution** errors whereby the recently imagined event becomes confused with the actual past. Researchers find it is particularly difficult to detect differences between recent imaging and childhood memory. For instance, Johnson, Foley, Suengas, and Payne (1988) asked participants to think of actual or imagined personal events from either the recent past or childhood and then rate them on a number of characteristics. They found far fewer significant differences between actual and imagined childhood events than for actual and imagined recent events.

A common result of having people imagine an experience is increased confidence that the event occurred. Garry, Manning, Loftus, and Sherman (1996) looked at the relationship between cues asking participants to imagine an experience and the later reporting of the event happening to them as a child. In their paradigm they asked participants to rate the likelihood certain childhood events happened to them on a life-events inventory (LEI) containing many experiences, for example, getting lost in a shopping mall. Two weeks later, half of the participants were instructed to imagine themselves as children experiencing several of these events, including some that had never happened to them. Only participants who performed the imaginative exercise reported substantial rises in confidence that both actual and illusory incidents had occurred. The researchers called this effect imagination inflation.

Experimental Investigation

Although there is empirical evidence that suggestions can influence childhood memory, a question arises as to whether it is possible for a marketer to exert an influence with suggestions in the form of advertising. The first study investigates whether autobiographical advertising can prompt consumers to image their childhood experiences so their memories become more consistent with the images evoked in the advertising. That first study focuses on a central childhood experience, visiting Disney World, and specifically shaking hands with Mickey Mouse. It is known from past research that pictures or images can trigger stronger remembering (Schacter, Johnson, Angell, & Gross, 1997), and that actions can be of superior value for prompting reconstruction because they typically form the unique attribute of a specific event (Anderson & Conway, 1993). Further, it is known that when people recount their past experiences they begin by visualizing perceptual details and embellish their memories based upon those details (Belli & Loftus, 1996). For that reason, the target ad incorporated various images from the park—from Disney's glistening castle to the mention of the theme song from "It's a Small World." The ad began with "Remember the

Magic" and describes a day in the park from a child's perspective, with the culmination being shaking hands with Mickey Mouse.

It is predicted that if the ad is part of the reconstruction process, the ad elements or images may be likely to appear as part of consumers' reconstructed memory of their visit, regardless of whether or not the events had actually happened. In addition, if the ad causes imaging of the childhood experience, then this imagination process will lead consumers to believe the ad-based experience of shaking hands with Mickey happened to them as a child—advertising inflation.

Experiment 1

The purpose of this study was to determine whether autobiographically focused advertising could directly affect how consumers remember a prior childhood experience. This is important for marketers because, although it is known that past experiences can be an important driver in future purchase, it is not known whether marketers can evoke or alter memories of childhood experiences through their advertising messages.

Method

Subjects

The participants were 107 undergraduates (64 female, 43 male) from a Midwestern university who received course credit for their involvement.

Design

A single-factor between-subjects design was used. Half the participants received the Disney ad, the other half received a control, non-Disney ad. The participants were randomly assigned to one of these conditions. Random assignment left 46 in the Disney ad condition, 51 in the control condition.

Materials Procedure

The experimental procedure was adapted from the Garry et al. (1996) imagination inflation paradigm. On the first week participants were given a list of 20 childhood events and asked to indicate whether or not the events had happened to them under the age of 10. They rated these on a 100-mm line where 0 = definitely did not happen, 100 = definitely did happen. The target item was "Met and shook hands with a favorite TV character at a theme resort." This item appeared fourth on the list. The LEI survey was given within several other experimental tasks. They were asked to come back the following week to finish one of those experiments.

The following week half were given the Disney ad, the other half the control ad, by another experimenter. They were encouraged to imagine themselves experiencing the situation appearing in the ad, and were given 5 minutes to write down how the ad made them feel and what it made them think about. Afterwards, participants rated the ad on four bipolar attitude scales anchored by: "unfavorable—favorable," "bad—good," "unpleasant—pleasant," and "negative—positive" on a 100-mm line, where a higher score indicates more favorable attitudes. They rated how involving the ad was for them, with the use of empathy measures adapted from the Wells *R* scale (1986): "I felt I was right there in the ad experiencing the situation again," "I really got involved in the feelings provoked by the ad," "While I was looking at the ad, I could easily put myself in the situation," and "While looking at the ad, I felt that the events were happening to me." These measures were anchored from 0 = "strongly disagree" to 100 = "strongly agree."

After a 5-minute distraction task, the original experimenter from Week 1 came in, appearing to be rather panicked, and said there had been a problem with coding the autobiographical data and could they please fill out the life-events inventory again.

After a 15-minute distraction task, participants were asked about their memories of Disney in a questionnaire delivered by a third experimenter. Participants were asked directly if they had ever visited Disney before they were 10 and if so, to describe their memory of that event. They were asked how well they remembered the event (1 = "not at all," 7 = "perfectly") whether the memory was pleasant (where –3 = "extremely unpleasant," 3 = "extremely pleasant"), the emotional involvement in the experience (1 = "nothing," 5 = "extreme"), centrality to their childhood (1 = "not central," 3 = "central"), and personal importance to their childhood (0 = "trivial," 100 = "very important"). These scales were adapted from Thompson et al. (1996). Last, as a means to assess demand characteristics, participants were asked what they thought the purpose of the experiment was, and whether or not they believed their memories of Disney had been influenced by the advertising.

Results

Coding Procedure

Two independent judges coded participants' reactions to the ads and the recall statements of their Disney experience. They had no knowledge of the experimental hypotheses. Their **interrater reliability** was 0.83 and an average was used for the analysis.

Autobiographical Effects of the Advertising

The judges looked at participants' written protocols to determine whether there was mention of a past experience, a report that the ad caused the participant to imagine or evoke his or her experience, or mention of future expectations regarding the resort. Out of the 46 participants who received the autobiographical ad, 30 (or 65%) mentioned memories of Disney World, 34 (or 74%) mentioned that the ad caused them to imagine the experience, and 29 (or 63%) mentioned future visits to the park. For instance, one participant wrote:

> It made me think back to when I was a kid and went to Disney World. It was great. I remembered eating all day long, riding on Space Mountain for the first time, and especially meeting Mickey Mouse! It made me want to beg my

parents to go there over Christmas break. I want to re-live the memories I had as a child.

As Baumgartner et al. (1992) found, this reliving can cause nostalgic feelings:

I felt very nostalgic, remembering what it was like the first time I was at Disney World. Disney World seems like a fantasyland "dreamlike" place to visit. A magical place where memories take place.

Even those who had not visited the park in the past were able to generate this imagination process: "It made me want to visit Disney World even more than I already want to. It describes it just like I imagine it to be."

Imagination Inflation

To reiterate, a major goal of Experiment 1 was to access whether exposure (plus imagination) to an advertisement about a product can increase participants' confidence that certain events occurred in their own past childhood experience with that product. The first analysis explored whether participants became more confident that the critical event occurred by examining whether LEI scores moved up or down, for the critical item "shaking hands with a TV character at a theme resort." The difference between Week 2 and Week 1 was the dependent measure—a score of 0 would indicate no memory change, a positive score a memory inflation, and a negative score a memory deflation.

Because the interest was in seeing if the ad could make the event more probable, people who were (at Week 1) quite certain that they had already experienced the shaking-hands event were eliminated from the data set. That left those who reported the shaking-hands incident had a low likelihood of occurrence on the first LEI, defined as a 0–50 on the line mark scale, to determine if the ad increased their confidence the event had occurred (as per Garry et al., 1996), which left 73 participants (32 control, 41 Disney). There are several ways to analyze this data. The first analysis looked at the number of people in each group that showed an increase, decrease, or same report on the LEI (see Figure 1). Significantly more people who received the Disney ad went up on the LEI, 90% versus 47% in the control, significantly different at $\chi_2(2, N = 73) = 17.3$, $p <.0001$. In addition, mean difference scores on the LEI were analyzed. A positive difference would indicate greater confidence the event had happened to them, a negative difference less confidence. The Disney group showed a more positive change, $M = 37.05$, than the control group, $M = -1.5$ significantly different at $t(71) = 5.93$, $p < .0001$. There were no significant differences on the other 18 items on the LEI test.

Another question of interest is which (if any) advertising measures would best predict the advertising/imagination inflation. Earlier work by Krugman (1967) suggests that autobiographical referencing may increase involvement, and Wells (1986) argues that traditional attitude-toward-ad measures may not effectively capture this effect. The four traditional ad-rating measures, where participants indicated their overall liking for the ad, loaded on one factor with coefficient alpha = .92 and were combined into an ad attitude/rating index. The Wells R involvement with ad measures, where participants indicated how

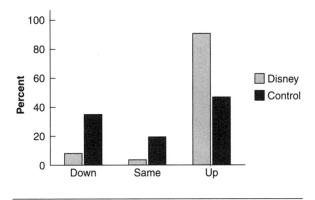

FIGURE 1 *Experiment 1: Change in LEI "shaking hands."*

emotionally involved they became in the ad-based situation, also loaded on one factor with coefficient of 0.90 and were combined to form an involvement index. Here it was found that the correlation between the ad attitude index and the LEI memory change was $r = .08$ and involvement in ad measures was $r = .31$, showing that in absence of the LEI change data, the Wells scale can capture the memory effects slightly better than traditional ad-attitude measures can.

Disney Memory

Thirty-four participants from the Disney ad group and 34 from the control group reported having visited a Disney park in the past. They were asked to describe and rate that visit on several scales. The two judges coded the recall statements on the number of words, independent thoughts, positive thoughts, negative thoughts, and elements from the ad that were mentioned. For the latter, the judges looked at the recall statements for usage of words from the ad (e.g., "magical") and actions from the ads (e.g. "cool rides" or hearing "It's a Small World"). One participant, who appeared to be heavily influenced by the advertising, wrote:

> Went on lots of different rides, met Mickey Mouse, watched the "Small World" show...hug.... Got sick from too much junk food, got drenched on log ride....

The ad had featured meeting Mickey Mouse, the "It's A Small World" song, and a variety of rides and food. That response would have scored a 4 on elements. Because some of these ad-suggested ideas may naturally appear in one's recall of Disney, the auto-biographical ad condition was compared to the control condition to assess whether the ad increased their appearance. There were no significant differences in the length or number of thoughts between the Disney/control condition; $M = 31$ words in the Disney condition, $M = 26$ in the control condition; $M = 4.4$ thoughts in the Disney condition, $M = 4.1$ in the control condition. There were significantly more positive thoughts ($M = 3.6$) in the Disney ad condition than in the control ($M = 2.8$, $t[66] = 2.07$, $p = .02$). There were no differences in negative thoughts; $M = 0.79$ in Disney, $M = 0.50$ in control, $t < 1$. There were more ad elements appearing in the recall in the ad condition ($M = 2.38$) than in the control ($M = 1.47$, $t[66] = 2.65$, $p = .005$).

Participants also rated their memory on several objective measures; means appear in Table 1. Those who received the Disney ad rated their memories as being more personally important, $t(66) = 1.93$, $p = .025$; better remembered, $t(66) = 3.11$, $p = .001$; more pleasant, $t(66) = 2.17$, $p = .015$; and more central to their childhood, $t 66) = 1.59$, $p = .055$ than those who did not receive the Disney ad. There were no significant differences in emotive aspects of recall, $t < 1$.

Demand

Participants were asked to guess the purpose of the experiments in order to assess demand factors. No one correctly responded that the advertising was intended to alter their childhood memories. Additionally, participants were asked whether the advertising helped them remember anything from their own experience that they might not otherwise have been able to remember. Forty-one participants who received the Disney ad said "no"; 5 said "yes." They were also asked if the ad they saw for Disney made them remember their ex-

TABLE 1 *Objective Memory Measures*

	Experiment 1	
	Disney	*Control*
Personal importance (0 = trivial, 100 = very important)	64	51
How well remembered (1 = not at all, 7 = perfectly)	4.8	3.9
Pleasantness of visit (–3 = extremely unpleasant, 3 = extremely pleasant)	2.4	2.0
Centrality to childhood (1 = not central, 3 = central)	2.2	1.7
Emotional involvement (1 = nothing, 5 = extreme)	3.6	3.5

	Experiment 2		
	Ariel	*Bugs*	*Nonautobiographical*
Personal importance (0 = trivial, 10 = very important)	5.6	5.5	5.0
How well remembered (1 = not at all, 7 = perfectly)	4.4	4.3	3.9
Pleasantness of visit (–3 = extremely unpleasant, 3 = extremely pleasant)	2.1	2.4	2.1
Centrality to childhood (1 = not central, 3 = central)	2.3	2.2	1.8
Emotional involvement (1 = nothing, 5 = extreme)	3.8	3.8	3.5

perience to be different than it really was. For instance, did the ad make them remember having a positive experience when in fact it was very negative? Forty-three participants said "no," and only 3 said "yes."

Discussion

The purpose of this study was to determine whether an autobiographical ad could make consumers more confident that they had experienced an advertised-suggested event as a child. It was found that autobiographical advertising can indeed induce this effect. The participants became more confident that they had shaken hands with a TV character after viewing the advertising than if they had not received that retrieval cue.

Figure 2 depicts three routes that could be happening as participants recalled the shaking-hands event, adapted from Haber and Haber (1996). Route 1 represents those who rated the shaking-hands experience high on both the LEI pre- and posttests; in other words, they did not need the ad to retrieve that memory, and those people were not included in the LEI analysis for that reason. Routes 2 and 3 are the most interesting with respect to the role autobiographical advertising has on cuing past experiences, for both routes represent those individuals that increased on the LEI test after receiving the Disney ad. The paradox of offering a retrieval cue is that it can help access both true and false memories (Spiegel, 1997). As Garry et al. (1996) note in their study of imagination inflation, some of the observed increases could be due to the ad providing an effective cue in surfacing a veridical memory. In other words, perhaps some participants at Week 1 forgot about shaking hands with Mickey and the ad helped surface that encounter. However, it is possible that the ad may have implanted that experience in consumers' minds.

It was impossible to determine whether in fact participants had ever shaken hands with Mickey Mouse, and thus is not clear whether Routes 2 or 3 were occurring. One way to determine this would be to get participants to remember an event that would have been impossible, for example, getting them to remember shaking hands with a character who became popular later, but did not exist at the time the participant would have been to a Disney park or, alternatively, feature a competitor's character (e.g., Warner Bros. Bugs Bunny), who would have never been in the park. If advertising leads people to claim an impossible experience, there would be evidence for the creation of false memories. This reasoning guided the design of Experiment 2.

Experiment 2

The purpose of this experiment was to determine whether false information in advertising about childhood experiences at Disney could make consumers believe those events had happened to them. Two types of false information were tested within the same ad format as used in Experiment 1: In one ad it was suggested that they had shaken hands with Bugs Bunny (a Warner Bros. character); in another ad it was suggested they had shaken hands with Ariel, the Little Mermaid (a Disney character not yet introduced at

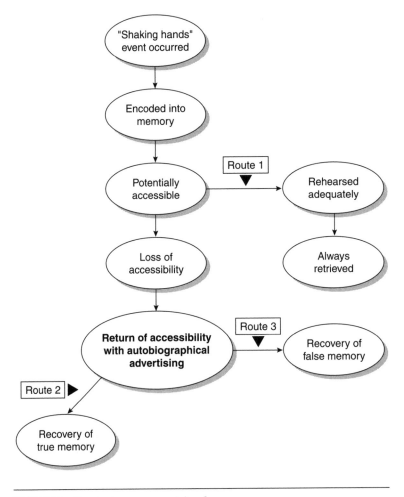

FIGURE 2   *Routes to memory retrieval.*

the critical childhood time period, before the age of 10). Bugs, meanwhile, was around during participants' childhood but would have never have been at a Disney resort. A non-autobiographical Disney ad served as a control group in order to investigate whether it is the autobiographical nature of the ad that is influencing consumers' past or the mere Disney mention that is triggering the results.[1] The nonautobiographical ad was more informational in nature (Puto & Wells, 1983), focusing on a new ride being offered at the park and providing information about how to order park tickets via the Web at a discount price.

---

[1]The researchers felt it was important to have all groups imagine the Disney experience to see what effect the autobiographical referencing had by just mentioning the Disney name, as other researchers have found spontaneous activation of autobiographical memories in the presence of advertising (Baumgartner et al., 1992).

Method

Subjects

The participants were 167 (104 female, 63 male) psychology undergraduates at a western university who received credit for their involvement.[2]

Materials and Procedure

The same basic procedure from Experiment 1 was followed, with some adaptations. Participants took the first LEI during a mass-testing situation and indicated whether or not they would be interested in participating in an upcoming ad study. Those who said "yes" were contacted and were assigned to one of the three ad conditions. Some screening occurred: Those who had visited Six Flags were eliminated to reduce a possible source-confusion error (Bugs Bunny does make an appearance at that park).

The target LEI measure was modified to "shaking hands with a cartoon character in a theme park" with a 10-point scale anchored by "definitely did not happen"/"definitely did happen." The Disney World focus was changed to Disneyland because of the higher likelihood that the students would have visited that California resort. All dependent measures were converted to numbered scales instead of the 100-mm line marks used in Experiment 1. The discrete numbering system simplified analysis.

The advertising measures were also the same as Experiment 1, but were measured on an 8-point scale, with higher values indicating greater liking or involvement. A few measures were added to determine whether in fact the false information had become a part of participants' childhood memories. The participants were asked to indicate with what confidence they had seen some characters at the park (with Bugs and Ariel being the target items buried within a set of other characters) and then to specifically remember what characters they had actually shaken hands with (again Bugs and Ariel were buried within a list). Specifically, they were asked to indicate their confidence that they had met the following characters, with Bugs appearing third and Ariel appearing fifth on a list of eight characters, and to put an "X" in front of characters they had actually met in person (e.g., shaking their hand); the Bugs and Ariel placement was the same on this list of eight characters.

Results

Autobiographical Effects of Advertising

The two autobiographical ads were more involving for participants, scoring higher than the non-autobiographical Disney ad on the Wells *R* scale index, formed as in Experiment 1 except that the scale now ranged from 1 to 8, with lower scores indicating less involvement.

---

[2]Differences in cell sizes in reported tests result from some participants skipping over measures. This did not occur frequently nor in an uneven distribution across conditions.

Means follow: 5.2 for the Ariel, 5.1 for the Bugs, 3.8 for the nonautobiographical Disney ad; a *t*-test comparison showed the two autobiographical ads were significantly higher than the nonautobiographical ad, $t(165) = 4.3, p < .0001$.[3]

The ad attitude/rating index showed no significant difference across the groups; the new range for attitude scale was 1 to 8, with lower values indicating less-favorable attitudes. Means follow: $M = 5.9$ Ariel, $M = 5.8$ Bugs, $M = 5.5$ nonautobiographical Disney, $F < 1$. Therefore, the Wells index can better differentiate types of advertising that influence memories than traditional ad-attitude measures.

Imagination Inflation

Recall that participants indicated how likely the target event, shaking hands with a cartoon character at a theme park, happened to them before the age of 10, on a 10-point scale, where 1 = "definitely did not happen" and 10 = "definitely did happen." They filled out the life-events inventory twice, once during the mass testing, and then again in a subsequent session. The discrete numbering scale allowed for a more precise segmentation than Experiment 1. Those who had indicated the event was unlikely to have happened to them (scoring 1–5 on the initial test) were eliminated, which left 106 participants (34 Ariel, 36 Bugs, 34 nonautobiographical ad condition). The interest was in determining if those individuals who had rated the event as being relatively unlikely would increase their confidence it had happened to them after seeing the false autobiographical suggestions in the advertising. Figure 3 depicts those individuals from each group and the direction of movement on the target LEI item, "shaking hands." All groups showed a tendency to increase but it was more pronounced in the conditions that received an autobiographical ad—76% in the Ariel condition, 78% in Bugs, and 62% in the nonautobiographical condition—the autobiographical groups being significantly more likely at $\chi^2 (1, N = 106) = 2.5, p = .05$. Mean movement on the LEI was also compared across groups, $M = 4.8$ for Ariel, 5.1 for Bugs, 3.8 for nonautobiographical Disney. Participants in the autobiographical ad conditions displayed significantly greater movement in their confidence that they had shaken hands than their nonautobiographical counterparts; $t(104) = 1.95, p = .05$.

As found in Experiment 1, the Wells R scale was more correlated with the change in LEI than the ad attitude scale, $r = 0.2$ Wells, $r = -.1$ ad attitude.

Disney Memory

All participants were asked to write about and rate their memory of their childhood experience at Disney; 46 in the Ariel condition, 56 in the Bugs condition, and 46 in the nonautobiographical condition did so. Those that received the autobiographical ads reported better

---

[3]Because the interest was in the difference between autobiographical and nonautobiographical advertising effects, the two autobiographical groups were combined after finding no significant difference between them in order to assess if they were different from the other type of ad. Another way to analyze this would be to run an ANOVA on the three groups and do post-hoc comparisons. This was done as well, with similar results. For simplicity, only the *t*-test results are reported. In these *t* tests pooled variance was used, and when directionality was predicted, one-tailed *p* values were reported. This technique was used throughout Experiment 2.

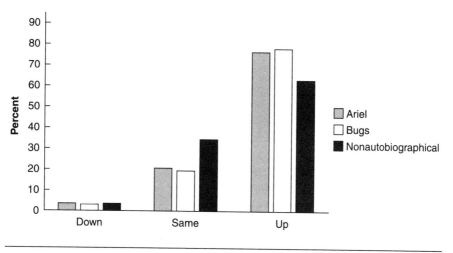

FIGURE 3 *Experiment 2: Change in LEI "shaking hands."*

clarity in their memories, $t(109) = 2.07$, $p = .02$; more emotional content, $t(111) = 1.64$, $p = .05$; more centrality of memory to childhood, $t(121) = 2.26$, $p = .01$; and more importance to their childhood, $t(110) = 1.76$, $p = .04$. There was no significant difference on pleasurable memories between conditions. Means appear in the bottom of Table 1.

False Memory

Participants were asked more directly about specific images (false ones) that may have happened on their childhood visit to the park. The interest was whether they would report greater confidence in having met or remembering shaking hands with either Ariel or Bugs if they received those respective ads. They were first asked to indicate confidence that they had met several characters at the park on a scale of 1 to 7, anchored by "not very confident" and "very confident." Confidence in meeting Bugs was $M = 2.7$ for the Bugs group, $M = 2.1$ for Ariel, $M = 2.2$ for the nonautobiographical Disney ad. A t-test comparison found the Bugs group to be more confident than the other groups that they had met him, $t(114) = 1.67$, $p = .04$. Participants were also asked whether they remembered specifically shaking hands with Bugs at the park as a child, 16% in the Bugs condition remembered doing so, compared to 7% in the Ariel group, and 7% in the nonautobiographical group. A comparison between the Bugs and other-ad conditions was significant, 16% versus 7%, $\chi^2(1, N = 131) = 2.6$, $p = .05$. In contrast, there was no significant difference between the Ariel-exposed group and other ad conditions on confidence they had met Ariel at the park, $M = 1.3$ for Ariel, $M = 1.8$ for Bugs, $M = 1.3$ for nonautobiographical Disney. However, there was a greater tendency for the subjects to believe they had shaken hands with Ariel as a child if they received the false ad: 7% of those in the Ariel condition remembered shaking her hand compared to 0% in the Bugs condition, and 4% in the nonautobiographical Disney condition; a comparison between the Ariel and other-ad groups was significant at $\chi^2 (1, N = 131) = 3.49$, $p = .03$.

Discussion

The main finding of this experiment is that featuring impossible events in autobiographical advertising can cause people to believe they had experienced the events. For example, 16% of people claimed that they shook hands with Bugs after receiving the false Bugs ad; 7% said they remembered meeting Ariel, a character that had not yet been introduced, after seeing an ad suggesting all children meet her at the park. Neither character would have been at the park during the participants' childhood, demonstrating that autobiographical ads can alter memories of the past. As found in Experiment 1, imagination inflation occurred, where people became more confident that the ad-suggested event had happened to them when they were children.

The Bugs ad was more effective in inducing this memory change. This could be because Bugs is a better-known character, and thus easier for participants to imagine during the ad exposure. For instance, in their study of imagining's effect on prediction of future actions, Sherman, Cialdini, Schwartzman, and Reynolds (1985) found that easier-to-imagine illnesses were judged as more likely to occur. Goff and Roediger (1998) found that as the number of imaginings of false experiences increased, so did the reported memories of participating in these events. Perhaps if participants had received several cues indicating the false characters were associated with Disney, there would be a higher reporting of impossible memories. There is some evidence to suggest this might be the case: There was a relationship observed between confidence in having memory of the shaking-hands experience, which was missing in the Ariel condition. This participant seemed to accept the Bugs ad, despite her initial feeling that it was incorrect:

> The first thing that went through my mind when looking at the ad was "why is Bugs Bunny on a Disneyland ad...isn't he a Warner Bros. character?" I'm still confused about whether he is or not, but oh well....

The advertising may make an event seem more plausible and help consumers develop (or amend) a script for the childhood experience, two factors thought to be important in generating a false memory (Pezdek, Finger, & Hodge, 1997).

General Discussion

The two studies provide empirical evidence for autobiographical advertising's influence on how consumers remember their past. Specifically, it was found that autobiographically focused advertising can make events (even impossible ones) seem more likely to have happened to consumers as children. In Experiment 1 it was found that an autobiographical ad increased consumers' confidence that they had shaken hands with Mickey Mouse in a before-age-10 visit to the park. There was no way to determine whether the ad had activated a true memory or created a new, false one. Experiment 2 found an increase in confidence that participants had experienced the ad-suggested scenario, but, in addition, found them more likely to believe they had met characters at the park who would not have been at Disney during their childhood.

The idea that autobiographical advertising can influence how consumers remember their past is a timely issue. Manufacturers like Ovaltine™, Alka Seltzer™, Maxwell House™, and Shake-n-Bake™ have begun to dig into their vaults from the 1950s and 60s to pull out nostalgic images from past advertising campaigns. Undeniably, such ads tap into some existing consumer memories from their childhood. Marketers had believed the process began and ended with the ads cuing actual past experiences, as Freud's general belief regarding the special status of the original memory has lingered.

But times are changing, and some marketers are beginning to realize that memories are constructive. Some have even benefited from the fact that their consumers' memories have been manufactured. Take, for example, Stewart's root beer. They report many adults seem to remember growing up drinking Stewart's frosty root beer in bottles. This is impossible, because the company only began full-scale distribution 10 years ago, and prior to that only fountain drinks were available. It could be that glass bottles adorned with sayings like "original" "old-fashioned" and "since 1924" provide consumers the illusion of a past that they might have shared as a child. In fact, the vice president of Stewart's marketing swears he remembers drinking their soda after Little League games in an area where distribution was unlikely, but admits, "Memories are always better when they're embellished" (Prince, 2000).

Although there is no direct evidence Disney altered memories through their "Remember the Magic" campaign, the evidence collected here suggests it is at least possible. The power of memory alteration is that consumers are not aware they have been influenced. The feeling associated with remembering a past event, of "seeing" the event unfold in their mind's eye, provides one the belief that how it is recollected is how it happened. Participants held this belief about the permanence of memory; most indicated that the ad had little (or no effect) on their recollections. One participant wrote:

> While I was reading it (the Disney ad) I was thinking that I have to take my children there someday because of the great memories that I have from there and probably always will have.

Most people are under the belief that memory is a permanent store and with hypnosis or other special techniques past information can be recovered (Loftus & Loftus, 1980). Autobiographical advertising, like hypnosis, allows the consumer to become personally involved in the message. Consumers, for the most part, enjoy the trip back in memory, and the marketer benefits from the positive affect brought forth by their role as memory guide. As a guide, the marketers' message has consequences on what consumers ultimately remember. Those who received the advertising were more confident the childhood experiences suggested in the advertising had happened to them.

Marketers can use autobiographical referencing to reestablish a personal relationship with their consumers. These autobiographical recollections serve important social and personal functions for consumers. For example, one participant wrote:

> It brought back memories indeed. I guess I thought the story-beginning was a bit cheesy but then I realize I do have to remember what the experience was like when I was younger. It made you want to run to a Walt Disney Resort, I must admit. It sounds like a lot of fun! The theme "Remember the Magic" I

think really caters to all ages, even adults, who may have forgotten what the "magic" was like—take me, for instance!

Another discussed the social aspects of this remembering process, writing that the ad "reminds them of happy memories and encourages them to share with others." Marketers can benefit on two counts by being the memory guide: directly, by influencing the consumer's attitude and purchase intention, and indirectly, by activating positive word-of-mouth regarding the brand.

Remembering is often a social activity in which people come to some agreement about the past (Hyman et al., 1995) and it is much more likely to take place in the context of friends, family, or advertising than with psychotherapists. In some sense, life is a continual memory alteration experiment where memories continually are shaped by new incoming information (Hyman et al., 1995). This brings forth ethical considerations. Is it all right for marketers to knowingly manipulate consumers' past? On one hand, the alteration will occur whether or not that was the intent of the marketer. And, in most cases, the advertiser is unlikely to try to plant a negative memory, as has been the issue with false memories of childhood abuse. On the other hand, there are ways in which the marketer can enhance the likelihood consumer memories will be consistent with their advertising messages. At the very least, consumers ought to be aware of that power.

Autobiographical referencing is one way to influence consumers' recollections. The ads employed in these studies accomplished that by providing consumers the imagery tools with which to build their memory. According to Reconstructionist theorist Frederic Bartlett (1932), an image becomes the device for picking bits out of schemes (of existing knowledge) and organizing it in such a way that decreases the variability in the reconstruction of the past situation. Typical ad rating scales may not be effective in determining whether an ad will or will not be successful in bringing forth consumer memories. This research found another scale, Wells *R,* to be slightly better in assessing the potential elaborative effects.

Limitations and Future Research

The subject pool was fairly homogeneous undergraduates. Generations exposed to similar media will become more homogeneous in the types of memories they recall. Different generations may have distinct time posts or markers that should be targeted for the Disney experience, for example, different characters or rides. Holbrook and Schindler (1996) find that there are critical periods for which particular experiences are imprinted and learning and affect are created for the brand or service. Childhood experiences may have been a critical period in the foundation of consumer's knowledge about Disney, though for other product categories different ages might be better suited for memory revision (e.g., drinking a particular beer in college). Future research should address which life periods should be targeted in autobiographical ads, depending on consumer age and product category.

The research environment also presents limitations. Participants were instructed to think about the advertising as it was presented to them. Such directed attention might not be representative of actual advertising exposures. Future research might vary the level of advertising exposure to determine how that influences the recollection process.

There are many opportunities for future investigations into this issue of memory alteration. For example, one avenue might look at what type of consumers are most likely to be influenced by autobiographical referencing. Forty-eight percent of the population is susceptible to hypnotic suggestion; these consumers might also be the ones most apt for brand memory distortion. The Disassociated Experience Scale (DES) has been fairly robust in capturing this effect (average *r* about 0.3).

Because Mickey Mouse is a well-known icon of Disney and is probably already a central part of consumer participants' script of visiting the park, the event of shaking hands may have been easier to imagine than with a lesser-known character (Ariel) or an unrelated character (Bugs). Not all participants in Experiment 2 easily accepted the false suggestion, as this participant wrote:

> Well first off I notice that Bugs Bunny is a Warner Bros. character rather than Walt Disney so in essence I feel a sense of false advertising here from the Disney company.

Previous work on false memories finds that very similar characters, for example, Mickey Mouse and Minnie, are easily substituted for one another in memory (Loftus, 1997). The participants had only one advertising exposure to associate these newer characters with Disney. It is quite possible that this research underestimates the true effects that autobiographical advertising has on shaping consumers' pasts because in the marketplace consumers may see the ads several times.

References

Ainsworth, M. D. (1985, Spring). Patterns of attachment. Clinical Psychologist, 38, 27–29.

Anderson, S. J., & Conway, M. A. (1993). Investigating the structure of auto-biographical memories. Journal of Experimental Psychology: Learning, Memory, & Cognition, 19, 1178–1196.

Bartlett, F. C. (1932). Remembering. Cambridge: Cambridge University Press. Baumgartner, H., Sujan, M., & Bettman, J. R. (1992). Autobiographical memories, affect and consumer information processing. Journal of Consumer Psychology, 1, 53–82.

Belli, R. F., & Loftus, E. F. (1996). The pliability of autobiographical memory: Misinformation and the false memory problem. In D. C. Rubin (Ed.), Remembering our past: Studies in autobiographical memory (pp. 157–179).

Boller, G. W. (1990). The vicissitudes of product experience: "Songs of our consuming selves" in drama ads. In M. E. Goldberg, G. J. Gorn, & R. W. Pollay (Eds.), Advances in consumer research (Vol. 17, pp. 621–625).

Braun, K. A. (1999). Postexperience advertising effects on consumer memory. Journal of Consumer Research, 25, 319–334.

Bruner, J. (1986). Actual minds, possible worlds. Cambridge, MA: Harvard University Press.

Garry, M., Manning, C. G., Loftus, E. F., & Sherman, S. J. (1996). Imagination inflation: Imagining a childhood event inflates confidence that it occurred. Psychonomic Bulletin & Review, 3, 208–214.

Goff, L. M., & Roediger, H. L. III. (1998). Imagination inflation for action events: Repeated imaginings lead to illusory recollections. Memory & Cognition, 26, 20–33.

Haber, R. N., & Haber, L. (1996). Antecedent conditions and operational definitions for recovered memory effects. Psychonomics Society Convention, Chicago.

Holbrook, M. B., & Schindler, R. M. (1996). Market segmentation based on age and attitude toward the past: Concepts, methods, and findings concerning nostalgic influences on customer tastes. Journal of Business Research, 37, 27–39.

Hyman, I. E., Husband, T. H., & Billings, F. J. (1995). False memories of childhood experiences. Applied Cognitive Psychology, 9, 181–197.

Hyman, I. E., & Pentland, J. (1996). The role of mental imagery in the creation of false childhood memories. Journal of Memory and Language, 35, 101–117.

Johnson, M. K., Foley, M. A., Suengas, A. F., & Raye, C. L. (1988). Phenomenal characteristics of memories for perceived and imagined autobiographical events. Journal of Experimental Psychology: General, 117, 371–376.

Krugman, H. E. (1967). The measurement of advertising involvement. Public Opinion Quarterly, 30, 349–356.

Lindsay, D. S., & Read, J. D. (1994). Psychotherapy and memories of childhood sexual abuse: A cognitive perspective. Applied Cognitive Psychology, 8, 281–338.

Loftus, E. F. (1997). Creating false memories. Scientific American, 277(3), 70–75.

Loftus, E. F., & Ketcham, K. (1994). The myth of repressed memory. New York: St. Martin's Press.

Loftus, E. F., & Loftus, G. R. (1980). On the permanence of stored information in the human brain. American Psychologist, 35, 409–420.

Loftus, E. F., & Pickrell, J. E. (1995). The formulation of false memories. Psychiatric Annals, 25, 720–725.

Marconi, J. (1996, October 21). Retro marketing helps brands gain new image. Marketing News, 30, p. 10.

Neisser, U., & Fivush, R. (1994). The remembered self: Construction and accuracy in the self narrative. Cambridge: Cambridge University Press.

Pezdek, K., Finger, K., & Hodge, D. (1997). Planting false childhood memories: The role of plausibility. Psychological Science, 8, 437–441.

Prince, G. W. (2000, March 15). Yesterday, today and tomorrow. Beverage Word, pp. 52–54.

Puto, C. P., & Wells, W. D. (1983). Informational and transformational advertising: The differential effects of time. In T. K. Kinnear (Ed.), Advances in consumer research (Vol. 11, pp. 638–643).

Roese, N. J. (2000). Counterfactual thinking and marketing: Introduction to the special issue. Psychology & Marketing, 17, 1.

Schacter, D. L. (1995). Memory distortion. Cambridge, MA: Harvard University Press.

Schacter, D. L., Koutstaal, W., Johnson, M. K., & Gross, M. S. (1997). False recollection induced by photographs: A comparison of older and younger adults. Psychology & Aging, 12, 203–215.

Schwarz, N. (1996). Cognition and communication. Mahwah, NJ: Lawrence Erlbaum.

Sherman, S. J., Cialdini, R. B., Schwartzman, D. F., & Reynolds, K. D. (1985). Imagining can heighten or lower the perceived likelihood of contracting a disease: The mediating effect of ease of imagery. Personality & Social Psychology Bulletin, 11, 118–127.

Spiegel, D. (1997). Memories: True and false. American Psychologist, 52, 995–996.

Sujan, M., Bettman, J. R., & Baumgartner, H. (1993). Influencing consumer judgments using autobiographical memories: A self-referencing perspective. Journal of Marketing Research, 30, 422–436.

Thompson, C. P., Skowronski, J. J., Larsen, S. F., & Betz, A. (1996). Autobiographical memory: Remembering what and remembering when. Mahwah, NJ: Lawrence Erlbaum.

Wells, W. D. (1986). Three useful ideas. In R. J. Lutz (Ed.), Advances in Consumer Research (Vol. 13, pp. 9–12). Provo, UT: Association for Consumer Research.

Introduction: Critical Thinking Questions _____

? How and why do advertisers "play off consumers' memories"? What is the aim of such advertising? Can you come up with some examples?

? What reason is there to expect that memory-evoking advertisements would alter the actual memory for certain childhood events?

? The researchers contend that "…early childhood brand relationships may set the stage for later adult brand relationships." Explain what they mean by this, and what the implications are for advertising.

? Describe the process whereby an imagined childhood experience (for an event that did not happen) could be remembered as happening. This memory failure is more likely to happen for events from the more distant past (i.e., childhood) than from the recent past. What evidence supports this?

? Describe the imagination inflation phenomenon, and how it has been demonstrated in research.

? What additional question did Experiment 2 address, and why did it involve Bugs Bunny?

Method: Critical Thinking Questions

? For each experiment, describe what you would have been asked to do, had you been a participant.

? For each experiment, name the independent variables, and their levels. Describe how each of these variables was operationalized. For each variable, state whether it was manipulated in a between-subjects or within-subjects fashion. How many conditions were there in the experiment?

? What was (were) the dependent variable(s) in each experiment?

? What aspects of the methodology were implemented to deal with possible confounds?

Results/Discussion: Critical Thinking Questions

? Did receiving an autobiographical ad about visiting Disney World influence participants' memories in Experiment 1? Explain, citing the relevant results.

? Further analyses in Experiment 1 investigated the effects of exposure to the ad on those participants who *had* actually visited the park. What were the differences between the groups who saw the ad and those who did not see the ad?

? The results of Experiment 1 indicate that autobiographical advertising can inflate judgments of confidence regarding whether events actually occurred. Describe the three possible "routes" to this increased confidence sketched in Figure 2.

? In Experiment 2, the experimenters attempted to have people falsely remember events—events that could not possibly have happened during their visit to Disneyland. Were they successful? Explain, citing the relevant results.

? Over the next few days, pay particular attention to the advertisements you come across, in any medium. Do any of them use autobiographical referencing? How so?

? Discuss the ethical debate concerning the use of advertising that evokes autobiographical remembering. Where do you stand on the relevant issues?

? Discuss some of the limitations that may qualify the researchers' conclusions.

? After reading this study, you may feel there are other issues or questions that would be worthwhile or intriguing to address. Pose one of these questions (other than those suggested by the authors) that could be investigated empirically.

Memory Suggestibility as an Example of the Sleeper Effect

Joe Underwood and Kathy Pezdek

Abstract

This study incorporates findings on both the sleeper effect and the suggestibility of memory and assesses the effect of source credibility and time delay on memory suggestibility. Subjects viewed a sequence of slides with four target items. A narrative followed, containing a misleading description of two target items; the other two items served as controls. The source of the narrative was attributed to either a 4-year-old boy (low-credibility source) or a memory psychologist (high-credibility source) who described the slides. A recognition memory test followed 10 min or 1 month later. The subjects in the low-credibility source condition falsely recognized significantly more misleading items in the delayed condition than in the immediate condition; in the high-credibility condition, the number of falsely recognized misleading items was high and did not differ between the delayed and the immediate conditions. This significant interaction between source credibility, time, and misled/control conditions on the rate of falsely recognizing misled items suggests that, with the passage of time, item and source information become less strongly associated in memory. The cognitive processes underlying the sleeper effect appear to be similar to those underlying memory suggestibility.

Conceptual Issues and Theoretical Questions

- What factors influence the suggestibility of memory?
- What are the joint effects of delay and source credibility on the suggestibility of memory?
- How do memory suggestibility effects relate to the well-established social psychology phenomenon termed the sleeper effect?

De-Jargonizing

- **suggestibility:** one's tendency to be influenced

Underwood, J., & Pezdek, K. (1998). Memory suggestibility as an example of the sleeper effect. *Psychonomic Bulletin and Review, 5,* 449–453. Reprinted by permission of Psychonomic Society, Inc.

- **source monitoring:** the memory processes involved in identifying the origin of some event
- **semantic features:** features of an event or memory that relate to meaning
- **perceptual/contextual features:** features of an event or memory that relate to sensations felt or surroundings experienced at that particular point in time

Psychological interest in the **suggestibility** of memory has increased dramatically in the past decade. This interest is due to both the concerns of the legal system regarding the reliability of child witnesses (Bottoms & Goodman, 1996; Ceci & Bruck, 1993) and the concerns about the validity of claims of recovered memories (Loftus, 1993). Although many memory researchers have reported that memories can be suggestively influenced (Belli, Lindsay, Gales, & McCarthy, 1994; Hyman, Husband, & Billings, 1995; Loftus & Palmer, 1974; Loftus & Pickrell, 1995; Pezdek, 1977), constraints on the construct of suggestibility have been noted (Ceci & Bruck, 1993; Lindsay, 1933; Pezdek, Finger, & Hodge, 1997; Pezdek & Greene, 1993; Pezdek & Roe, 1994). This study examined the interaction of two such constraints on suggestibility—source credibility and time delay.

Although the effect of the interaction of source credibility and time delay on the suggestibility of memory has not been investigated, the effect of this interaction on communication effectiveness has been thoroughly researched. In a study by Hovland and Weiss (1952), subjects evaluated two presentations, one given by a communicator of high credibility and the other given by a communicator of low credibility. Although the presentations were identical, the subjects rated the *high-credibility* communicator as significantly more effective than the *low-credibility* communicator. When the researchers tested the subjects 4 weeks later, however, the ratings of the low-credibility communicator had increased, and the difference between the two credibility conditions was no longer significant. The researchers labeled this phenomenon the *sleeper elect.* This effect occurs when the impact of information from a source low in credibility increases over time (Hovland, Lumsdaine, & Sheffield, 1949). Although many researchers rejected the sleeper effect when they failed to replicate the findings of Hovland and Weiss (see, for example, Gillig & Greenwald, 1974), many researchers have since replicated the effect when carefully controlling their procedures (Hannah & Sternthal, 1984). Currently, researchers have accepted the existence of the sleeper effect and have moved ahead to focus on why the effect occurs and under what conditions (Mazursky & Schul, 1987).

The dominant interpretation of the sleeper effect is based on the availability–valence hypothesis. According to this hypothesis, the cognitive availability of relevant issues at the time of recall determines how an individual will judge the effectiveness of a message. The availability of the issues depends both on the recency of information and on the degree of cognitive elaboration (e.g., the number and type of related associations that are activated at encoding). As posited by Hannah and Sternthal (1984), when an individual reads a message, the individual encodes two potential pieces of information into memory—the message and the credibility of the source of the message. The relative availability of both pieces of information, however, is dependent on the actual encoding process. Specifically, if the information is elaborated on during encoding, the information becomes relatively more available for later recall. The elaboration is particularly effective if the individual uses the self as a reference when encoding the information (Mazursky & Schull, 1987). The elaboration becomes particularly relevant as more time passes from the initial encoding to the time of recall. If an individual recalls a message soon after reading it, the recency of the encoding ensures that the message and the source are available in memory. With the passage of time, however, the message and the source become less strongly associated in memory. The elaborated message, then, will have a relatively greater chance of being available than the nonelaborated source, so that, when the message is recalled, the source is less likely to be remembered (Hannah & Sternthal, 1984; Mazursky & Schul, 1987). In the study by Hovland and Weiss (1952), subjects initially rejected the low-credibility communicator, because the message and its source were strongly associated in memory. After a month, however, the message and its source were less strongly associated, so the subjects did not reject the low-credibility communicator.

The availability–valence hypothesis was developed to explain the impact of time and source credibility on communication effectiveness. In this study, however, we apply these underlying concepts to the study of memory suggestibility. When misleading information is suggested to subjects, this increases the probability that they will later falsely recognize this information as true. The probability that subjects will be misled by the suggested information is greater if the source of the misleading information is attributed to a high-credibility source rather than to a low-credibility source. Dodd and Bradshaw (1980) showed subjects a video of an automobile accident. Later, each was provided a transcript of an eyewitness account that contained three false presuppositions. This account was attributed either to an innocent bystander (neutral source) or to the driver of the car that caused the accident (biased source). Subjects incorporated the presupposition into memory if they thought the source of the presupposition was neutral, but not if they thought the source was biased. Similarly, Smith and Ellsworth (1987) reported that adults were more likely to be misled by a high- than by a low-credibility source.

Lampinen and Smith (1995) found similar results when they showed a videotaped interview to children ranging from 3 to 5 years of age. The interview contained either an adult (high-credibility condition), a silly adult (low-credibility condition), or a child (low-credibility condition), each of whom provided either misleading information or unbiased information. In the high-credibility condition, the children were misled; there was a significant difference in accuracy between the children in the misled condition and those in the control condition. In the low-credibility condition, there were no significant differences in accuracy between the misled and unbiased conditions. Thus, when the subjects were provided with misleading information, they were more likely to be suggestively influenced by the misleading information if the source of the information was credible. In contrast, the subjects were not suggestively influenced by the misleading information if the source of the information was not credible. Similar findings have also been reported by Ceci, Ross, and Toglia (1987), with children as subjects.

Although researchers have shown, then, that source credibility does affect memory suggestibility, no researchers have studied the effect of the interaction of source credibility and time delay on memory suggestibility. In this study, it is posited that, much as in the sleeper effect, in the suggestibility paradigm, a misleading item and its original source will become less strongly associated in memory as time passes. As the association weakens with time delay, the probability that subjects will be misled by information suggested by a low-credibility source will increase and approach the probability of being misled by information suggested by a high-credibility source. The probability that subjects will be misled by information suggested by a high-credibility source is predicted to be similar in the immediate and delayed test conditions.

In this study, the past findings of both the sleeper effect and memory suggestibility studies were incorporated in order to examine the effect of source credibility and time delay on memory suggestibility. Specifically, subjects viewed two slide sequences that each contained two target slides. After the slides were presented, the subjects read a narrative that contained a misleading description of two of the target slides (one for each slide sequence). The source of the narrative was attributed to either a high-credibility source or a low-credibility source. Half of the subjects completed a recognition test 10 min later, and the other half completed a recognition test 1 month later. The major prediction was that the number of falsely recognized misleading items would be greater in the misled condition than in the control condition and that the difference between the rate at which the subjects falsely recognized the misleading items in the misled verses the control condition would be greater in the delayed condition than in the immediate condition for the low-credibility source but would not differ between the delayed condition and the immediate condition for the high-credibility source.

Method

Subjects and Design

The subjects were 111 undergraduate students from colleges in the metropolitan Los Angeles area. All students participated in a classroom setting. The subjects ranged in age from 18 years to 33 years ($M = 19.76$ years, $SD = 2.90$); 61 were female, 47 were male, and 3 did not specify gender. The design was a 2 (source credibility) × 2 (time) × 2 (misled vs. control condition) mixed factorial design, with the first two factors varied between subjects. Each subject received both misled and control items. The subjects participated in groups, each of which was randomly assigned to one of four conditions arrived at by combining the first two variables. The numbers of subjects in these groups were as follows: high-credibility immediate test, $n = 31$; high-credibility delay test, $n = 25$; low-credibility immediate test, $n = 28$; and low-credibility delay test, $n = 27$.

Procedure

The procedure consisted of a presentation phase, in which two slide sequences were presented; a suggestion phase, in which two postevent narratives were read; and a recognition memory test phase. Prior to the presentation phase the subjects were told that they would view a sequence of slides and that afterward they would be asked questions about what they saw. Each group of subjects was presented both slide sequences, counterbalanced across groups for order of presentation. The slides were presented at a rate of 3 sec each. There was a brief break between presenting the two slide sequences that was only long enough for changing slide trays. After viewing both slide sequences, the subjects completed a 10-min distractor task and were then read the two narratives, one after the other, without a break. They were instructed to visualize the slides while reading the narrative, in order to foster cognitive elaboration of the suggested information. A different 10-min distractor task followed the suggestion phase. The subjects in the immediate test condition then completed the recognition memory test. The subjects in the delayed test condition completed the recognition memory task 1 month later. In all conditions, the researcher stressed that the subjects should not talk to each other about the slides, because they would be asked questions about the slides at another time.

Materials

The Presentation Slide Sequence.   Two slide sequences developed by Pezdek and Roe (1995) were used. One sequence of 26 photographs depicted a young woman preparing and baking a cake. She mixed ingredients, used various utensils and containers, and opened various doors, cabinets, and drawers. The other sequence of 26 slides depicted a man walking around a construction site as he prepared to work on a house. He carried and used various tools, toolboxes, and other construction equipment. There were two target slides in each sequence. In the kitchen sequence, the two target slides were (1) a picture of the women opening a drawer and pulling out a *spoon* and (2) a picture of the women opening a cabinet and pulling out a *plate*. In the construction sequence, the two target slides were (1) a picture of the man reaching down and picking up a *hammer* and (2) a picture of the man bending down and picking up a *brick*.

The Postevent Narrative.   In the suggestion phase, a narrative summarizing each of the two sequences was read by the subjects. Each of the two narratives contained a control description of one target slide and a misleading description of the other target slide, (the *spoon* was described as a *fork* or the *plate*, was described as a *cup*, and the *hammer* was described as a *screwdriver* or the *brick* was described as a *rock*). The control description used the, generic word *something* to describe the target item, so the actual target item was never repealed in the narrative. The assignment of each target item to the misled or control condition was counterbalanced across subjects, In the low-credibility source condition, the subjects were told, "The narratives were created by the four-year-old son of the man and woman in the slide sequences. The child watched the slides and then told us what he remembered seeing. The narratives are a paraphrased version of what he had described." In the high-credibility source condition, the subjects were told, "The narratives were created by a memory psychologist who described the slide sequence as he slowly watched it."

The Recognition Memory Test.   A recognition memory test was completed by each subject. The test consisted of 12 questions, randomly arranged and presented in the same order to all of the subjects. Subjects responded *yes* or *no* to each question. Each of the four target slides was referenced by 3 test questions. The 3 questions were worded identically, except for a key word that referred to either (1) the target item ("Did the lady reach into the kitchen drawer and pull out a *spoon*?"), (2) the misleading item ("Did the lady reach into the kitchen drawer and pull out a *fork*?"), or (3) a foil item ("Did the lady reach into the kitchen drawer and pull out a *knife?*"). It was possible for subjects to respond yes to any number of the 3 test questions that referenced each target sequence. The test was presented in writing, and the subjects were instructed not to go back and change any answers, once a response had been marked.

Results

Presented in Table 1 are the mean number of yes responses per subject for the misleading, target, and foil items, as a function of the source credibility, time, and misled/control conditions. The effects for each of the three types of test items were analyzed separately, using a 2 (source credibility) × 2 (time) × 2 (misled/control) mixed factorial analysis of variance (ANOVA). The level of significance for all tests is $p < .05$.

The major predictions involve the subjects' responses to the misleading test items. As predicted, the main effects of time and the misled/control condition were significant in the anticipated directions [$F(1,107) = 34.52$, $MS_e = 15.95$, and $F(1,107) = 39.12$, $MS_e = 13.95$, respectively]. The only other significant effect involving the responses to the misleading test items was the predicted interaction of source × time × misled/control [$F(1,107) = 4.18$, $MS_e = 1.49$]. The interaction is presented in Figure 1. As predicted, in the low-credibility condition, the difference between the rate at which subjects falsely recognized the misled items as old in the misled versus the control condition was greater in the delayed condition than in the immediate condition. In the high-credibility condition, the difference between the rate at which subjects falsely recognized the misled items as old in the misled versus the control condition was relatively high and similar in the immediate and the delayed test conditions. Separate 2 (time) × 2 (misled/control) ANOVAs were conducted on the high- and low-credibility conditions separately. Whereas the time × misled/control condition interaction was significant in the analysis of the low-credibility condition [$F(1,52) = 4.6$, $MS_e = 2.4$], this interaction was not significant in the analysis of the high-credibility condition ($F = 1.03$).

Separate 2 (credibility) × 2 (time) × 2 (misled/control) ANOVAs were also conducted on the responses to target and foil test items. As can be seen in Table 1, the accuracy rate for recognizing target items was relatively high. None of the effects involving the target items was significant, although the source × time × control/misled interaction approached

TABLE 1   *Mean Number of "Yes" Responses Per Subject on Recognition Test (Maximum Mean = 2.00)*

		Misleading Items		Target Items		Foil Items	
Source	*Condition*	*Immediate*	*Delay*	*Immediate*	*Delay*	*Immediate*	*Delay*
Low credibility	control	0.18	0.34	1.39	1.22	0.21	0.37
	misled	0.54	1.33	1.14	1.48	0.21	0.56
High credibility	control	0.19	0.30	1.32	1.20	0.42	0.52
	misled	0.94	1.12	1.19	1.04	0.35	0.56

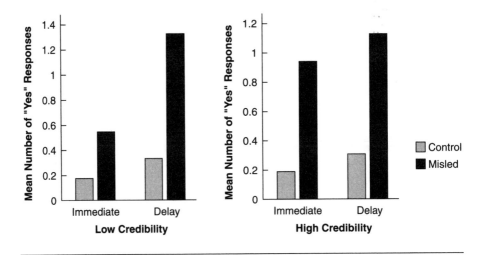

FIGURE 1   *Mean number of yes responses to misleading test items per subject as a function of source credibility, time, and misled/control conditions.*

significance $[F(1,107) = 2.86, MS_e = 1.01, p < .09]$. For the responses to the foil items, only the main effect of time was significant $[F(1,107) = 7.22, MS_e = 2.22]$.

The rate of responding yes was compared for misleading and foil test items in the misled condition only to assess whether the subjects were discriminating between their false alarm rate to these two types of new items. The number of recognized foil items ($M = 0.41$, $SD = 0.56$) was significantly lower than the number of recognized misleading items $[M = 0.97, SD = 0.78, t(110) = 6.12, p < .001]$. This suggests that the recognition of the misleading items specifically resulted from reading the intervening narrative, not from general effects of interference or simple memory decay. Otherwise, the number of recognized foil and misleading items, none of which were actually viewed in the slide sequence, would have been similar.

Discussion

This study tested the hypothesis that misleading information and the source of the misleading information will become less strongly associated as time passes, thus increasing the probability that a subject will be suggestively misled, especially by material from a low-credibility source. This hypothesis was confirmed. Consistent with the availability–valence explanation for the sleeper effect, when tested immediately, the subjects in the high-credibility condition falsely recognized more misleading items than did the subjects in the low-credibility condition. Because of the recency of the encoding, the misleading items were still associated with the source of the misleading information at the time of testing. In the 1 month delay condition, however, the subjects were more likely to be suggestively misled by the misleading narrative, with similar high false alarm rates for misleading items in both the low- and high-credibility source conditions. This result is attributed to the disassociation between item and source information in memory in the delayed condition. This significant interaction between source credibility, time, and misled/control conditions on the rate of responding yes to misled items suggests that, with the passage of time, item and source information become less strongly associated in memory. Thus, the cognitive processes underlying the sleeper effect appear to be similar to those underlying memory suggestibility.

The interpretation of memory suggestibility effects indicated above is related to the **source monitoring** interpretation of Johnson and her colleagues (see, e.g., Johnson, in press). According to this view, in suggestibility experiments, at the time of test, subjects have access to representations of both the original information and the suggested information, but confuse which was presented when. According to Johnson, source memory will be reduced by anything that disrupts the binding of the **semantic** and the **perceptual/contextual features** of to-be-encoded informally at encoding or afterward. Although, in the present study, it is the credibility of the suggestive source that is forgotten over time, nonetheless, the two interpretations are similar in that both attribute suggestibility error to the availability of source information at the time of test.

The impact that the sleeper effect has on memory, especially memory suggestibility, deserves careful consideration. In today's technological world, people are becoming daily consumers of massive amounts of information. Ideally, one would hope that people can discern between information that is highly credible and information that is not credible. This study suggests that, initially, people can correctly discriminate between high- and low-credibility sources of information and are not likely to be misled by information from a low-credibility source. However, as time passes, their ability to resist being misled by information from a low-credibility source diminishes. This decrease in accuracy can have serious implications. In court cases, jurors should initially be able to correctly decide which evidence is credible and which evidence is not credible. In extremely long trials, however, jurors could be persuaded by misleading evidence from a low-credibility witness, especially if a knowledgeable attorney asks them to cognitively elaborate on this evidence during the trial to make it more memorable. Also, a month after initial viewing, less credible news programs, such as tabloid programs, would have the same impact as highly credible news programs, even when presenting deceptive stories. The scientific field is also not genuine. If a scientist reads an article or study that includes misleading or misinterpreted results, the scientist may initially give little credence to the study. After the passage of time, however, the scientist might be discovered repeating the results of the study, without remembering the poor credibility of the source from which the information was obtained.

References

Belli, R. F., Lindsay, D. S., Gales, M. S., & McCarthy, T. T. (1994). Memory impairment and source misattribution in postevent misinformation experiments with short retention intervals. *Memory & Cognition,* **22,** 40–54.

Bottoms, B. L., & Goodman, G. S. (Eds.) (1996). *International perspectives on child-abuse and child testimony.* Newbury Park, CA: Sage.

Ceci, S. J., & Bruck, M. (1993). Suggestibility of the child witness: A historical review and synthesis. *Psychological Bulletin,* **113,** 403–439.

Ceci, S. J., Ross, D. F., & Toglia, M. P. (1987). Suggestibility of children's memory: Psycholegal implications. *Journal of Experimental Psychology: General,* **116,** 38–49.

Dodd, D. H., & Bradshaw, J. M. (1980). Leading questions and memory: Pragmatic constraints. *Journal of Verbal Learning & Verbal Behavior,* **19,** 695–704.

Gillig, P. M., & Greenwald, A. G. (1974). Is it time to lay the sleeper effect to rest? *Journal of Personality & Social Psychology,* **29,** 132–139.

Hannah, D. B., & Sternthal, B. (1984). Detecting and explaining the sleeper effect. *Journal of Consumer Research,* **11,** 632–642.

Hovland, C. I., Lumsdaine, A. A., & Sheffield, F. D. (1949). *Experiments in mass communication.* Princeton, NJ: Princeton University Press.

Hovland, C. I., & Weiss, W. (1952). Source credibility and effective communication. *Public Opinion Quarterly,* **16,** 635–650.

Hyman, I. E., Jr., Husband, T. H., & Billings, F. J. (1995). False memories of childhood experiences. *Applied Cognitive Psychology,* **9,** 181–197.

Johnson, M. K. (in press). Source monitoring and memory distortions. In L. Squire & D. Schacter (Eds.), *Biological and psychological perspectives on memory and memory disorders.* New York: American Psychiatric Press.

Lampinen, J. M., & Smith, V. L. (1995). The incredible (and sometimes incredulous) child witness: Child witnesses' sensitivity to source credibility cues. *Journal of Applied Psychology,* **80,** 621–627.

Lindsay, D. S. (1993). Eyewitness suggestibility. Current Directions in *Psychological Science,* **2,** 86–89.

Loftus, E. F (1993). The reality of repressed memory. *American Psychologist,* **48,** 518–537.

Loftus, E. F., & Palmer, J. C. (1974). Reconstruction of automobile destruction: An example of the interaction between language and memory. *Journal of Verbal Learning & Verbal Behavior,* **13,** 585–589.

Loftus, E. F., & Pickrell, J. E. (1995). The formation of false memories. *Psychiatric Annals,* **25,** 720–725.

Mazursky, D., & Schul, Y. (1987). The effects of advertisement encoding on the failure to discount information: Implications for the sleeper effect. *Journal of Consumer Research,* **15,** 24–35.

Pezdek, K. (1977). Cross-modality semantic integration of sentence and picture memory. *Journal of Experimental Psychology,* **3,** 515–524.

Pezdek, K., Finger, K., & Hodge, D. (1997). Planting false childhood memories: The role of event plausibility. *Psychological Science,* **8,** 437–441.

Pezdek, K., & Greene, J. (1993). Testing eyewitness memory: Developing a measure that is more resistant to suggestibility. *Law & Human Behavior,* **17,** 361–369.

Pezdek, K., & Roe, C. (1994). Memory for childhood events: How suggestible is it? *Consciousness & Cognition,* **3,** 374–387.

Pezdek, K., & Roe, C. (1995). The effect of memory trace strength on suggestibility. *Journal of Experimental Child Psychology,* **60,** 116–128.

Smith, V. L., & Ellsworth, P. C. (1987). The social psychology of eyewitness testimony: Misleading questions and communicator expertise. *Journal of Applied Psychology,* **72,** 294–300.

Introduction: Critical Thinking Questions _____

? Describe the sleeper effect. How does it demonstrate an interaction between the credibility of a source and delay between message encoding and message retrieval?

? Discuss how the availability–valence hypothesis accounts for the sleeper effect.

? Describe the effects of source credibility on the effects of misleading information, as revealed in earlier studies discussed by the authors.

? How do the researchers apply the sleeper demonstrated effect in communication effectiveness to the suggestibility effect demonstrated in memory?

Method: Critical Thinking Questions _____

? Describe what you would have been asked to do, had you been a participant in the experiment

? Name the independent variables in the experiment, and their levels. Describe how each of these variables was operationalized. For each variable, state whether it was manipulated in a between-subjects or within-subjects fashion. How many conditions were there in the experiment?

? What was (were) the dependent variable(s) in the experiment?

? What aspects of the methodology were implemented to deal with possible confounds?

Results/Discussion: Critical Thinking Questions _____

? Describe the pattern of results found for the misleading items. Do these results indicate a sleeper effect? Explain. Describe the pattern of results found for the target and foil items.

? Was the availability-valence account supported? Explain.

? The authors discuss the ramifications of the sleeper effect for the effectiveness of testimony in court cases. Discuss these ramifications, and how poor evidence or a poor witness may nonetheless influence a jury.

? Give an everyday example of the interaction between source credibility and delay. How might you be influenced by a source of information that's less than reliable?

? After reading this study, you may feel there are other issues or questions that would be worthwhile or intriguing to address. Pose one of these questions (other than those suggested by the authors) that could be investigated empirically.

Twins Dispute Memory Ownership

A New False Memory Phenomenon

Mercedes Sheen, Simon Kemp, and David Rubin

*Abstract*_____

In three experiments, we examined a new memory phenomenon: disputed memories, in which people dispute ownership of a memory. For example, in one disputed memory each of the twins recollected being sent home from school for wearing too short a skirt, although only one of them was actually sent home. In Experiment 1, 20 sets of same-sex adult twins were asked to produce a memory for each of 45 words, and most twins spontaneously produced at least one disputed memory. In Experiment 2, 20 different sets of same-sex adult twins rated disputed memories as higher in recollective experience, imagery, and emotional reliving than nondisputed memories. In Experiment 3, siblings who were close in age as well as same-sex friends were also found to have disputed memories, but less often than twins.

Conceptual Issues and Theoretical Questions _____

- How commonly are autobiographical memories disputed by twins?
- Are certain types of memories more likely to be disputed than others?
- Are memories of disputed ownership limited to twins?
- What are the roles of visual imagery and viewer perspective in producing disputed memories?

De-Jargonizing _____

false memory: a memory representation of an event that, in reality, did not occur

monozygotic twins: twins who develop from the same fertilized egg; identical twins

dizygotic twins: twins who develop from two separate fertilized eggs; fraternal twins

Sheen, M., Kemp, S., & Rubin, D. (2002). Twins dispute memory ownership: A new false memory phenomenon. *Memory and Cognition, 29*, 779–788. Reprinted by permission of Psychonomic Society, Inc.

source monitoring: the memory processes involved in identifying the origin of some event

misinformation effect: the phenomenon whereby misleading information presented after some event distorts memory for that original event

unconscious plagiarism: a failure of source monitoring, in which a person unwittingly takes credit for an idea that originated elsewhere

Galton's method of semantic cuing: procedure for investigating autobiographical memory; involves using single word cues (e.g., banana) as cues for a person to relate an autobiographical memory

spaced rehearsal: multiple encodings that are spread out over time

episodic memory: memory for previous events, complete with recall of contextual detail

semantic memory: memory representations of general knowledge; recall lacks contextual detail

deja vu: a phenomenological experience in which a person believes some event has taken place before, when such an occurrence is very unlikely

tip-of-the-tongue phenomenon: a phenomenological experience in which the answer to some general knowledge query seems imminent, but retrieval is blocked

schematic knowlege: generalized knowledge about some place, thing, or event

Our autobiographical memories define who we are and tie us to our personal histories. Imagine, then, what it is like when someone else claims your personal memories as their own. Personal and anecdotal evidence suggest that the ownership of memories is occasionally disputed by twins, and our aim in the present paper was to investigate this phenomenon.

Twins have long been used as participants in psychological research, mainly in the realm of behavior genetics and trait personality (Carver & Scheier, 2000). We focused on using twins as participants as a starting point in the experiment of disputed memories because (1) we have observed disputed memories anecdotally in twins; (2) twins often look similar to each other, allowing for perceptual confusion in imagery within the twins; (3) twins look similar to each other, allowing for perceptual confusions in others who might innocently implant a **false memory;** (4) twins are siblings of the same age and thus share an unusually large proportion of their histories, and hence they have more chance to generate disputed memories; and (5) twins, particularly **monozygotic twins,** tend to assimilate their personalities (Plomin, DeFries, & McClearn, 1990).

Our aim in this early stage of the research was not to ascertain the accuracy of the memories, nor to resolve questions of who owned them. Instead we focused on such questions as the following: Do twins have disputed memories, and if so, how often? Are monozygotic twins more likely to report disputed memories than **dizygotic twins?** What kinds of memories are disputed? Are these disputed memories similar between twins? Do they differ from ordinary, nondisputed memories? Is the possession of disputed memories limited to twins?

The present research can be seen as an example of the increasing interest that researchers have shown in the last 15 years in the fallible nature of autobiographical memory. Much emphasis has been placed on the reconstructive processes involved in recollecting personal memories and on the cognitive processes involved in making autobiographical memory errors (Hyman, 1999). Studies that have focused on memory errors include research on **source monitoring** failures (Johnson, 1988; Johnson & Raye, 1981; Pope, 1996), the creation of false memories (Hyman & Billings, 1998), the **misinformation effect** (Loftus, 1979, 1992; Zaragoza & McCloskey, 1989), loss and distortion of memory content (Bahrick, 1979), and **unconscious plagiarism** (Bink, Marsh, Hicks, & Howard, 1999).

Disputed memories differ from memory errors studied by other researchers in that the major detail that is in dispute is who the protagonist in the event is, a detail that is at the heart of the definition and use of self in autobiographical memory. From the existing literature on autobiographical memory, several factors emerge as being of possible importance for our understanding of this phenomenon. For example, people frequently cite reports of visual imagery to support the authenticity of their autobiographical memories. They argue that because they can "see it as plain as day" or "as if it were happening right now," they must be correctly remembering a past event (Rubin, 1998). In fact, false reports of visual imagery have been almost trivially easy to induce in laboratory settings (Hyman & Pentland, 1996; Roediger, McDermott, & Goff, 1997). Research has also shown that participants report visual imagery when the image is either inferred (Loftus & Hoffman, 1989) or schema-based (Brewer & Pani, 1983; Brewer & Treyens, 1981). Hence, in our second experiment we paid attention to the imagery that was reported as present in the disputed memories.

One aspect of an image is whether the experience is recalled from the individual's own *field* of view or from the standpoint of a third-party *observer*. Nigro and Neisser (1983) demonstrated that the point of view taken during recollection was related to the purpose of recall, the characteristics of the original experience, and the time elapsed between event and recall. They proposed that memories recalled from the observer's perspective must, by their very nature, be reconstructed, because the original event must have been experienced from the field perspective. Their results suggested that older or less emotional memories are recalled from the observer's perspective and that more recent or highly emotional memories are recalled from the field perspective. The participants in our second experiment were asked to report on whether they recalled their memories through their own eyes or through the eyes of an observer.

An important methodological issue concerns how disputed memories should be elicited. Clearly, there would be much less risk of demand characteristics influencing the results if twins produced memories in response to **Galton's method of semantic cuing** (Crovitz & Shiffman, 1974; Galton, 1880; Rubin, 1982) without mention of disputed memories. This method, however, has disadvantages: It is not possible for the cue words to cover every situation that might give rise to a disputed memory. The cue word method does, however, allow for a base-line measure of the frequency and types of memories that are disputed. There is also some advantage in applying a traditional autobiographical memory research tool to a new area of research.

An alternative way of eliciting disputed memories is simply to ask people whether or not they have experienced disputed memories with others and then to collect data on those memories. This method acts as a good catchall for collecting data on disputed memories, but there is, of course, the risk that demand characteristics might encourage participants to report a higher number of disputed memories than they have in fact actually experienced.

The last matter that needed to be considered was whether or not the occurrence of disputed memories is exclusive to twins. Do other sets of the population, such as siblings, also experience this kind of memory error?

In view of these methodological concerns, we conducted three experiments on this memory phenomenon: In the first experiment reported here, we used the cue word method of eliciting autobiographical memories. This experiment was carried out to determine whether disputed memories could be uncovered without participants' being specifically prompted for them. The second experiment involved asking twins directly whether they had experienced disputed memories with their co-twins, and these memories were compared with their shared nondisputed memories (i.e., shared autobiographical memories on whose ownership both agreed) using a questionnaire devised by Rubin, Schrauf, and Greenberg (1999). This questionnaire focuses on different properties and component processes of mental experience that are central to autobiographical memory, such as visual imagery and belief in one's memory, and it asks participants to report on the phenomenal characteristics of their autobiographical memories.

The scales in the questionnaire are intended to measure many properties of autobiographical memory; several were suggested by theories of autobiographical memory. For example, we attempted to assess the importance of belief in one's memory (Ross, Buehler, & Karr, 1998) by having participants respond on a seven-point scale to the question "I believe the event in my memory really occurred in the way I remember it and that I have not imagined or fabricated anything that did not occur." Other scales represent theoretical elements such as rehearsal—particularly **spaced rehearsal,** which Bahrick (1979) suggested greatly improved retention levels—**episodic/semantic memory** (Tulving, 1972), auditory and visual imagery (Reisberg, 1992), reliving of emotions (Christianson, 1996), and significance of the memory (Pillemer, 1998).

In the third experiment, we administered a brief questionnaire to non-twins to see whether they too would report having experienced disputed memories.

Experiment 1

Method

Twenty sets of same-sex twins, (16 female) were recruited through advertisements in the local media and by posters around the university. They had a mean age of 27 years and a median age of 20 (range, 16–56). Eleven sets were monozygotic twins, and 9 sets were dizygotic. Upon initial contact, the twins were told that the experiment was about personal memory in twins and that they would be asked to provide autobiographical memories in response to the presentation of common words. They were then asked to contact their co-twins to arrange a convenient time when both of them could be interviewed together. The interviews took place in one of the twins' homes. After a few moments' introduction, permission to audio record the interview was obtained and recording commenced. The participants were briefly interviewed about their lives as twins and were asked whether they were monozygotic or dizygotic twins. Two sets of twins reported that their zygosity had never been determined, but that they had been raised to believe they were identical twins, and, given their similarity in appearance, they were recorded as monozygotic twins. After this brief informal interview, the participants were again told that the experiment was on autobiographical memory in twins, and they were instructed to come up with a specific autobiographical memory of a late childhood or early adolescent event (from the ages of 8–12) that they had experienced. The twins were asked to take turns providing the first memory for each cue word. The 45 cue words, selected to cue common events, were presented randomly, and whenever the participants provided a general memory in response to presentation of a cue word they were prompted by the interviewer for an event-specific memory. These sessions typically took 1–2 h.

Results

The 20 sets of twins reported 36 disputed memories in total; 14 had disputed memories with their twin and 6 had no disputed memories. The mean number of disputed memories reported was 1.8 (range, 0–14), and the age of the twins at the time at which the event had occurred varied from 5 to 14, with a median age of 8 years. Chi-square analysis performed on both gender and zygosity showed no significant differences in the number of disputed memories that the twins reported. Brief descriptions of the disputed memories reported by fourteen sets of twins are shown in Table 1.

One of the interesting results of Experiment 1 was how many new disputed memories were discovered through the context of the experiment. Of the 36 disputed memories, 21 were discovered as disputed in the context of the experiment, and 15 were known to have been disputed prior to the experiment. Table 2 shows the distribution of new and old disputed memories together with a rating of whether the disputed memory was for a negative, positive, or neutral event.

Disputed memories were reported for 21 of the 45 cue words. The cue word *accident* produced five disputed memories; *birthday* produced four disputed memories; *being in trouble* elicited three disputed memories; *fairground, church, picnic, sport, bicycle,* and *car* elicited two disputed memories; and *swings, barbecue, Christmas, clothing, grandparents, restaurant, fireworks, boat, holiday, pet, first day at school,* and *doctor* each produced one disputed memory.

Experiment 2

Method

Forty people responded to newspaper advertisements for same-sex twins to take part in an experiment on autobiographical memory. (The advertisement did not mention disputed memories, and none of the people from Experiment 1 took part in Experiment 2.) Thirty-one of these respondents were women, and 9 were men. The respondents were given the example of the disputed memory described in the abstract, in which both twins dispute

TABLE 1 *Description of Disputed memories for Cue Word Experiment*

Participant and Zygosity	Age Now	Age at Disputed Memory	Cue Word	Description of Memory
A mz	21	5	Bicycle	Both believe they were pushed off their bike by their cousins
A mz	21	6	Bicycle	Both had a recurring dream of Singapore during war
A mz	21	5	Swing	Both think they swung across a pond on a vine and fell in pond
A mz	21	6	Accident	Both think they got a nail in their foot
A mz	21	11	Barbecue	Both think they were asked to do a display dive at school
A mz	21	5	Accident	Both think the other was chased by a swarm of wasps
A mz	21	8	Christmas	Disagree about who discovered Xmas presents in parents' closet
A mz	21	11	Fair	Both think they came 12th in an international cross country race
A mz	21	7	Church	Argue over who disobeyed superstition and pointed at the moon
A mz	21	12	Clothing	Both think the other wore a terrible outfit and was caught by a boy
A mz	21	6	Grandparents	Argue over who got caned by their grandmother for something the other twin did
A mz	21	14	Restaurant	Who went for lunch with their mum and had a worm in her meal
A mz	21	5	Fireworks	Rabbit lantern catching on fire during Chinese Festival
A mz	21	12	Boat	Argue over who was in boat with their father when they saw a tiger shark
B mz	54	7	Picnic	Disagree about who threw a sandwich away on a picnic
B mz	54	9	Picnic	Disagree about which one of them used to habitually squish pound cake in their hands
E dz	16	8	Trouble	One of them got into severe trouble for something the other did
F dz	20	8	Accident	Argue over who got a nail in their foot
F dz	20	8	Accident	Both say the other ate half the contents of a mustard jar and was sick
F dz	20	5	Birthday	Both think they got their ear glued to their head by a birthday party guest
H dz	17	13	Holiday	Disagree over who befriended a girl while they were on holiday

(continued)

125

TABLE 1   Continued

Participant and Zygosity	Age Now	Age at Disputed Memory	Cue Word	Description of Memory
I mzm	19	12	Sport	Both think it was their name that their rugby coach got wrong during an important match
J mz	17	5	Pet	Both think the other twin used to grab their dog by its testicles
K mz	17	9	Car	Argue over who, on a trip in a car, threw up over everyone
K mz	17	5	1st day at school	Argue over what each other wore during their first day at school
L dz	21	7	Sport	Argue over who played goal attack during a game of kiwi netball
M dz	19	6	Birthday	Disagree about who got a particular present that they both loved
M dz	19	10	Car	Disagree as to who was in the back seat of car during accident
Nmzm	16	9	Fair	Disagree about who went on a roller coaster at a fairground
P mz	54	8	Accident	Disagree about who fell over when a wheel came off rollerskate
P mz	54	10	Birthday	Both think they were the one not invited to a friend's birthday party
P mz	54	7	Birthday	Disagree about whose head got dunked when bobbing for apples
P mz	54	8	Trouble	Both say the other was the one who stole lollies from a shop
R dz	29	9	Trouble	Argue over who got into a fight in the playground at school
S mzm	56	13	Doctor	Both think they fell off a tractor and sprained their wrists
S mzm	56	8	Church	Both think the other got in trouble for throwing things in Church

Note: mz, monozygote; dz, dizygote; m, male.

who was sent home from school for wearing too short a skirt. The respondents were then asked whether they had experienced a disputed memory. Of the original 40, 25 females and 1 male reported that they disputed at least one memory with their twin. A test of proportion showed no significant (at the $p < .05$ level) difference between the 65% of twins who re-

TABLE 2 *Number of New and Old Disputed Memories*

Number of Disputed Memories	No. of twins	Old Dispute	New Dispute	Positive	Neutral	Negative
0	6	—	—	—	—	—
1	7	4	3	2	3	2
2	4	3	5	—	3	5
3	1	2	1	—	1	2
4	1	2	2	—	—	4
14	1	4	10	2	3	9
Totals	20	15	21	4	10	22

sponded positively on this question and the 70% of twins in Experiment 1 who came up with at least one disputed memory during the cue word procedure. Chi-square analysis showed that female twins were significantly more likely to report having had disputed memories than male twins ($\chi^2(1) = 7.95, p < .01$].

Owing to difficulties in availability (it was not always possible to interview both of the twins), only 19 sets of female and 1 set of male twins took part in the subsequent experiment. The participants were asked to contact their twins to discuss the research and in particular to think of as many memories as possible for which they believed ownership was disputed. Ten sets of twins were monozygotic (identical) and 10 dizygotic (fraternal). Their ages at the time of the experiment ranged from 17 to 52 years, with a median age of 24.

Meetings took place at one of the twins' houses or in a meeting room at the university. The first author asked the twins to provide 10 autobiographical memories in total—up to 5 disputed memories, with the remainder memories that were shared but whose ownership was not in dispute. For example, if the twin pair had 2 disputed memories, they were then asked to provide 8 nondisputed memories. For a memory to be included, both twins had to confirm that they had a clear recollection of the event. The twins were then asked to come up with a one-sentence description of each memory, beginning with the disputed memories. The researcher recorded the one-sentence descriptions on the top of a separate questionnaire for each twin.

Once this was complete, each twin was given the 10 autobiographical memory questionnaires and was asked to complete them. They did this individually in isolation. They were asked to consider each memory one at a time and to complete the disputed memory questionnaires first. The whole process typically took an hour, after which the twins were thanked for their time and were asked to contact the researcher if they recalled any further disputed memories.

The autobiographical memory questionnaires were adapted from those devised and used by Rubin et al. (1999). Each questionnaire contained 15 statements about the memory that were to be responded to on a 7-point scale (see the Appendix). In addition, the respondents were asked how old they were at the time of the event, and whether when they recalled the event, they imagined it through their own eyes (*field*) or from the perspective of an *observer.*

For the disputed memories only, the twins were also asked six additional questions: Who was present during the event, what they were doing at the time, how did they come to be there, how old they were when the event took place, and what they were doing immediately before and after the event?

Results

In total, the twins produced 33 disputed memories. Eight sets of twins reported having 1 disputed memory, 11 sets reported 2 disputed memories, and 1 set reported 3 disputed memories. Brief descriptions of disputed memories recalled by each of the pairs of twins are shown in Table 3. A chi-square test $[\chi^2(1) = 0.3, n.s.]$ indicated that zygosity did not affect the number of disputed memories that the twins reported. The age of the twins when the events occurred varied from 5 to 22, with a median age of 10 years. Thus the incidents were recalled mainly from late childhood or adolescence. At one extreme, one set disputed a memory for an event that occurred 6 months previously; another set disputed the memory for an event that had occurred 46 years before.

An attempt to code the disputed memories failed to reveal any consistent themes in the events. The twins generally agreed on most of the details surrounding the event. Forty-five percent (15 out of 33) of the disputed memories were for events that occurred at home, and 51% (17 out of 33) involved people other than the twins.

In total, the twins reported 167 nondisputed memories. The mean age of the twins' disputed memories was 12.5, and the mean age of their nondisputed memories was 11.9. Seventy-four percent of the disputed memories and 64 per cent of the nondisputed memories were recalled from the field perspective, and a test of proportion showed no significant difference between them (at the $p < .05$ level). Of the 33 disputed memories, 16 were recalled by both twins from their own field of view, 10 were recalled by one twin from the field and the other from an observer's point of view, and 7 were recalled by one twin from the field view while the other could not tell.

Table 4 shows the means of the ratings assigned to the disputed and nondisputed memories by the twins. The table shows systematic differences between the types of memory. As we noted earlier, many researchers have defined imagery as a central component of recollection, (Brewer, 1986, 1996; Rubin, 1996, 1998; Tulving, 1983, 1985; Wheeler, Stuss, & Tulving, 1997). In this context, it is important to note that the disputed memories were rated higher on many of the scales intended to assess either recollection (e.g., reliving, and remember vs. know) and some aspect of sensory imagery (e.g., hearing, seeing, setting, and spatial layout). These memories were also rated as having a significantly greater *real* component and as producing more of the *emotion* originally felt. In brief, although the memories must have been partially fabricated for at least half of the sample, the measures of memory quality provide no indication of this.

All but one of the scales measuring recollection, imagery, and emotional reliving were significantly higher for the disputed memories, and none of the other scales were. The differences in recollection and in imagery and emotional reliving cannot have been

TABLE 3 *Disputed Memories for Each Pair of Twins: Experiment 2*

Twin Pair	Age Now	Age at Memory	Sex	Zygosity	Description of Memory
F	17	10	F	Mz	We both think we were the one who was sick and missed a week of school
P	18	9	F	Mz	We argue over who won the spelling prize at school, I say it was me
		18	F	Mz	At Nana's funeral I sat with mum and she sat in the pew behind with dad
C	19	11	F	Mz	I was sleepwalking and walked into the dining room while dad was having breakfast
		19	F	Mz	It was me who got my drivers license on my 19th birthday
A	21	7.5	F	Mz	One of us forgot to give dad a very important phone message
		5.5	F	Mz	We were told not to touch an envelope on the dining table but one of use sealed it and got into trouble from dad
T	22	8	F	Mz	She peeked at our Christmas presents and told me what they were
		10	F	Mz	We were both in the same class but I felt sick and had to leave and threw up in the hallway
D	23	5	F	Mz	We were playing with building blocks and my brother x came over and knocked them over
		8	F	Dz	I (not my sister) ran into a clothesline and cut my head
J	23	12	F	Dz	I got smacked by a very strange girl who thought I was my twin sister
K	23	10	F	Dz	We both think we were the one who had to have a wart removed
E	24	14	F	Dz	I went alone with my mother to pick up x
		22	F	Dz	It was my meal that was awful and had to be sent back to the kitchen
I	24	9	F	Dz	We argue over who won a freestyle swimming race in a competition
		15	F	Dz	We were getting a drink from the fridge and she knocked over a jug of orange juice that went all over the carpet.
L	24	8	F	Dz	I got a hot water bottle with rabbits' ears on it for our birthday, hers didn't have rabbits' ears
		14	F	DZ	I caught a fish when we went on holiday in x, she says she caught it
S	25	10	F	Mz	We were skiing together and I broke my ski and had to walk down
G	26	8	M	Dz	We were playing on our bikes when our neighbour pushed me off my bike
		17	M	Dz	He thinks he made a tie-saving tackle in final but it was me
O	26	12	F	Dz	I had really bad chicken pox when I was young, she had it mildly
Q	28	11	F	Dz	I stayed alone in the tent after she went inside because she was cold

(continued)

TABLE 3   **Continued**

Twin Pair	Age Now	Age at Memory	Sex	Zygosity	Description of Memory
N	32	15	F	Mz	We both say that we danced with x all night at the school dance
H	42	6	F	Mz	She thinks it was her but it was me who got the dolls' house as a gift
		12	F	Mz	I was the only one who played in the school marching band
		12	F	Mz	Mum and dad didn't know, but I (not her) was on the stairs watching a movie
M	42	14	F	Mz	I lost my sister's earring, I remember feeling my ear and it was gone
		7	F	Mz	We were in a dairy and I stole sweets from the shop and the man told our parents
R	46	6	F	Dz	We disagree about who knocked over a huge plant and got in trouble
		6	F	Dz	We always wore different colour clothing and it was me who had the yellow raincoat, she had the blue one
B	52	5.5	F	Mz	She ran away from home, mum and I searched frantically for her

Note: For Age at Memory, when the twins disagreed about their ages, means were used. Twins were tested in the order of the lettering. Mz, monozygote; Dz, dizygote.

due to differences in perceived significance of the event, reported rehearsal, language in the memory, or narrative coherence. Of special note is the observation that the disputed memories were no less believed than the nondisputed memories even though both twins realized that one of them was wrong. These observations are consistent with the reality-monitoring literature in which increased imagery leads to greater belief in a memory (Johnson & Raye, 1981), but they offer little encouragement to those who would use detailed imagery to separate "true" from "false" memories. It could be argued that the higher ratings for disputed memories were merely a reflection of the twins' attempts to convince themselves (or the interviewer) that the memory was indeed theirs. It could further be argued that the methodology was partly to blame for the higher ratings for disputed memories. It seems unlikely, however, that these account solely for the higher ratings and it also does not explain why ratings on certain of the scales, indeed scales central to theories of recollection, showed significant differences while other ratings did not.

The six open-ended questions asking each twin about the 33 disputed memories were analyzed to see whether the twins agreed, disagreed, or appeared to answer each question in different ways (for example, the twins sometimes answered the question "What were you doing immediately prior to the event?" in ways that suggested they had slightly different understandings of what "immediately" might mean in this context). This analysis was performed by two independent raters who achieved 82% agreement on their first coding and then resolved their differences by discussion.

TABLE 4 *Mean Disputed and Nondisputed Memory Ratings*

Scale	Disputed	Nondisputed	t value
Recollection			
Reliving	5.5	4.7	4.31***
Actually remember the event	6.1	5.7	2.62*
I travel back to the time	5.0	4.8	.82
Imagery and Emotion			
Hear in my mind	4.8	4.3	2.12*
See in my mind	6.0	5.3	4.81***
Recall the setting	6.1	5.7	2.52*
I know its spatial layout	5.1	4.6	2.66*
Feeling the emotion now	5.4	4.8	2.41*
Language and Narrative			
Talking in the event	4.5	4.3	.87
The event comes to me in words	4.2	4.1	.54
Coherent story	4.7	4.8	−.26
Significance, Belief, and Rehearsal			
Significant for my life	4.4	4.3	.46
Event really occurred as I remember it	6.2	5.8	1.95
I have thought and talked about it	4.3	4.1	1.46
Talked about it with twin	4.6	4.3	.88

Note: Results of a two-tailed t test ($df = 19$; random factor = sets of twins) are shown. *$p < .05$; **$p < .01$; ***$p < .001$. A similar t test conducted with *individuals* as the random factors found the same 7 (and only 7) significant differences, although for "Actually remember the event," $p < .01$. All variables are measured on a scale from 1 to 7, where 7 denotes more of the quality.

The twins agreed about who else was present in 78% of the disputed memories and disagreed in 13%. (The remaining 9% of the answers indicated a tendency to answer in different ways.) In answer to what they were doing, they agreed in 94% of the memories and disagreed in 3%. They agreed about how they came to be there for 78% and disagreed for 6%. They agreed about their age at the time for 81% of the memories and disagreed for 9% of them. They agreed on what they were doing immediately prior to the event for 53% of the memories and what they did immediately after the event for 56% of them. Disagreements for these two questions were 19% and 22% of the memories, respectively. Thus there was good agreement on most aspects of the memory except who the protagonist was.

Pearson correlations between the different rating scales were calculated separately for disputed and nondisputed memories, an analysis that was performed twice—once using different individuals and once using different memories as the data points. However, neither the correlations themselves nor factor analyses based on them revealed any interesting oddities regarding the disputed memories.

Experiment 3

Method

A questionnaire was distributed to 69 students during class time. The questionnaire began as follows:

> We are carrying out an experiment of disputed memories and are currently gathering data on the issue. A disputed memory is a memory in which two people as on most of the details of what happened but disagree on to whom the event occurred. One such example of this occurred when two girls argued over which of them got sent home from school for wearing too short a skirt. They agreed on most of the details of the incident and agreed that only one of them was sent home but both believe they were the person who was actually sent home. Everyone makes mistakes in their memories, the kind of memory that we are looking for is when you get the memory mostly right except that *the event never happened to you but did happen to someone else.*

The questionnaire then asked the participants whether they had ever experienced this kind of memory. The participants were asked to describe any such instances and to provide details if possible about the incident, including when it occurred, who the dispute was with, and how many other such instances they could think of. They were then asked for demographic information.

Results

Of the 69 participants, 6 reported having experienced a disputed memory. Three disputed the memory with siblings and 3 with same-sex friends. Table 5 shows summary details of the reported disputed memories and provides details of each group of participants. We assumed that all of the participants had friends and thus counted the number of disputed memories between friends and siblings and whether they were the same or different gender. In order to compare these participants with twins, we also sorted them by whether they had a sibling 2 years or less apart.

Because the twins in Experiment 2 were also given a description of a disputed memory, a direct comparison between the results can be made. A test of proportion between the percentage of twins reporting disputed memories in Experiment 2 (65%) and the percentage of respondents with close siblings reporting disputed memories in Experiment 3 (8%) is significant at the $p < .001$ level. Thus, although other people have disputed memories, twins are significantly more likely to experience them.

Discussion

The primary goal of these experiments was to establish the existence of disputed memories in twins. Anecdotal evidence had suggested that these memories existed, and our results

TABLE 5   *Number of Disputed Memories Reported in Experiment 3*

Type of Person With Whom Memory Was Disputed	No. of Participants	No. of Disputed Memories	Percentage of Disputed Memories
	Experiment 2		
Twins same-sex	40 (38 f)	26	65
	Experiment 3		
Sibling < 2 years same sex	22 (15 f)	2	9
Sibling < 2 years different sex	16 (10 f)	1	6
Sibling > 2 years same sex	9 (5 f)	0	0
Sibling > 2 years different sex	14 (8 f)	0	0
Friends same sex	69 (46 f)	3	4
Friends different sex	69 (46 f)	0	0

Note: f, females.

confirm the anecdotes and indicate that disputed memories are a relatively common occurrence among twins. One of the most intriguing aspects of the studies is that despite a major shift in methodology, disputed memories of similar kinds occurred in all three studies. This suggests that disputed memories are a stable and reliable memory error, that they occur frequently among twins, and that they are open to empirical investigation with a variety of methodologies.

The change in methodology did affect the findings on gender differences. As noted earlier, in Experiment 1 we found no significant differences in the number of disputed memories male and females reported. In Experiment 2, however, we did find a significant effect for gender. This difference can in part be explained by looking at the shift in methodology and the qualitative data that emerged from Experiment 1. During the cue word experiment, 75% of the disputed memories the male twins produced were *new* disputes, that is, they were not aware that the memory was in dispute, and both had always assumed that the memory was their own. This may be compared with the 56% of new disputed memories that female twins discovered during the cue word experiment. Given that most of the male twins' disputed memories were discovered only in the context of the cue word experiment, it is hardly surprising that only 1 in 9 males reported disputed memories in Experiment 2 (i.e., when they were asked directly whether they had experienced disputed memories with their twin, they were unaware they had any). The data from Experiment 3 support this further: No males reported having experienced a disputed memory. Possible reasons for these differences lie outside the realm of this paper, but it seems likely that because female twins talk to each other more than male twins do (Koch, 1966), they were thus more likely to discover that some of their shared memories are disputed at a higher rate than males. When, during the cue word experiment, male twins were encouraged to talk about past events together, they reported the same number of disputed memories as did female twins. In a large-scale experiment of twins, Koch showed that, in comparison with female twins, males were more withdrawn, subdued, and socially apprehensive as well as less adequate in speech and possessed of fewer interests. This could explain some of our findings on gender differences and disputed memories.

The types of autobiographical memories that were disputed by the twins do not appear, in content, to be very different from their nondisputed memories. In particular, the disputed memories in Experiment 2 had no more personal significance than did the nondisputed memories. In retrospect, this may not be surprising. It would seem unlikely, for example, that one respondent could incorrectly claim a twin's memory of being hit by a car or getting straight As in school, because independent verification would be relatively easy to find. Indeed, it is likely that twins have already resolved many of the memory disputes that can be resolved, and that those that remain, especially when, as in Experiment 2, they are already known to be disputed, are those that cannot be readily resolved.

One pair of 52-year-old twins disagreed about which of them had made a dramatic attempt at running away from home at the age of 6. Both recalled sitting in the back of the car while the mother frantically searched the streets for the missing twin. There are two surprising aspects to this disputed memory. First, of all the 33 disputed memories reported in Experiment 2, this was the only one in which both twins recalled their *opposite* as being the protagonist in the memory as opposed to themselves. Second, an incident such as this would become part of a family's history, so it seems unusual that a critical detail such as who actually ran away could be confused. Research has shown not surprisingly, that unique or important events from our lives are recalled better than neutral events (Wagenaar, 1986a, 1986b), although, as Linton (1982) noted in her longitudinal experiment of her own autobiographical memory, an event's salience changes over time, making the memory less accessible to recollection.

One of the most intriguing aspects of Experiment 2 was the relatively small number of disputed memories that the twins reported. Upon initial contact, many of the participants recognized the phenomenon immediately and said that they had had many arguments with their twin over disputed memories in the past, but during the actual interviews most twins could only recall one or two disputed memories. Indeed the participants often reported frustration that they could not recall further disputed memories. As one commented, "I can't believe this, I can't remember any more. We have had so many arguments over lots of memories. She is always stealing them from me and I get so mad!" Of further interest is that the disputed memories were discovered only during talking at a later date about the event that the memory concerned, whether between the twins themselves or with a third party. It appears, therefore, that disputed memories are a naturally occurring phenomenon that are discovered rather rarely and by accident, and this conclusion is supported by the number of new disputed memories discovered through the course of the cue word experiment and suggests that twins likely have many more undiscovered disputed memories. The anecdotal evidence from the participants who took part in Experiment 2 supports the view that details of disputed memories are hard to recall, in much the same way that other unusual memory incidences such as **déjà vu** or **tip-of-the-tongue** would be.

The twins who took part were aware that one of them must have had a non-veridical recollection of the event that they remembered, but it would be hard to pick this from the qualities that were ascribed to the memories in Experiment 2. This is particularly evident in the high ratings on the various scales that assessed the imagery present in the memory and the vividness of it, which have been defined as central to autobiographical memory (Brewer, 1986). One might also note that both disputed and nondisputed memories were usually reported from the *field* perspective.

The interpretation of the differences in qualia that we found between the disputed and nondisputed memories in Experiment 2 is a little unclear. Do, for example, disputed memories receive higher imagery ratings because memories that are more easily "seen in one's mind" are more likely to be disputed? Or do the disputes that the twins have had lead to more imagery, possibly as part of an attempt to assert one's ownership, possibly in part as a consequence of being asked about them by the experimenter? In theory, this issue might be resolved by first obtaining the imagery ratings and then later attempting to discover whether the memory is disputed, but the relative small number of disputed memories would make this a difficult undertaking.

In his research on the creation of false memories, Hyman (1999) suggests that three cognitive processes are involved in the process of creating false memories: Event acceptance, imagery/narrative creation, and source-monitoring error. He argues, first, that an event has to be deemed plausible for it to be accepted as a possible memory. Second, an image or narrative has to be formed. People often combine **schematic knowledge** with personal experiences and current demands to construct an image or narrative of the event; and tying the event to self-knowledge, for example, makes false memory construction more likely. Finally, a source-monitoring error must be made: A person may think an event plausible and may even be able to tell a story about the event, but that person may still not think the event an actual memory. Phenomenal characteristics of the constructed memory affect whether a source-monitoring error is made. Clearer images, and greater level of affect and self-involvement, for example, increase the chance that the memory will be regarded as legitimate. In the case of disputed memories in twins, it could be argued that the first two cognitive processes take place automatically, thereby making twins more susceptible to disputed memories. The event surrounding the disputed memory *has* occurred, and therefore event acceptance is automatic. A narrative or image has been created, either by both twins having been present and having seen the event occur or by their having heard or told the story to someone else. It is also possible that the twin with the non-veridical recollection of the event has heard someone else who confused the twins' identities (which is a common occurrence for twins; see Nairn, 1994) tell the story. Studies on behavior genetics show clear evidence that twins tend to assimilate their personalities to a far greater degree than siblings do (Plomin et al., 1990). It is possible that this assimilation of personalities and a shared combination of personal experience and schematic knowledge explain the *higher frequency of disputed memories* in twins than in close siblings. A further possibility is that twins are not only similar to each other but are so used to sharing things that they also share each other's memories. When they do not have their own particular memories, they use their twin's personal memories, unconsciously or otherwise, as a default.

Previous research (e.g., Brewer, 1988; Gruneberg & Sykes, 1993) has generally found a good relationship between accuracy and confidence judgments of autobiographical memories. Laboratory experiments have also shown that belief is reliably related to accuracy (Tulving & Thomson, 1971; Wagenaar, 1986a, 1986b). The twins who took part in this experiment were aware that one of them had a nonveridical memory (Greenwald, 1980; Johnson & Raye, 1981) for the disputed event, yet neither twin was willing to concede that his or hers was the false memory. As in previous research, they were unwilling to "give up" their autobiographical memories, considering them to be true accounts of past experiences even when presented with contrary evidence (Brewer, 1986; Neisser & Harsch, 1993).

References

Bahrick, H. P. (1979). Maintenance of knowledge: Questions about memory we forgot to ask. *Journal of Experimental Psychology: General,* **108,** 296–308.

Bink, M. L, Marsh, R. L., Hicks, J. L. & Howard, J. D. (1999). The credibility of a source influences the rate of unconscious plagiarism. *Memory, 7,* 293–308.

Brewer, W. F. (1986). What is autobiographical memory? In D. C. Rubin (Ed.), *Autobiographical memory* (pp. 25–49). Cambridge: Cambridge University Press.

Brewer, W. F. (1988). Memory for randomly sampled autobiographical events. In U. Neisser & E. Winograd (Eds.), *Remembering reconsidered: Ecological and traditional approaches to the study of memory* (pp. 21–90). Cambridge: Cambridge University Press.

Brewer, W. F. (1996). What is recollective memory? In D. C. Rubin (Ed.), *Remembering our past* (pp. 19–66). Cambridge: Cambridge University Press.

Brewer, W. F., & Pani, J. R. (1983). The structure of human memory. In G. H. Bower (Ed.), *The psychology of learning and motivation: Advances in research and theory* (Vol. 17, pp. 1–38). New York: Academic Puss.

Brewer, W. F., & Treyens, J. C. (1981). Role of schemata in memory for places. *Cognitive Psychology,* **13,** 207–230.

Carver, C. S., & Scheir, M. F. (2000). *Perspectives on personality* (4th ed.). Boston: Allyn & Bacon.

Christianson, S. A. (1996). Emotional events and emotions in autobiographical memory. In D. C. Rubin (Ed.), *Remembering our past* (pp. 218–243). Cambridge: Cambridge University Press.

Crovitz, H. F., & Schiffman, H. (1974). Frequency of episodic memories as a function of their age. *Bulletin of the Psychonomic Society,* **4,** 517–518.

Galton, F. (1880). Statistics of mental imagery. *Mind,* **5,** 301–318.

Greenwald, A. G. (1980). The totalitarian ego: Fabrication and revision of personal history. *American Psychologist,* **35,** 603–618.

Gruneberg, M. M., & Sykes, R. N. (1993). The generalisability of confidence–accuracy studies in eyewitnessing. *Memory,* **1,** 185–189.

Hyman, I. E, Jr. (1999). Creating false memories. In E. Winograd, R. Fivush, & W. Hirst (Eds.), *Ecological approaches to cognition: Essays in honor of Ulric Neisser* (pp. 75–84). Mahwah, NJ: Lawrence Erlbaum.

Hyman, I. E., Jr., & Billings, F. J. (1998). Individual differences and the creation of false childhood memories. *Memory,* **6,** 1–20.

Hyman, I. E. Jr., & Pentland, J. (1996). The role of mental imagery in the creation of false childhood memories. *Journal of Memory & Language,* **35,** 101–117.

Johnson, M. K. (1988). Reality monitoring: An experimental phenomenological approach. *Journal of Experimental Psychology: General,* **117,** 390–394.

Johnson, M. K., & Raye, C. L. (1981). Reality monitoring. *Psychological Review,* **88,** 67–85.

Koch, H. L. (1966). *Twins.* Chicago: University of Chicago Press.

Linton, M. (1982). Transformations of memory in everyday life. In U. Neisser (Ed.), *Memory observed: Remembering in natural contexts* (pp. 77–91). San Francisco: W. H. Freeman.

Loftus, E. E. (1979). The malleability of human memory. *American Scientist, 67,* 312–320.

Loftus, E. F. (1992). When a lie becomes memory's truth: Memory distortion after exposure to misinformation. *Current Directions in Psychological Science,* **1,** 121–123.

Loftus, E. F., & Hoffman, H. G. (1989). Misinformation and memory: The creation of new memories. *Journal of Experimental Psychology: General,* **118,** 100–104.

Nairn, D. K. (1994). *Emotion in twins: An exploratory experiment.* Unpublished Masters thesis. New Zealand: University of Canterbury.

Neisser, U., & Harsh, N. (1993). Phantom flashbulbs: False recollections of hearing the news about Challenger. In E. Winograd & U. Neisser (Eds.), *Affect and accuracy in recall: Studies of "flash-bulb" memories* (pp. 9–31). New York: Cambridge University Press.

Nigro, G., & Neisser, U. (1983). Point of view in personal memories. *Cognitive Psychology,* **15,** 467–482.

Pillemer, D. B. (1998). What is remembered about early childhood events. *Clinical Psychology Review,* **18,** 895–913.

Plomin, R., DeFries, J. C., & McClearn, G. E. (1990). *Behavioral genetics: A primer* (2nd ed). New York: W. H. Freeman.

Pope, K. S. (1996). Memory, abuse, and science: Questioning claims about the false memory syndrome debate. *American Psychologist,* **51,** 957–974.

Reisberg, D. (Ed.) (1992). *Auditory imagery.* Hillsdale, NJ: Erlbaum.

Roediger, H. L., III, McDermott, K. B., & Goff, L. M. (1997). Recovery of true and false memories: Paradoxical effects of repeated testing. In M. A. Conway (Ed.), *Recovered memories and false memories: Debates in psychology* (pp. 118–149). Oxford: Oxford University Press.

Ross, M., Buehler, R., & Karr, J. W. (1998). Assessing the accuracy of conflicting autobiographical memories. *Memory & Cognition,* **26,** 1233–1244.

Rubin, D. C. (1982). On the retention function for autobiographical memory. *Journal of Verbal Learning & Verbal Behavior,* **21,** 21–38.

Rubin, D. C. (Ed.). (1996). *Remembering our past.* Cambridge: Cambridge University Press.

Rubin, D. C. (1998). Beginning of a theory of autobiographical remembering. In C. P. Thompson & D. J. Herrmann (Eds.), *Autobiographical memory: Theoretical and applied perspectives.* Mahwah, NJ: Erlbaum.

Rubin, D. C., Scrauf, R. W., & Greenberg, D. L. (1999). *Remembering, reliving, and believing autobiographical memories: Inter- and intra-individual analyses.* Unpublished manuscript.

Tulving, E. (1972). Episodic and semantic memory. In E. Tulving & W. Donaldson (Eds.), *Organization of memory* (pp. 381–403). New York: Academic Press.

Tulving, E. (1983). *Elements of episodic memory.* New York: Oxford University Press.

Tulving, E. (1985). How many memory systems are there? *American Psychologist,* **40,** 385–398.

Tulving, E., & Thomson, D. M. (1971). Retrieval processes in recognition memory: Effect of associative context. *Journal of Experimental Psychology,* **87,** 116–124.

Wagenaar, W. A. (1986a). My memory: A study of autobiographical memory over six years. *Cognitive Psychology,* **18,** 225–252.

Wagenaar, W. A. (1986b). People and places in my memory: A experiment on cue specificity and retrieval from autobiographical memory. In M. M. Gruneberg & P. E. Morris (Eds.), *Practical aspects of memory: Current research and issues* (pp. 228–233). New York: Wiley.

Wheeler, M. A., Stuss, D. T., & Tulving, E. (1997). Towards a theory of episodic memory: The frontal lobes and autonoetic consciousness. *Psychological Bulletin,* **12,** 331–354.

Zaragoza, M. S., & McCloskey, M. (1989). Misleading postevent information and recall of the original event: Further evidence against the memory impairment hypothesis. *Journal of Experimental Psychology: Learning, Memory & Cognition,* **13,** 36–44.

Appendix

Questionnaire from Experiment 2

1. As I remember the event I feel as though I am *reliving* it [*not at all* to *as clearly as if it were happening right now*].

2. As I remember the event I can *hear* it in my mind [*not at all* to *as clearly as if it were happening right now*].

3. As I remember the event, I can *see* it in my mind [*not at all* to *as clearly as if it were happening right now*].

4. As I remember the event, I or other people are *talking* [*not at all* to *as clearly as if it were happening right now*].

5. As I remember the event, I can feel now the *emotion* I felt then [*not at all* to *as clearly as if it were happening right now*].

6. As I remember the event, I can recall the *setting* where it occurred [*not at all* to *as clearly as if it were happening right now*].

7. Sometimes people know something happened to them without being able to actually remember it. As I think about the event I can actually *remember* it rather than just knowing that it happened [*not at all* to *as much as any memory*].

8. As I remember the event, it comes to me in *words* [*not at all* to *as much as any memory*].

9. As I remember the event, I feel that I *travel* back to the time when it happened, that I am a participant in it again, rather than an outside observer tied to the present [*not at all* to *as much as any memory*].

10. As I remember the event, it comes to me in words or in pictures as a *coherent* story or episode and not as an isolated fact, observation or scene [*not at all* to *as much as any memory*].

11. As I remember the event, I know its spatial *layout* [*not at all* to *as clearly as f it were happening right now*].

12. This memory is *significant* for my life because it imparts an important message for me or represents an anchor, critical juncture or turning point [*not at all* to *as much as any memory*).

13. I believe the event in my memory *really* occurred in the way I remember it and that I have not imagined or fabricated anything that did not occur [*100% imaginary* to *100% real*].

14. Since it happened, I have *thought* or talked about this event [*not at all* to *as often as any event in my life*].

15. Since it happened, I have talked about this event with my *twin* [*not at all* to *as often as any event in my life*].

Introduction: Critical Thinking Questions

? What factors make twins an especially good source of data for an investigation of disputed memories?

? Distinguish a *field view* of a memory from an *observer view* of a memory. Why must observer memories be reconstructed, at least to some extent?

? Contrast the methods that might be used to elicit disputed memories, citing the disadvantages of each. Which do the authors employ in the present study?

Method: Critical Thinking Questions

? Describe the general procedure employed in Experiment 1. Describe what occurred in the twin interview, and how autobiographical memories were elicited.

? How did the memory elicitation in Experiment 2 differ from Experiment 1? Describe what occurred in the twin interview.

? Describe the critical difference in participants and methodology employed in Experiment 3. What would you have been asked to do, had you been a participant in this study?

Results/Discussion: Critical Thinking Questions _____

? How commonly were memories disputed in Experiment 1? What were some of the characteristics of the disputed memories in relation to old/new and positive/negative/neutral?

? Did the disputed memories from Experiment 2 seem to differ from the non-disputed memories? Why might this have been the case? (The discussion section should help in answering this question.)

? Table 4 presents the results of Experiment 2, and summarizes some of the qualitative characteristics of the disputed memories (e.g., imagery, sense of reliving). Based on this data, the researchers contend that "…although the memories must have been partially fabricated for at least half the sample, the measures of memory quality provide no indication of this." Explain what they mean. (The discussion section should help in answering this question.)

? In Experiment 2, did the fact that a memory was disputed by a pair of twins lead to decreased confidence in the memory for one or both twins? Why might this have happened?

? What do the results of Experiment 1 and 2 indicate about how disputed memories are discovered? Explain how the results indicate this.

? What did Experiment 3 reveal about the incidence of disputed memories in siblings?

? There seemed to be an interaction between the methodologies used to elicit disputed memories and gender. Describe the nature of this interaction, and possible reasons for it.

? The authors discuss three processes involved in false memory creation (from Hyman, 1999). Describe each of these processes, and how they may underlie disputed memories in twins.

? After reading this study, you may feel there are other issues or questions that would be worthwhile or intriguing to address. Pose one of these questions (other than those suggested by the authors) that could be investigated empirically.

3

Language Processes

Overhearing a Language During Childhood

Terry Kit-fong Au, Leah M. Knightly, Sun-Ah Jun, and Janet S. Oh

Abstract

Despite its significance for understanding of language acquisition, the role of childhood language experience has been examined only in linguistic deprivation studies focusing on what cannot be learned readily beyond childhood. This study focused instead on long-term effects of what can be learned best during childhood. Our findings revealed that adults learning a language speak with a more nativelike accent if they overheard the language regularly during childhood than if they did not. These findings have important implications for understanding of language-learning mechanisms and heritage-language acquisition.

Conceptual Issues and Theoretical Questions

- What role does input timing (the period during which someone is exposed to particular aspects of a language) play in learning the language?
- Does minimal early experience with a language (i.e., simply overhearing it) serve as preparation for learning the language more easily later, relative to those who do not receive early exposure?
- Does overhearing a language aid perception, production, or both?

De-Jargonizing

phonology: the analysis of the basic sounds that make up spoken language

morphosyntax: the rules that dictate how morphemes (basic units of word meaning) may be combined

voiced and voiceless stop: voicing relates to what the vocal cords do when the airflow disruption of speech stops. If the vocal cords vibrate at this point, the phoneme is termed voiced (e.g., /b/). If the vocal cords vibrate *after* the disruption stops, it's termed voiceless (e.g., /p/).

Au, T. K., Knightly, L. M., Jun, S., & Oh, J. S. (2002). Overhearing a language during childhood. *Psychological Science, 13,* 238–243. Copyright © 2002 by Blackwell Publishing. Reprinted by permission.

phonemic patterns: patterns of speech for basic units of speech

phonetic level: acoustic properties of the speech signal

phonological level: letter and letter-like (e.g., "th" sounds in the speech signal)

phonological rule: the acoustic properties of basic speech sounds (similar to letters) that leads the hearer to classify the sounds into different categories (e.g., a "v" or a "b")

implicit memory: memory for some event that is reflected unconsciously, often as a subtle change in behavior or task performance

The prevailing wisdom is that children cannot learn a language by merely overhearing it (Pinker, 1994; Rice, 1983; Sachs, Bard, & Johnson, 1981; Snow et al., 1976). Yet little is known about what might best reveal the effects of childhood overhearing, namely, later acquisition of an overheard language. Finding such effects would benefit current understanding of language-learning mechanisms (Au & Romo, 1907),

Consider the timing of input. If deprived of early linguistic input, children generally do not fully acquire a language—especially its phonology and morphosyntax—even when input is available later (e.g., Curtiss, 1977; Flege, 1987; Flege, Yeni-Komshian, & Liu, 1999; Johnson & Newport, 1989; Newport, 1990; Oyama, 1976). This implies that language learners can best make use of relevant input during certain maturational states. Despite its significance, input timing has thus far been investigated only in linguistic deprivation studies focusing on what cannot be learned readily beyond childhood. The study of childhood overhearing reported here constitutes a first step in exploring long-term effects of what can be learned readily during childhood. Specifically, it explored whether adults learning a language would have more nativelike mastery of its **phonology** and **morphosyntax** if they overheard the language regularly during childhood than if they did not.

This study also has applied implications. Although there are advantages to being bilingual (e.g., Taylor, Meynard, & Rheault, 1977), raising bilingual children in a predominantly monolingual environment such as the United States is not easy (Taylor, 1987; Wong-Fillmore, 1991). Is there any point for bilingual parents so situated to try? If childhood experience with a language—even if incomplete or discontinued—turns out to help older learners master that language, the answer would be "yes" after all. It would then also make sense for policymakers to allocate more resources to language programs for young children.

Our study focused on phonology and morphosyntax because these aspects of language seem easy for children to acquire and difficult for adults to master. They are therefore good candidates for revealing long-term effects of childhood overhearing.

Phonology

Much can be learned from hearing a language. Hearing the ambient language helps preverbal infants learn about its characteristic intonational and rhythmic patterns (Dehaene-Lambertz &

Houston, 1998; Mehler, Dupoux, Nazzi, & Dehaene-Lambertz, 1996). Although all newborns seem alike in how they categorize speech sounds, they learn to group distinct speech sounds into consonants and vowels that are relevant to their ambient language during their first year of life (Eimas, Siqueland, Jusczyk, & Vigorito, 1971; Jusczyk, 1997; Kuhl & Iverson, 1995; Werker & Tees, 1984). Once acquired, such perceptual categories appear to persist even years after exposure to the language has ended (e.g., because of emigration; Tees & Werker, 1984).

But becoming a native listener is one thing; passing oneself off as a native speaker (even only in accent) is another. This chasm may appear wider than it is, however. Improving perception could improve production because accurate speech perception may help language learners modify their speech to emulate native speakers (Best, 1994; Flege, 1995; Kuhl & Meltzoff, 1982). Indeed, an intensive training regimen designed to help Japanese adults hear /r/ and /l/ in English accurately improved not only their perception, but also their production of these consonants (Bradlow, Pisoni, Akahane-Yamada, & Tohkura, 1997); such improvements were still evident 3 months after training (Bradlow, Akahane-Yamada, Pisoni, & Tohkura, 1999). Thus, overhearing a language during childhood might help adults learn to speak that language with a more nativelike accent, even if they start learning it in earnest well past childhood.

To test this idea, we compared adult learners of Spanish who had overheard Spanish regularly during childhood with those who had no regular exposure to Spanish until around age 14. If childhood overhearing has measurable benefits for an adult learner's Spanish accent, the childhood overhearers should sound better than the typical late second-language (L2) learners. We also compared these two groups with native Spanish speakers to see how nativelike they sounded. We should note one caveat: "Pure" overhearers are difficult to find. The overhearers in our study typically could say some words and commonly used phrases in the overheard language. Fortunately, the typical late L2 learners in this study could also do this because they had been living in a city with a substantial Latino presence (Los Angeles). We nonetheless assessed all participants' childhood speaking experience to get more systematic information.

Method

Participants

Using a detailed language-background questionnaire and follow-up interview, we screened approximately 200 college students enrolled in 2nd-year Spanish language classes. We identified 11 childhood overhearers and many typical late L2 learners. The childhood overhearers reported that they had overheard informal Spanish spoken by native speakers for at least several hours ($M = 9.3$ hr, $SE = 3.7$ hr) each week for at least 3 years between birth and age 6; such overhearing experience became less frequent afterward (e.g., $M = 3.7$ hr/week, $SE = 1.2$ hr/week between ages 6 and 12). They had spoken and had been spoken to in Spanish minimally (e.g., occasional Spanish words or short phrases embedded in English utterances) until they started taking Spanish classes around age 14.

The typical late L2 learners had minimal exposure (i.e., spending less than an hour each week around someone who uttered at most isolated Spanish words or short phrases) or had no regular exposure to Spanish until they started taking Spanish classes around age 14. Twelve typical late L2 learners were randomly selected within the constraints that they match our overhearer sample roughly in both gender composition and the Spanish instructors to which they were assigned. All of the overhearers and typical late L2 learners were enrolled in a 2nd-year Spanish class at the University of California, Los Angeles; none had been regularly exposed to any language other than English and Spanish. The two groups did not differ reliably in the mean number of years of Spanish classes in either high school (3.8 and 4.5 years, respectively) or college (0.66 and 0.75 year). Ten native speakers of Spanish were also recruited from the same university to serve as another comparison group.[1] The mean age and gender composition were 21.7 years and 70% women for the native speakers, 19.7 years and 82% women for the overhearers, and 18.9 years and 67% women for the typical late L2 learners. Written informed consent was obtained from all participants.

Self-reports of childhood Spanish experience corresponded well with reports from independent informants.[2] For additional corroboration, we assessed the participants' knowledge of childhood slang in Spanish. Because childhood slang is typically used by native speakers around children, the ability to produce and understand childhood slang could be a good indicator of childhood experience with a language. For slang production, participants read 20 expressions in English (e.g., *cry baby, pacifier, dry crust in the eyes*) and were asked to "say aloud what these words mean in Spanish slang or informal Spanish as you would hear them at home, in the neighborhood, or in a school yard." For slang comprehension, participants heard 40 childhood slang terms in Spanish (e.g., *chiqueado,* "spoiled child"; *las escondidas,* "hide-and-seek") read by a native Spanish speaker and were asked to say in English what the words meant. The test was self-paced, and the responses were audiotaped and later transcribed and compared against a list of acceptable responses compiled by a team of native Spanish speakers who spoke a variety of dialects commonly found in southern California. As expected, the native speakers produced and understood childhood slang in Spanish extremely well. The overhearers did significantly worse than the native speakers but still reliably better than the typical late L2 learners (Table 1). Together with the self-reports, these findings suggest that the overhearers' childhood experience with Spanish, in terms of speaking and understanding, was rather limited.

Stimuli

Participants were asked to read aloud 36 Spanish sentences presented on a computer screen. Each sentence contained a target word in the frame, *Diga* _____ *por favor*

[1]Using language-background data, two coders independently categorized each of the 33 participants as native, overhearer, typical late L2 learner, or not classifiable. They agreed on 94% of the cases ($\kappa = .93$), resolving any disagreements through discussion. Two native Spanish speakers in our lab listened to speech samples of the 10 self-identified native speakers and confirmed the self-reported native-speaking competence.

[2]We asked each participant to help us contact someone who would know about his or her childhood experience with Spanish. Independent informant reports were obtained for 4 of the 11 overhearers, confirming that they heard Spanish spoken by native speakers regularly during childhood and spoke Spanish minimally (i.e., no more than isolated words or short phrases occasionally). Informant reports were obtained for 3 of the 12 typical late L2 learners, confirming that they had no regular exposure to Spanish during childhood.

("Say _____ please"). The target words contained **voiceless stops** /p, t, k/ and **voiced stops** /b, d, g/ in either word-initial (e.g *tacos, beso*) or word-medial (e.g., *notar, jabón;* see Table 2) position.

Procedure

Each sentence was presented on a computer screen for 3 s. Participants were instructed to say each sentence naturally, as if they were speaking to someone in Spanish. They were also asked to stress the second word in the sentence (i.e., the target word) and not to pause between words. The 36 sentences were presented three times and in random order. The utterances were audiotaped using a head-mounted microphone and a Marantz PMD-222 or PMD-430 professional recorder. Participants were tested individually in a small room lined with acoustical foam.

Phonology Assessment

We use the term "phonology" in a broad sense meaning "sound" contra to grammar. We examined accent at both the phonetic level (using acoustical measurements, namely, *voice onset time,* VOT) and the phonological level (namely, phonemic patterns and a **phonological rule**).

At the **phonetic level,** we focused on VOT for voiceless stop consonants (/p, t, k/) because it is a widely used and informative phonetic measure for assessing phonology in people's first language and in L2 acquisition (e.g., Eimas et al., 1971; Williams, 1979). Simply put, VOT refers to the time from the release of a stop consonant (e.g., when the lips open in saying /p/) to the onset of voicing (vocal cord vibration) of the following vowel. The VOT for /p, t, k/ is typically 30 to 50 ms longer in English than in Spanish (e.g., Lisker & Abramson, 1964). If overhearing Spanish during childhood helps an adult learner's Spanish accent, overhearers should produce /p, t, k/ with a more nativelike, and hence shorter, VOT than typical late L2 learners.

At the **phonological level,** our assessment capitalized on a robust difference between Spanish and English phonology. When a Spanish voiced stop (/b, d, g/) appears between two vowels, it becomes lenited. That is, the air flow is only partially blocked rather than completely cut off. To the untrained ear of a native English speaker, a lenited Spanish /b/ sounds somewhat like a "v," and a lenited Spanish /d/ sounds somewhat like the "th" in the English word *this*. These phonological rules apply to /b, d, g/ appearing in intervocalic contexts both within a word (e.g., the /b/ *in sabor*) and across words (e.g., the /b/ in *Diga beso…*). These rules do not exist in English. If childhood overhearing helps adult learners master these rules, overhearers should produce Spanish /b, d, g/ as lenited consonants in intervocalic contexts more often than typical late L2 learners.

The "Diga…por favor" utterances were digitized (at a sampling rate of 12.5 kHz), and the spectrograms were analyzed by trained researchers who were not aware of the speakers' prior experience with Spanish. VOT was measured for all target voiceless stops. The target voiced stops were each categorized as either a stop or a lenited consonant (distinguished by an abrupt or a gradual change, respectively, in amplitude between the consonant and following vowel). To assess measurement and coding reliability, two researchers independently analyzed approximately 12% of the data. The differences between measurers on mean VOT were minimal, ranging from 2.5 to 3.7 ms for individual participants. The percentages of agreement between coders on categorizing voiced stops ranged from 92% to 97% for individual participants (κs: .70–.92).

To see if any benefits of childhood overhearing can be detected by the average native speaker, we asked 28 native speakers to give accent ratings on the target consonants (e.g., the /p/ in *pase*) in the 36 "Diga…por favor" sentences produced by 29 of the 33 participants in the main study (7 native speakers, 10 overhearers, and 12 typical late L2 learners).[3] Each native speaker rated one token from a third of each participant's 36 sentences on a 5-point scale (1 = *very strong foreign accent, definitely nonnative;* 2 = *strong foreign accent;* 3 = *noticeable foreign accent;* 4 = *slight foreign accent;* 5 = *no foreign accent, definitely native*), in 12 blocks of sentences with each block containing the same sentence (e.g., *Diga pase por favor*) produced by all 29 participants. Each rater heard a representative subset of the 36 stimulus words, containing one exemplar of each phoneme-and-position combination (e.g., /b/ in word-initial position). The sentences were digitized at 12.5 kHz and presented over headphones in random order within each block. The interrater reliability was very high (average accent scores for individual participants: intraclass $R = .98$).

Results

If overhearing Spanish during childhood helps the accents of adults learning Spanish, overhearers should produce voiceless stops (/p, t, k/) with more nativelike, and hence shorter, VOTs than typical late L2 learners. As shown in Table 1, the overhearers were virtually native-like by this measure for the word-initial position; their VOT was reliably shorter than the typical late L2 learners', $F(2, 30) = 8.4$, $p < .001$. A similar, although not statistically reliable, pattern was seen in the word-medial position, $F(2, 30) = 2.3$, $p > .1$. The typical late L2 learners' VOT pattern—longer VOT in word-initial than word-medial position—mirrors the initial-strengthening phenomenon in English (Fougeron & Keating, 1997). Their pattern differed reliably from the native speakers' and the childhood overhearers' (Table 1), $F(1, 20) = 6.6$, $p < .05$, and $F(1, 21) = 6.2$, $p < .05$, respectively, for the Position X Group interaction; the latter two groups were virtually identical, $F(1, 19) = 0.12$. These findings suggest that although typical late L2 learners cue the boundary of a **prosodic word** in Spanish by lengthening VOT, as they do in English, overhearers cue the word boundary as native Spanish speakers do.

If childhood overhearing helps adult learners master phonological rules in the target language, overhearers should produce Spanish /b, d, g/ as lenited consonants in both within-word and across-word intervocalic contexts reliably more often than typical late L2 learners. This was exactly what we found (Table 1), $Fs(2, 30) > 10$, $ps < .001$, for both intervocalic contexts.

Finally, the overhearers' accents were judged by the native-speaker raters to be reliably more nativelike than the typical late L2 learners' (Table 1), $Fs(2, 26) > 27$, $ps < .001$.

These findings suggest that lasting benefits of overhearing a language during childhood are measurable by phonetic analyses and are psychologically real to the average na-

---

[3]The raters were self-identified and verified native speakers of Spanish recruited at the University of California, Los Angeles (see footnote 1 for the verification procedure). To date, we have accent ratings on only 29 participants.

TABLE 1   *Participants' performance on tests of Spanish abilities*

Measure	Native speakers	Childhood overhearers	Typical late L2 learners
Childhood slang			
Production	79_a (10)	17_b (3)	3_c (2)
Comprehension	88_a (4)	22_b (4)	3_c (10)
Voice onset time (ms)			
Word-initial voiceless stops	19.3_a (1.1)	19.6_a (2.5)	36.2_b (4.8)
Word-medial voiceless stops	22.4_a (1.2)	23.4_a (4.0)	31.2_a (3.4)
Percentage lenited			
Word-initial voiced stops	43_a (9)	24_a (8)	1_b (1)
Word-medial voiced stops	72_a (3)	63_a (8)	23_b (5)
Accent rating			
Voiceless stops	4.3_a (0.06)	3.5_b (0.12)	2.2_c (0.15)
Voiced stops	4.4_a (0.08)	3.3_b (0.15)	2.7_c (0.12)
Morphology production			
Gender agreement	93_a (4)	70_b (5)	68_b (6)
Number agreement	92_a (5)	88_a (4)	85_a (5)
Grammaticality judgement			
Accuracy	94_a (1)	64_b (2)	63_b (3)
Reaction time (ms)	$1,042_a$ (190)	$2,475_b$ (374)	$2,209_{a,b}$ (304)

Note: For the measures of childhood slang, morphology production, and accuracy of grammaticality judgement, the table indicates the mean percentage correct. Accent ratings were on a 5-point scale, with higher ratings indicating more nativelike pronunciation. Standard errors are given in parentheses. Within a row, means with the different subscripts were not reliably different from each other according to Tukey's HSD test, two-tailed, $p < .05$. Number with the same subscript were not reliably different from each other.

tive speaker of that language.[4] Such benefits seem to come with no costs to the overhearers' dominant-language phonology: VOT measurements of the overhearers' word-initial English /b/ and /p/ suggested nativelike pronunciation[5]

[4]We did not assess speech sound perception because of the results of a pilot study of categorical perception of Spanish /t/ and /d/ using stimuli created at Haskins Laboratories. Surprisingly, even native speakers (who had been bilingual in Spanish and English since early childhood, like the native speakers in the main study) used the "English" VOT boundary. Although a more Spanish-like boundary was obtained from several monolingual Spanish speakers, we ended this line of pursuit because of the floor effects obtained with the bilingual native Spanish speakers.

[5]We collected production data on English word-initial /b/ and /p/ from 5 native speakers, 6 overhearers, and 7 typical late L2 learners who had participated in the Spanish phonology assessment. They were asked to say, "Take a _____ once again," with *beggar, bonnet, pepper,* and *pocket* as target words. Their mean VOTs were, respectively, 11 ms, 11 ms, and 10 ms for /b/, and 56.8 ms, 49.1 ms, and 51.3 ms for /p/ (SEs: 4.0–6.5 ms). These results are comparable to published results from monolingual native English speakers (e.g., Eimas et al., 1971; Lisker & Abramson, 1964). Analyses of variance revealed no reliable group differences for either the voiced or the voiceless stops, $Fs(2, 15) < 1$, suggesting all three groups were equally nativelike. Interestingly, their mean VOTs for initial /p/ in Spanish were 13.4 ms ($SE = 1.3$), 9.3 ms ($SE = 1.4$), and 31.1 ms ($SE = 10.9$), respectively. So, both the native speakers and the overhearers shortened their VOT by about 40 ms going from English to Spanish, resulting in a mean VOT comfortably within the range of published estimates for native Spanish speakers (4–16 ms; e.g., Lisker & Abramson, 1964; Williams, 1979). By contrast, the typical late L2 learners shortened their VOT by only about half as much, resulting in a mean VOT well outside the range produced by native speakers.

TABLE 2 *Stimulus words for phonology production*

Word-initial set: *base, beca, beso, datos, deja, día, gallo, gato, goma, pase, pena, peso, tacos, teja, tía, callo, caso, coma*

Word-medial set: *cabeza, jabón, sabor, nadar, pedido, rodar, hogar, pagó, pegó, zapeta, vapor, tapón, matar, metido, notar, tocar, sacó, pecó*

An important question remains: Does the amount of childhood overhearing matter? The language-background data on the 11 overhearers allowed us to estimate the amount of overhearing per week ($M = 9.3$ hr, $SE = 3.7$ hr) and the duration of overhearing at least 3 or 4 hr per week ($M = 3.5$ years, $SE = 0.9$ year) between birth and age 6. As it turned out, these estimates were not reliably related to our phonological measures summarized in Table 1 (rs ranging from $-.29$ to $.25$, ps $> .38$, two-tailed; 9 of the 12 rs went against the predicted direction). However, given the relatively small sample size and crude estimates, it remains an open question whether the amount of childhood overhearing—above and beyond a few hours a week for a few years—actually matters.

Morphosyntax

Can childhood overhearers "soak up" the small grammatical markers (e.g., the ubiquitous *-os* and *-as* endings of nouns, adjectives, and determiners in Spanish signaling masculine and feminine plural, respectively) the way they acquire a good accent?

Method

Participants

The same participants from the phonology assessment participated in the morphosyntactic assessment.

Stimuli and Procedure

To assess morphosyntax production, we elicited Spanish noun phrases to examine number and gender agreement among determiners, adjectives, and nouns (e.g., the plural marker *s* and masculine marker *o* in *los pianos blancos,* "the white pianos"). Participants were asked to complete five simple four-piece jigsaw puzzles verbally. Each puzzle was presented on a computer screen for 18 s, with a puzzle frame (showing numbered spaces for the pieces) appearing above the four puzzle pieces. There was a picture of one or two colored objects on each puzzle piece. To complete a puzzle, participants had to say aloud, for instance, "Pon los pianos blancos en cuatro, pon la vacs negra en tres,..." ("Put the white pianos in four, put the black cow in three,..."). The noun phrases needed to specify the puzzle pieces varied in number (singular vs. plural) and gender (feminine vs. masculine) marking.

The puzzles were designed to elicit four combinations of number and gender markers. For example, one puzzle included pieces depicting a black piano (*el piano negro*: singular masculine), a black cow (*la vacs negra*: singular feminine), two white pianos (*los pianos blancos*: plural masculine), and two white cows (*las vacas blancas*: plural feminine). Participants' responses were audiotaped and independently transcribed by two native Spanish speakers; a third native speaker resolved any discrepancies. Then two native speakers coded the determiner-noun agreement and noun-adjective agreement independently, with any discrepancies resolved by a third native speaker. (Disagreement between any pair of transcribers or coders occurred in less than 5% of the words or codes.) Our prediction was that if childhood overhearing helps adult learners speak with correct basic morphosyntax, such as number and gender agreement in noun phrases, the overhearers would do better than the typical late L2 learners.

We also assessed these participants' ability to detect morphosyntactic errors in other people's speech. They listened to 33 grammatical sentences and 33 similar but ungrammatical sentences. Each ungrammatical sentence contained an error in marking in one of these categories: number or gender agreement in noun phrases (e.g., *la flores, *el carro blanca*), number or person agreement in verbs (e.g., *Marta corren, *nosotros comienzan*), tense-aspect marking in verbs (e.g., *Dentro de cuatro años, soy un abogado*), negation (e.g., *El conoce a nadie*), or indirect object (e.g., *El enseña a nosotros*). The 66 sentences were each presented twice over headphones in a random order. The test was self-paced, and participants indicated their responses ("grammatical" or "ungrammatical") by pressing a button on a button box. (The stimuli are available upon request.)

Results

On both morphosyntax tasks, the overhearers and the typical late L2 learners performed virtually equally (Table 1). In the case of morphosyntax production, both groups performed worse than the native speakers in marking gender agreement, $F(2, 25) = 5.7$, $p < .01$, but they were quite nativelike in marking number agreement, $F(2, 25) < 1$. The overhearers and the typical late *L2* learners were comparable in both the accuracy and the reaction times of their grammaticality judgments. The native speakers judged with almost perfect accuracy, and they were reliably more accurate than the other two groups, $F(2, 27) = 33.3$, $p < .001$. The native speakers were also faster than the overhearers ($p < .05$) and marginally faster than the typical late L2 learners ($p = .063$), $F(2, 27) = 4.4$, $p < .05$. These findings converge to reveal no measurable benefits of childhood overhearing in morphosyntax, in sharp contrast to the sizable benefits in phonology.

Discussion

This study complements linguistic deprivation studies in highlighting the importance of childhood language experience. Although waiting until adulthood to learn a language almost guarantees a bad accent, having overheard the target language during childhood seems to lessen this predicament substantially. This study also speaks to other fundamental questions about language development. One such question is, how might the nature of childhood experience affect language acquisition? Our findings on childhood overhearing suggest that even incomplete language experience during childhood can have lasting benefits. These findings add to the body of evidence on how perception might affect production in phonological development: Deaf infants' babbling typically starts late and never becomes sophisticated (e.g., Oller & Eilers, 1988), experimental intervention aimed at improving speech perception also improves production (Bradlow et al., 1997, 1999), and overheating a language regularly during childhood helps adult learners speak that language with a better accent.

What underlying mechanisms might mediate the relation between childhood overhearing and adult learners' accents? Recall that the childhood overhearers in our study also spoke a little—mostly isolated words and short phrases—as children. Could their limited speaking experience have joined force with regular overhearing experience to tune their perceptual-motor system during childhood, thereby "inoculating" them against having a heavy foreign accent when learning the language in high school or college? Growing up in a heritage-language context might also contribute to childhood overhearers' ethnic identity, which could in turn contribute to the lasting benefits of childhood overhearing documented in this study. It is therefore important to sort out how early minimal speaking experience and cultural identity might mediate the relation between childhood language experience and later language development.

Our study explored a new approach to investigating how the timing and nature of input might affect language acquisition. The variety of naturally occurring incomplete and discontinued childhood language experience offers a valuable window onto language-learning mechanisms. For instance, by studying adult learners who spoke their heritage language during early childhood before becoming virtually monolingual in the majority language, researchers could learn whether, and how, early experience with a language establishes a learner's mental representation of the language in some fundamental and long-lasting way (Chocks, 1981), and how much **implicit** childhood **memory** for the structure of a language can be recovered through language reacquisition. By studying adults who regularly heard their heritage language during childhood but spoke only the majority language, researchers could learn how much of a language can be acquired with little or no corrective feedback. Our study on childhood overhearing is just a first step into this virtually uncharted territory in the study of language acquisition.

References

Au, T. K., & Romo, L. F. (1997). Does childhood language experience help adult learners? In H. C. Chen (Ed.), *The cognitive processing of Chinese and related Asian languages* (pp. 417–441). Hong Kong: Chinese University Press.

Best, C. T. (1994). The emergence of native-language phonological influences in infants: A perceptual assimilation model. In J. C. Goodman & H. C. Nusbaum (Eds.), *The development of speech perception: The transition front speech sounds to spoken words* (pp. 167–224). Cambridge, MA: MIT Press.

Bradlow. A. R., Akahane-Yamada, R., Pisoni, D. B., & Tohkura, Y. (1999). Training Japanese listeners to identify English /r/ and /l/: Long-term retention of learning in perception and production. *Perception & Psychophysics, 61,* 977–985.

Bradlow, A. R., Pisoni, D. B., Akahane-Yamada, R., & Tohkura, Y. (1997). Training Japanese listeners to identify English /r/ and /l/: Some effects of perceptual teaming on speech production. *Journal of the Acoustical Society of America, 101,* 2299–2310.

Chomsky, N. (1981). *Lectures on government and binding.* Dordrecht, Netherlands: Foris.

Curtiss, S. (1977). *Genie: A psycholinguistic study of a modern-day "wild child."* New York: Academic Press.

Dehaene-Lambertz, G., & Houston, D. (1998). Faster orientation latencies toward native language in two-month-old infants. *Language and Speech, 41,* 21–43.

Eimas, P. D., Siqueland, E. R., Jusczyk, P., & Vigorito, J. (1971). Speech perception in infants. *Science, 171,* 303–306.

Flege, J. E. (1987). A critical period for learning to pronounce foreign languages? *Applied Linguistics, 8,* 162–177.

Flege, J. E. (1995). Second language speech learning: Theory, findings, and problems. In W. Strange (Ed.), *Speech perception and linguistic experience: Issues in cross-language research* (pp. 233–272). Baltimore: York Press.

Flege, J. E., Yeni-Komashian, G. H., & Liu. S. (1999). Age constraints on second-language acquisition. *Journal of Memory and Language, 41,* 78–104.

Fougeron, C., & Keating, P. A. (1997). Articulatory strengthening at edges of prosodic domains. *Journal of the Acoustical Society of America, 101,* 3728–3740.

Johnson, J. S., & Newport, E. L. (1989). Critical period effects in second language learning: The influence of maturational state on the acquisition of English as a second language. *Cognitive Psychology, 21,* 60–99.

Jusczyk, P. W. (1997). *The discovery of spoken language.* Cambridge, MA: MIT Press.

Kuhl, P. K., & Iverson, P. (1995). Linguistic experience and the "perceptual magnet effect." In W. Strange (Ed.), *Speech perception and linguistic experience: Issues in cross-language research* (pp. 121–154). Baltimore: York Press.

Kuhl, P. K., & Meltzoff, A. N. (1982). The bimodal perception of speech in infancy. *Science, 218,* 1138–1141.

Lisker, L., & Abramson, A. (1964). A cross-language study of voicing in initial stops: Acoustical measurements. *Word, 20,* 384–422.

Mehler, J., Dupoux, E., Nazzi, T., & Dehaene-Lambertz, G. (1996). Coping with linguistic diversity: The infant's viewpoint. In J. L. Morgan & K. Demuth (Eds.), *Signal to syntax: Bootstrapping form speech to grammar in early acquisition* (pp. 101–116). Mahwah, NJ: Erlbaum.

Newport, E. L. (1990). Maturational constraints on language learning. *Cognitive Science, 14,* 11–28.

Oller, D. K., & Eilers, R. E. (1988). The role of audition in infant babbling. *Child Development, 59,* 441–449.

Oyama, S. (1976). A sensitive period for the acquisition of a nonnative phonological system. *Journal of Psycholinguistic Research, 5,* 261–283.

Pinker, S. (1994). *The language instinct.* New York: Morrow.

Rice, M. (1983). The role of television in language acquisition. *Developmental Review, 3,* 211–224.

Sachs, J., Bard, B., & Johnson, M. L. (1981). Language learning with restricted input: Case studies of two hearing children of deaf parents. *Applied Psycholinguistics, 2,* 33–54.

Snow, C. E., Arlman-Rupp, A., Hassing. Y., Jobse, J., Joosten, J., & Vorster, J. (1976). Mothers' speech in three social classes. *Journal of Psycholinguistic Research, 5,* 1–20.

Taylor, D. M. (1987). Social psychological barriers to effective childhood bilingualism. In P. Homel, M. Palij, & D. Aaronson (Eds.), *Childhood bilingualism: Aspects of linguistic, cognitive, and social development* (pp. 183–195). Hillsdale, NJ: Erlbaum.

Taylor, D. M., Meynard, R., & Rheault, E. (1977). Threat to ethnic identity and second language learning. In H. Giles (Ed.), *Language, ethnicity and intergroup relations* (pp. 99–116). New York: Academic Press.

Tees, R. C., & Werker, J. F. (1984). Perceptual flexibility: Maintenance or recovery of the ability to discriminate non-native speech sounds. *Canadian Journal of Psychology, 38,* 579–590.

Werker, J. F., & Tees, R. C. (1984). Cross-language speech perception: Evidence for perceptual reorganization during the fast year of life. *Infant Behavior and Development, 7,* 49–63.

Williams, L. (1979). The modification of speech perception and production in second-language learning. *Perception & Psychophysics, 26,* 95–104.

Wong-Fillmore, L. (1991). When learning a second language means losing the first. *Early Childhood Research Quarterly, 6,* 323–346.

Introduction: Critical Thinking Questions _____

? If it turns out that there are benefits from early exposure to a language for later language learning, how might this knowledge help parents who want to raise a bilingual child?

? What perceptual abilities can be acquired from hearing a language? What empirical evidence exists to expect these abilities to transfer to language production?

? Outline the conditions tested in the experiment, and the major predictions that follow from the idea that overhearing a language aids in its later learning.

Method: Critical Thinking Questions _____

? What were the criteria for selecting participants for the "overhearers" condition, the late L2 learners condition, and the control condition?

? In the phonology study, what was the purpose of assessing participants' ability to understand childhood slang in Spanish? What were the researchers attempting to assess? What did the assessment show?

? In the phonology study, describe the measures used to assess the phonetic and phonological abilities of the participants. What were the predictions for "overhearers" and late L2 learners for the phonetic and phonological assessments?

? In the morphosyntax study, the researchers assessed "morphosyntactic" competence in two different ways. (a) Describe the puzzle assembly task and how it assessed this competence. What were the independent variables manipulated within this task? (b) Describe how the error detection task assessed morphosyntactic competence.

Results/Discussion: Critical Thinking Questions _____

? Describe the results of the phonology study. What did each measure show with regard to the phonological proficiency of (a) native speakers, (b) childhood overhearers, and (c) late language learners. Was the predicted pattern obtained?

? What were the results of the morphosyntax study? Was the predicted pattern obtained?

? What mechanism do the researchers propose to explain the relation between childhood overhearing and adult learners' accents? Why do the childhood learners' accents seem "less foreign" than later language learners?

? Explain how incomplete childhood language experience could be a valuable window into the basic processes of language acquisition. Do the same for discontinued childhood language experience.

? After reading this study, you may feel there are other issues or questions that would be worthwhile or intriguing to address. Pose one of these questions (other than those suggested by the authors) that could be investigated empirically.

Listeners' Uses of um *and* uh *in Speech Comprehension*

Jean E. Fox Tree

Abstract

Despite their frequency in conversational talk, little is known abort how ums *and* uhs *affect listeners' on-line processing of spontaneous speech. Two studies of* ums *and* uhs *in English and Dutch reveal that hearing an* uh *has a beneficial effect on listeners' ability to recognize words in upcoming speech, but that hearing an* um *has neither a beneficial nor a detrimental effect. The results suggest that* um *and* uh *are different from one another and support the hypothesis that* uh *is a signal of short upcoming delay and* um *is a signal of a long upcoming delay.*

Conceptual Issues and Theoretical Questions

- Dysfluencies in speaking (e.g., saying "um" or "uh"), although prevalent in everyday conversation, are generally portrayed quite negatively. But might they serve a purpose?
- Do pauses in conversational speech serve some sort of signaling function?
- Do the pause indicators *um* and *uh* differ in their function?

De-Jargonizing

syntactic structure: how the words in a sentence are arranged grammatically

discourse structure: the sensible arrangement of words and sentences in a passage of prose

on-line speech comprehension: the process of ongoing understanding while processing spoken language

lexicon: the mental representations that correspond to the words with which we're familiar; our mental dictionary

Fox Tree, J. E. (2001). Listeners' use of *um* and *uh* in speech comprehension. *Memory and Cognition, 29,* 320–326. Reprinted by permission of Psychonomic Society, Inc.

word integration: the assimilation of a word into the syntactic and semantic representation of a sentence

nonpropositional information: information that does not relate to the content of the topic being discussed (*um*s and *uh*s may provide such nonpropositional information)

coarticulation: the precise sound of a given phoneme is impacted by surrounding phonemes

parsing: sentence comprehension process that involves breaking a sentence down into its component phrases

Hardly a conversation goes by without an *um* or an *uh;* but despite their frequency, they are often considered undesirable and unnecessary. People take courses to learn how to avoid saying them, reporters strike them from verbatim accounts of what someone has said, and professional broadcasters digitally splice them out of interviews. Perhaps because of their disagreeable status, *um*s and *uh*s have been overlooked by or excluded from models of speech comprehension. The possible effects that *um*s and *uh*s might have on on-line speech comprehension were tested across two languages—English and Dutch.

Ums and Uhs as Signals of Upcoming Delay

One proposal for the function of *um*s and *uh*s is that they serve as signals of upcoming delay (Clark, 1994; Clark & Wasow, 1998; Smith & Clark, 1993). When people are thinking of answers to factual questions, they say *um* when the delay before answering is going to be long and *uh* when the delay is going to be short (Clark, 1994; Clark & Wasow, 1998; Smith & Clark, 1993). This proposed function might be what underlies a number of disparate proposals about the functions of *um*s and *uh*s, such as that they mark **syntactic structure** or **discourse structure** (Maclay & Osgood, 1959; Martin, 1967; Sweets, 1998), that they indicate a desire to maintain control of the floor (Maclay & Osgood, 1959; Rochester, 1973; Schegloff, 1981; Siegman, 1979), or that they indicate a speaker's speech production trouble, including the need for more time to plan upcoming speech (Christenfeld, Schacter, & Bilous, 1991; Jefferson, 1974; Kasl & Mahl, 1987; Levelt, 1989; Martin, 1967; Reynolds & Paivio, 1968; Schacter, Christenfeld, Ravina, & Bilous, 1991; Siegman, 1979; Tannenbaum, Williams, & Hillier, 1965). In all these cases, *um*s and *uh*s might serve as forewarnings of delays associated with these processes, instead of forewarning the actual processes.

As indicators of varying lengths of delay, *um* and *uh* may have different effects on **on-line speech comprehension.** For example, as an indicator of a brief delay, *uh* could focus the listener's attention on immediately upcoming information; but an indicator of a longer delay might not be as useful to listeners. When expecting a minor delay after hearing *uh,* it is to a listener's advantage to focus on upcoming speech in anticipation of a continuation. But when expecting a major delay after hearing *um,* it might not be useful to focus on upcoming speech. One reason for this is that it might be a long time before the speaker begins to talk again, and it might not be possible for listeners to maintain heightened attention for that long. A second reason is that a major delay after *um* might arise from problems that are not benefitted by a listener's heightened attention. For example, listeners may gain no benefit from heightening their attention if speakers are having trouble conceptualizing what they want to say. Yet another twist is that anticipated major delays might even shift the focus from listeners' anticipation of upcoming speech. Listeners may play active roles in helping speakers complete their ideas (from Jefferson, 1974, p. 186); for example,

(1) Ken: I like driving. I really do. I enjoy it very much.

   Louis: I used to like it until I became the complete sl-uhm. (1.0)

   Ken: 'Slave'? Yeah.

They may help speakers advance the topic (adapted from Svartvik & Quirk, 1980; asterisks indicate overlapped speech); for example,

(2) C: I remember it over aunt Matty. One was always having to find out how many steps there were in places, before one knew whether one could take her there. This house for instance, there are thirteen up to this room

   D: yes, but I really meant not so much that, which is bad enough as you know, but places where there are one or two or three steps

   C: yes. right, I'm sure

   D: um up and down to *places*

   C: *m* (pause)

   D: um

   C: ramps

   D: yes, the people are doing a lot with ramps.

So, even though they both signal delay, *um* and *uh* might have different effects on *on-line comprehension* because of the different lengths of delays they signal.

How Ums and Uhs Might Affect On-Line Speech Comprehension

The present studies tested one level of comprehension, on-line sentence processing—in particular, listeners' incorporation of spoken words into a representation of what was said. Hearing *um* or *uh* could affect on-line comprehension in three ways: There could be no effect, a detrimental effect, or a beneficial effect.

There are two different reasons that *um*s and *uh*s can be predicted to have no effect on on-line comprehension. One is that they might be filtered out of the speech stream before **word integration** begins. *Um*s and *uh*s have predictable *F0 frequencies within clauses* (Shriberg & Lickley, 1992, 1993), which might set them apart from the rest of a person's speech, allowing a processor to detect and remove them before they are even sent to the **lexicon** for identification, even before *word incorporation* can take place. If *um*s and *uh*s are automatically filtered out, people should have a difficult time noticing them in speech, and they do (Christenfeld, 1995, Lindsay & O'Connell, 1995; Martin, 1971; Martin & Strange, 1968). However, people can notice them when they want to (Christenfeld, 1995), showing that an automatic filter must at times be nonautomatic and under conscious control. The automatic filter proposal is especially attractive for theories of *um* and *uh* function that describe them as being by-products of the speech production process without their having any implications for the listener (Martin, 1971; Martin & Strange, 1968).

Another reason *um*s and *uh*s can be predicted to have no effect on on-line comprehension is that they might function at a different level of comprehension. Instead of being filtered out, *um*s and *uh*s might be processed and noted without their influencing on-line *word integration.* This proposal is especially attractive for theories of *um* and *uh* function that describe them as being involuntary emotional reactions to nervousness or stress (Lalljee & Cook, 1969, 1973; see also Christenfeld & Creager, 1996, and Rochester, 1973, for reviews of relevant research). Listeners might notice them and recognize the speaker's state, which in turn might influence listeners' interpretations of speaker intention and the shared conversational goals, yet they might not have any effect on on-line word recognition or integration.

In contrast to the no-effect predictions, there are at least two reasons to predict that *um*s and *uh*s could be disruptive to on-line comprehension. One reason concerns the filter hypothesis. It is possible that *um*s and *uh*s are filtered out, but that the filtering process is disruptive. The identification of *um*s and *uh*s in the speech stream, the flagging of them as **nonpropositional information,** and the inhibition of their incorporation into discourse can take time. This would mean that every time an *um* or *uh* is encountered, the on-line speech processor is slowed.

The second reason *um*s and *uh*s might be disruptive has nothing to do with filtering, but rather with failed attempts at incorporation. Several models of speech comprehension propose that, in understanding speech, people identify words, assign them grammatical roles, and then connect them to a syntactic representation of the utterance that is built word by word, as speech is being heard (for reviews, see Carroll, 1994; Mitchell, 1994). *Um*s and *uh*s would pose a serious stumbling block to these systems because they cannot be combined with surrounding words to form syntactic constructions (Clark & Fox Tree, 2000). Speech comprehension systems might try to incorporate them, and when can't, they resort to repair procedures to recover from the misparses. Both the disruptive filter proposal and the stumbling block proposal are especially attractive for theories of *um* and *uh* function that describe them as unwanted speech disruptions (see Postma, Kolk, & Povel, 1990, for discussion).

Finally, there is reason to believe that *um*s and *uh*s have beneficial effects on comprehension. As signals of upcoming delay, *um*s and *uh*s could benefit on-line speech comprehension by prompting listeners to pay more attention to upcoming speech. This benefit would be lost if *um*s and *uh*s were absent. This proposal fits well with the findings that *um*s and *uh*s affect listeners' off-line interpretations of talk (Brennan & Williams, 1995; Christenfeld 1995; Fox Tree, 1999).

To test how *um*s and *uh*s affect on-line speech processing, I compared how long it took listeners to detect a word in a speech stream after a spontaneously produced *um* or *uh* with how long it took them to detect the same word when the *um* or *uh* had been digitally excised. In this task, the people listen for a word in an utterance and pressed a button if they hear that word. The speed at which they press the button is related to their ability to integrate information up to that point (Fox Tree, 1995; Fox Tree & Schrock, 1999; Marslen-Wilson & Tyler, 1980). If *ums* and *uhs* are disruptive to on-line comprehension, word monitoring should be slower after an *um* or *uh* than when the *um* or *uh* has been excised. But, if *ums* and *uhs* are beneficial for speech processing, word monitoring should be faster after an *um* or an *uh* than when the *um* or *uh* has been excised. If they are neither detrimental nor beneficial, there should be no effect.

Experiment 1
English Ums *and* Uhs

Method

Participants

Thirty-four native English speakers from the University of California participated in this experiment in exchange for course credit.

Materials

The materials were taken from the spontaneous speech of students telling face-to-face stories to each other. The corpus was collected by Herbert Clark at Stanford University. The materials consisted of a stretch of speech from one speaker that contained at least one spontaneously occurring *um* or *uh,* which was followed immediately by a word that had not occurred earlier in the stimulus (i.e., the *post-um-or-uh-word*). Each stimulus began at the beginning of an idea and finished with a completed thought.

Eighty-eight stimuli were selected: 40 critical stimuli, 40 filler stimuli, and 8 practice stimuli. All stimuli were similar in length and content. In the critical stimuli, the post-um-or-uh-word was the target word. In the filler stimuli, a target word was chosen that was similar semantically and, if possible, phonologically to the post-um-or-uh-word but that did not occur in the stimulus (e.g., if *question* were the post-um-or-uh-word, *query* could be the target word). Target words were chosen from a variety of form classes and were one to four syllables long. The filler stimuli helped ensure that the participants did not adopt a strategy of immediately responding after hearing an *um* or *uh*. This strategy would not work in this case because the stimuli contained 24 *ums* and 17 *uhs* in addition to the 20 *ums* and *uhs* of interest that each participant heard (see the Design section).

Eight of the critical *ums* and eight of the critical *uhs* (40% of the critical stimuli) were matched on the local syntactic constituent structure immediately surrounding the fillers and targets. For example,

(3) Um: And he said why sure well what kind of *um* price range are you looking for?

Uh: Then he also toi-sold her on *uh* a couple of *uh* furniture items for the ant.

Matching was done to test the role of syntactic location in causing any effects found. For example. if *uhs* usually occur within clauses and *ums* between clauses, as has been found in one Dutch corpus (Swerts, 1998), *uh*s might be more noticeable than *um*s and therefore have a stronger effect. *Um*s and *uh*s tested in the present experiment occurred both within and between clauses.

For each of the critical stimuli and for half the filler stimuli, second versions were created in which the critical *um* or *uh* was digitally excised. The *um* or *uh* was not replaced by a pause, although any pauses preceding or following the *um* or *uh* were retained. The technique of creating edited versions of materials kept constant a number of variables that might otherwise have influenced comparisons between speech with and without *um*s and *uh*s, such as target word frequency or pronunciation, prosodic stress, or syntactic construction. The only difference across conditions was whether or not there was an *um* or an *uh,* as well as any processing time associated with the lengths of each (350 msec on average).

Detectability of Editing

A follow-up study tested whether the listeners were able to detect editing in the stimuli. The 80 critical stimuli were divided into two lists, each containing 10 unedited *um* items, 10 edited *um* items, 10 unedited *uh* items, and 10 edited *uh* items. Twenty people who did not participate in the main experiment listened to each list, 10 per list. These participants indicated on an answer sheet whether they thought each trial had been edited. They were asked to "spot the splice" where the materials may have been digitally edited. Two practice trials helped them understand the instructions. The participants performed no better than chance at identifying the edited speech. The inability of the listeners to detect editing is consistent with listeners' inability to detect editing in other similar studies (Fox Tree, 1995; Fox Tree & Schrock, 1999). Although it is possible that splicing can be detected beneath conscious awareness, such detection would be too unsystematic to drive the effects found here; in other similar studies, the edited conditions were sometimes responded to more quickly, sometimes more slowly, and sometimes in the same amount of time as the unedited conditions (Fox Tree, 1995, Fox Tree & Schrock, 1999).

Design

Two lists were created. List 1 contained the practice stimuli, 10 unedited critical *um* stimuli, 10 unedited critical *uh* stimuli, 10 edited critical *um* stimuli, 10 edited critical *uh* stimuli, and 40 filler stimuli. List 2 contained the same practice and filler stimuli, but had the edited versions of the List I unedited critical stimuli and the unedited versions of the List 1 edited critical stimuli. The randomized order of presentation was the same across lists. Each participant listened to only one list and therefore heard only one version of each stimulus (a within-subjects and within-items counterbalanced design).

Procedure

Each trial had the following structure. First, a 500-msec tone was heard indicating that the participants should focus their attention on the computer screen. The tone was followed by a 500-msec silence. A word then appeared on the computer screen for 1,000 msec, followed by a 1,000-msec silence, after which a sound file was played. The participants held the word in memory while they listened to the sound file and immediately pressed a button in front of them if they heard the word. Critical stimuli elicited buttonpresses: filler stimuli did not. Reaction times (RTs) were measured from the onset of the target words in milliseconds. Response times timed out after 1,500 msec. All stimuli played to the end, regardless of whether a button was pressed. There was a 1,500-msec silence between trials. The experiment lasted about half an hour.

Results

Three items were removed from the analyses, one because of an experimental error and two because they were not responded to by more than 20% of the participants. The low response items were the first and last items in the stimulus list and, in addition, contained target words that might have been hard to hear. Response times more than two standard deviations from the mean were treated as outliers and removed from the analyses (4% of the data). This eliminated both false alarms and misses. There was no difference in error rates across conditions [unedited *um*: 3.8%, edited *um*: 3.2%, F_1 (1,33) = 0.48, n.s.; F_2 (1,18) = 0.03, n.s.; unedited *uh*: 5.5%, edited *uh*: 4.7%, F_1 (1,33) = 0.04, n.s., F_2 (1,17) = 0.29, n.s.].

The main finding was that there was a significant difference in the participants' speed at recognizing target words following *uh*s compared with their speed at recognizing the same words when the *uh*s had been excised [F_1 (1,33) = 13.77, p = .00 1; F_2 (1,17) = 5.93, p < .05], but there was no significant difference for the *um*s [F_1 (1,33) = 0.52, n.s.; F_2 (1,18) = 0.41, n.s.]. Means and standard deviations are presented in Table 1.

A number of other possible differences between *um*s and *uh*s can be ruled out as factors causing the different effects of *um* and *uh*. One is the length of the *um*s or *uh*s: If the *uh*s had been longer, the listeners might have paid more attention to them than to the *um*s. In fact, the *um*s tended to be longer than the *uh*s. The *um*s were on average 384 msec long (range, 205–557 msec) and *uh*s were on average 327 msec long [range, 214–451 msec; t(35) = 1.93, p – .06].

A second difference is the amount of pausing before and after *um*s and *uh*s: If the *uh*s had longer pauses surrounding them, they might have been more prominent in the speech stream. But the pauses before and after *um*s and *uh*s did not vary systematically in this set of sentences [average pause before *um* was 362 msec, average pause before *uh* was 349

TABLE 1 *Summary of Means (SD) for English* **Ums** *and* **Uhs** *Averaged Across Participants and Items in Milliseconds*

	Unedited		Edited		
	M	**SD**	**M**	**SD**	**Difference**
Um	561	132	548	126	13
Uh	554	121	601	121	−47

msec, $t(35) = .09$, n.s.; average pause after *um* was 334 msec, average pause after *uh* was 355 msec; $t(35) = -.13$, n.s.].

A third possible difference is where the *um*s and *uh*s were located: If the *uh*'s effect was due to its position, the effect should be stronger for the more wide ranging, unmatched *uh* stimuli than for the constrained, matched *uh* stimuli. Similarly, if *um*'s lack of an effect was due to its position, an effect might appear with those *um*s that match the syntactic location of the *uh*s. But there was no interaction between the presence or absence of *um* or *uh* and whether the stimuli were matched or not [editing × matching; *um*: $F_1 (1,33) = 0.0$, n.s., $F_2(1,17) = 0.10$, n.s., one item was removed from analysis because of low response; *uh*: $F_1 (1,33) = 0.07$, n.s., $F_2(1,16) = 0.45$, n.s., two items were removed from analysis because of low response and experiment error]. Although it may be true that *um*s and *uh*s vary in usual location of occurrence and that the present experiment might have had a different proportion of typical to atypical *um*s versus *uh*s, this variance cannot account for the results found here.

A fourth possible difference is in the target words that followed the *um*s and *uh*s: If *uh* targets were less frequent words, more softly spoken, or longer, maybe they would benefit more from a preceding filler. But there was no difference between the overall RTs to *um* targets and *uh* targets [mean RT *um*, 551, *SD*, 92; mean RT *uh*, 567, *SD*, 89; $t(35) = .55$, n.s.]. So, functionally, targets occurring after *um* and *uh* can be treated as being similar enough to not be considered as the cause of the effects found here.

A fifth possible difference is in the pauses in the edited conditions. After the *um*s and *uh*s were edited out, the original pauses that preceded or followed them were retained in the edited items. Instead of *uh*s' benefitting recognition, the pauses might have slowed recognition. Of course, this does not explain why no similar detrimental effect of pauses was found for the *um* items, given that the amount of pausing before and after *um*s and *uh*s was similar. In fact, there was no correlation between the differences in RTs across conditions and the amount of pausing that remained in the edited conditions (pause before *um* or *uh* plus pause after; $r = .19$, $p = $ n.s.).

A related alternative explanation is that the differences between *um*s and *uh*s were due to **coarticulation** effects. If targets after *uh* are more likely to be coarticulated with the *uh* than are targets after *um,* removing the *uh* could also remove some important word recognition information. Although the listeners could not detect the editing, they might nonetheless have been deprived of crucial acoustic cues, but only in the *uh* conditions. This explanation can be ruled out by considering that only four *um*s and four *uh*s did not have a pause between them and the targets. Even without intervening pauses, coarticulation effects would be surprising, given that *um*s and *uh*s are never cliticized onto the next word (Clark & Fox Tree, 2000).

Discussion

The present study provides evidence that *uh*s are beneficial to listener's abilities to recognize words in upcoming speech. Neither beneficial nor detrimental effects were found for *um*s. Several alternative explanations for these results have been ruled out; that is, the results were not due to (1) differences in the editing quality across *um* and *uh* stimuli, (2) the lengths of the *um*s and *uh*s, (3) the amount of pausing before or after the *um*s and *uh*s,

(4) the syntactic position of the *um*s and *uh*s, or (5) characteristics of the targets following *um*s and *uh*s. The effect also cannot be due to a listener strategy of responding positively immediately after hearing an *uh*. There were many other *uh*s in the materials, both in the critical stimuli and the filler stimuli, so this strategy would have failed more often than it would have succeeded. It is also unlikely that the listeners adopted the strategy of responding faster only after *uh* but not after *um*.

Experiment 2 attempted to replicate these findings cross-linguistically. A further discussion of why *um*s and *uh*s differ is in the General Discussion section.

Experiment 2
Dutch Ums *and* Uhs

Method

Participants

The participants were 32 native Dutch speakers from the Max Planck Institute participant pool. They were each paid FL8.50 for their participation.

Materials

The materials were taken from the spontaneous speech of students describing abstract figures to an experimenter who acted as a silent listener. The corpus was collected by Nanda Poulisse at the Max Planck Institute for Psycholinguistics (Poulisse, 1989). The selection and preparation of the materials were similar to those in Experiment 1, except that there were 10 additional filler stimuli, targets ranged from one to six syllables, and 50% of the critical stimuli were syntactically matched.

Detectability of Editing

In the Dutch detection study, the listeners followed along with a transcript and were allowed to hear each stimulus up to six times. Twelve participants (6 per list) listened to each stimulus and were instructed to mark on the transcript where they thought it might have been digitally manipulated. A practice trial and discussion of that trial helped them understand the instructions.

The listeners greatly overestimated the amount of editing in this task. Overall, 90% of the stimuli were judged to have been edited at some point, when in fact only 50% had been edited. Among the edited stimuli, 27.5% of the edits were detected. However, on no item was editing accurately detected by all 6 participants who heard it, and on nine items, none of the participants detected the editing. Importantly, there was no difference in the delectability of editing between *um* stimuli and *uh* stimuli [on average, 1.9 participants detected an edit in an *um* stimulus, and 1.4 detected an edit in an *uh* stimulus; $t(38)$—1.25. n.s., i.e., 32% of the *um* stimuli and 23% of the *uh* stimuli were judged to have been edited].

Design

The design was the same as that in Experiment 1, except that there were 10 additional filler stimuli.

Procedure

The procedure was the same as that in Experiment 1, except that the tone was followed by a 1,500-msec silence, the word appeared for 715 msec, and the word was followed by a 285-msec silence.

Results

Response times more than two standard deviations from the mean were treated as outliers and removed from the analyses (7% of the data). This eliminated both false alarms and misses. There was no difference in error rates across conditions [unedited *um,* 5.9%, edited *um,* 7.4%, F_1 (1,31) = 0.66, n.s., F_2 (1,19) = 0.63, n.s.; unedited *uh,* 6.6%, edited *uh,* 8.2%, F_1 (1,31) = 0.62, n.s., F_2 (1,19) = 1.11, n.s.].

The results replicated those of Experiment 1: There was a significant difference in the listeners' speed at recognizing the target words following *uh*s compared with their speed at recognizing the same words when the *uh*s were excised [F_1 (1,31) = 7.5, *p* = .01; F_2 (1,19) = 4.28, *p* = .05]; there was no significant difference for the *um*s [F_1 (1,31) = 0.04, n.s.; F_2(1,19) = 0.35, n.s.]. Means and standard deviations are presented in Table 2.

Once again, many alternative explanations for the differences between *um*s and *uh*s can be ruled out. One is that, if the *uh*s were longer, listeners might have paid more attention to them than to the *um*s. In fact, the *um*s were longer [average length of *um* was 615 msec, average length of *uh* was 476 msec; *t*(38) = 2.20, *p* < .05]. Another alternative is that the amount of pausing before and after the *um*s and *uh*s could have caused the effect. In contrast to the English materials, in the Dutch materials, pausing occurred more often before and after *um*s than before and after *uh*s [average pause before *um* was 592 msec, before *uh,* 181 msec; *t*(38) = 2.77, *p* <.01; after *um,* 412 msec, after *uh,* 199 msec; *t*(38) = 1.92, *p* =.06]. This extra pausing should have highlighted the presence of an *um,* yet the *um*s had no effect on the listeners' word recognition. There was also no correlation between the differences in RTs across conditions and the amount of pausing remaining in the edited conditions (*r* =

TABLE 2 *Summary of Means (SD) for Dutch* **Um***s and* **Uh***s Averaged Across Participants and Items in Milliseconds*

	Unedited		Edited		
	M	*SD*	*M*	*SD*	*Difference*
Um	585	119	591	96	–6
Uh	506	84	534	76	–28

.12, p = n.s.). Another alternative is that the location of the *um*s and *uh*s could have driven the effects. But there was no interaction between the presence or absence of *um* or *uh* and whether the stimuli were matched or not [i.e., editing x matching; *um:* F_1 (1,31) = 0.20, n.s., F_2(1,18) = 0.75, n.s.; *uh:* F_1(1,31) = 0.04, n.s., F_2(1,18) = 0.01, n.s.].

One alternative explanation that cannot be ruled out, as it has been for the English materials, is that there was something about the target words that varied systematically across the *um* and *uh* items. Overall RTs to the *um* targets were slower than to the *uh* targets [mean RT *um,* 589 msec, SD = 128; mean RT *uh,* 522 msec, SD = 69; t(29.38) = 2.03, p = .05]. Of course, given the number of post hoc tests (on length of *um* or *uh,* pausing, syntactic location), a p level of .05 might be considered suspect. The slowness of *um* target recognition was not caused by a loss of articulatory information: 16 targets after *um* had an intervening pause (7 targets after *uh* also had an intervening pause). Although it is possible that an effect of *um* on upcoming targets was drowned out by slower processing, this would not explain why no effect of *um* was found in the English experiment.

Discussion

Experiment 2 replicated cross-linguistically the results of Experiment 1 that showed that *uh*s were beneficial to the listeners' recognition of words in upcoming speech, with *um*s being neither beneficial nor detrimental. As before, many alternative explanations were ruled out; that is, the results were not driven by (1) differences in the editing quality across the *um* and *uh* stimuli, (2) the lengths of the *um*s and *uh*s, (3) the amount of pausing before or after the *um*s and *uh*s, or (4) the syntactic position of the *um*s and *uh*s. Unlike the English targets, the Dutch targets after *um* were recognized more slowly than were the targets after *uh* (at p = .05, without a Bonferroni correction). Future investigation will clarify what the implications this has for the differences between *um* and *uh.*

General Discussion

In two word-monitoring studies, in two different languages, *uh*s were found to increase the speed at which listeners were able to recognize words in upcoming speech, whereas *um*s were found to have no effect on the listeners' speed of recognition. The fact that *um*s and *uh*s are frequently avoided in speech or edited from reported speech suggests that there may be something wrong with them. Against this backdrop, it is surprising that *um*s and *uh*s do not inhibit on-line processing and, even more surprising that *uh*s aid processing.

There are two alternative explanations for the present findings. According to the editing account, it is not that *uh*s speed up RTs, but that editing slows them. Even if people cannot overtly detēct editing, their RTs may still be hindered by an editing by-product that occurs beneath overt awareness. According to the *time-to-target account,* splicing out *um*s and *uh*s shortens the processing time available to listeners, slowing responses in the edited conditions. Both accounts are unlikely for several reasons.

The editing account is unlikely because (1) it cannot explain why editing has not always yielded a negative effect, either in prior studies (see Fox Tree, 1995; Fox Tree &

Schrock, 1999) or in the present studies, in which only the *uh* stimuli would have been so affected; (2) it cannot explain why similar effects were found in both English and Dutch, despite stimulus variation that could have presumably affected such an editing by-product, such as the fact that the materials were from two languages that sound different phonologically, and that the stimuli were created by using different digitizing and editing systems and were played on different kinds of audio equipment; and (3) it cannot explain why RTs are sometimes faster in edited conditions (see Fox Tree, 1995). The difficulty in explaining why a hypothetical subdetection editing signal would hinder responses in only certain situations leads to a rejection of the editing account.

The time-to-target account is unlikely because (1) there was no correlation between pausing and RT differences in either experiment; (2) in other similar experiments, whether the edited item was replaced by a pause or not had no affect on the results (Fox Tree, 1995; Fox Tree & Schrock, 1999); and (3) it cannot explain why slowing would occur only for the *uh*s and not for the *um*s; this is especially problematic given that the *um*s tended to be longer than the *uh*s, which means that more processing time would have been lost in the edited versions of the *um* stimuli, incorrectly predicting a stronger effect for *um*s. Given the lack of concordance between the processing time predictions and the three outcomes listed above, this account has been rejected.

The present results pose problems for **parsing** models that describe parsing as a process that involves identifying words in the speech stream, assigning them grammatical roles, and fitting them into syntactic representations. According to these models, the occurrence of an *um* or an *uh* should lead to parsing failure since they do not combine with surrounding words to form syntactic constructions. The negative reputation of *um*s and *uh*s in the public eye fits nicely with this predicted negative influence on word recognition. The problems for these, models posed by the nondetrimental effects found here may seem to be easily overcome by an automatic filtering system account, in which *um*s and *uh*s are detected and filtered out before the processes of word identification and syntactic construction begin. This filtering process should be effortless and have no effect on processing. Unfortunately, an automatic filtering system would also remove the demonstrated benefits of *uh*.

The present results are consistent with the proposal that *um*s and *uh*s signal different lengths of upcoming delay. The brief delays signaled by *uh* heighten listeners' attention for upcoming speech. The longer delays after *um* do not appear to alter listeners' attention in the same way, either because heightened attention is not as useful when the length of delay is indeterminant, or because listeners focus their attention elsewhere in an effort to help speakers get their thoughts out, or for some other reason.

The present research strongly suggests that utterances with *um*s and *uh*s excised cannot automatically be considered better versions of the originals. In fact, cleaned-up versions might be lacking important information that listeners use to process spontaneous speech. Instead of their being undesirable, speakers may choose to use one or the other, and addressees seem to make use of the distinction.

References _____

Bennan, S. E., & Williams, W. (1995). The feeling of another's knowing: Prosody and filled pauses as cues to listeners about the metacognitive states of speakers. *Journal of Memory & Language,* **34,** 383–398.

Carroll, D. W. (1994). *Psychology of language* (2nd ed.). Pacific Grove, CA: Brooks/Cole.

Christenfeld, N. (1995). Does it hurt to say um? *Journal of Nonverbal Behavior,* **19,** 171–186.

Christenfeld, N., & Creager, B. (1996). Anxiety, alcohol, aphasia, and ums. *Journal of Personality & Social Psychology,* **70,** 451–460.

Christenfeld, N., Schacter, S., & Bilous, F. (1991). Filled pauses and gestures: It's not coincidence. *Journal of Psycholinguistic Research,* **20,** 1–10.

Clark, H. H. (1994). Managing problems in speaking. *Speech Communication,* **15,** 243–250.

Clark, H. H., & Fox Tree, J. E. (2000). Uh *and* um as *English words.* Manuscript in preparation.

Clark, H. H., & Wasow, T. (1998). Repeating words in spontaneous speech. *Cognitive Psychology,* **37,** 201–242.

Fox Tree, J. E. (1995). The effects of false starts and repetitions on the processing of subsequent words in spontaneous speech. *Journal of Memory & Language,* **34,** 709–738.

Fox Tree, J. E. (1999). *Between-turn pauses and ums.* Paper presented at the International Conference of Phonetic Sciences Satellite Meeting on Disfluencies, Berkeley, CA.

Fox Tree, J. E., & Schrock, J. C. (1999). Discourse markers in spontaneous speech: Oh what a difference an oh makes. *Journal of Memory & Language,* **40,** 280–295.

Jefferson, G. (1974). Error correction as an interactional resource. *Language in Society,* **3,** 181–199.

Kasl, S. V., & Mahl, G. F. (1987). Speech disturbances and experimentally induced anxiety. In G. F. Mahl (Ed.), *Explorations in non-verbal and vocal behavior* (pp. 203–213). Hillsdale, NJ: Erlbaum.

Lalljee, M. G., & Cook, M. (1969). An experimental investigation of the function of filled pauses in speech. *Language & Speech,* **12,** 24–28.

Lalljee, M. [G.], & Cook, M. (1973). Uncertainty in first encounters. *Journal of Personality & Social Psychology,* **26,** 137–141.

Levelt, W. J. M. (1989). *Speaking: From intention to articulation.* Cambridge, MA: MIT Press.

Lindsay, J., & O'Connell, D. C. (1995). How do transcribers deal with audio recordings of spoken discourse? *Journal of Psycholinguistic Research,* **24,** 101–115.

Maclay, H., & Osgood, C. E. (1959). Hesitation phenomena in spontaneous English speech. *Word,* **75,** 19–44.

Marslen-Wilson, W., & Tyler, L. K. (1980). The temporal structure of spoken language understanding. *Cognition,* **8,** 1–71.

Martin, J. G., (1967). Hesitations in the speaker's production and listener's reproduction of utterances. *Journal of Verbal Learning & Verbal Behavior,* **6,** 903–909.

Martin, J. G. (1971). Some acoustic and grammatical features of spontaneous speech. In D. Horton & J. Jenkins (Eds.), *The perception of language* (pp. 47–68). Columbus, OH: Merrill.

Martin, J. G., & Strange, W. (1968). The perception of hesitation in spontaneous speech. *Perception & Psychophysics,* **3,** 427–438.

Mitchell, D. C. (1994). Sentence parsing. In M. A. Gernsbacher (Ed.). *Handbook of psycholinguistics* (pp. 375–409). San Diego: Academic Press.

Postma, A., Kolk, H., & Povel, D. J. (1990). On the relation among speech errors, disfluencies, and self-repairs. *Language & Speech,* **33,** 19–29.

Poulisse, W. (1989). *The use of compensatory strategies by Dutch learners of English.* Doctoral dissertation, de Katholieke Universiteit te Nijmegen.

Reynolds, A., & Paivio, A. (1968). Cognitive and emotional determinants of speech. *Canadian Journal of Psychology,* **22,** 164–175.

Rochester, S. R. (1973). The significance of pauses in spontaneous speech. *Journal of Psycholinguistic Research,* **2,** 51–81.

Schacter, S., Christenfeld, N., Ravina, B., & Bilous, F. (1991). Speech disfluency and the structure of knowledge. *Journal of Personality & Social Psychology,* **60,** 362–367.

Schegloff, E. A. (1981). Discourse as an interreactional achievement: Some uses of 'uh huh' and other things that come between sentences. In D. Tannen (Ed.), *Georgetown University round table on languages and linguistics, 1981,* Washington, DC: Georgetown University Press.

Shriberg, E. E., & Lickley, R. J. (1992). *The relationship of filled-pause F0 to prosodic context.* Paper presented at the IRCS Workshop on Prosody in Natural Speech, University of Pennsylvania.

Shriberg, E. E., & Lickley, R. J. (1993). Intonation of clause-internal filled pauses. *Phonetica,* **50,** 172–179.

Siegman, A. W. (1979). Cognition and hesitation in speech. In A. W. Siegman & S. Feldstein (Eds.), *Of speech and time* (pp. 151–178). Hillsdale, NJ: Erlbaum.

Smith, V. L., & Clark, H. H. (1993). On the course of answering questions. *Journal of Memory & Language,* **32,** 25–38.

Svartvik, J., & Quirk, R. (Eds.). (1980). *A corpus of English conversation.* Lund: Gleerups.

Swerts, M. (1998). Filled pauses as markers of discourse structure. *Journal of Pragmatics,* **30,** 485–496.

Tannenbaum, P. H., Williams, F., & Hillier, C. S. (1965). Word predictability in the environments of hesitations. *Journal of Verbal Learning & Verbal Behavior,* **4,** 134–140.

Introduction: Critical Thinking Questions

? What are the differerences between the delays found after *uh* and those found after *um,* and how might these differences affect speech comprehension?

? How might the major delay signified by *um* lead the listener to shape the ensuing conversation?

? The author cites an automatic filter proposal whereby ums and uhs "…might be filtered out of the speech stream before word integration begins." If such a filter did exist, what should we see in people's processing of *um*s and *uh*s? Explain. What does empirical evidence suggest about such a filter? Explain.

? Describe the two reasons why *um*s and *uh*s may be harmful to on-line speech comprehension.

? Discuss the logic behind the researcher's choice of a word identification task for assessing the effects of *um*s and *uh*s on comprehension. What are her hypotheses?

Method: Critical Thinking Questions

? For each experiment, describe what you would have been asked to do, had you been a participant in the experiment.

? Name the independent variables in each experiment, and their levels. Describe how each of these variables was operationalized. For each variable, state whether it was manipulated in a between-subjects or within-subjects fashion. How many conditions were there in the experiment?

? What was (were) the dependent variable(s) in each experiment?

? What aspects of the methodology were implemented to deal with possible confounds?

Results/Discussion: Critical Thinking Questions

? What was the effect of *uh*s or *um*s on the recognition of upcoming words? Explain the relevant pattern of results.

? The results of these studies are problematic for which models of speech comprehension? Explain why the results cannot be accounted for by these models.

? Which views do the results support? Explain how the results support these views.

? What is the general conclusion about the popular practice of removing *um*s and *uh*s from one's speech? Explain.

? After reading this study, you may feel there are other issues or questions that would be worthwhile or intriguing to address. Pose one of these questions (other than those suggested by the authors) that could be investigated empirically.

Working Memory, Inhibitory Control, and Reading Disability

Penny Chiappe, Lynn Hasher, and Linda S. Siegel

Abstract

The relationships among working memory, inhibitory control, and reading skills were studied in 966 individuals, 6–49 years old. In addition to a standardized measure of word recognition, they received a working memory (listening span) task in the standard, blocked format (three sets containing two-, three-, or four-item trials) or in a mixed format (three sets each containing two-, three-, and four-item trials) to determine whether scores derived from the standard format are influenced by proactive interference. Intrusion errors were investigated in order to determine whether deficits in working memory were associated with the access, deletion, or restraint functions of inhibitory control. The results indicated that deficits in working memory were characteristic of individuals with reading disabilities at all ages. These deficits may be associated with the access and restraint functions of inhibition. Working memory skills increased until the age of 19. The blocked format showed a gradual decline in adulthood whereas the mixed format did not. The different patterns suggest that the decline in working memory skills associated with aging may result from growing inefficiencies in inhibitory control, and not diminished capacity.

Conceptual Issues and Theoretical Questions

- What are the relative roles of storage and processing capabilities of working memory in reading?
- How do individual differences in the storage and processing capabilities of working memory relate to reading disability?
- What is the locus of the deficits observed in those with reading disabilities?
- To what extent does a failure of inhibitory processing play in reading disability?

Chiappe, P., Hasher, L., & Siegel, L. S. (2000). Working memory, inhibitory control, and reading disability. *Memory and Cognition, 28,* 8–17. Reprinted by permission of Psychonomic Society, Inc.

De-Jargonizing

processing capacity (of working memory): the capacity of working memory to be engaged in cognitive processes such as rehearsal or inhibition

storage capacity (of working memory): the capacity of working memory to hold a certain amount of information

homophone: a word that has the same sound as another, but a different meaning (e.g., *reed* and *read*)

homonym: a word that is identical to another in sound *and* spelling, but with a different meaning (e.g., *bear* can refer to the action of carrying, or to the animal)

negative priming: an inhibitory effect whereby responses are slowed to stimuli that have been previously presented, but ignored.

garden-path stories: story in which the reader builds a strong expectation that is ultimately violated by the text (i.e., the reader is *led up the garden path*)

proactive interference: occurs when information already encoded in memory impairs the encoding of new information

blocked procedure (for listening span task): reading span procedure in which trials of the same length are presented together (i.e., blocked), and followed by a block of trials of a different length (a series of trials of length two, followed by a series of trials of length three, followed by a series of trials of length four)

mixed procedure (for listening span task): reading span procedure in which trials of different lengths are interspersed (trial of length two followed by a trial of length three followed by a trial of length four)

phonological processing: processing of speech sounds

automaticity: effortless processing of a well-practiced task

grapheme–phoneme correspondences: the relationship between the printed form of a word (i.e., its basic visual patterns, or graphemes) and the spoken form of a word (i.e., its basic sounds, or phonemes)

ascending order (span task): reading span procedure in which shorter trials are followed by successively longer trials (two reading span trials, then three, then four)

descending order (span task): reading span procedure in which longer trials are followed by successively shorter trials (two reading span trials, then three, then four)

Working memory refers to the cognitive processes involved in the temporary storage of information while an individual is simultaneously processing incoming information or retrieving information from long-term storage. As such, it is thought to underlie a number of cognitive processes, such as reading, problem solving, and learning (see, e.g., Baddeley, 1983, 1986; Daneman & Carpenter, 1980).

Working memory has been conceptualized as consisting of a central processor, known as the central executive, which controls a number of subsidiary systems that operate on and store specific information about the items being processed (Baddeley, 1983). An important feature of working memory is that it has limited capacity. Its limited capacity may be considered a limited pool of attentional resources or a finite work space that must be shared between processing and data storage (Tirre & Peña, 1992). From this perspective, when more demands are placed on the central executive, fewer cognitive resources remain available for the subsidiary systems.

In 1980, Daneman and Carpenter introduced the reading span task as a measure of functional working memory available for reading. This task was designed to assess both the **storage** and **processing components** of working memory. In the reading span task and its variants, participants read or listened to a series of unrelated sentences and comprehended each sentence while preparing to recall the final word of each sentence at the end of the set. As the number of sentences increased, demands on working memory were also assumed to increase.

An important contribution of Daneman and Carpenter's (1980) reading span measure is its capacity to assess both the storage and the processing components of working memory. Given the limited capacity, individuals who experience difficulties processing the primary task (e.g., reading or listening comprehension) would need to devote more resources or capacity to processing sentences. Consequently, they would have fewer resources available to maintain the target words in memory. Conversely, individuals who are skilled at processing sentences are expected to have greater resources available for the storage task.

In fact, working memory capacity varies as a function of individual differences and age (see, e.g., Daneman & Carpenter, 1980; Gick, Craik, & Morris, 1988; Hasher & Zacks, 1988; Siegel & Ryan, 1988). For example, individuals with reading disabilities experience significant difficulties with working memory (Siegel, 1994; Siegel & Linder, 1984; Siegel & Ryan, 1988; Swanson, 1993, 1994). Similar difficulties in working memory have been reported for disabled readers in Chinese (So & Siegel, 1997), Hebrew (Geva & Siegel, in press), Italian (De Beni, Palladino, Pazzaglia, & Cornoldi, 1998), and Portuguese (Da Fontoura & Siegel, 1995).

In addition, working memory capacity has been shown to vary across the lifespan. For example, working memory performance has been shown to increase throughout childhood and adolescence, and then decline gradually through adulthood until age 50 (Siegel, 1994). According to some developmental theorists, growth in functional working memory through childhood is the result of increases in working memory capacity (e.g., Case, Kurland, & Goldberg, 1982; Hitch & Halliday, 1983). Similarly, according to the reduced capacity view, the resources individuals have available for the storage and processing of information diminish as they grow older. As a result, older individuals demonstrate performance decrements on measures of working memory (see, e.g., Babcock & Salthouse, 1990; Campbell & Charness, 1990; Gick et al., 1988; Light & Anderson, 1985; Morris, Gick, & Craik, 1988; Salthouse & Babcock, 1991; Wingfield, Stine, Lahar, & Aberdeen, 1988). Thus, changes in working memory performance across the lifespan have been attributed to changes in working memory capacity.

Recently, an alternative interpretation of the data showing reductions of working memory span with age and with reading skill has been offered by Hasher and her colleagues (Hasher, Stoltzfus, Rumpa, & Zacks, 1991; Hasher & Zacks, 1988; Hasher, Zacks, & May, 1999) and by Gernsbacher and her colleagues (Gernsbacher, 1990; Gernsbacher & Faust, 1991). These researchers have hypothesized that age-related cognitive deficits, and possibly individual differences related to reading skill, may result from inefficient inhibitory control of attention. For example, comparisons of more and less skilled university-age readers revealed that less skilled readers were less efficient at rejecting inappropriate meanings of ambiguous words and incorrect forms of **homophones,** ignoring words and pictures and revising incorrect inferences (Gernsbacher & Faust, 1991; Gernsbacher, Varner, & Faust, 1990; Whitney, Ritchie, & Clark, 1991). Similarly, less skilled readers tended to accept meanings of **homonyms** that were not implied by the sentence context more slowly than more skilled readers (Gernsbacher & Robertson, 1995). Because the less skilled readers activated contextually appropriate information with greater strength than the more skilled readers, Gernsbacher attributed the less skilled readers' poorer reading comprehension to less efficient suppression mechanisms.

Relatedly, declines in working memory associated with aging have been attributed to decreases in the ability to suppress irrelevant or no-longer-relevant information rather than decreases in working memory capacity. For example, the phenomenon of **negative priming** is seen in tasks requiring responses to target items in the presence of distractors. Responses to items that have been switched from distractors to targets tend to be slower as a result of inhibition. Although young adults tend to show negative priming, older adults often do not (Kane, May, Hasher, & Rahhal, 1997; May, Kane, & Hasher, 1995; Stoltzfus, Hasher, Zacks, Ulivi, & Goldstein, 1993). Similarly, investigations using **garden-path stories** revealed that although older adults were as likely as young adults to encode the correct interpretation, they were more likely to maintain the original, incorrect interpretation (Hamm & Hasher, 1992). The failure to inhibit the initial, incorrect interpretation results in difficulties in recalling the stories (Zacks & Hasher, 1988). Thus, the decline in working memory associated with aging may result from deficits in the inability to clear from working memory information that is irrelevant or information that is no longer relevant.

There are three ways in which inhibition may control the contents of working memory (Hasher et al., 1999). These functions are access, deletion, and restraint. Inhibition may control access to working memory by preventing any activated but goal-irrelevant information from entering working memory. In this manner, inhibition restricts access to working memory to goal-relevant information. Inhibition also controls the contents of working memory by deleting or suppressing the activation of irrelevant information or information that was once relevant and is no longer relevant. Thus, the deletion function of inhibition removes irrelevant information from the working memory buffer. Failures of the deletion function would lead to **proactive interference,** a disrupted pattern of recall produced by competition among relevant and irrelevant events at retrieval. Finally, inhibitory processes serve a restraining function by preventing strong responses from immediately seizing control of thought and action effectors so that other, less probable, responses can be considered. Thus, the restraining function of inhibition suppresses erroneous interpretations of text and language. Taken together, these functions ensure that information in the memory buffer is restricted to goal-relevant information.

Hasher and colleagues (Hasher et al., 1999) suggested that the decline in working memory performance associated with aging is caused in part by diminished inhibitory control. Older adults tend to show greater proactive interference than younger adults (Kane & Hasher, 1996). Because older adults are more susceptible to proactive interference, their working memory spans may be reduced. Thus, age differences in working memory spans may result from diminished inhibitory control with aging. According to this view, if the influence of proactive interference can be reduced, age differences in working memory span should be diminished. In fact, Hasher and her colleagues eliminated age differences in working memory span by changing the usual span procedure so as to reduce proactive interference (May, Kane, Hasher, & Valenti, 1996). One way to reduce proactive interference involved increasing the distinctiveness of each trial in a working memory task by administering a unique, nonverbal 90-sec distractor task after each trial. After the distractor task had been administered, older adults' working memory spans were as large as the spans of younger adults. These findings cannot be accounted for by limited capacity models alone. Therefore, failures of inhibitory control do seem to play an important role in working memory performance, at least that of older adults.

The central purpose of the current study was to examine the extent to which the inhibitory control hypothesis may account for differences in working memory based on age and reading skill. The working memory performance of people who ranged in age from 6 to 49 was studied. These people had been given one of two versions of the working memory task. In Experiment 1, participants were given the listening span task in the standard **blocked procedure,** whereas a **mixed procedure** was used in Experiment 2. Deficit in inhibitory control was assessed through the analysis of errors. Errors associated with aging have been hypothesized to reflect failures of the deletion and restraining functions of inhibitory control. Therefore, intrusion errors that were either previous targets (reflecting failures of deletion) or new words (reflecting failures of restraint) were hypothesized to increase with age.

In addiction to examining the relationship between age, error patterns, and span scores, the present study was able to assess this relationship for people with and without reading disabilities. In the current study, participants with reading disabilities were characterized by deficits in word recognition. However, in much of the research investigating the relationship between inhibitory control and reading skill, the less skilled readers were not individuals with reading disabilities. They were university students who read within the normal range of adult reading skill (see, e.g., Gernsbacher & Faust, 1991; Gernsbacher & Robertson, 1995; Gernsbacher et al., 1990; Whitney et al., 1991). Although deficits in suppression mechanisms interfered with reading comprehension among normal adult readers, there is little evidence that impaired inhibitory control is related to the deficient word recognition skills associated with reading disability. In fact, there is considerable evidence that impairments in **phonological processing** inhibit the development of fluent word recognition among disabled readers of all ages (e.g., Bruck, 1990, 1992; Bruck & Treiman, 1990; Perfetti, 1985; Rack, Snowling, & Olson, 1992; Share, 1995; Siegel & Ryan, 1988; Stanovich & Siegel, 1994). Consequently, individuals with reading disabilities tend to have limited **automaticity** in word recognition and are dependent on slow, capacity-draining word recognition processes (Stanovich, 1986). Although limited working memory capacity may interfere with the slow, demanding processes involved in word recognition for disabled readers, impairments in inhibitory control may also contribute to poor word recognition. For example, because disabled readers are less skilled at applying appropriate **grapheme–phoneme correspondences** (Chiappe & Siegel, 1999), disabled readers must inhibit inappropriate grapheme–phoneme correspondences. Failures to inhibit incorrect candidate pronunciations may further impair performance in word recognition. Therefore, it is possible that deficits in inhibitory control interfere with the word recognition of disabled readers.

Experiment 1

Method

Participants

The analyses presented here combined the data from adults and children who participated in one of a series of published and unpublished studies (e.g., Chiappe & Siegel, 1999; Shafrir & Siegel, 1992; Siegel, 1994). This total sample included 665 individuals—351 skilled readers and 314 individuals with reading disabilities. Participants from these studies had been recruited from schools, universities, colleges, and community agencies; some were volunteers from the community. The sample was predominantly middle class. All participants had been educated in English. Participants were classified as disabled reader if they had scores below the 26th percentile on the Wide Range Achievement Test (WRAT; Jastak & Jastak, 1978; WRAT–R, Jastak & Wilkinson, 1984; WRAT–3, Wilkinson, 1994) and an IQ > 79 on an abbreviated version of the Wechsler Intelligence for Children (WISC–R; Sattler, 1982; Weschler, 1974) or the Wechsler Adult Intelligence Scale—Revised (WAIS–R; Silverstein, 1992; Weschler, 1974) that included the Vocabulary and the Block Design subtests.

Participants were arbitrarily divided into five age groups: 6–9, 10–19, 20–29, 30–39, and 40–49. The numbers of skilled readers (first number in parentheses) and disabled readers (second number in parentheses) within each age group were: 6–9 (98, 108), 10–19 (85, 68), 20–29 (99, 81), 30–39 (43, 45), and 40–49 (26, 12).

Reading Tests

The reading subtest of the Wide Range Achievement Test (WRAT, WRAT–R, or WRAT–3) tested individuals' ability to read single words in isolation.

Working Memory

The blocked design of the listening span task was based on the procedure developed by Daneman and Carpenter (1980). The experimenter read to participants sentences each of which was missing its final word. Participants supplied the missing word and attempted to repeat all the set's missing words on completion of the set. Sets contained two, three, or four sentences. Each set size, or level, contained three trials. To reduce difficulties in word retrieval, the sentences were selected so that the final word was virtually predetermined. None of the participants experienced difficulties in providing the final word. Examples of sentences were as follows: "In a baseball game, the pitcher throws the ___; "On my two hands, I have ten ___." Participants then attempted to repeat the two words that they had selected, in this case, *ball* and *fingers*. The task was discontinued when an individual failed all three items at a given level.

An absolute span score was calculated for each participant using the procedure developed by Engle and his colleagues (Engle, Cantor, & Carullo, 1992; Engle, Nations, & Cantor, 1990). To calculate the absolute span score, the number of words recalled on perfectly recalled trials was summed. In perfectly recalled trials, participants were not penalized for recalling the words in an incorrect order. Thus, if a participant perfectly recalled all three trials of Set Length 2, two trials of Set Length 3, and recalled none of the trials with a set length of four perfectly, the absolute span score would be 12. The highest possible absolute span score was 27.

Error Analyses

Because the purpose of this study was to evaluate the role of inhibition in working memory, two types of errors, no responses (or omissions) and intrusion errors, were analyzed. Omissions were analyzed as a proportion of all errors. That is, the number of items for which the participant did not provide a response was divided by the total number of target words that were not recalled correctly. Intrusion errors occurred when participants misrecalled a target word and provided another word as the response. Three categories of mutually exclusive errors were considered. The first type of error, current nonfinal (CNF) intrusions, were errors in which the response was a word from the current trial but was not one of the target words. CNF intrusions reflected deficient inhibition that resulted in increased entry into working memory of irrelevant information. The second type of error, previous (P) intrusions, were responses in which either target words or nonfinal words from earlier trials were recalled. Previous intrusions reflect proactive interference that may result from the failure to inhibit information once it has become irrelevant. Finally, extraneous (E) intrusions were errors in which the response was a word that had not been presented in the current or previous trials. Extraneous intrusions may reflect deficiencies in the restraining function of inhibition. The total number of intrusion errors and the raw score of each type of error were used as dependent variables.

Results

The results for the absolute span scores are shown in Figure 1 and the two left columns in the top portion of Table 1. A 5 (age) × 2 (reading group) analysis of variance (ANOVA) indicated significant main effects of age [$F(4,655) = 104.21, p < .001$] and reading group [$F(4,655) = 33.40, p < .001$]. The interaction between age and reading group was also significant [$F(4,655) = 3.77, p < .01$]. This blocked version of the working memory task revealed an increase in working memory capacity for both skilled and disabled readers until age 20, at which point scores started to decline. This pattern of performance is consonant with the literature (Siegel, 1994). Individual comparisons for each age group (*t* tests) indicated that skilled readers had higher scores than disabled readers at each age level. In general, there were significant differences between the first three adjacent age groups (under 10, 10–19, and 20–29). The scores of children under 10 were significantly lower than those of the other groups, while the scores of the 10–19 age group were significantly higher than those of all other groups. The interaction was determined both by a greater increase in working memory performance for skilled readers than for disabled readers as they went

TABLE 1 Mean Span Scores, Error Rates, and Standard Deviations on the Blocked and Mixed Designs of the Working Memory Task as a Function of Age and Reading Skill

| | Absolute Span | | | | No Response | | | | Total Intrusion | | | | Current Nonfinal Intrusions | | | | Previous Final Intrusion | | | | Extraneous Intrusions | | | |
| | Skilled Readers | | Disabled Readers | | Skilled Readers | | Disabled Readers | | Skilled Readers | | Disabled Readers | | Skilled Readers | | Disabled Readers | | Skilled Readers | | Disabled Readers | | Skilled Readers | | Disabled Readers | |
Age	M	SD	M	SD	M	SD	M	SD	M	SD	M	SD	M	SD	M	SD	M	SD	M	SD	M	SD	M	SD
									Blocked Design															
6–9	5.16	4.81	4.85	5.32	.89	.17	.89	.12	1.48	1.39	1.42	1.62	0.79	0.92	0.74	1.10	0.39	0.74	0.35	0.78	0.31	0.66	0.32	0.68
10–19	18.06	6.63	14.25	5.77	.78	.31	.78	.23	.81	1.06	1.29	1.32	0.44	0.64	0.72	0.83	0.22	0.61	0.38	0.65	0.15	0.48	0.19	0.47
20–29	16.67	6.38	12.54	5.61	.79	.30	.76	.24	.81	0.99	1.64	1.59	0.40	0.67	1.1	1.31	0.35	0.61	0.42	0.95	0.05	0.22	0.21	0.49
30–39	15.16	6.78	12.87	5.21	.73	.27	.80	.19	1.28	1.22	1.44	1.41	0.77	0.81	1.1	1.16	0.40	0.73	0.24	0.53	0.12	0.32	0.11	0.32
40–49	15.50	7.23	9.67	6.88	.78	.27	.81	.17	0.92	1.09	2.0	1.65	0.73	0.92	1.33	1.23	0.19	0.40	.33	.78	0	0	.33	0.49
									Mixed Design															
6–9	5.76	4.22	3.13	3.15	.77	.19	.69	.20	2.55	2.29	4.76	3.77	1.31	1.75	3.03	3.03	0.79	1.12	0.71	1.34	0.45	0.76	1.02	1.23
10–19	8.44	4.76	3.88	4.47	.73	.27	.68	.22	2.69	2.98	4.63	3.90	1.44	2.28	3.25	2.89	1.13	1.09	0.75	0.86	0.13	0.50	0.63	1.09
20–29	13.94	6.12	7.47	5.15	.68	.24	.64	.25	1.61	1.29	4.00	4.26	0.61	0.70	3.0	3.93	0.78	0.88	0.79	1.32	0.22	0.43	0.21	0.54
30–39	14.00	6.75	9.96	6.82	.66	.31	.60	.30	1.81	1.74	3.33	2.73	0.65	0.80	2.07	2.06	0.96	1.25	1.07	1.39	0.19	0.49	0.19	0.40
40–49	15.30	8.21	6.40	5.13	.67	.31	.60	.19	1.10	1.00	5.40	3.78	0.60	0.70	3.60	2.70	0.30	0.68	1.40	1.14	0.20	0.42	0.40	0.55

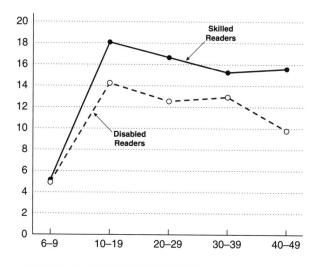

FIGURE 1   *Absolute span scores as a function of age and reading skill on the blocked version of the working memory task.*

from the youngest age group to the 10–19 group, and by a decline in performance seen in disabled readers in the 40–49 age group. This decline was not shown by skilled readers.

Error Analyses

No Responses.   The proportion of no responses is shown in the top half of Table 1. All dependent variables were analyzed using 5 (age) × 2 (reading group) ANOVAs. The rate of no responses differed significantly among the five age groups [$F(4,624) = 8.59, p < .001$]. However, neither the main effect of reading group [$F(1,624) < 1$, n.s.] nor the age × reading group interaction was significant [$F(4,419) < 1$, n.s.]. Post hoc comparisons (Fischer's PLSD) indicated that children under 10 committed more no response errors than did all groups of older participants; there were no differences in omission rates as a function of reading skill.

Total Intrusions.   The mean number of intrusion errors is shown in the top half of Table 1. Skilled readers produced fewer intrusion errors than disabled readers [$F(1,655) = 14.60$, $p < .001$]. Although there was no effect of age [$F(4,655) = 2.18$, n.s.], the age × reading group interaction was significant [$F(4,655) = 3.40, p < .01$]. The interaction was determined by a decline in intrusions produced by skilled readers between the ages of 10 and 29 that was not shown by disabled readers.

Current Nonfinal Intrusions.   The mean number of CNF intrusions is shown in the top half of Table 1. There was a significant main effect of age [$F(4,655) = 2.71, p < .05$]. Post hoc comparisons (Fischer's PLSD) indicated that adolescents between the ages of 10 and 19 produced significantly fewer CNF intrusion errors than participants older than 29.

Skilled readers produced fewer CNF intrusions than disabled readers [$F(1,655) = 15.82$, $p < .001$]. The age × reading group interaction was also significant [$F(4,655) = 3.66$, $p < .01$]. The interaction was determined by a decline in CNF intrusions produced by skilled readers between the ages of 10 and 29 that was not shown by disabled readers.

Previous Intrusions.   The mean number of P intrusions is shown in the upper portion of Table 1. The P intrusion rates did not differ significantly among the five age groups [$F(4, 655) < 1$, n.s.] or the two reading groups [$F(1,655) < 1$, n.s.]. The age × reading group interaction was not significant [$F(4,655) < 1$, n.s.].

Extraneous Intrusions.   The mean number of E intrusions is shown in the two right columns in the top half of Table 1. There was a significant main effect of age [$F(4,655) = 4.46$, $p < .01$]. Post hoc comparisons (Fischer's PLSD) indicated that children under the age of 10 produced significantly more E intrusion errors than did all the other participants. Skilled readers produced fewer E intrusions than did disabled readers [$F(1,655) = 5.08$, $p < .01$]. The age × reading group interaction was not significant [$F(4,655) = 1.24$, n.s.].

Discussion

At each age, skilled readers had higher listening span scores than did disabled readers. Thus, difficulties in working memory for disabled readers extend beyond childhood into adolescence and adulthood These findings are consistent with the literature (Siegel, 1994). Deficits in inhibitory control may contribute to disabled readers' lower span scores. Overall, disabled readers produced more intrusion errors than skilled readers. In fact, CNF intrusions and E intrusions were particularly difficult for disabled readers, suggesting that disabled readers were less efficient in the access and restraint functions of inhibition. Deficits in the access and restraint functions of inhibition would permit irrelevant information increased entry into working memory. However, proactive interference, as indicated by P intrusions, was not problematic for disabled readers. Thus, the current findings suggest that deficits in the access and restraint functions of inhibitory control may contribute to the difficulties experienced by disabled readers in working memory.

The current study revealed that working memory performance increased steadily through childhood and adolescence and then gradually declined after age 20 (which is consistent with Siegel, 1994). The results of the error analyses provided mixed support for the inhibitory control hypothesis. Adolescents between the ages of 10 and 19 produced fewer CNF errors (which would indicate failures in the access function of inhibition) than did adults older than 29. However, the significant interaction for the CNF errors suggests that disabled readers do not experience the increased efficiency in the access function of inhibition between the ages of 10 and 29 that is experienced by skilled readers. In contrast, the error patterns of the P intrusions and E intrusions did not support the inhibitory control hypothesis. In fact, there was no effect of age for the previous intrusions. Similarly, although young children produced more E errors than adolescents and adults, participants older than 10 produced E errors with comparable frequency. Thus, the error analysis suggests that only the access function of inhibitory control may account for the decline in working memory performance associated with aging.

Experiment 2

The data from Experiment 1 suggest that deficits in working memory performance associated with reading disability may result from inefficient inhibitory control. The deficits in the access and restraint functions of inhibitory control among individuals with reading disabilities were consistent with evidence of deficient suppression mechanisms among university students who were less skilled readers (Gernsbacher & Faust, 1991; Gernsbacher et al., 1990). However, Experiment 1 provided limited support for the hypothesis that age-related declines in working memory performance were caused by deficits in inhibitory control. Although older adults showed impairments in the access function of inhibition, there was no relationship between aging and the deletion or restraint functions of inhibition. These results were surprising in light of other studies showing that the effects of proactive interference increase with age (e.g., Kane & Hasher, 1996; May et al., 1996).

Another way of addressing the hypothesis that declines in working memory spans result from diminished inhibitory control is by changing the procedure for administering the working memory task. If declines in working memory are the result of deficient inhibitory control, then changing the procedure to minimize proactive interference should reduce age differences. In fact, Hasher and her colleagues eliminated age differences in working memory spans by making such alterations. For example, although adults aged 60 and older had lower span scores than young adults when span measures were presented in the typical **ascending order,** age differences completely disappeared when span measures were presented in **descending order** (May et al., 1996). Similarly, older adults' working memory spans were as large as those of young adults when the distinctiveness of each trial was enhanced by administering a 90-sec nonverbal distractor task after each trial (May et al., 1996). Although deficits in inhibitory control may play an important role in working memory for adults over 60, it is less clear whether such deficits influence the working memory performance of middle-aged adults. Similarly, it is less clear whether altering the procedure would benefit poor readers to the same extent as older adults.

The purpose of Experiment 2 was to further examine the role of inhibition in working memory. The role of inhibitory control was assessed in two ways. First, the inhibitory control hypothesis was tested by presenting the working memory span task using a mixed design in which three sets of trials each contained two, three, and four sentences. Because the inhibitory control hypothesis proposes that inhibition would be diminished for individuals susceptible to proactive interference when trials are distinctive, support for the inhibitory control hypothesis would take the form of diminished effects of aging on the span measure when the mixed design of the listening span was administered. In addition, the error analysis used in Experiment 1 was used to assess the role of inhibitory control in working memory.

Method

Participants

The analyses presented here are based on the combined data from adults and children who participated in one of a series of published and unpublished studies (e.g., Gottardo, Stanovich, & Siegel, 1996; Siegel, 1994). This total sample included 331 individuals—137 skilled readers and 194 disabled readers. Participants from these studies had been recruited from schools, universities, colleges, and community agencies, or they were volunteers from the community. The sample was predominantly middle class. All participants had been educated in English. Participants were classified as reading disabled if they had scores below the 26th percentile on the WRAT (or the WRAT–R or the WRAT–3) and an IQ > 79 on an abbreviated version of the WISC–R or the WAIS–R that included the Vocabulary and the Block Design subtests.

Participants were arbitrarily divided into five age groups: 6–9, 10–19, 20–29, 30–39, and 40–49. The numbers of skilled readers (first number in parentheses) and disabled readers (second number in parentheses) within each age group were as follows: 6–9 (67, 127), 10–19 (16, 16), 20–29 (18, 19), 30–39 (26, 27), and 40–49 (10, 5).

Reading Tests

The reading subtest of the WRAT (or the WRAT–R or the WRAT–3) was administered.

Working Memory

Gottardo et al.'s (1996) adaptation of Daneman and Carpenter's (1980) listening span task was used as the mixed design. Participants were required to listen to a series of sentences and decide whether each was true or false. After listening to each of the sentences in a set, participants attempted to recall the final word of each sentence in the set. As in the blocked design used in Experiment 1, there were three trials containing two sentences, three trials with three sentences, and three trials with four sentences. However, unlike the blocked design, trials of the same length were not blocked. Instead, each of the three sets contained a two-item trial followed by a three-item trial, and ended with a four-item trial. An absolute span score was calculated for each participant using the procedure described in Experiment 1. The maximum score was 27.

Error Analysis

Errors on the listening span task were classified using the procedure outlined in Experiment 1. Using the procedures described above, the relative proportion of no response errors was calculated, as well as the raw scores for the total intrusions, CNF intrusions, P intrusions, and E intrusions.

Results

The results for the absolute span scores are shown in the two left columns in the lower portion of Table 1 and in Figure 2. A 5 (age) × 2 (reading group) ANOVA indicated significant main effects of reading group [$F(1,321) = 49.68, p <.001$] and age [$F(4,321) = 35.31, p <.001$]. The interaction between age and reading group was significant [$F(4,321) = 2.42, p < .05$]. The mixed version of the working memory task revealed an increase in working memory capacity for both skilled and disabled readers throughout the life span. This pattern of performance is in contrast with the pattern revealed in Experiment 1. Individual

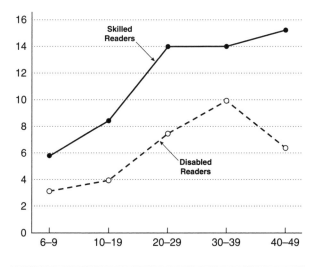

FIGURE 2   *Absolute span scores as a function of age and reading skill on the mixed version of the working memory task.*

comparisons for each age group (*t* tests) indicated that skilled readers had higher scores than disabled readers at each age level. In general, there were significant differences between the first three adjacent age groups (under 10, 10–19, and 20–29). The scores of children under 10 were significantly lower than those of the other groups, and the scores of the 10–19 age group were significantly lower than those of the 20–29, 30–39, and 40–49 groups. The interaction was determined by both a greater increase in working memory performance for skilled readers than for disabled readers as they went from the youngest age group to the 10–19 group, and by a decline in performance seen in poor readers in the 40–49 age group. However, this decline was not shown by skilled readers. In sum, reading span scores increased with age for both skilled readers and disabled readers between the ages of 6 and 29. Thereafter, span scores leveled off for skilled readers and declined for disabled readers.

Error Analyses

No Responses.   The proportion of no responses is shown in the lower half of Table 1. The proportion of no response errors was analyzed using a 5 (age) × 2 (reading group) ANOVA. No response rates declined significantly across the five age groups [$F(4,317) = 2.77, p < .05$]. There was a tendency for skilled readers to produce a greater proportion of no responses [$F(1,317) = 3.27, p < .07$]. The age × reading group interaction was not significant [$F(4,317) < 1$, ns.]. Post hoc comparisons (Fischer's PLSD) indicated that adults in the *30–39* group produced fewer no response errors than did children under 10 and adolescents 10–19 years old.

Total Intrusions.   The mean number of intrusion errors is shown in the bottom half of Table 1. Disabled readers produced more intrusion errors than did skilled readers [$F(1, 321) = 24.41, p < .001$]. There were no significant differences among the age groups [$F(4, 321) = 1.59$, n.s.], and the interaction between age and reading group was not significant [$F(4,321) < 1$, n.s.].

CNF.   The mean number of CNF intrusions is shown in the lower portion of Table 1. The mean number of CNF intrusions was analyzed using a 5 (age) × 2 (reading group) ANOVA. Disabled readers produced more CNF intrusions than did skilled readers [$F(1, 321) = 27.03, p < .001$]. There were no significant differences among the age groups [$F(4, 321) = 1.28$, n.s.], and the interaction between age and reading group was not significant [$F(4,321) < 1$, n.s.].

P Intrusions.   The mean number of P intrusions is shown in the lower portion of Table 1. The P intrusion rates did not differ significantly among the five age groups [$F(4,321) < 1$, n.s.] or the two reading groups [$F(1,321) < 1$, n.s.]. The age × reading group interaction was not significant [$F(4,321) < 1$, n.s.].

E Intrusions.   The mean number of E intrusions is shown in the two right columns in the lower half of Table 1. Disabled readers produced more E intrusions than did skilled readers [$F(4,321) = 5.47, p < .001$]. The main effect of age approached significance [$F(4,321) = 2.96, p < .08$]. Post hoc comparisons (Fischer's PLSD) suggested that children under the age of 10 produced more E intrusions than adults between the ages of 20–49. The interaction was not significant [$F(4,321) = 1.55$, n.s.].

Discussion

Skilled readers consistently earned higher listening span scores than disabled readers. These results are consistent with the findings of Experiment 1. The failure of the mixed design to eliminate differences between skilled readers and disabled readers suggests that disabled readers' deficits in working memory cannot be attributed to proactive interference. Further, there was no suggestion that disabled readers produced more P intrusions than skilled readers, although P intrusions are considered an index of proactive inhibition. Together, these two findings indicate that disabled readers' difficulties in working memory are not the result of deficits in the deletion function of inhibition. In contrast, individuals with reading disabilities demonstrated difficulties in both the access and the restraint functions of inhibition, since they produced more CNF and E errors than did skilled readers. These findings, which were convergent with those of Experiment 1, suggest that disabled readers have difficulties in screening out irrelevant information. Thus, deficits in the access and restraint functions of inhibitory control may contribute to the lower listening span scores of disabled readers.

Although the standard blocked design used in Experiment 1 revealed that working memory performance increased steadily until adolescence, and then gradually declined after age 20, the mixed design did not reveal such a decline, except for poor readers. In fact, with the mixed design of the working memory task, adults over the age of 19 had significantly higher span scores than children and adolescents. However, the span scores for each group of adults did not differ. These findings, together with those of May et al. (1996), suggest that proactive interference plays an important role in the decline of working memory performance associated with aging. Both the procedural changes used in the present study and the changes used by May et al. (1996) demonstrated that working memory spans would not decline with age if proactive interference was minimized. Similarly, the results of the error analyses suggest that the mixed design reduced differences associated with aging with respect to the role of inhibition in working memory. In fact, none of the error categories revealed evidence for the decline in inhibitory control associated with aging using the mixed design. Therefore, decreases in working memory associated with aging might be attributed to declines in inhibitory control rather than declines in capacity.

General Discussion

The current study investigated the role of proactive interference in working memory in two main ways. The role of inhibitory control was considered in relation to reading skill and in relation to age. Each will be discussed in turn.

At each age, there were differences between skilled and disabled readers on the working memory tasks, suggesting that difficulties in working memory for disabled readers extend beyond childhood into adolescence and adulthood. The finding of a persistent working memory deficit through the life span of disabled readers is consistent with the literature (Siegel, 1994). Deficient suppression mechanisms control may have contributed to disabled readers' lower span scores. In fact, both the standard blocked and mixed designs of the listening span task revealed deficits in the access and restraint functions of inhibitory control among disabled readers. That is, disabled readers had greater difficulty in preventing irrelevant information from entering working memory. However, disabled readers' impairments in inhibition did not include greater susceptibility to proactive interference. For example, although the mixed design was expected to reduce the influence of proactive interference on memory span, differences between skilled readers and disabled readers remained. Similarly, disabled readers did not have difficulties with the deletion functions of inhibitory control, as indicated by the fact that they produced previous final word intrusions with the same frequency as skilled readers. Therefore, the current study extends evidence of deficient suppression mechanisms among normally achieving university students who are less skilled comprehenders (e.g., Gernsbacher & Faust, 1991; Gernsbacher & Robertson, 1995; Gernsbacher et al., 1990; Whitney et al., 1991) to populations of individuals with reading disabilities.

The two working memory tasks revealed very different patterns in terms of the declines in working memory associated with aging from adolescence to midlife. Although both designs showed increases in performance with increasing age through childhood and adolescence, the patterns of performance diverged in adulthood. The blocked design showed a decline after age 20 (which is consistent with Siegel, 1994), whereas the mixed design did not. Similarly, the absence of age effects in the error data in Experiment 2 suggest that the mixed design reduced the effects of inhibition. These findings suggest the importance of inhibitory control for older adults. Simply changing the procedure of the listening span to diminish proactive interference resulted in improved performance for middle-aged adults as well as young adults. Thus, the span data are consistent with other studies suggesting that declines in working memory reported for older adults may result from difficulties in inhibiting irrelevant information rather than declines in working memory capacity (Hartman & Hasher, 1991; Hasher & Zacks, 1988; Hasher et al., 1999; May et al., 1996).

However, the error analyses using the blocked format of the working memory task provided only mixed support for the relation between inhibitory control and aging. The error patterns revealed for the CNF intrusions, which were hypothesized to reflect failures in the access function of inhibition, were consistent with the inhibitory control hypothesis. The greater frequency of CNF intrusions among participants older than 29 suggests that the older adults experienced greater difficulties in preventing goal-irrelevant information from entering working memory. However, the relationship between the efficiency of the access function of inhibitory control and age was restricted to skilled readers. The frequency of CNF errors was unrelated to age among disabled readers, who showed general impairments in denying goal-irrelevant information access into working memory. In contrast, although P intrusions were hypothesized to reflect failures in the deletion function of inhibition and to lead to proactive interference, older adults produced as many P intrusion errors as younger participants did in both experiments. These findings are surprising in light of other studies that have shown greater susceptibility to proactive interference in older adults (e.g., Kane & Hasher, 1996). Finally, there was little evidence of declines in the restraint function of inhibition. Therefore, the errors produced using the blocked design provided evidence for the hypothesis that decreases in working memory associated with aging may be attributed to declines in the access function of inhibitory control rather than declines in capacity.

In summary, deficits in working memory are characteristic of disabled readers throughout the life span. Working memory skills develop through childhood and adolescence; however, the standard blocked design revealed declines in middle adulthood whereas the mixed design did not. The different patterns suggest that the decline in working memory skills associated with aging may result from growing inefficiencies in inhibitory control rather than diminished capacity. These declines were associated with growing inefficiencies in the access function of inhibition. In contrast, disabled readers' difficulties in working memory result from smaller working memory capacity in addition to difficulties in restricting access to the working memory system to relevant information.

References

Babcock, R. L., & Salthouse, T. A. (1990). Effects of increased demands on age differences in working memory. *Psychology & Aging, 5,* 421–428.

Baddeley, A. D. (1983). Working memory. *Philosophical Transactions of the Royal Society of London: Series B,* **302,** 311–324.

Baddeley, A. D. (1986). *Working memory.* London: Oxford University Press.

Bruck, M. (1990). Word-recognition skills of adults with childhood diagnoses of dyslexia. *Developmental Psychology,* **26,** 439–454.

Bruck, M. (1992). Persistence of dyslexics' phonological awareness deficits. *Developmental Psychology,* **28,** 874–886.

Bruck, M., & Treiman, R. (1990). Phonological awareness and spelling in normal children and dyslexics: The case of initial consonant clusters. *Journal of Experimental Child Psychology, 50,* 156–178.

Campbell, J. I. D., & Charness, N. (1990). Age-related declines in working-memory skills: Evidence from a complex calculation task. *Developmental Psychology, 26,* 879–888.

Case, R., Kurland, D. M., & Goldberg, J. (1982). Operational efficiency and the growth of short-term memory span. *Journal of Experimental Child Psychology, 28,* 386–404.

Chiappe, P., & Siegel, L. S. (1999). Phonological awareness and reading acquisition in English and Punjabi-speaking Canadian children. *Journal of Educational Psychology, 91,* 20–28.

Da Fontoura, H. A., & Siegel, L. S. (1995). Reading, syntactic, and working memory skills of bilingual Portuguese–English Canadian children. *Reading & Writing: An Interdisciplinary Journal, 7,* 139–153.

Daneman, M., & Carpenter, P. A. (1980). Individual differences in working memory and reading. *Journal of Verbal Learning & Verbal Behavior, 19,* 450–466.

De Beni, R., Palladino, P., Pazzaglia, R., & Cornoldi, C. (1998). Increases in intrusion errors and working memory deficit of poor comprehenders. *Quarterly Journal of Experimental Psychology, 51A,* 305–320.

Engle, R. W., Cantor, J., & Carullo, J. J. (1992). Individual differences in working memory and comprehension: A test of four hypotheses. *Journal of Experimental Psychology: Learning. Memory; & Cognition, 18,* 972–992.

Engle, R. W., Nations, J. K., & Cantor, J. (1990). Is "working memory capacity" just another name for word knowledge? *Journal of Educational Psychology, 82,* 799–804.

Gernsbacher, M. A. (1990). *Language comprehension as structure building.* Hillsdale, NJ: Erlbaum.

Gernsbacher, M. A., & Faust, M. E. (1991). The mechanism of suppression: A component of general comprehension skill. *Journal of Experimental Psychology: Learning, Memory, & Cognition, 17,* 245–262.

Gernsbacher, M. A., & Robertson, R. R. W. (1995). Reading skill and suppression revisited. *Psychological Science, 6,* 165–169.

Gernsbacher, M. A., Varner, K. R., & Faust, M. E. (1990). Investigating differences in general comprehension skill. *Journal of Experimental Psychology: Learning, Memory, & Cognition, 16,* 430–445.

Geva, E., & Siegel, L. S. (in press). The role of orthography and cognitive factors in the concurrent development of basic reading skills in bilingual children. *Reading & Writing: An Interdisciplinary Journal.*

Gick, M. L., Craik, F. I. M., & Morris, R. G. (1988). Task complexity and age differences in working memory. *Memory & Cognition, 16,* 353–361.

Gottardo, A., Stanovich, K. E., & Siegel, L. S. (1996). The relationships between phonological sensitivity, syntactic processing, and verbal working memory in the reading performance of third-grade children. *Journal of Experimental Child Psychology, 63,* 563–582.

Hamm, V. P., & Hasher L. (1992). Age and the availability of inferences. *Psychology & Aging, 7,* 56–64.

Hartman, M., & Hasher, L. (1991). Aging and suppression: Memory for previously relevant information. *Psychology & Aging, 6,* 597–594.

Hasher, L., Stoltzfus, E. R., Rumpa, B., & Zacks, R. T. (1991). Age and inhibition. *Journal of Experimental Psychology: Learning, Memory, & Cognition, 17,* 163–169.

Hasher, L., & Zacks, R. T. (1988). Working memory, comprehension, and aging: A review and a new view. In G. H. Bower (Ed.), *The psychology of learning and motivation* (Vol. 22, pp. 193–225). San Diego: Academic Press.

Hasher, L., Zacks, R. T., & May, C. P. (1999). Inhibitory control, circadian arousal, and age. In D. Gopher & A. Koriat (Eds.), *Attention and performance XVII: Cognitive regulation of performance: Interaction of theory and application* (pp. 653–675). Cambridge, MA: MIT Press.

Hitch, G. J., & Halliday, M. S. (1983). Working memory in children. *Philosophical Transactions of the Royal Society of London: Series B, 302,* 325–340.

Jastak, J. R., & Jastak, S. R. (1978). *Wide range achievement test.* Wilmington, DE: Jastak Associates.

Jastak, S., & Wilkinson, G. S. (1984). *Wide range achievement test—revised.* Wilmington, DE: Jastak Associates.

Kane, M. J., & Hasher, L. (1996). Interference. In G. Maddox (Ed.). *Encyclopedia of aging* (2nd ed.). New York: Springer-Verlag.

Kane, M. J., May, C. P., Hasher, L., & Rahhal, T. (1997). Dual mechanisms of negative priming. *Journal of Experimental Psychology: Human Perception & Performance, 23,* 632–650.

Light, L. L., & Anderson, P. A. (1985). Working-memory capacity, age, and memory for discourse. *Journal of Gerontology, 40,* 737–747.

May, C. P., Kane, M. J., & Hasher, L. (1995). Determinants of negative priming. *Psychological Bulletin,* **118,** 35–54.

May, C. P., Kane, M. J., Hasher, L., & Valenti, M. (1996, November). *Proactive interference and working memory span.* Paper presented at the annual meeting of the Psychonomic Society, Chicago.

Morris, R. G., Gick, M. L., & Craik, F. I. M. (1988). Processing resources and age differences in working memory. *Memory & Cognition,* **16,** 362–366.

Perfetti, C. A. (1985). *Reading ability.* New York: Oxford University Press.

Rack, L. P., Snowling, M. J., & Olson, R. K. (1992). The nonword reading deficit in developmental dyslexia: A review. *Reading Research Quarterly,* **27,** 28–53.

Salthouse, T. A., & Babcock, R. L. (1991). Decomposing age differences in working memory. *Developmental Psychology,* **27,** 763–776.

Sattler, J. M. (1982). *Assessment of children's intelligence and special abilities* (3rd ed.). Boston: Allyn & Bacon.

Shafrir, U., & Siegel, L. S. (1992). *Subtypes of learning disabilities in adolescents and adults.* Unpublished manuscript, Ontario Institute for Studies in Education, Toronto.

Share, D. L. (1995). Phonological recoding and self-teaching: *Sine qua non* of reading acquisition. *Cognition,* **55,** 151–218.

Siegel, L. S. (1994). Working memory and reading: A lifespan perspective. *International Journal of Behavioral Development,* **17,** 109–124.

Siegel, L. S., & Linder, B. A. (1984). Short-term memory processes in children with reading and arithmetic teaming disabilities. *Developmental Psychology,* **24,** 28–37.

Siegel, L. S., & Ryan, E. B. (1988). Development of grammatical sensitivity, phonological, and short-term memory skills in normally achieving and learning disabled children. *Developmental Psychology,* **24,** 28–37.

Silverstein, A. B. (1982). Two- and four-subtest short forms of the Wechsler Adult Intelligence Scale— Revised. *Journal of Counseling & Clinical Psychology,* **50,** 415–415.

So, D., & Siegel, L. S. (1997). Learning to read Chinese: Semantic, syntactic, phonological and short-term memory skills in normally achieving and poor Chinese readers. *Reading & Writing: An Interdisciplinary Journal,* **9,** 1–21.

Stanovich, K. E. (1986). Matthew effects in reading: Some consequences of individual differences in the acquisition of literary. *Reading Research Quarterly,* **21,** 360–407.

Stanovich, K. E., & Siegel, L. S. (1994). Phenotypic performance profile of children with reading disabilities: A regression-based test of the phonological-core variable-difference model. *Journal of Educational Psychology,* **86,** 24–53.

Stoltzfus, E. R., Hasher, L., Zacks, R. T., Ulivi, M. S., & Goldstein, D. (1993). Investigations of inhibition and interference in younger and older adults. *Journal of Gerontology: Psychological Sciences,* **48,** 179–188.

Swanson, H. L. (1993). Individual differences in working memory: A model testing and subgroup analysis of learning-disabled and skilled readers. *Intelligence,* **17,** 285–332.

Swanson, H. L. (1994). Short-term memory and working memory: Do both contribute to our understanding of academic achievement in children and adults with learning disabilities? *Journal of Learning Disabilities,* **27,** 34–50.

Tirre, W. C., & Peña, C. M. (1992). Investigation of functional working memory in the reading span test. *Journal of Educational Psychology,* **84,** 462–472.

Wechsler, D. (1974). *Manual for the Wechsler intelligence scale for children–Revised.* New York: Psychological Corp.

Wechsler. D. (1981). *Manual for the Wechsler adult intelligence scale–Revised.* New York: Psychological Corp.

Whitney, P., Ritchie, B. G., & Clark, M. B. (1991). Working-memory capacity and the use of elaborative inferences in text comprehension. *Discourse Processes,* **14,** 133–146.

Wilkinson, G. S. (1994). *Wide range achievement test–3.* Wilmington, DE: Jastak Associates.

Wingfield, A., Stine, E., Lahar C. J., & Aberdeen, J. S. (1988). Does the capacity of working memory change with age? *Experimental Aging Research,* **14,** 103–107.

Zacks, R. T., & Hasher, L. (1988). Capacity theory and the processing of inferences. In L. L. Light & D. M. Burke (Eds.), *Language, memory and aging* (pp. 154–170). New York: Cambridge University Press.

Introduction: Critical Thinking Questions _____

? Briefly describe the reading span task, and how it attempts to separate the processing and storage components of working memory.

? Explain the reason why the differences observed in working memory performance across the lifespan could be due to changes in the capacity of working memory.

? The researchers think that perhaps "…inefficient inhibitory control of attention" may be responsible for the deficits seen in those with reading disability. Explain what they mean with a few examples.

? Inhibitory processes are important in determining what information is being processed in working memory. The researchers delineate three inhibitory processes: *access, deletion,* and *restraint.* Briefly describe each of these processes.

? Why would the reduction of proactive interference result in a lessening of age-related differences in working memory span? Explain, citing the relevant discussion and experimental results.

? How might deficits in working memory capacity impact the word recognition processes of a reading-disabled reader?

? In Experiment 2, why did the researchers expect the use of a mixed design on the reading span task to lessen age-related deficits?

Method: Critical Thinking Questions _____

? For each experiment, describe what you would have been asked to do, had you been a participant in these experiments.

? For each experiment, name the independent variables, and their levels. Describe how each of these variables was operationalized. For each variable, state whether it was manipulated in a between- or within-subjects fashion. How many conditions were there in the experiment?

? What was (were) the dependent variable(s) in each experiment?

? In Experiment 1, describe the different types of errors (*CNF, P,* and *E* intrusions) that were noted for each participant. How do these different types of errors allow the researchers to tease apart different inhibitory processes?

Results/Discussion: Critical Thinking Questions _____

? For Experiment 1, briefly describe the pattern of results with regard to span differences between skilled and disabled readers, and how these differences changed (or failed to change) over the lifespan.

? For Experiment 1, which of the three inhibitory processes discussed in the introduction seems to be central to (1) problems seen in those with reading disabilities and (2) age-related changes in reading? What evidence supports these conclusions and why?

? In Experiment 2, researchers switched to a mixed design in order to increase distinctiveness. What effect did they expect this would have? Was this result found? What does this indicate about the working memory deficits found in disabled readers? Do other results converge on this conclusion? If so describe the result.

? What did the results of Experiment 2 indicate about age-related declines in working memory? Explain.

? The researchers argue that the results of both experiments converge on the conclusion that disabled readers' deficits in working memory stem from problems in the *access* and *restraint* functions of inhibition, rather than the *deletion* function. Explain how they come to this conclusion.

? In discussing age-related changes in working memory span, the researchers contend that their results fit with the view that minimizing proactive interference eliminates age-related working memory deficits. Explain how they come to this conclusion.

? After reading this study, you may feel there are other issues or questions that would be worthwhile or intriguing to address. Pose one of these questions (other than those suggested by the authors) that could be investigated empirically.

In Search of Gender Neutrality

Is Singular They *a Cognitively Efficient Substitute for Generic* He?

Julie Foertsch and Morton Ann Gernsbacher

*Abstract*_____

With increasing frequency, writers and speakers are ignoring grammatical proscription and using the plural pronoun they *to refer to singular antecedents. This change may, in part, be motivated by efforts to make language more gender inclusive. In the current study, two reading-time experiments demonstrated that singular they is a cognitively efficient substitute for generic he or she, particularly when the antecedent is nonreferential. In such instances, clauses containing* they *were read (a) much more quickly than clauses containing a gendered pronoun that went against the gender stereotype of the antecedent, and (b) just as quickly as clauses containing a gendered pronoun that matched the stereotype of the antecedent. However, with referential antecedents, for which the gender was presumably known, clauses containing singular* they *were not read as quickly as clauses containing a gendered pronoun that matched the antecedent's stereotypic gender.*

Conceptual Issues and Theoretical Questions _____

- Which pronoun is best for referring to an earlier antecedent within a text?
- Can a plural pronoun be used in place of a singular pronoun with no loss in comprehension?
- How quickly are different referential pronouns understood while reading a text?
- Do the effectiveness of male and female pronouns depend on whether they're used to refer to stereotypically male and female antecedents?

De-Jargonizing _____

antecedent: a word that, when repeated, is replaced by a pronoun ("Greg" and "Bridget" in the following sentences: Greg and Bridget went to a movie. *They* both really enjoyed *it*.)

Foertsch, J., & Gernsbacher, M. A. (1997). In search of gender neutrality: Is singular *they* a cognitively efficient substitute for generic *he? Psychological Science, 28,* 106–111. Copyright © 1997 by Blackwell Publishing. Reprinted by permission.

anaphor: the word used to refer back to an earlier antecedent (i.e., *they* and *it* in the preceding sentences)

nonreferential antecedent: an antecedent that does not refer to a specific person or entity

indefinite determiners: determiners (e.g., a, an) that do not refer to a specific person or entity

referential antecedent: an antecedent that does refer to a specific person or entity

prescriptive grammar: the rules that define correct and incorrect word arrangement

> In speech we often solve the problem of the generic he by [using] a plural pronoun...as in *Everyone brought their books to class.* But this construction violates the expectations of most readers, so it should be avoided in writing. (Fowler & Aaron, 1983, p. 195)

In spite of proscriptions like this one, using the plural pronoun *they* to refer to a singular person of unknown gender has become ubiquitous, even in writing (Bodine, 1975; MacKay, 1980; Meyers, 1990; Valian, 1977). Ever since generic *he* fell out of favor for being gender biased and presumptive, speakers and writers have been looking for a reasonable alternative (Beardsley, 1973; Bodine, 1975; Flanagan & Todd-Mancillas, 1982; Nilsen, 1984; Spencer, 1978). More and more often, singular *they* is the pronoun of choice.

As ungrammatical as this shift may be, the justification for it is quite clear. The generic *he* that grammarians prescribe is typically perceived as referring to a male, not as being all-inclusive (Khosroshahi, 1989; Kidd, 1971; MacKay & Fulkerson, 1979; Martyna, 1978a; Moulton, Robinson, & Elias, 1978; Silvera, 1980). To counter this inequity, many writers and editors have adopted the policy of using *he or she* in place of generic *he,* even though this construction is awkward when used repeatedly. Other alternatives include using *s/he,* which works only in print, or replacing generic *he* with the generic *she,* a form of linguistic affirmative action.

The alternative examined in the current study, using *they* as a singular pronoun, has been considered by a number of researchers (Bodine, 1975; MacKay, 1980; Martyna, 1978a, 1978b; Valian, 1977). For some situations, singular *they* has even received grammarians' endorsement. Since 1970, grammar handbooks have struggled with the fact that singular *they* seems more natural than generic *he* in certain situations, and most now begrudgingly allow writers to use *they* as a pronoun for two limited classes of singular **antecedents: indefinite pronouns** like *anybody* or *someone* and corporate nouns like *the shop* or *Seattle* (Zuber & Reed, 1993). Of course, *they* used in this way is still in some sense "plural": Indefinite pronouns refer to any person from a group of unspecified persons, and corporate nouns refer to groups of people who form a functional unit.

However, using *they* to refer to an individual of known or unknown gender is still considered problematic. As Strunk and White's (1979) *Elements of Style* asserts, "The furor recently raised about *he* would be more impressive if there were a handy substitute for the word. Unfortunately, there isn't, or at least no one has come up with one yet" (p. 61). However, according to the experiments reported here, a handy substitute for generic he has already been found: namely, singular *they*. Aided by society's increasing resistance to biased language, this genderless singular pronoun has become firmly embedded in the American lexicon (Meyers, 1990). Indeed, it is unclear whether many of the people who now choose to use singular *they* realize that it is "ungrammatical."

How does using *they* as a singular pronoun affect comprehension? The only way to know for sure is through empirical research. In the experiments reported here, the processing cost of using singular *they* in various contexts was measured through the reading times of university undergraduates. As an experiment by Kerr and Underwood (1984) had already demonstrated, readers fixate longer on pronouns that are somehow surprising than on pronouns that are consistent with expectations. In Kerr and Underwood's study, participants read sentences that contained gender-stereotyped antecedents (e.g., *the surgeon, the nurse),* each followed by a gender-specific pronoun that either matched or mismatched the stereotypic gender of the antecedent. Readers were consistently slower reading sentences in which the gender of the pronoun and the gender implied by the antecedent did not match. By this same logic, if using singular *they* is confusing and incurs additional cognitive processing, readers would be slowed when reading a clause that uses *they* to refer to a singular antecedent. Thus, our experiments compared how quickly the pronouns *he, she,* and *they* were read and understood in sentences with antecedents that were stereotypically masculine (e.g., truck *driver*), stereotypically feminine (e.g., *nurse*), gender neutral (e.g., *runner*), or indefinite pronouns (e.g., *anybody*).

In both experiments, readers read three-clause sentences that contained a human antecedent in the first clause and a pronoun referring to that antecedent in the second clause. Readers proceeded through the sentences one clause at a time, pressing a button marked "Continue" when they were ready to advance. In this way, we obtained a reading time for each clause. As in Kerr and Underwood's (1984) experiments, we expected reading times for the clause containing the pronoun to be slower when the pronoun's gender did not match the implied gender of the antecedent. The question of interest was how quickly clauses containing *they* would be read in comparison to clauses containing either *he* or *she*. We reasoned that if *they* is considered an inappropriate or surprising **anaphor** to use with a singular antecedent, comprehenders should be significantly slower reading the clauses containing *they* than the clauses containing *he* or *she*. Therefore, if comprehenders were not significantly slowed when encountering the pronoun *they* with a singular antecedent, the argument that singular *they* "violates the expectations of most readers" would not be empirically supported. Such a result would demonstrate that singular *they* has become an acceptable substitute for generic *he* in the minds of our readers.

Experiment 1

In Experiment 1, participants read 72 three-clause sentences in a self-paced reading task and indicated their agreement or disagreement with the opinion expressed in each sentence. The sentences in Experiment 1 contained **nonreferential antecedents** in the form of common nouns modified by **indefinite determiners,** as in Examples 1 through 3, or indefinite pronouns, as in Example 4.

1. A truck driver should never drive when sleepy,
   even if *he/she/they* may be struggling to make a delivery on time,
   because many accidents are caused by drivers who fall asleep at the wheel.
2. A nurse should have an understanding of how a medication works,
   even if *he/she/they* will not have any say in prescribing it,
   because nurses must anticipate how a patient will respond to the medication.
3. A runner should eat lots of pasta the night before a race,
   even if *he/she/they* would rather have a steak,
   because carbohydrates provide fuel for endurance events, while proteins do not.
4. Anybody who litters should be fined $50,
   even if *he/she/they* cannot see a trashcan nearby,
   because littering is an irresponsible form of vandalism and should be punished.

After each sentence, readers saw a "True or False?" prompt and pressed a button to respond.

The first independent variable was the type of antecedent read in the first clause. The antecedents were stereotypically masculine nouns, stereotypically feminine nouns, neutral nouns, or indefinite pronouns. The second independent variable was the pronoun that appeared in the second clause: *he, she,* or *they.* The dependent variable was the reading time for the clause containing the pronoun. In view of Kerr and Underwood's (1984) results, we anticipated that reading times for sentences that had gender-stereo-typed antecedents (masculine or feminine) would be slowest when the pronoun mismatched the gender stereotype of its antecedent and fastest when the pronoun matched the gender stereo-type of its antecedent. In short, we predicted that *they* would serve as a cognitively efficient compromise. For example, in cases in which the singular antecedent is assumed—but not known—to be female (e.g., *nurse*), using singular *they* to refer to that antecedent might actually be less disruptive than using generic *he.*

For sentences that had neutral or indefinite antecedents, we predicted that reading times for clauses with *they* would be no slower than—and perhaps somewhat faster than—reading times for clauses with *he* or *she.* Our reasoning for this prediction was as follows: First, because of the increased occurrence of singular *they* in colloquial English, sentences that use *they* to refer to an indefinite or gender-neutral singular antecedent are no longer unexpected or surprising. Second, with neutral and indefinite antecedents, clauses containing *they* might be read even faster than clauses containing *he* or *she* because the pronoun *they* adds no new information, whereas the pronouns *he* and *she* seem to specify the gender of an antecedent whose gender was not previously known. Any additional information provided by an anaphor increases processing time (Foertsch & Gernsbacher, 1994; Garnham, 1981, 1984; Garrod & Sanford, 1977). Hence, if the reader has not made a presumption about the gender of the antecedent, or if the reader's presumption does not match the gender that is then specified by the pronoun, the reader will be slower processing a clause that uses a gender-specific pronoun.

Method

Participants

The participants were 87 undergraduates in an introductory psychology course at the University of Wisconsin-Madison. All participants were native English speakers.

Materials

The experimental stimuli were 72 three-clause sentences.[1] The first clause always began with a masculine, feminine, or neutral common noun modified by an indefinite determiner, or with an indefinite pronoun.[2] Care was taken to ensure that nothing in this first clause other than the intended referent could be referred to using the pronouns *he, she,* or *they.* The second clause began with the words "even if," followed by the pronoun *he, she,* or *they.* The verb in the second clause was unmarked for number so that its form was identical regardless of the pronoun used. The third clause, beginning with "because," provided a justification for the opinion expressed in the first two clauses and was included as a buffer so that reading time for the crucial second clause would not be contaminated by a reader's wrap-up processing at the end of each sentence.

The 72 experimental sentences were presented in the same order to all participants. This order was random with the exception that sentences of the same antecedent type (masculine, feminine, neutral, or indefinite pronoun) did not appear more than twice consecutively, and sentences using the same pronoun (*he, she,* or *they*) did not appear more than three times consecutively. Three material sets were created so that each sentence appeared with a different pronoun in each material set. The experiment was conducted as a within-subjects design, with each antecedent type appearing with each pronoun a total of six times per material set.[3]

Procedure

Participants were tested in separate cubicles containing computer screens with three-button response pads. At the beginning of a session, participants read instructions that appeared on their screens. Participants were instructed that they would read a series of three-clause sentences presented one clause at a time, and that they were to advance through each sentence by pressing the "Continue" button. After reading the last clause of each sentence and

---

[1]A list of the sentences used in both experiments is available on request.

[2]A norming study with 40 subjects was conducted to compile a set of common nouns that are typically perceived as referring to a masculine feminine, or neutral entity. Participants rated a list of 82 common noun that described various roles or occupations using a 10-point Likert scale ranging from 1, *Male,* to 10, *Female.* The mean rating for each common noun was calculated. Any noun rated between 1 and 3.5 was classified as "masculine," any noun rated between 4.5 and 6.5 was classified W "neutral," and any noun rated between 7.5 and 10 was classified a: "feminine." Stimuli for each of the three common-noun categories were selected from this set. The fourth category, indefinite pronouns, comprised *everyone, everybody, anyone, anybody, someone,* and *somebody,* each used a total of three times.

[3]Subsequent analyses found no differences in how participants responded to the three material sets, so means are collapsed across material set in the reported analyses of both experiments.

pressing the "Continue" button, the words "True or False?" would appear on the screen. Participants were told to indicate their agreement with the opinion expressed in the sentence by pressing either a button labeled "True" or a button labeled "False." Participants were given three example sentences with which to practice this procedure. After practicing, participants signed informed consent sheets, and the experimenter began the presentation of experimental stimuli.

Each clause of each sentence appeared flush-left in the center of the computer screen. A clause remained on the screen until the participant pressed the "Continue" button or until 20 s elapsed. A 250-ms blank period intervened between consecutive clauses. After participants read the last clause of a sentence and pressed the "Continue" button, the "True or False?" prompt appeared on the screen and remained until the participant responded or 20 s elapsed. A 1.5-s blank period intervened between sentences.

Results and Conclusions

To control for variability in the number and length of words between conditions, reading times for the critical second clauses were divided by the number of characters in each clause.[4] The mean per-character reading times for the three pronoun conditions for each of the four types of antecedent are displayed in Figure 1.

Within-subjects analyses of variance (ANOVAs) with pronoun and material set as factors were performed for each of the four types of antecedent. For both feminine and masculine antecedents, clauses containing opposite-gender pronouns were read most

---

[4]Analyses were also performed using the whole-clause and per-word reading times. Because the results were essentially the same, only the results of per-character analyses are reported.

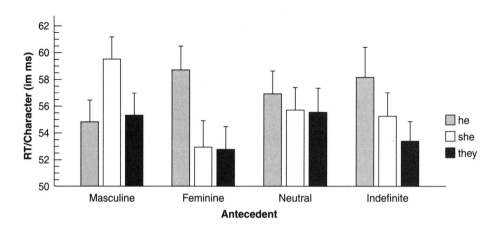

FIGURE 1   *Effects of antecedent type (masculine, feminine, neutral, or indefinite) and pronoun (he, she, or they) on per-character reading time (RT) when sentences were used nonreferentially (Experiment 1).*

slowly. However, clauses containing same-gender pronouns and singular *they* were read with equal facility. More specifically, for masculine antecedents, *she* clauses ($M = 59.5$, $SE = 2.05$) were read significantly more slowly than either *he* clauses ($M = 54.8$, $SE = 1.77$) or *they* clauses ($M = 55.3$, $SE = 1.77$), $F_1(2, 168) = 5.14$, $p = .007$; $F_2(2, 34) = 5.37$, $p = .009$; $\min F'(2, 116) = 2.63$, $p < .05$. In contrast, for masculine antecedents, *he* clauses and *they* clauses were read with equal facility, $F < 1$. For feminine antecedents, *he* clauses ($M = 58.7$, $SE = 1.66$) were read significantly more slowly than either *she* clauses ($M = 52.9$, $SE = 1.64$) or *they* clauses ($M = 52.7$, $SE = 1.67$), $F_1(2, 168) = 11.37$, $p < .0001$; $F_2(2, 34) = 4.87$, $p = .014$; $\min F'(2, 67) = 3.41$, $p < .05$; *she* clauses and *they* clauses were read with equal facility, $F < 1$. Apparently, singular *they* is readily substituted for the same-gender pronoun in sentences in which the antecedent has a strong gender bias.

When the sentence's antecedent was neutral, *he* clauses ($M = 56.9$, $SE = 1.75$), *she* clauses ($M = 55.7$, $SE = 1.73$), and *they* clauses ($M = 55.5$, $SE = 1.86$) were all read with equal facility, $F < 1$. Finally, when the sentence's referent was an indefinite pronoun, singular *they* was the pronoun of choice: *They* clauses ($M = 53.4$, $SE = 1.50$) were read faster than either *she* clauses ($M = 55.3$, $SE = 1.86$) or *he* clauses ($M = 58.2$, $SE = 2.23$), $F_1(2, 168) = 4.41$, $p < .0001$; $F_2(2, 34) = 4.97$, $p = .014$; $\min F'(2, 122) = 2.34$, $p < .05$; planned comparisons show that only the difference between *they* and *he* is significant, $p < .004$. It was anticipated that singular *they* would be the most readily accepted pronoun with indefinite pronoun antecedents like *anyone* because even grammar books have endorsed this usage. Interestingly, with indefinite pronoun antecedents, *she* clauses had a marginally significant advantage over *he* clauses, $p = .081$, suggesting that members of our liberal-minded student body may have been reacting to the perceived chauvinism of using *he* in sentences in which the referent supplies no gender information.

Experiment 2

Experiment 1 demonstrated that singular *they* can be a cognitively efficient substitution for generic *he* or generic *she* when the nonreferential antecedent is either an indefinite pronoun or a common noun with an indefinite determiner. Experiment 2 investigated whether similar results would be found with *referential antecedents*. In Experiment 2, we removed the indefinite pronoun sentences and modified the remaining masculine, feminine, and neutral antecedents to make them referential, giving the reader the impression that each sentence was about a specific person whose gender was presumably known. To accomplish this, the antecedents were modified by the definite determiner *that*, as in Example 5; by first-person possessives, as in Example 6; or by indicators that the antecedent was personally known to the speaker, as in Example 7:

5. That truck driver shouldn't drive when sleepy,
    even if *he/she/they* may be trying to make a delivery on time,
    because many accidents are caused by drivers who fall asleep at the wheel.
6. My nurse was able to explain how my medication would affect me,
    even though *he/she/they* had no say in prescribing it,
    because nurses must anticipate how patients will respond to medication.

7. A runner I knew always ate lots of pasta the night before a race,
   even when *he/she/they* would've rather had a steak,
   because carbohydrates provide fuel for endurance events, while proteins do not.

After reading each sentence, participants responded to a yes/no question, such as "Do you agree?" We assume that speakers and writers are less likely to use singular *they* in situations in which the antecedent's gender is known than in situations in which the antecedent is a hypothetical person of indeterminate gender. The question of interest was whether readers are sensitive to this difference.

Method

Participants

The participants were 108 undergraduates in an introductory psychology course at the University of Wisconsin-Madison. None had participated in Experiment 1. All participants were native English speakers.

Materials

The experimental stimuli were 54 three-clause sentences expressing opinions about the behavior of specified persons in particular situations. The sentences were based on those used in Experiment 1 except that each antecedent was made more specific (i.e., referential) by modifying it as illustrated in Examples 5 through 7. A norming study with 30 subjects ascertained that the resulting antecedents were overwhelmingly comprehended as referring to "one particular person" and were rarely if ever perceived as plural. After the third clause of each sentence, participants read a yes/no question pertaining to the sentence. About one third of the questions asked whether the participant agreed with the opinion or behavior expressed in the sentence, about one third asked if anything similar had ever happened to the participant, and about one third asked if the participant agreed with a proposed course of action.

Procedure

The procedure was the same as in Experiment 1 except that participants responded to a yes/no question instead of the "True or False?" prompt after each sentence.

Results and Conclusions

As in Experiment 1, the dependent variable was the percharacter reading time for the second clause. The mean percharacter reading times for the three pronoun conditions for each of the three types of antecedent are displayed in Figure 2.

Within-subjects ANOVAs with pronoun and material set as factors were performed for each of the three types of antecedent. For masculine antecedents, same-gender *he* clauses resulted in the fastest reading times ($M = 51.7$, $SE = 1.28$), and opposite-gender *she*

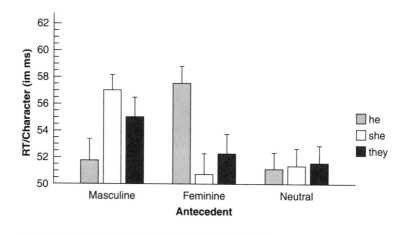

FIGURE 2   *Effects of antecedent type (masculine, feminine, or neutral) and pronoun (**he, she,** or **they**) on per-character reading time (RT) when sentences were used referentially (Experiment 2).*

clauses resulted in the slowest reading times ($M = 57.0$, $SE = 1.56$), whereas *they* clauses had an intermediate reading time ($M = 55.0$, $SE = 151$), $F_1(2, 210) = 12.76$, $p < .0001$; $F_2(2, 34) = 3.84$, $p = 031$; $\min F'(2, 57) = 2.96$, $p < .05$. As in Experiment 1, planned comparisons showed the reading times for *she* clauses to be significantly slower than the reading times of *he* clauses, $p < .05$. However, in contrast to Experiment 1, the reading times for *they* clauses, though marginally faster than those for *she* clauses, $p = .065$, were also significantly slower than those for *he* clauses, $p < .05$. The feminine antecedents showed a similar pattern: Same-gender *she* clauses resulted in the fastest reading times ($M = 50.7$, $SE = 1.16$), and opposite-gender *he* clauses in the slowest reading times ($M = 57.8$, $SE = 1.66$), whereas *they* clauses had an intermediate reading time ($M = 52.2$, $SE = 1.41$), $F_1(2, 210) = 19.38$, $p < .0001$; $F_2(2, 34) = 8.87$, $p = .0008$; $\min F'(2, 70) = 6.08$, $p < .05$. Planned comparisons showed reading times for the *he* clauses to be significantly slower than the reading times of either the *she* clauses or the *they* clauses, $p < .05$, but *they* clauses were also marginally slower than *she* clauses, $p = .10$.

Thus, when the antecedents are referential, singular *they* is no longer as efficient as a gendered pronoun that matches the gender stereotype of the antecedent. For example, in sentences in which the antecedent suggests a male and the explicitness of the modifiers suggests the informant is talking about a particular person whose gender should be known, using *they* as an anaphor produces almost as much of a slowdown as using *she*. Looking at the neutral antecedents, in contrast, we see no such disadvantage for clauses using *they*. As in Experiment 1, there were no significant differences in the reading times for *he* clauses ($M = 51.1$, $SE = 1.24$), *she* clauses ($M = 51.3$, $SE = 1.35$), and *they* clauses ($M = 515$, $SE = 1.40$), $F < 1$.

The results from these experiments support the contention that singular *they* is an acceptable substitution for gender-specific pronouns with nonreferential antecedents, which are quite possibly ambiguous as to gender. In contrast, singular *they* is less acceptable with referential antecedents, for which there should be no ambiguity about genders.[5] The only difference between the sentences in Experiments 1 and 2 was the specificity of the antecedents. Experiment 1 used nonreferential antecedents such as "A student who…" or "A sailor who…," which suggested that a hypothetical person was being discussed. In effect, these sentences discussed Xs in general—an entire class of people rather than a particular person. For this reason, it is perhaps not surprising that the pronoun *they*—a technically plural pronoun—was readily accepted for all four antecedent types. Indeed, when the antecedent was an indefinite pronoun, readers actually processed singular *they* faster than *he* or *she,* and the rules of **prescriptive grammar** have already been changed to accommodate this apparent preference. According to these same rules, using *they* to refer to a singular common noun is not acceptable, but our college-age readers did not seem to care. Indeed, singular *they* has become so common that postexperiment surveys of our readers revealed 51% did not believe that using *they* in place of *he* or *she* is ungrammatical.

In Experiment 2, when the antecedents were used referentially, singular *they* was not processed quite as readily. The antecedents in these sentences implied a specific person whose gender was presumably known. Undoubtedly, using the nonspecific *they* when *he* or *she* should be readily applicable seems unnecessarily opaque, and the reading times of our participants reflected this. The fact that *they* clauses were read more slowly than gender-matched-pronoun clauses suggests that using *they* with referential antecedents seems out of place. Indeed, using *they* in such cases might imply that the writer or speaker is trying to conceal the gender of the person being talked about, which is likely to give the reader or listener pause.

A norming study we performed using our experimental materials sheds further light on the status of singular *they* in the minds of our undergraduate readers. When the readers were asked to provide a pronoun for each experimental sentence, spontaneous use of singular *they* was common. For the nonreferential antecedents used in Experiment 1, 70% of the readers used *they* to refer to an indefinite pronoun at least once, and 57% used *they* to refer to a singular common noun at least once (most frequently the nouns were gender neutral). In contrast, for the referential antecedents used in Experiment 2, only 20% of the readers used *they* to refer to a singular common noun at least once.

Taken together, the results of these two experiments demonstrate that the increased use of singular *they* is not problematic for the majority of readers. We propose that in those few cases in which its use is considered surprising, the delays seen in comprehension are due not to the pronoun's ungrammaticality or to uncertainty over the intended referent, but to the suspicious opacity of using a nongendered pronoun for an antecedent whose gender is presumably known.

References

Beardsley, E. L. (1973). Referential generalization. *Philosophical Forum, 5,* 285–293.
Bodine, A. (1975). Androcentrism in prescriptive grammar: Singular "they," sex-indefinite "he," and "he or she." *Language in Society, 4,* 129–146.

[5]A between-experiments ANOVA showed that gender-matched pronouns (those that matched the gender stereotype of their antecedent) had a larger advantage over singular *they* in Experiment 2 than in Experiment 1, as reflected by a marginally reliable interaction, $F(1,193) = 3.23, p = .07$.

Flanagan, A. M., & Todd-Mancillas, W. R. (1982). Teaching inclusive generic pronoun usage: The effectiveness of an authority innovation-decision approach vs. optional innovation-decision approach. *Communication Education, 31,* 275–284.

Foertsch, J., & Gernsbacher, M. A. (1994). In search of complete comprehension: Getting "minimalists" to work. *Discourse Processes, 18,* 271–296.

Fowler, H. R., & Aaron, J. E. (1983). *The Little, Brown handbook* (3rd ed.). Glenview, IL: Scott, Foresman.

Garnham, A. (1981). Anaphoric reference to instances, instantiated and non-instantiated categories: A reading time study. *British Journal of Psychology, 72,* 377–384.

Garnham, A. (1984). Effects of specificity on the interpretation of anaphoric noun phrases. *Quarterly Journal of Experimental Psychology, 36A,* 1–12.

Garrod, S., & Sanford, A. (1977). Interpreting anaphoric relations: The integration of semantic information while reading. *Journal of Verbal Learning and Verbal Behavior, 16,* 77–90.

Karr, J. S., & Underwood, G. (1984). Fixation time on anaphoric pronouns decreases with congruity of reference. In A. G. Gale & F. Johnson (Eds.), *Theoretical and applied aspects of eye movement research* (pp. 110–136). Amsterdam: Elsevier Science.

Khosroshahi, F. (1989). Penguins don't care, but women do: A social identity analysis of a Whorfian problem. *Language in Society, 18,* 505–525.

Kidd, V. (1971). A study of the images produced through the use of the male pronoun as the generic. *Moments in Contemporary Rhetoric and Communication, 1,* 25–30.

MacKay, D. G. (1980). On the goals, principles, and procedures for prescriptive grammar. Singular they. *Language in Society, 9,* 349–367.

MacKay, D. G., & Fulkerson, D.C. (1979). On the comprehension and production of pronouns. *Journal of Verbal Learning and Verbal Behavior, 18,* 661–673.

Martyna, W. (1978a). *Using and understanding the generic masculine: A social-psychological approach to language and the sexes.* Unpublished doctoral dissertation, Stanford University, Stanford, CA.

Martyna, W. (1978b). What does "he" mean? *Journal of Communication, 28,* 131–138.

Meyers, M. (1990). Current generic pronoun usage: An empirical study. *American Speech, 65,* 228–237.

Moulton, J., Robinson, G., & Elias, C. (1978). Sex bias in language use. *American Psychologist, 33,* 1032–1036.

Nilsen, A. P. (1984). Winning the great he/she battle. *College English, 46,* 151–157.

Silvera, J. (1980). Generic masculine words and thinking. *Women's Studies International Quarterly, 3,* 165–178.

Spencer, N. J. (1978). Can "she" and "he" coexist? *American Psychologist, 33,* 782–783.

Strunk, W., Jr., & White, E. B. (1979). *The elements of style* (3rd ed.). New York: Macmillan.

Valian, V. (1977). Linguistics and feminism. In F. Ellison, J. English, & M. Vetterling (Eds.), *Feminism and philosophy* (pp. 154–166). Totowa, NJ: Littlefield, Adams.

Zuber, S., & Reed, A. M. (1993). The politics of grammar handbooks: Generic *he* and singular *they*. *College English, 55,* 515–530.

Introduction: Critical Thinking Questions

? Explain why the use of generic *he* is considered unacceptable. What alternatives have been offered? Why are these alternatives not completely satisfactory?

? What does the research investigating the match or mismatch between antecedent and pronoun indicate about comprehension in these two situations?

? How was the task used to investigate the effects described in the previous question used in the current studies? What predictions can be made about the effect of using *they* as a referential pronoun within this task?

? In what cases might the use of *they* actually be *less* disruptive (i.e., faster reading times or equivalent reading times) than the use of *he* or *she*? Why?

? What change to the basic procedure was made for Experiment 2, and what was the purpose of the change?

Method: Critical Thinking Questions _____

? For each experiment, describe what you would have been asked to do, had you been a participant.

? For each experiment, name the independent variables, and their levels. Describe how each of these variables was operationalized. For each variable, state whether it was manipulated in a between-subjects or within-subjects fashion. How many conditions were there in the experiment?

? What was (were) the dependent variable(s) in each experiment?

? What aspects of the methodology were implemented to deal with possible confounds?

Results/Discussion: Critical Thinking Questions _____

? Describe the results from Experiments 1 and 2 regarding the substitution of singular *they* for gender-consistent pronouns (e.g., substituting *they* for *she* with nurse). for gender inconsistent pronouns (substituting *they* for *he* with nurse). What does this indicate about using singular *they* as a substitute for *he* or *she* in these circumstances?

? Describe the results for the use of *she, he,* or singular *they* when the antecedent is neutral (Experiment 1 and 2) and indefinite (e.g., anyone) (Experiment 1)? What does this indicate about using singular *they* as a substitute for *he* or *she* in these circumstances?

? Come up with your own example of (a) a sentence in which the use of *they* would have no effect, or a beneficial effect on comprehension, and (b) a sentence in which the use of *they* would have a detrimental effect on comprehension.

? After reading this study, you may feel there are other issues or questions that would be worthwhile or intriguing to address. Pose one of these questions (other than those suggested by the authors) that could be investigated empirically.

4

Reasoning, Decision Making, and Problem Solving

Birds of a Feather Flock Conjointly (?)

Rhyme as Reason in Aphorisms

Matthew S. McGlone and Jessica Tofighbakhsh

*Abstract*_____

We explored the role that poetic form can play in people's perceptions of the accuracy of aphorisms as descriptions of human behavior. Participants judged the ostensible accuracy of unfamiliar aphorisms presented in their textually surviving form or a semantically equivalent modified form. Extant rhyming aphorisms in their original form (e.g., "What sobriety conceals, alcohol reveals") were judged to be more accurate than modified versions that did not preserve rhyme ("What sobriety conceals, alcohol unmasks"). However, the perceived truth advantage of rhyming aphorisms over their modified forms was attenuated when people were cautioned to distinguish aphorisms' poetic qualities from their semantic content. Our results suggest that rhyme, like repetition, affords statements an enhancement in processing fluency that can be misattributed to heightened conviction about their truthfulness.

Conceptual Issues and Theoretical Questions _____

- To what degree are aphorisms (pithy little sayings) believed, and what factors influence whether they seem credible or not?
- To what degree does the familiarity of these sayings play a role in whether people accept them as true?
- To what degree do aesthetic qualities (e.g., alliteration and rhyme) of the sayings play a role in whether people accept them as true?
- Can people make a distinction between the aesthetic value of a saying and its actual truth value?

McGlone, M. S., & Tofighbakhsh, J. (2000). Birds of a feather flock conjointly (?): Rhyme as reason in aphorisms. *Psychological Science, 11,* 424–428. Copyright © 2000 by Blackwell Publishing. Reprinted by permission.

De-Jargonizing

propositional content: propositions are statements about relations between events and objects. The propositional content of an aphorism refers to the actual claim that the aphorism makes

prime word: priming refers to the facilitation of one word or concept through the presentation of another related word. For example, presenting the word "nurse" facilitates the identification of the word "doctor;" in this case, "nurse" is a prime word

lexical activation: the process whereby a concept's representation in memory is activated

graphemic correspondence: the degree to which the visual pattern of a word (i.e., the printed letters) relates to another (e.g., the graphemic correspondence between *house* and *mouse* is high)

misattribution: coming to an errant conclusion about the cause of an event

Aphorisms are succinct statements that offer observations and advice about universal human concerns such as happiness (e.g., "Better to be happy than wise"), health ("An apple a day keeps the doctor away"), and friendship ("Birds of a feather flock together"). Although they enjoy a reputation among laypeople as distillations of age-old psychological wisdom, aphorisms are commonly characterized by psychologists as dubious generalizations to be contrasted with more precise scientific descriptions of human behavior (Gibbs & Beitel, 1995; Teigen, 1986). To this end, many introductory psychology textbooks draw attention to the existence of apparently contradictory pairs of aphorisms such as "Birds of a feather flock together" versus "Opposites attract" and "Out of sight, out of mind" versus "Absence makes the heart grow fonder" (Baron, Byrne, & Kantowitz, 1980; Taylor & Manning, 1975). Presumably, a set of statements about behavior can be considered scientifically "accurate" only if each statement's truth conditions can be operationalized and the statements do not contradict each other (Downy, Wall, & Peters, 1981). However, the notorious vagueness of aphorisms makes specification of their truth conditions especially difficult. For example, what conditions must be satisfied for the statement "Haste makes waste" to be true? Which forms of urgent action constitute "haste"? How does one distinguish a priori between a situation in which "Haste makes waste" is good advice and one in which "He who hesitates is lost" would be more appropriate? If the persuasive force of an aphorism depended critically on the clarity of its truth conditions, we should find it surprising that people invest any belief in such statements.

Given the murkiness of aphorisms' truth conditions, why might people believe that such statements describe human behavior accurately? One important factor is an aphorism's familiarity (Higbee & Millard, 1983). For example, consider the well-worn observation that "opposites attract." American college students not only are highly familiar with this aphorism, but also judged it to be a more accurate description of companion selection than novel statements that entail the same claim (e.g., "People with divergent interests and personalities tend to be drawn to one another"; McGlone & Necker, 1998). The conflation of familiarity and accuracy in aphorisms is consistent with experimental demonstrations of the influence of repetition on people's judgments of statements with uncertain truth value (Bacon, 1979; Begg, Anas, & Farinacci, 1992; Begg & Armour, 1991; Hasher, Goldstein, & Toppino, 1977). For example, Hasher et al. (1977) found that repetition of unsubstantiated trivia statements (e.g., "Divorce is found only in technically advanced societies") produced a systematic shift in their rated truth value: Repeated statements were judged as more likely to be true than nonrepeated statements. Begg et al. (1992) characterized this and other demonstrations of the "illusory truth" effect as evidence that a fluency heuristic operates in people's judgment of a statement's truth; repetition increases a statement's familiarity, and the processing fluency that familiarity affords the statement is misattributed to belief in its propositional truth (cf. Whittlesea, 1993). Although fluency of this sort might contribute to people's belief in conventional aphorisms such as "Haste makes waste," it does not encourage belief in unfamiliar aphorisms such as "Variety prevents satiety." Yet unfamiliar aphorisms often seem to have a "ring of truth" as well, their dubious truth conditions notwithstanding. What characteristics of unfamiliar aphorisms might contribute to this perception?

The present study focuses on the role that aesthetic properties of an aphorism can play in people's (specifically, readers') perceptions of its truthfulness. Although these statements' reputation as kernels of psychological wisdom may be dubious, their reputation as verbal art forms is well deserved. Aphorisms employ many of the aesthetic devices exalted in poetry, including metaphor, (e.g., "Oppression is the mother of liberty"), alliteration ("Fortune favors the fool"), assonance ("A rolling stone gathers no moss"), and rhyme ("Haste makes waste"; Gibbs & Beitel, 1995; Odlin, 1986). Traditionally, literary scholars have classified these devices as aspects of aphoristic form that are separate from propositional content (e.g., Goodwin & Wenzel, 1979). In his seminal work on structuralist poetics, Culler (1975) acknowledged this distinction by suggesting that the rhetorical effectiveness of an aphorism depends on the "observable accuracy of its meaning" (i.e., content) and "the aesthetic pleasure afforded by its form" (p. 143).

Although the distinction between content and form clearly has analytic value, it has not been established that readers routinely separate the contributions that these components make to their overall appreciation of an aphorism (McGlone & Tofighbakhsh, 1999). For example, consider how readers might respond differently to "Variety prevents satiety" and a slightly modified version of this statement, "Variation prevents satiety." The two statements do not differ appreciably in **propositional content,** but the former has an aesthetic element (i.e., repetition of the stressed vowel and subsequent speech sounds in two or more words, or rhyme; Brogan, 1994) that the latter does not. If readers distinguish between the propositional content of the aphorism and its poetic form, then there should be no difference in the perceived accuracy of the rhyming and nonrhyming versions. However, rhyme, like familiarity, can increase the fluency with which words forming a statement are recognized and understood (Meyer, Schvaneveldt, & Ruddy, 1975; Rubin, 1995). For example, Meyer et al. (1975) found that people are faster to judge that a string of letters presented visually is a word if it is preceded by a rhyming **prime word** than if it is preceded by a nonrhyming prime. This effect is observed even when the prime word is presented auditorily, suggesting that **lexical activation** (as opposed to simple **graphemic correspondence**) is the locus of facilitation (Hillinger, 1980). If, as Begg et al. (1992) have argued, people base their judgments of a statement's accuracy in part on the fluency with which the statement is processed, then the fluency that rhyme affords an aphorism may confer upon the statement a perceived truth advantage over a semantically equivalent non-rhyming version. Such an advantage would indicate that the traditional analytic distinction between a statement's "rhyme and reason" (i.e., form and content) is not always appreciated by readers; in some circumstances, rhyme may be treated *as* reason.

In this article, we report an experiment exploring the influence of poetic form on people's perceptions of aphorisms' accuracy as descriptions of human behavior. This experiment tested two distinct hypotheses. First, we hypothesized that people would misattribute the processing fluency produced by an aphorism's rhyming form to heightened conviction about the statement's accuracy (following Begg et al., 1992), relative to a semantically equivalent nonrhyming version of the aphorism. Second, we predicted that this **misattribution** would be attenuated when people were prompted to attribute processing fluency to its actual source (cf. Schwarz & Clore, 1996; Whittlesea, Jacoby, & Girard, 1990). Specifically, we expected that people advised to distinguish aphorisms' poetic qualities from their propositional content would be less prone to exhibit the "rhyme as reason" effect.

Method

Participants

For participating in this experiment, 120 Lafayette undergraduates received extra credit in a course they were taking. Twenty participated in the materials check and 100 in the experiment proper. All were native English speakers.

Materials

Initially, 50 rhyming and 50 nonrhyming aphorisms were selected from published aphorism collections using the following criteria: (a) The aphorism was an advisory or descriptive statement about human behavior (as opposed to a value judgment or opinion, which people might be hesitant to judge as accurate or inaccurate); (b) it was not similar in meaning to another selected aphorism; and (c) it was unfamiliar to the authors. For each extant (i.e., textually surviving) rhyming aphorism (e.g., "What sobriety conceals, alcohol reveals"), a modified version was created by replacing one of the rhyming words with a close synonym that did not rhyme with any of the other words in the statement (e.g., "What sobriety conceals, alcohol unmasks"). For each extant nonrhyming aphorism (e.g., "Benefaction is the most difficult weapon to conquer"), a modified version was created by replacing a content word with a close synonym that did not rhyme with any of the other words in the statement (e.g., "Benefaction is the most difficult weapon to overcome").[1] The extant non-rhyming aphorisms and their modified counterparts were included in the stimulus materials to control for the possibility that a perceived truth advantage for an extant rhyming

---

[1]Although it would have been ideal to construct modified rhyming versions of the extant nonrhyming aphorisms (thus putting assignment of statements to the rhyming and nonrhyming conditions under the experimenter's control), it was impossible in most cases for us to create such versions that adequately preserved the meaning of the originals.

aphorism over a nonrhyming version might be attributable not to rhyme per se, but rather to modification of the statement's textually surviving form. We expected that if the latter were true, we would observe a truth advantage for the extant nonrhyming aphorisms over their modified counterparts as well.

On the basis of a pilot experiment ($n = 20$), we chose 30 pairs (original plus modified version) from each of the rhyming and nonrhyming aphorism sets. A pair was selected only if all participants indicated that (a) they could not recall having read or heard the original aphorism in the past and (b) they did not perceive a difference in meaning between the original and modified versions. Examples of the selected pairs are presented in Table 1. Two lists were created from these materials. Each list contained 60 aphorisms; 15 extant rhyming aphorisms in their original form and 15 in modified (i.e., nonrhyming) form, and 15 extant nonrhyming aphorisms in their original form and 15 in modified form. Only one version of each extant aphorism appeared in each list. Although the order in which the aphorisms appeared was randomized, a given aphorism and its modified form were in the same position in their respective lists.

Design and Procedure

This experiment employed a $2 \times 2 \times 2$ design with aphorism type (extant rhyming or nonrhyming) and version (original or modified) as within-subjects factors and instruction condition (control or warning) as a between-subjects factor. Upon arrival in the laboratory, participants were randomly assigned to one of the aphorism lists and an instruction condition. The first page of each questionnaire indicated that the experiment was part of a larger study exploring the psychological theories implied by English aphorisms and provided instructions for the accuracy ratings. Participants were instructed to read each aphorism carefully and then to rate the degree to which they perceived the aphorism as "an accurate description of human behavior," on a scale from 1 (*not at all accurate*) to 9 (*very accurate*).

TABLE 1 *Examples of the Aphorism Pairs*

Original version	*Modified version*
Extant rhyming aphorisms	
Woes unite foes.	Woes unite enemies.
What sobriety conceals, alcohol reveals.	What sobriety conceals, alcohol unmasks.
Life is mostly strife.	Life is mostly struggle.
Caution and measure will win you treasure.	Caution and measure will win you riches.
Variety prevents satiety.	Variation prevents satiety.
Extant nonrhyming aphorisms	
Fools live poor to die rich.	Fools live poor to die wealthy.
Power grows mightier with each trial.	Power grows mightier with each challenge.
Short pleasure, long repentance.	Short pleasure, long regret.
He who rides a tiger is afraid to dismount.	He who rides a tiger is afraid to get off.
Good intentions excuse ill deeds.	Good intentions excuse ill acts.

In the control-instructions condition, the instructions did not include any mention of or ad-monition concerning the distinction between aphorisms' poetic qualities and their ostensi-ble accuracy. In contrast, instructions in the warning condition specifically cautioned participants to base their accuracy judgments "only on the claim that the statement makes about behavior, not the poetic quality of the statement's wording." This caveat was pre-sented in boldface type in the instructions, and was further emphasized by the observation that "a statement might strike you as quite poetic, but not particularly accurate; on the other hand, a statement might strike you as quite accurate, but not particularly poetic."

After participants in both conditions completed the accuracy ratings, they were asked the following yes/no question: "In your opinion, do aphorisms that rhyme describe human behavior more accurately than those that do not rhyme?" After responses to this question were recorded, participants were debriefed regarding the true purpose of the ex-periment. On average, the experimental sessions lasted 25 min.

Results

Initial analyses did not reveal main effects or interactions involving stimulus list, so subse-quent analyses collapsed across this factor. Separate analyses of variance were conducted on the ratings data treating participants (F_p) and items (F_i) as random factors. Analyses of the accuracy ratings indicated that, overall, there were no reliable differences in mean rat-ings between extant rhyming and nonrhyming aphorisms (5.51 and 5.45, respectively) or original and modified versions (5.63 and 5.35), $p > .10$ in both cases. However, participants in the control-instructions condition generated slightly higher ratings overall than those in the warning condition (5.68 and 5.26), $F_p(1, 98) = 2.79$, $p < .08$, and $F_i(1, 58) = 2.63$, $p < .12$. This marginal effect was moderated by a reliable Aphorism Type × Version × Instruc-tion Condition interaction, $F_p(1, 98) = 7.84$, $p < .01$, and $F_i(1, 58) = 5.58$, $p < .02$. The rel-evant means are presented in Figure 1. Planned analytical comparisons (Keppel, Saufley, & Tokunaga, 1992) were used to investigate differences among the means. As we pre-dicted, participants who were not cautioned to distinguish aphorisms' semantic content

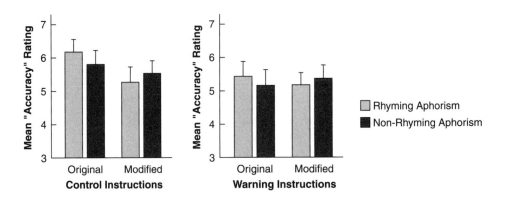

FIGURE 1 *Mean accuracy ratings by aphorism type, version, and instruction condition.*

from their poetic qualities (the control-instructions condition) assigned higher accuracy ratings to the original rhyming aphorisms than their modified counterparts (6.17 and 5.26), $F_p(1, 98) = 12.77$, $p < .01$, and $F_i(1, 58) = 8.62$, $p < .03$; however, they assigned comparable ratings to the original and modified nonrhyming aphorisms (5.79 and 5.51), $F_p(1, 98) = 1.21$, $p > .10$, and $F_i(1, 58) = 0.82$. The fact that the difference in ratings between aphorism versions was reliable for the extant rhyming aphorisms, but not the nonrhyming aphorisms, suggests that the difference is attributable specifically to manipulation of rhyme in the former and not simply to the modification of their textually surviving form.[2]

Participants in the warning condition exhibited a markedly different pattern of accuracy ratings. The original rhyming aphorisms were assigned reliably lower accuracy ratings in this condition than in the control condition (5.42 and 6.17), $F_p(1, 98) = 4.79$, $p < .05$, and $F_i(1, 58) = 4.26$, $p < .05$. In addition, in the warning condition, there were no reliable differences in participants' ratings for original and modified versions of the extant rhyming aphorisms (5.42 and 5.17), $F_p(1, 98) = 0.96$, and $F_i(1, 58) = 0.65$, or of the extant nonrhyming aphorisms (5.14 and 5.36), $F_p(1, 98) = 0.75$, and $F_i(1, 58) = 0.52$. Thus, bringing the distinction between an aphorism's poetic qualities and semantic content to participants' attention had the desired effect of thwarting their tendency to conflate fluency with perceived accuracy. However, there is no evidence that this tendency in the control condition stemmed from an explicit belief that rhyming aphorisms are more accurate than nonrhyming ones. When asked if they held such a belief, all participants in both conditions responded "no" (and many gave us quizzical looks).

Discussion

In *The Gay Science,* Nietzsche (1878/1986) attributed the origin of poetry to a primitive belief that rhythm and rhyme could confer magical powers to the words of prayers, carrying them "closer to the ears of the gods." Although this superstition was dismissed long ago in most cultures, Nietzsche observed that "even now...the wisest among us are still occasionally fooled by rhythm—if only insofar as *we sometimes consider an idea truer because it has a metrical form and presents itself with a divine spark and jump*" (pp. 139–140, emphasis added). Our results offer some support for Nietzsche's claim: Participants conflated the rhyme and perceived accuracy of aphorisms unless they were explicitly instructed to distinguish the statements' semantic content from their poetic qualities. This occurred despite the fact that participants did not read the aphorisms aloud, which would have made those that rhymed especially salient. Among the prosodic poetic devices (e.g., alliteration, assonance), rhyme is the first that children learn to appreciate and one that adults routinely notice even during silent reading (Hayes, Chemelski, & Palmer, 1982).

---

[2]A second possibility is that the perceived truth advantage was attributable in part to modification of the rhyming aphorisms' meter. It proved difficult in many cases for us to create modified versions of these aphorisms in which rhyming words were replaced with synonyms that had the same number of syllables and stress pattern as the replaced words, thereby preserving both the meanings and the meter of the statements; however, we were able to do this for 14 of the 30 rhyming aphorisms used (see examples in Table 1). We found no differences in the pattern of accuracy ratings for these aphorism pairs and those in which the modified version preserved only the meaning of the original. Thus, we tentatively conclude that the meter confound did not contribute appreciably to the effect reported.

Thus, it is not surprising that participants discriminated between the rhyming and non-rhyming aphorisms in the stimulus lists. What *is* surprising is that they discriminated between these forms in terms of accuracy, even though none of them reported believing that rhyme confers a truth advantage on such statements. Psychologists have documented that people are often unaware of factors that influence their judgments (e.g., Nisbett & Wilson, 1977). However, barring an unconscious belief in the magical power of rhyme on the part of our participants, what accounts for the rhyme-as-reason effect?

We suggest that this effect is a product of the enhanced processing fluency that rhyme affords an aphorism such as "What sobriety conceals, alcohol reveals" relative to a semantically equivalent nonrhyming version. Although enhanced processing fluency is often the consequence of repeated exposure to a stimulus (Begg et al., 1992; Jacoby & Kelley, 1987), it can also be produced by factors in the present stimulus environment. For example, manipulations of fluency such as adjusting the figure-ground contrast or presentation duration of a stimulus produce misattributions akin to those generated by repetition manipulations (Reber, Winkielman, & Schwarz, 1998; Whittiesea, 1993). When these manipulated factors are brought to people's attention, misattribution of processing fluency to other psychological dimensions (e.g., liking, familiarity) is attenuated (Whittlesea et al., 1990). In the same fashion, our participants misattributed processing fluency to a perceived truth advantage of rhyming aphorisms over nonrhyming versions; however, when they were cautioned to distinguish an aphorism's poetic form from its semantic content, the advantage was significantly reduced.

Although we have explored the rhyme-as-reason effect within the narrow domain of antiquated sayings, it clearly can occur in contemporary communications as well. Consider defense attorney Johnnie Cochran's celebrated plea to the jury during O. J. Simpson's criminal trial: "If the gloves don't fit, you must acquit!" Journalists have focused almost exclusively on the mnemonic value of rhyme in this statement: Rhyme increased the likelihood that jurors would rehearse, remember, and thus apply Cochran's directive (Buckley, 1997). However, the fluent quality of the statement undeniably overshadows its dubious proposition—after all, the jury was obligated to consider all of the presented evidence, not just the tight gloves! We wonder how persuasive the jury might have found this proposition had Cochran proclaimed, "If the gloves don't fit, you must find him not guilty!"

References

Bacon, F. T. (1979). Credibility of repeated statements: Memory for trivia. *Journal of Experimental Psychology: Human Learning and Memory, 5,* 241–252.

Baron, R. A., Byrne, D., & Kantowitz, B. H. (1980). *Psychology: Understanding behavior.* New York: Holt, Rinehart, & Winston.

Begg, I. M., Anas, A., & Farinacci. S. (1992). Dissociation of processes in belief: Source recollection, statement familiarity, and the illusion of truth. *Journal of Experimental Psychology: General, 121,* 446–458.

Begg, I. M., & Armour, V. (1991). Repetition and the ring of truth. *Journal of Experimental Psychology: General, 121,* 446–458.

Brogan, T. V. F. (1994). *The new Princeton handbook of poetic terms.* Princeton, NJ: Princeton University Press.

Buckley, C. (1997). *Wry martinis.* New York: Harper Perennial.

Culler, J. (1975). *Structuralist poetics.* Ithaca, NY: Cornell University Press.

Dowty, D. R., Wall, R. E., & Peters, S. (1981). *Introduction to Montague semantics.* Boston: Reidel.

Gibbs, R. W., & Beitel, D. (1995). What proverb understanding reveals about how people think. *Psychological Bulletin, 118,* 133–154.

Goodwin, P. D., & Wenzel, J. W. (1979). Proverbs and practical reasoning: A study in sociologic. *Quarterly Journal of Speech, 65,* 289–302.

Hasher, L., Goldstein, D., & Toppino, T. (1977). Frequency and the conference of referential validity. *Journal of Verbal Learning and Verbal Behavior, 16,* 107–112.

Hayes, D. S., Chemelski, S. M., & Palmer, M. (1982). Nursery rhymes and prose passages: Preschoolers' liking and short-term retention of story events. *Developmental Psychology, 96,* 211–222.

Higbee, K. L., & Millard, R. J. (1983). Visual imagery and familiarity ratings for 203 sayings. *American Journal of Psychology, 96,* 211–222.

Hillinger, M. L. (1980). Priming effects with phonemically similar words: The encoding-bias hypothesis reconsidered. *Memory & Cognition, 8,* 115–123.

Jacoby, L. L., & Kelley, C. M. (1987). Unconscious influences of memory of a prior event. *Personality and Social Psychology Bulletin, 13,* 314–336.

Keppel, G., Saufley, W. H., & Tokunaga, H. (1992). *Introduction to design and analysis* (2nd ed.). New York: W. H. Freeman.

McGlone, M. S., & Necker, R. (1998). *The perils of paraphrase.* Unpublished manuscript. Lafayette College, Easton, PA.

McGlone, M. S., & Tofighbakhsh, J. (1999). The Keats heuristic: Rhyme as reason in aphorism interpretation. *Poetics, 26,* 235–244.

Meyer, D. E., Schvaneveldt, R. W., & Ruddy. M. G. (1975). Loci of contextual effects on visual word recognition. In P. M. Rabbit & S. Domic (Eds.), *Attention and Performance, Volume V* (pp. 98–118). London: Academic Press.

Nietzsche, F. (1986). *The gay science.* New York: Mentor. (Original work published 1878)

Nisbett, R. E., & Wilson, T. D. (1977). Telling more than we can know: Verbal reports of mental processes. *Psychological Review, 84,* 231–259.

Odlin, T. (1986). Language universals and constraints on proverbial form. *Proverbium, 3,* 125–151.

Reber, R., Winkielman P., & Schwarz, N. (1998). Effects of perceptual fluency on affective judgments. *Psychological Science, 9,* 45–48.

Rubin, D. C. (1995). *Memory in oral traditions: The cognitive psychology of epic, ballads, and counting-out rhythms.* Oxford, England: Oxford University Press.

Schwarz, N., & Clore, G. L. (1996). Feelings and phenomenal experiences. In E. T. Higgins & A. Kruglanski (Eds.), *Social psychology: Handbook of basic principles* (pp. 433–465). New York: Guilford.

Taylor, D. A., & Manning, S. A. (1975). *Psychology: A new perspective.* London: Van Nostrand.

Teigen, K. H. (1986). Old truths or fresh insights? A study of students' evaluations of proverbs. *British Journal of Social Psychology, 25,* 43–49.

Whittlesea, B. W. A. (1993). Illusions of familiarity. *Journal of Experimental Psychology: Learning, Memory, and Cognition, 6,* 1235–1253.

Whittlesea, B. W. A., Jacoby, L. L., & Girard, K. (1990). Illusions of immediate memory: Evidence of an attributional basis for feelings of familiarity and perceptual quality. *Journal of Memory and Language, 29,* 716–732.

Introduction: Critical Thinking Questions _____

? The authors contend that the "illusory truth" of a saying may be the result of a fluency heuristic. Explain this claim, and how it relates to the effects that the familiarity of an aphorism might have on the perception of its truth value.

? The authors state that "rhyme may be treated as reason" in the case of aphorisms. Explain what they mean, and describe how it relates to the earlier discussion of processing fluency.

? Describe the authors' two major hypotheses.

Method: Critical Thinking Questions _____

? Describe what you would have been asked to do, had you been a participant in the experiment.

? Name the independent variables in the experiment and their levels. Describe how each of these variables was operationalized. For each variable, state whether it was manipulated in a be-tween- or within-subjects fashion. How many conditions were there in the experiment?

? What was (were) the dependent variable(s) in the experiment?

? What aspects of the methodology were implemented to deal with possible confounds?

Results/Discussion: Critical Thinking Questions _____

? Describe the pattern of results obtained (a) in the warning condition and (b) in the control con-dition. Did the results support the authors' original hypothesis? Can people separate rhyme from reason?

? Does the effect of rhyme on the perception of aphorism accuracy appear to be conscious or un-conscious? Explain.

? The authors relate their findings to the (in)famous Johnnie Cochran quip "If it doesn't fit, you must acquit." In what other contexts do you most often encounter communicators attempting to take advantage of the "rhyme as reason" effect? Find some examples. How might you test the persuasive influence of such phrases in the laboratory?

? After reading this study, you may feel there are other issues or questions that would be worth-while or intriguing to address. Pose one of these questions (other than those suggested by the authors) that could be investigated empirically.

Parents Explain More Often to Boys than to Girls during Shared Scientific Thinking

Kevin Crowley, Maureen A. Callanan,
Harriet R. Tenenbaum, and Elizabeth Allen

*Abstract*_____

Young children's everyday scientific thinking often occurs in the context of parent-child interactions. In a study of naturally occurring family conversation, parents were three times more likely to explain science to boys than to girls while using interactive science exhibits in a museum. This difference in explanation occurred despite the fact that parents were equally likely to talk to their male and female children about how to use the exhibits and about the evidence generated by the exhibits. The findings suggest that parents engaged in informal science activities with their children may be unintentionally contributing to a gender gap in children's scientific literacy well before children encounter formal science instruction in grade school.

Conceptual Issues and Theoretical Questions _____

- How are children informally exposed to scientific principles and concepts, and how does this exposure influence their later learning?
- What factors may underlie the gender gap that exists in measures of science achievement?
- Do girls and boys differ in the amount and quality of informal exposure to scientific principles?

Crowley, K., Callanan, M. A., Tenenbaum, H. R., & Allen, E. (2001). Parents explain more often to boys than to girls during shared scientific thinking. *Psychological Science, 12,* 258–261. Copyright © 2001 by Blackwell Publishing. Reprinted by permission.

Prior to their first science instruction in school, many children are exposed to science through informal educational contexts such as museums, television shows, Web pages, and books (Gelman, Massey, & McManus, 1991; Korpan, Bisanz, Bisanz, Boehme, & Lynch, 1997). Children often participate in these activities in the company of their parents, yet little is known about how families learn in informal science settings. In particular, little is known about whether boys and girls experience informal science in the same ways.

Girls in the United States continue to lag behind boys on many measures of science achievement (O'Sullivan, Reese, & Mazzeo, 1997). One reason often cited to account for gender gaps in science achievement is differential teacher-student discourse in classrooms. Teachers have been described as more likely to encourage boys than girls to ask questions, make integrative comments, and explain (American Association of University Women, 1995; Jones & Wheatley, 1990; Kelly, 1988). Although interventions in response to such findings have often been targeted at teacher bias, the effect may be driven at least in part by differences in volunteer rates between boys and girls (Altermatt, Jovanovic, & Perry, 1998). Regardless of why the difference occurs, the logic of the claim with respect to science education is that the reflective thinking involved in answering questions and constructing explanations leads boys to develop deeper conceptual knowledge about science and greater interest in science.

Could a similar gender difference characterize parent-child conversations during informal science learning? No prior study has examined this question directly, although findings from two literatures are relevant. One set of findings comes from developmental psychology. In studies of the development of children's gender roles, families are often observed during play. The most consistent finding in this literature is that if parents use different interaction styles with boys and girls, the difference is usually linked to the parents' perception of whether the play activity is gender-appropriate for boys or for girls (Leaper & Gleason, 1996; Lytton & Romney, 1991; McGillicuddy-de Lisi, 1988); this is particularly true in the case of fathers (Siegal, 1987). To the extent that parents see science as a stereotypically male activity, these findings suggest that parents may show differences in how they interact with boys and girls while engaged in informal science activities.

A second set of relevant findings comes from the literature on museum learning. Historically, studies of learning in museums have focused on nonverbal behaviors such as the length of time visitors stay engaged with an exhibit (Dierking & Falk, 1994). The few studies of museum activity that have focused on parent-child conversation provide suggestive but inconclusive evidence that parents may be more likely to talk to boys than girls while using exhibits (e.g., Cone & Kendall, 1978; Diamond, 1994).

The current study focused on whether parents explain more often to boys than to girls while using interactive science exhibits in a museum. Explanations include talk about causal relations, analogies, and scientific principles. Our focus on explanations was motivated by prior studies showing that when children, undergraduates, or professional scientists focus on building explanations during scientific thinking, they develop more coherent theories, are better at interpreting evidence, and are better at transferring knowledge to solve new problems (e g., Chi, de Leeuw, Chiu, & LaVancher, 1994; Dunbar; 1995; Okada & Simon, 1997). Furthermore, by the time children enter school, they have already constructed naive scientific theories to account for biological, psychological, physical, and geological events and entities (Wellman & Gelman, 1998). Children's developing explanations for the causal and relational structure of their everyday environments are thought to be core mechanisms in creating and organizing these theories (Callanan & Oakes, 1992; Carey, 1985). Thus, to the extent that parents help children build explanations about science during informal science activities, they may facilitate children's scientific problem-solving skills, as well as aid them in constructing and revising naive theories about science.

Method

Participants

After the data-reduction procedure described in the next section, the final sample included 298 interactions, each from a different family: 65 involving fathers with 1 or more boys, 34 involving fathers with 1 or more girls, 78 involving mothers with boys, 54 involving mothers with girls, 42 involving mothers and fathers with boys, and 25 involving mothers and fathers with girls. Of the 185 families including boys, the youngest boy was 1 to 3 years old in 88 families, 4 to 5 years old in 66 families, and 6 to 8 years old in 31 families. Of the 113 families with girls, the youngest girl was 1 to 3 years old in 43 families, 4 to 5 years old in 41 families, and 6 to 8 years old in 29 families.

Data Collection and Reduction

Video cameras and wireless microphones were set up at 18 interactive science exhibits in a California children's museum. Exhibits demonstrated content from biology, physics, psychology, geography, or engineering and could be successfully manipulated by a single child (i.e., no exhibit necessarily required parent or staff participation). Data were collected on 26 days spaced over a 30-month period, including weekends and weekdays, in the summer and during the school year.

Researchers greeted families entering the museum, explained that they were videotaping as part of a research project, and asked parents for written consent to participate (more than 90% agreed). Children in consenting families wore stickers coded to identify their ages. This was the only contact the research team had with the families. If, in the natural course of their visit, children wearing stickers chose to engage an exhibit under study, the engagement was videotaped.

Videotapes were segmented into nonoverflapping interactions beginning when the first child from a family—the *target child*—engaged an exhibit and ending when he or she disengaged. The next target child was the first child from a new family who engaged the exhibit after all members of the previous target child's family had disengaged. Thus, each interaction was a unique slice of time capturing the complete engagement of a particular target child at an exhibit. Because our focus was on parent-child interaction, children appearing on the videotape were not designated as targets if they visited exhibits without their parents. There was no difference between the percentage of boys (27.3%) versus girls (26.9%) who visited exhibits without parents.

This procedure initially yielded 351 independent family interactions. Because we were interested in preschool and young elementary school children, we excluded 13 families with no children younger than 9 years old. Because we were interested in parent-child interactions, we excluded one interaction in which a museum staff member talked to the family while they were engaged with an exhibit. Finally, because interactions including only boys or girls provide the most direct test of potential gender differences, we excluded 39 families in which boys and girls engaged an exhibit together. Thus, the final sample included 298 families.

Coding of Conversation and Action

Conversations were coded for whether parents explained an exhibit, gave directions, or talked about evidence:

- A conversation was coded for *explanation* if a parent talked about causal connections within the exhibit interface (e.g, "When you turn that fast, it makes more electricity" at an exhibit including a hand-cranked generator), about relations between observed phenomena and more general principles (e.g., "You see all those colors because the bubble reflects different kinds of light" at an exhibit where visitors can pull a sheet of bubbles up in front of a black background), or about analogies to related phenomena (e.g., "This is just like that one time when our plants died because we forgot to water them" during a time-lapse video of withering bean sprouts).
- A conversation was coded for *giving directions* if parents gave directions on exhibit use that did not establish any causal, analogical, or principled connections (e.g., "Put your hands on those sensors" at an exhibit that measures a visitor's heartbeat).
- A conversation was coded for *talking about evidence* if parents spoke about evidence that could be observed at the exhibit, that is, if they made reference to visual, auditory, or tactile information that did not establish any causal, analogical, or principled connections (e.g., "There's the crankshaft!" at an exhibit where a telepresence robot roves underneath a stationary fire truck).

Actions were coded for who initiated engagement with the exhibit and whether the target child directly manipulated the exhibit:

- Whether the child, parent, or both initiated engagement was defined by who appeared first at the exhibit on the videotape. Researchers turned on the videotape as the target child approached an exhibit, so initiation was often recorded. When the tape recording began with both parents and children already at an exhibit, we did not code initiation.
- The target child was determined to have directly manipulated an exhibit if he or she successfully completed at least one of the core exhibit manipulations. Core manipulations were actions that effected change in ways consistent with the educational goals of the exhibit. Simply touching an exhibit was not sufficient.

Coding was conducted by multiple raters. Reliability was assessed by having 20% of the interactions coded by more than one rater. Agreements exceeded 86%.

Results

Analysis of nonverbal measures of children's activity suggested that, regardless of gender, children took an active role in choosing and using the interactive science exhibits. First, boys and girls were not significantly different in whether they initiated engagement: Engagement was child initiated in 78% of interactions including boys, compared with 74% of interactions including girls. Second, the vast majority of both boys (96%) and girls (99%) were actively involved in manipulating the exhibits. Third, the mean length of time children remained engaged with an exhibit also showed no significant difference between boys ($M = 107$ s, $SD = 117$ s) and girls ($M = 88$ s, $SD = 93$ s), $t(288) = 1.43$, n.s. When 13 outliers greater than 2 standard deviations above the mean were excluded, mean engagement times for boys (M-86 s, $SD = 68$ s) and girls ($M = 83$ s, $SD = 69$ s) were virtually identical.

In contrast, boys were three times more likely than girls to hear explanations from their parents. Parents used at least one explanation in 29% of interactions with boys compared with 9% of interactions with girls, $\chi^2(1, N = 298) = 16.50$, $p < .0001$. This difference was almost completely accounted for by boys hearing many more explanations of causal connections (22% of interactions) than girls (4%). All children were unlikely to hear explanations including general principles (3% for boys, 5% for girls) or analogies (6% for boys, 3% for girls). (Subtotals exceed totals because some parents used more than one kind of explanation.)

Figure 1 shows the percentage of interactions that included explanations, first by the parents' gender and then by the age of the child. As shown in Figure 1a, differences in the frequency of explanations to boys versus girls were most extreme in father-child interactions, $\chi^2(1, N = 99) = 10.34$, $p < .01$, but were also present in mother-child interactions, $\chi^2(1, N = 132) = 5.58$, $p < .05$. When both parents were present, the difference was in the same direction but did not reach significance.[1]

As shown in Figure 1b, differences in the frequency of explanation were relatively stable across all ages of children in the study. Of the 298 interactions, 51 included a target child and one or more siblings who were in different age groups. In these cases, the age of the youngest child was used to assign an age to each interaction. Parents explained more often to boys than girls, regardless of whether children were 1 to 3 years old, $\chi^2(1, N = 131) = 7.27$, $p < .01$; 4 to 5 years old, $\chi^2(1, N = 107) = 4.63$, $p < .05$; or 6 to 8 years old, $\chi^2(1, N = 60) = 4.90$, $p < .05$. Assigning age based an the oldest child rather than the youngest child produced similar findings, all χ^2s > 4.10, all ps $< .05$.

The gender difference observed in parents' explanation did not characterize other kinds of talk by parents. Parents were equally likely to talk about how to manipulate exhibits when interacting with boys (66%) and girls (60%), $\chi^2(1, N = 298) = 1.01$, n.s, and were equally likely to talk about the visual, auditory, or tactile information available from exhibits when interacting with boys (66%) and girls (57%), $\chi^2(1, N = 298) = 2.59$, n.s. No differences emerged when data were broken down by gender of parents, age of youngest child, or age of oldest child, all χ^2s < 3.5, all ps $> .05$.

---

[1]Explanations were coded in 25% of interactions with both parents: Mothers explained in 13% of those interactions, fathers in 5%, and both mothers and fathers in 7%.

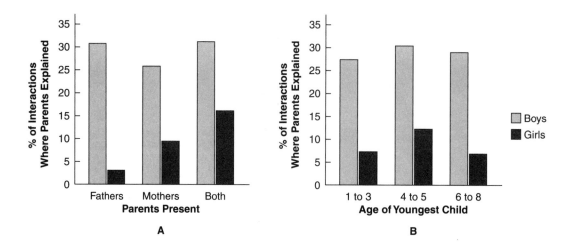

FIGURE 1 *Percentage of parent–child interactions in which parents explained interactive science exhibits in a museum. Explanations were coded when parents talked about causal relations within exhibits, scientific principles illustrated by exhibits, or analogical connections between exhibits and real-world devices or events. Percentage of interactions with explanations is shown as a function of whether children were with fathers, mothers, or both (a) and as a function of the age of the youngest child involved in the interaction (b). Results are shown separately for boys and girls.*

Why did parents explain more often to boys than girls? It is possible that, much like teachers in the classroom (Altermatt et al., 1998), parents in the museum explained more often to boys because boys asked more questions. If this were true, we would expect parents' explanations to have often been preceded by children's questions. However, we found that children who heard explanations rarely asked questions of any kind. In the 10 s prior to the first explanation offered by a parent, only 8% of boys and 6% of girls asked any kind of question. In the 60 s prior to the first explanation, only 13% of boys and 13% of girls asked any kind of question.

Discussion

This study demonstrated that parents were more likely to explain to boys than to girls during informal science activity. Parents brought their daughters to a museum, engaged interactive science exhibits with them, talked about what to do with exhibits, and talked abort what to perceive from exhibits; however, the crucial step of providing an explanatory context for the experience was primarily reserved for boys. The findings are especially noteworthy because we observed differences in the rate of parents' explanation to children as young as 1 to 3 years old, suggesting that parents may be involved in creating gender bias in science learning years before children's first classroom science instruction.

Compared with explanation as defined in philosophy or pedagogy (Leinhardt & Schwarz, 1997), explanation as we defined it was simple, incomplete, and mundane—no more than a few words uttered by a parent at an appropriate moment during the ongoing activity. Such "explanatoids" are offered when relevant evidence is the focus of joint parent-child attention and thus may serve the function of providing children an on-line structure for parsing, storing, and making inferences about evidence as it is encountered (Crowley & Galco, 2001). Although we located this study in a museum, the essential properties of the activity characterize many of the everyday activities in which early scientific and technical thinking are first constructed—building with blocks, mixing watercolors, or figuring out how a new computer game works, for example. The hypothesis that explanation from parents shapes what children learn from such activities is consistent with earlier laboratory work showing that simple adult explanations lead to deeper children's learning and that, without adult assistance, children are unlikely to construct explanations on their own (Crowley & Siegler, 1999; Göncü & Rogoff, 1998; Krascum & Andrews, 1998; Siegler, 1995).

Parents who involve children in informal science activities not only provide an opportunity for children to learn factual scientific information, but also provide opportunities for children to engage in scientific reasoning, to develop an interest in learning more about science, and to develop a sense that practicing the habits of scientific literacy is an important priority. Until the design of informal science contexts recognizes and addresses gender differences in parents' explanation, the full potential of informal science learning to interest and involve girls in science will remain unrealized.

References

Altermatt, E. R., Jovanovic, J., & Perry, M. (1998) Bias or responsivity? Sex and achievement-level effects an teaches' classroom questioning practices. *Journal of Educational Psychology, 90,* 516–517.

American Association of University Women (1995). *How schools shortchange girls.* Washington, DC: National Education Association.

Callanan, M. A., & Oakes, L. A. (1992). Preschoolers' questions and parents' explanations: Causal thinking in everyday activity. *Cognitive Development, 7,* 213–233.

Carey, S. (1985). *Conceptual change in childhood.* Cambridge, MA: MIT Press.

Chi, M. T. H, de Leeuw, N., Chiu, M.-H., & LaVancher, C. (1994). Eliciting self-explanations improves understanding. *Cognitive Science, 18,* 439–477.

Cone, C. A., & Kendall, K. (1978). Space, time, and family interaction: Visitor behavior at the Science Museum of Minnesota. *Curator, 21,* 245–258.

Crowley, K., & Galco, J. (2001). Everyday activity and the development of scientific thinking. In K. Crowley, C. D. Schunn, & T. Okada (Eds.), *Designing for for science: Implications from everyday, classroom, and professional settings* (pp. 393–413). Mahwah, NJ: Erlbaum.

Crowley, K., & Siegler, R. S. (1999). Explanation end generalization in young children's strategy learning. *Child Development, 70,* 304–316.

Diamond, J. (1994). Sex differences in science museums: A review. *Curator, 37,* 17–24.

Dierking, L. D., & Falk, J. H. (1994). Family behavior and learning in informal science settings: A review of the research. *Science Education, 78,* 57–72.

Dunbar, K. (1995). How scientists really reason: Scientific reasoning in real-world laboratories. In R. J. Sternberg & J. E. Davidson (Eds.), *The nature of insight* (pp. 365–395). Cambridge MA: MIT Press.

Gelman, R., Massey, C. M., & McManus, M. (1991). Characterizing supporting environments for cognitive development: Lessons from a children's museum. In L. B. Resnick, J. M. Levine, & S. D. Teasley (Eds.), *Perspectives on socially shared cognition* (pp. 226–256). Washington, DC: American Psychological Association.

Göncü, A., & Rogoff, B. (1998). Children's categorization with varying adult support. *American Educational Research Journal, 35,* 333–349.

Jones, M. G., & Wheatley, J. (1990). Gender differences in teacher–student interactions in science class-rooms. *Journal of Research in Science Teaching, 27,* 861–874.

Kelly, A. (1988). Gender differences in teacher-pupil interactions: A meta-analytic review. *Research in Education, 39,* 1–23.

Korpan, C. A., Bisanz, G. L. Bisanz, J., Boehme, C., & Lynch M. A. (1997). What did you learn outside of school today? Using structured interviews to document home and community activities related to science and technology. *Science Education, 81,* 651–662.

Krascum, R. M., & Andrews, S. (1998). The effects of theories on children's acquisition of family-resemblance categories. *Child Development, 69,* 333–346.

Leaper, C., & Gleason, J. B. (1996). The relationship of play activity and gender to parent and child sex-typed communication. *International Journal of Behavior Development, 19,* 689–703.

Leinhardt, G., & Schwarz, B. (1997). Seeing the problem: An explanation from Pólya. *Cognition and Instruction, 15,* 395–434.

Lytton, H., & Romney, D. M. (1991). Parents' differential socialization of boys and girls: A meta-analysis. *Psychological Bulletin, 109,* 267–296.

McGillicuddy-de Lisi, A. V. (1988). Sex differences in parental teaching behaviors. *Merrill-Palmer Quarterly, 34,* 147–162.

Okada, T., & Simon, H. A. (1997). Collaborative discovery in a scientific domain. *Cognitive Science, 21,* 109–146.

O'Sullivan, C. Y., Reese, C. M., & Mazzeo, J. (1997). *NAEP 1996 science report card for the nation and the states.* Washington, DC: National Center for Education Statistics.

Siegal, M. (1987). Are sons and daughters treated more differently by fathers than by mothers? *Developmental Review, 7,* 183–209.

Siegler, R. S. (1995). How does cognitive change occur: A microgenetic study of number conservation. *Cognitive Psychology, 25,* 225–273.

Wellman, H., & Gelman, S. (1998). Knowledge acquisition in foundational domains. In D. Kuhn & R. S. Siegler (Eds.), *Handbook of child psychology: Cognition, perception, and language* (pp. 523–573). Now York: Wiley.

Introduction: Critical Thinking Questions

? How might teacher-student discourse in schools be related to the gender gap that exists in science achievement scores?

? What does the developmental psychology literature indicate about the likelihood that the teacher-student discourse addressed in the previous question exists at home—that is, in parent-child interactions? How might these interactions produce gender differences in science interest and ability?

? What does research on museum learning indicate about possible gender differences in parent-child interaction?

? The present study focuses on *explanations*—what types of descriptions make up an explanation? Why do the authors choose to focus on this level of discourse?

Method: Critical Thinking Questions

? Describe the age and sex breakdown of the sample.

? How were data collected for analysis? What did the researchers term a "target child," and how did this relate to the data collection procedure?

? Discuss each of the coding categories developed by the researchers, with an explanation of each.

? Although the study is descriptive (rather than experimental), there are critical variables that one could (loosely) label as "independent variables." What are these critical variables—the variables that the researchers believe impact the interaction between parents and children? (You will need to look at the results section to help you answer this question.)

Results/Discussion: Critical Thinking Questions _____

? Some behaviors of boys and girls revealed no gender differences. Describe these behaviors. Also some of the interactions between parents and children revealed no gender differences. Describe these behaviors.

? How did explanations vary as a function of parent gender and child gender? Were the observed interactions consistent with the researchers' hypothesis? How did the researchers determine if these explanations were initiated by the children? What did they find?

? The authors term the sort of explanations given by parents "explanatoids." Explain this term, and what functions these explanatoids might have.

? Take a trip to a science museum and see if you observe differences in the ways that parents interact with girls and boys. For coding practice, see if you can (unobtrusively, of course) observe these interactions, and classify them according to the authors' categories (explanations, giving directions, and talking about evidence).

? After reading this study, you may feel there are other issues or questions that would be worthwhile or intriguing to address. Pose one of these questions (other than those suggested by the authors) that could be investigated empirically.

"I Knew We Would Win"

Hindsight Bias for Favorable and Unfavorable Team Decision Outcomes

Therese A. Louie, Mary T. Curren, and Katrin R. Harich

*Abstract*_____

This study examined hindsight bias for team decisions in a competitive setting in which groups attempted to outperform each other. It was anticipated that, because of self-serving mechanisms, individuals would show hindsight bias only when decision outcomes allowed them to take credit for their own team's success or to downgrade another team for being unsuccessful. MBA students playing a market simulation game made hindsight estimates regarding the likelihood that either their own or another team would perform well. Consistent with a self-serving interpretation, when decision outcomes were favorable individuals evaluating their own team, but not those evaluating another, showed hindsight bias. When outcomes were unfavorable individuals evaluating their own team did not show hindsight bias, but those evaluating another team did. Discussion focuses on implications of hindsight bias in team decision-making settings.

Conceptual Issues and Theoretical Questions _____

- How does the hindsight bias (the tendency to believe that you "knew it all along") operate in situations that involve competition?
- How does the hindsight bias operate in the context of team (as opposed to individual) decision making?
- Does the hindsight bias change as a function of whether someone is an observer of, or actor within, a given situation?
- Does the hindsight bias change, depending on whether the outcomes in question are favorable or unfavorable?

Louie, T. A., Curren, M. T., & Harich, K. R. (2000). "I knew we would win": Hindsight bias for favorable and unfavorable team decision outcomes. *Journal of Applied Psychology, 85,* 264–272. Copyright © 2000 by the American Psychological Association. Reprinted with permission.

De-Jargonizing

postdictions: estimates of the likelihood of some event, made *after* the event has already occurred

a priori likelihood: independent estimation of likelihood

external attribution: determining the cause of some event to be due to situational causes (i.e., environment)

internal attribution: determining the cause of some event to be due to dispositional factors (i.e., personality)

In the 1970s, the Washington Public Power Supply System (WPPSS), a consortium of public utilities, planned to build seven nuclear power plants to meet energy needs that were forecasted to grow by 7% per year (Baden, 1995). Up through the early 1980s more than 27,000 investors bought bonds supporting the project. During that time, however, higher energy prices prompted consumers to insulate water heaters and lower thermostats. As a result of these consumption changes and advances in technology, the demand for power grew by only 1–2%. Ultimately, just one of the seven nuclear power plants was completed, so in 1983 WPPSS defaulted on bonds worth $2.25 billion. Investors decided to sue. As a group they were involved in lawsuits that continued well into the 1990s. WPPSS claimed throughout the process that the default was unfortunate but not highly foreseeable. In contrast, investors claimed that WPPSS should have known that the demand for power would change such that there would no longer be a need for large-scale high-technology projects.

The different perspectives held by the two sides of the WPPSS fiasco bring to mind the question of how outcome information can bias the perception of what individuals would or should have known at the time that a decision was originally made. In particular, research indicates that hindsight distortion can influence post-outcome perceptions (Fischhoff, 1975). This bias occurs when outcomes seem more inevitable in hindsight than they did in foresight. Referred to as the "knew-it-all-along effect," hindsight bias occurs when individuals feel as if they would have predicted the outcome to events better than they actually did, or better than they actually would have had they been asked to make a forecast. The bias occurs when individuals are asked to recall original predictions (Fischhoff & Beyth, 1975) and even when individuals are specifically asked to ignore outcome information (Fischhoff, 1977).

In terms of legal strategy, it made sense for WPPSS to state that the default was not foreseeable and for investors to claim it was. Yet, because of mechanisms that influence hindsightful reasoning, it is also possible that each team to some degree truly believed their position. Although hindsight bias has been studied extensively, a review of research to date reveals no studies that have investigated whether or why competitors show hindsight bias. Given the prevalence of team decision making, an understanding of factors that influence hindsight bias in such settings would presumably be of theoretical and practical interest. This research investigated the extent of bias that individuals show both for their own and for competing teams' decision outcomes.

Background

Hindsight Bias

Hindsight distortion is a pervasive bias that has occurred in a variety of political, managerial, military, and health care settings (for a review, see Christensen-Szalanski & Willham, 1991, and Hawkins & Hastie, 1990). For example, Bukszar and Connolly (1988) asked research participants to read a managerial case that described a group's decision to expand a company. One set of participants was asked to make predictions regarding the likelihood that the decision would result in a favorable or an unfavorable outcome. The remaining participants read about the same event but were additionally told that either a favorable or an unfavorable outcome had actually occurred. These participants then made "**postdictions**": they estimated the **a priori likelihood** of occurrence of the two outcomes. As expected, participants who had received outcome information, relative to those who had not, assigned higher likelihoods of occurrence to the particular outcome they received.

Bukszar and Connolly (1988) used a between-subjects hindsight design wherein participants made either predictions or postdictions. Using a different approach, Fischhoff and Beyth (1975) tested hindsight bias with a within-subject design wherein participants were asked to make both types of estimates. When making postdictions, these participants were asked to remember their original predictions. In some respects the within-subject design is a more rigorous test of hindsight effects. It may be easier for individuals to recall closely their own predictions—and hence to show little or no bias—than it is for them to estimate what they think they would have predicted. Even with the more conservative within-subject task, Fischhoff and Beyth's (1975) research participants showed hindsight bias.

Although Bukszar and Connolly's (1988) work indicated that individuals show hindsight bias when observing a group's decision, the WPPSS example suggests the question of how individuals display the bias when evaluating their own group's decision. Uninvestigated in past work is how individuals show hindsight bias when they participate in, instead of observe, a group or team effort.

Team Members' Perspectives

When individuals are asked to make hindsight estimates for their own team's outcome, it might be reasoned that—similar to Bukszar and Connolly's (1988) participants—they would show the bias for favorable as well as unfavorable decision outcomes. Yet when making hindsight estimates for their own, instead of another, team's decision individuals have heightened personal relevance. Investigations of hindsight bias in more self-relevant settings suggest that individuals do not show the bias indiscriminately (Louie, 1999; Mark & Mellor, 1991). Instead, they show the bias selectively for favorable outcomes.

For example, Mark and Mellor (1991) used a naturally occurring situation to investigate how personal relevance influences hindsight bias. They asked three teams of individuals to make postdictions regarding the foreseeability of a layoff: laid-off workers, workers who kept their jobs through the layoffs, and community members. The first, set of participants rated the layoff as less foreseeable than the second set, which in turn rated the layoff as less foreseeable than the third set. As the personal relevance of the layoff increased, hindsight bias decreased.

Mark and Mellor (1991) interpreted their results as consistent with the influence of the self-serving bias. Self-serving mechanisms prompt individuals to take credit for favorable outcomes and avoid blame for unfavorable outcomes (Bradley, 1978; Wortman, Costanzo, & Witt, 1973). Whereas the former may encourage hindsight effects (e.g., "I knew my decision would result in a favorable outcome"), the latter may dampen the bias (e.g., "The unfavorable decision outcome was not foreseeable and was not my fault"). The laid-off individuals may not have shown the bias because they wanted to avoid blame for an outcome that was unfavorable to them.

Another explanation for Mark and Mellor's (1991) findings is that the laid-off individuals were surprised at the outcome and that their astonishment prevented feelings of foreseeability. This interpretation is consistent with the findings of research investigating the influence of surprise (e.g., Hoch & Loewenstein, 1989; Ofir & Mazursky, 1997). However, to further support a self-serving interpretation, research efforts (Louie, 1999) found that (a) participants who received favorable outcomes displayed hindsight bias, but not when their inclination to take credit for success was suppressed, and (b) those who received unfavorable outcomes did not show hindsight effects and made more **external** than **internal attributions** for the outcome. These findings provided additional support that self-serving mechanisms can influence hindsight effects in addition to any reactions of surprise.

Curren, Folkes, and Steckel (1992) found that when individuals strive together at a team decision, they show group-serving attributions that parallel the individual-level self-serving bias. Therefore, we proposed that individuals would show hindsight bias when their team decision outcomes were favorable, but not when the outcomes were unfavorable. It is worthwhile to note that some group research findings suggest a different pattern of hindsight effects. Schlenker and Miller (1977) found that individuals whose judgments were combined into a team decision distanced themselves from unfavorable team outcomes. In such settings, the distancing process may prompt individuals to show hindsight bias for unfavorable outcomes (e.g., "I am not really involved in the team, and I knew the outcome would be unfavorable"). Given the possibility of individual dissociation, it is worthwhile to examine whether team members show a pattern of hindsight bias similar to that shown by individual decision makers.

In summary, if individuals involved in team decision making feel more personal relevance than those who are not involved, and if heightened relevance triggers self-serving mechanisms, then team members may show hindsight bias when their decision outcomes are favorable but not when they are unfavorable. The latter finding would be consistent with the WPPSS officials' perspective that they could not have foreseen the bond default. Similar to Curren et al.'s (1992) work, these ideas are tested in this research using a naturally existing, personally relevant setting. Management students who were divided into 10 decision-making teams made predictions and postdictions for their performance on a graded class assignment.

Competing Team Members' Perspectives

The setting for this research provided an additional opportunity to explore how self-serving mechanisms influence hindsight bias. It is possible to examine how individuals react to other teams' decision outcomes in a competitive setting in which groups want to outperform one another. To illustrate, suppose that of the 10 teams mentioned above, the members of the first 5 teams were asked to make hindsight estimates for the performance outcome of the last 5 teams. Although the performance outcome of the last 5 teams would not be directly self-relevant to members of the first 5 teams, in a competitive setting other teams' outcomes would not be completely irrelevant or inconsequential. It is interesting to consider how hindsight bias would be displayed for other teams' outcomes given a game-type environment, as it presumably has implications in professional environments where resources and awards are allocated competitively.

There is reason to believe that in competitive settings, self-serving tendencies may have opposite effects when individuals evaluate another, rather than their own, team. Research findings suggest that individuals give others less credit for favorable outcomes, and more blame for unfavorable outcomes, than they do for themselves (for a review, see Taylor & Brown, 1988). In addition, Taylor and Koivumaki (1976) found that attributions regarding specified others can differ depending upon the role the others have in the life of the person making the attribution. For example, the researchers found that spouses and friends were more likely to be seen as causing positive behaviors than were strangers and acquaintances. Their research findings differ from those of other work wherein participants were asked to make attributions for an anonymous group (e.g., "most students," or "most people"); in the latter situation, attributions were generally neutral with regard to whether the other individuals caused favorable or unfavorable outcomes (Mirels, 1980).

If attributions for close others are similar to those for oneself, and if attributions for a group of anonymous others are neutral, it is reasonable to propose that attributions are quite dissimilar when the self–other relationship becomes not only more distant but oppositional. This might be especially so for situations similar to that used in this study, in which team performances were interdependent. Accordingly, individuals may exhibit hindsight bias when observing another team's unfavorable outcome (e.g., "I knew they would not do well") but not when witnessing another's favorable outcome (e.g., "I did not foresee that they would do so well"). Building on past work in which participants were unconcerned observers of another team's performance (e.g., Bukszar & Connolly, 1988), this research examined hindsight bias in settings in which team participants want themselves, but not others, to succeed.

Measuring Team Members' Hindsight Bias and Self-Serving Mechanisms

The main focus of this research was to examine how individuals show hindsight bias for team decision outcomes in a competitive and personally consequential setting. Another way that this work builds on hindsight bias studies in self-relevant settings is that the bias was examined using the stringent within-subject design. Mark and Mellor (1991) measured postdictions only, and Louie (1999) used a between-subjects design. The present study provides a strong test of self-serving effects on hindsight bias by asking individuals to make, then recollect, their predictions.

In this research it is desirable to include measures to assess whether the decision outcome information does indeed prompt self-serving mechanisms. It is difficult, however, to measure such processes with direct questions (e.g., "How are you affected by the outcome information?") because self-protecting mechanisms might allow participants to deny successfully any negative reactions. In achievement settings researchers have overcome this issue by using participants' evaluations of the research tasks as indirect measures of self-serving activity (for a review, see Taylor & Brown, 1988). For example, individuals have shown self-serving mechanisms by positively evaluating tasks that allowed them to dwell on favorable rather than unfavorable feedback.

Therefore, in this work the participants' reactions to the outcome information were assessed through their feelings about the task of making postdictions. If outcomes are favorable and participants are influenced by self-serving mechanisms, those reviewing their own team's decisions (who would react positively to their own success) should show more interest in making postdictions than those reviewing another team's decision. In contrast, when outcomes are unfavorable, participants reviewing their own rather than another's past decision should react more negatively to the task of making postdictions.

In summary, we hypothesized that when individuals received favorable outcome information they (a) would show hindsight bias for their own, but not for another, team's decision outcome and (b) would react more favorably to the task of making postdictions when reviewing. their own, rather than another, team. In contrast, when participants received unfavorable outcome information they (a) would show hindsight bias for another, but not their own, team's decision outcome and (b) would react more negatively to the task of making postdictions for their own rather than another team.

Method

Overview

As stated above, this study was conducted in a personally relevant setting wherein student teams' performances on a decision-making task affected their course grades. The context for this research was a marketing strategy computer simulation game called MARK-STRAT (Larreche & Gatignon, 1990). This game was deemed an appropriate context for this study because both academics and managers believe MARKSTRAT constitutes a realistic environment in which students can become actively involved in making managerial decisions (Kinnear & Wammer, 1987). Also, using this game, Curren et al. (1992) demonstrated that self-serving mechanisms (as measured with rating scales) are triggered in team decision-making settings. In MARKSTRAT, teams of students are assigned to one of five business firms. With the goal of strengthening their market position, the members of each firm meet together regularly to make a series of managerial decisions. As with real-world companies, a MARKSTRAT firm's performance depends on its own decisions and those of the other firms. The players in this study received weekly feedback about their performance, such as their team's proportion of total dollar sales or market share.

Participants

Seventy-one MBA students, enrolled in a marketing course, participated in this study. They had an average of 2 years' work experience. As stated above, the students in each firm made managerial decisions jointly. In contrast, they responded to the research materials individually and were assured anonymity.

Procedure

Participants were told that the study was being conducted to explore the dynamics of managerial decision making. When the study questionnaires were distributed, the instructor was running separate MARKSTRAT simulation games, referred to as Game I and Game II each with five teams or firms, A through E. For the study, the players were instructed to make hindsight estimates regarding a specific target firm's marketshare performance. That is, at the start of the games, each participant was asked to review the first set of decisions made by those in the target firm he or she was assigned to evaluate. The participant was then asked to make predictions about the target firm's upcoming market-share performance.

One week after making predictions, and after the game administrator had run the market simulation, the participants were individually presented with the decision information that they reviewed earlier. This time, however, they also received updates regarding the target firm's actual performance. After being reminded that they had made predictions a week earlier, they then made postdictions (i.e., were asked to recall their pre-outcome estimates) regarding the target firm's market share.

Independent Variables

Self and other team evaluation conditions. The participants were divided into "self" and "other" team evaluation conditions. Players in the self-evaluation condition were asked to make estimates regarding the market share of their own firm. The remaining players were assigned to the other-evaluation condition. These participants provided estimates for a firm participating in a MARKSTRAT game other than their own. For example, in the other-evaluation condition a participant in Game I, Firm A, made hindsight estimates for the team decision of the participants in Game II, Firm A.

It is important to note that each participant in the other-evaluation condition did not compete directly in the same MARKSTRAT game with participants in the team he or she evaluated. For example, those in Game I, Firm A did not evaluate those in Game I, Firm B. Informing individuals of firm decisions within the same game would have compromised the integrity of the assignment, as part of the task was for each team to anticipate how firms in the same game would behave. Showing a participant the decision of a firm in the same game would be like giving a football player an opposing team's playbook. However, all teams from both games were opponents in that their performance influenced their course grade. They were informed that the two teams that achieved the best performance in the class as a whole (not just in their particular game) received a grade of A for their game, the next two received an A–, and so on down to the worst two teams. In this manner, teams competed against each other not only in their respective games but also against every other team in the class. For this reason, all firms wanted to perform the best and did not want other firms to do well.

Favorable and unfavorable outcome conditions. To test the influence of outcome information, firms were divided into those that received favorable and those that received unfavorable feedback. Outcome favorableness was measured by the direction in which the target firm's market share changed after the initial decisions were implemented. Because an objective of the game was for players to increase their firm's standing, players who evaluated target firms that had increases in market share were in the favorable-outcome condition, and those who evaluated target firms that had decreases in market share were in the unfavorable-outcome condition.

Dependent Variables

Hindsight Estimates.   Before receiving outcome information, participants predicted the likelihood that the target firm's market share would increase, decrease, and stay the same. Participants were instructed that their estimates should sum to 100%.

A week after making predictions, the participants were informed of their target firm's actual market share performance (either that market share had increased or decreased, as no firm's share remained the same). They were reminded that they had previously made predictions about the outcomes and then were asked to recall to the best of their ability what they had predicted. The instructions emphasized that participants should ignore outcome information when making postdictions.

Interest in Postdiction Task.   Two measures were used to provide evidence of participants' self-serving activity upon receiving outcome information. After making postdictions, participants were asked the extent to which they thought the postdiction questionnaire was interesting. They responded on a scale of 1 (*not at all interesting*) to 10 (*very interesting*). Then participants were instructed to explain why they felt the postdiction questions were or were not interesting. Thus, both close-ended and open-ended measures were used to find evidence of the self-serving bias.

Results

Prediction and Postdiction Scores

Three participants did not complete the postdiction task and were eliminated from the analysis. Similar to the procedure used in other within-subject hindsight studies (Campbell & Teaser, 1983; Haslam & Jayasinghe, 1995; Wood, 1978) the remaining participants' likelihood estimates were combined so that each participant had one prediction and one postdiction score. We simplified the prediction estimates by calculating the net likelihood of an increase. The likelihood of a market share increase was multiplied by 1, the likelihood of a decrease was multiplied by −1, and the likelihood of market share staying the same was multiplied by 0. The resulting three numbers were summed to form each participant's prediction score. A participant who predicted that the target firm's market share had a 50% chance of increasing, a 30% chance of decreasing, and a 20% chance of staying the same had a prediction score of 20. The same calculations were made for the postdiction estimates. In this coding scheme, participants who were informed that their target firm's market share increased showed hindsight bias if the postdiction score exceeded the prediction score. In contrast, for unfavorable outcomes (i.e., reduced market share) a drop in the net likelihood of an increase from prediction to postdiction reflected hindsight bias.

The changes between the participants' predictions and postdictions were analyzed across evaluation conditions using a repeated measures analysis of variance, with firm membership as a factor in the model. Because outcome favorableness was based on the actual results of the market simulation game, it was not appropriate to use it as a factor, as this would have required random assignment to the outcome conditions. Therefore, the analysis was conducted first for those in the favorable-outcome condition, then separately for those in the unfavorable-outcome condition.

Favorable-Outcome Condition

Hindsight Findings.   The mean prediction and postdiction scores for the favorable- and unfavorable-outcome conditions are presented in Table 1. A favorable outcome is represented by an increase in market share. A repeated measures analysis of variance (ANOVA) revealed a significant within-subject main effect of prediction versus postdiction score that was qualified by a significant within-subject interaction of these estimates across the evaluation conditions, $F(1, 29) = 11.02, p < .01, \omega^2 = .19$. We anticipated that participants receiving favorable outcome information would show hindsight bias for their own, but not another, team's decision. As we expected, a within-subject test of the difference between prediction and postdiction scores revealed that self-evaluation participants showed the bias: their mean net postdiction score for an increase in market share exceeded their mean prediction score, $t(14) = 3.72, p < .01, d = 0.73$. In contrast, and also as we anticipated, other-evaluation condition participants did not show the bias, as their mean postdiction score for their target firm did not differ significantly from their prediction score, $t(17) = 0.29, ns, d = 0.04$.

There is further evidence that self-evaluation condition participants shifted their estimates according to the nature of the outcome information. As can be seen in Table 1, their

TABLE 1   *Mean Hindsight Estimates*

Measure	Net likelihood of an increase	
	Prediction	*Postdiction*
Favorable-outcome condition		
Self-evaluation ($n = 15$)[a]	16.00 (33.34)	39.33 (30.81)
Other evaluation ($n = 18$)	−1.39 (28.48)	−0.28 (27.89)
Unfavorable-outcome condition		
Self-evaluation ($n = 17$)	14.12 (30.37)	16.18 (30.80)
Other evaluation ($n = 18$)[a]	0.00 (45.86)	−17.22 (30.78)

Note: Numbers in parentheses are standard deviations.
[a]Means in this row differ at $p < .05$.

mean prediction score did not differ significantly from that of other-evaluation partici-pants, $t(31) = 1.52$, *ns, d* $= 0.56$. Yet the self-evaluation participants' mean postdiction score was significantly higher, $t(31) = 4.02, p < .01, d = 1.35$. In support of a hindsight ef-fect, we found that after self-evaluation participants received favorable outcome informa-tion, they felt more strongly than did other-evaluation participants that they had previously predicted a favorable outcome.

Interest in Postdiction Questions.   The mean ratings for the favorable-outcome partici-pants' level of interest in the postdiction questions are presented in Table 2. The data are consistent with the view that, relative to other-evaluation participants, self-evaluation par-ticipants reacted more positively to the outcome information. As we anticipated, partici-pants rated the task of making postdictions as more interesting when evaluating their own instead of another firm's decision, $t(31) = 2.52, p < .05, d = 0.82$.

We also analyzed the participants' open-ended remarks about their interest in the postdiction questions. The responses for the favorable- and unfavorable-outcome teams were shuffled randomly together and then analyzed by two independent coders. Both coders were undergraduates who were trained to categorize open-ended responses. They were not informed of the research hypotheses or the experimental conditions. After the coders counted the total number of thoughts for each participant, they coded the content of the comments. Most of the responses, as we had requested, were about the postdiction questionnaire. These responses were separated into those that were positive about the ma-terials (e.g., "This provides insight into the decision-making process,"), and those that were negative (e.g., "This survey is given in conditions that make it relatively useless"). A third category was added to accommodate miscellaneous comments that were irrelevant to the postdiction questionnaire (e.g., "R & D [research and development], sales, and re-search all have an impact on the team result"). Agreement between the coders was 81% with all discrepancies resolved through discussion.

Analysis of the favorable-outcome participants' open-ended responses across the self- and other-evaluation conditions revealed no significant differences in the total number of thoughts, $t(31) = 0.50$, *ns, d* $= 0.19$. We anticipated that compared with other-evaluation par-ticipants, self-evaluation participants would have more positive comments about the post-diction questions. However, the self-evaluation participants did not have a significantly higher mean number of positive comments, $t(31) = 0.72$, *ns, d* $= 0.30$. There were also no differences across evaluation conditions in the mean number of negative thoughts, $t(31) = 0.88$, *ns, d* $= 0.37$, or the mean number of miscellaneous thoughts, $t(31) = 0.82$, *ns, d* $= 0.33$.

In short, the self-evaluation participants had a higher rated level of interest in the postdiction task than did the other-evaluation participants, but an analysis of the open-ended responses revealed no greater number of positive comments. There is partial sup-porting evidence that the former participants' hindsight bias was based on their positive re-action to the outcome information.

Unfavorable-Outcome Condition

Hindsight Findings.   For unfavorable-outcome-condition participants, hindsight bias was displayed if the mean postdiction score that market share will increase was lower than

TABLE 2   *Treatment Means for Reaction to Postdiction Task*

	Evaluation condition	
Measure	*Self*	*Other*
Favorable-outcome condition		
n	15	18
Interest rating[a]	6.13	4.28
	(2.10)	(2.37)
Total number of thoughts	0.53	0.72
	(0.92)	(1.02)
Positive comments about postdiction questionnaire	0.20	0.39
	(0.56)	(0.70)
Negative comments about postdiction questionnaire	0.13	0.28
	(0.35)	(0.46)
Miscellaneous comments	0.20	0.05
	(0.56)	(0.24)
Unfavorable-outcome condition		
n	17	18
Interest rating	5.00	5.56
	(1.73)	(2.03)
Total number of thoughts	1.35	0.72
	(1.32)	(0.96)
Positive comments about postdiction questionnaire	0.29	0.17
	(0.59)	(0.38)
Negative comments about postdiction questionnaire[a]	1.00	0.33
	(1.12)	(0.59)
Miscellaneous comments	0.06	0.22
	(0.24)	(0.43)

Note: Numbers in parentheses are standard deviations.
[a]Means in this row differ at $p < .05$.

the mean prediction score. A repeated measures ANOVA revealed a significant within-subject interaction effect for the prediction and postdiction scores across evaluation conditions, $F(1, 31) = 4.90$, $p < .05$, $\omega^2 = .08$. As we anticipated, self-evaluation participants did not show hindsight distortion for their own team's unfavorable outcomes. As can be seen by the means presented in Table 1, within-subject tests revealed that the self-evaluation participants' mean postdiction score was not significantly different from their mean prediction score, $t(16) = 0.23$, *ns*, $d = 0.07$. In contrast, and as we anticipated, the other-evaluation participants showed hindsight bias for another team's unfavorable outcome because their mean postdiction score was lower and significantly different from their mean prediction score, $t(17) = 2.34$, $p < .05$, $d = 0.44$.

Similar to the analysis for the favorable outcome team, an examination of the pattern of predictions and postdictions revealed that the differences between the self- and other-evaluation participants occurred after the presentation of outcome information. As can be seen in Table 1, the mean prediction scores do not differ significantly across the evaluation conditions, $t(33) = 0.71$, *ns*, $d = 0.36$. However, relative to the self-evaluation participants, the other-evaluation participants' mean postdiction score was significantly lower, $t(33) = 2.96$, $p < .01$, $d = 1.08$. In support of the notion of a hindsight effect, after receiving outcome information, other-evaluation participants felt more strongly than did self-evaluation participants that they had predicted unfavorable outcomes.

Interest in Postdiction Questions. As can be seen in Table 2, and contrary to our expectations, the self-evaluation participants did not rate the experimental task as significantly less interesting than the other-evaluation participants after receiving unfavorable outcome information, $t(33) = 0.81$, *ns*, $d = 0.30$.

However, the participants' open-ended comments were consistent with the view that the self-evaluation participants reacted more negatively to the postdiction questions than the other-evaluation participants did. Although the total number of thoughts across the two evaluation conditions was not significantly different, $t(33) = 1.56$, *ns*, $d = 0.55$, self-evaluation participants provided a higher mean number of negative comments than did other-evaluation participants, $t(33) = 2.49$, $p < .05$, $d = 0.75$. There were no significant differences across self- and other-evaluation participants in the mean number of positive thoughts, $t(33) = 0.51$, *ns*, $d = 0.24$, or the mean number of miscellaneous thoughts, $t(33) = 1.54$, *ns*, $d = 0.46$. Whereas the favorable-outcome self-evaluation participants showed a more positive reaction to the postdiction task through the rating scale measure, the unfavorable-outcome self-evaluation participants showed a more negative reaction through open-ended comments.

Supplementary Hindsight Analysis

Although the hindsight findings are consistent with a self-serving interpretation, it is worthwhile to note potential limitations of the hindsight measure and to provide additional support for the findings. As in past work (e.g., Leary, 1981), the dependent variable was constructed as a net likelihood of an increase score because it standardized participants' likelihood estimates into a measure that represented the optimism (or lack thereof) they felt about their target firm. Yet this measure is potentially problematic because it is a difference score. For example, difference scores are less reliable than individual component scores when the latter are positively correlated (Peter, Churchill, & Brown, 1993). This particular issue is not a problem in this study because the participants' likelihood estimates for an increase and a decrease were negatively correlated ($r = -.73$), which enhances reliability (Peter et al., 1993, footnote 3). One might also say that because the hypothesized effects were found, credence is given to the validity of the measure. Nonetheless, it is worthwhile to examine the data in a manner that does not incur the errors caused by combining likelihood estimates.

We analyzed the data again using another representation of the dependent measure. One can examine predictions and postdictions by focusing on the outcome that meets the objective of the event of interest (e.g., Connolly & Bukszar, 1990; Schkade & Kilbourne, 1991). For this study, the relevant likelihood estimate would be the one that corresponds with the objective to increase market share. When we analyzed the data focusing on the likelihood of an increase estimate, the findings remained the same as when using the net likelihood of an increase score. For those who received favorable outcome information, participants in the self-evaluation condition showed a significant amount of hindsight bias in the difference between their predictions and postdictions ($M = 18.33$, $SD = 15.99$), $t(14) = 4.44$, $p < .01$, $d = 1.17$. Participants in the other-evaluation condition did not ($M = 1.11$, $SD = 12.43$), $t(17) = 0.38$, ns, $d = 0.07$. For those who received unfavorable outcome information, self-evaluation participants did not show a significant amount of hindsight bias ($M = -0.29$, $SD = 21.61$), $t(16) = -0.06$, ns, $d = 0.02$. The other-evaluation participants did show a significant amount of bias ($M = -10.56$, $SD = 19.17$), $t(17) = 2.34$, $p < .05$, $d = .54$.

To further explore the findings, the data were examined one final way using the original net likelihood of an increase score. Instead of investigating the results for the favorable- and unfavorable-outcome conditions separately, we pooled the data together and analyzed them with a regression. The participants were divided into two groups. A hindsight group was composed of participants who we anticipated would show a significant amount of bias (i.e., those in the self-evaluation/favorable-outcome and other-evaluation/unfavorable-outcome conditions). A no-hindsight group was composed of the participants who were not expected to show the bias (i.e., those in the self-evaluation/unfavorable-outcome and other-evaluation/favorable-outcome conditions). The differences between the prediction and postdiction scores were regressed on these dummy variables. As we expected, participants in the hindsight group showed a significant amount of hindsight bias; the estimated coefficient was 20.00, which was statistically significant ($p < .01$). Participants in the no-hindsight group did not show a significant amount of bias. The estimated coefficient for that group was -0.43 ($p > .90$). The difference between the two groups (i.e., 20.43) was significant ($p < .01$).

The hindsight results were consistent across three measurement approaches, and when the dependent variable was and was not measured as a difference score. (Complete details of the two supplementary analyses are available from the authors.) Together, the findings provide support for the anticipated effects.

Discussion

Hindsight Bias in Team Decision-Making Settings

Taken together, the self- and other-evaluation findings strongly support the notion that self-serving mechanisms can influence hindsight bias when individuals evaluate team decision outcomes in personally relevant settings. First, consistent with past findings (Louie, 1999; Mark & Mellor, 1991) but applied to a team decision-making setting, the self-evaluation participants showed hindsight bias only when their outcomes were favorable. If the favorable-outcome participants had been asked to update their predictions based on outcome information, then it would have been appropriate for them to make postdictions that were influenced by outcome information. However, because they were asked not to revise but to recall their original predictions, and because their recollection was biased in the direction of outcome information, there is evidence of a systematic hindsight effect.

Second, this study investigated hindsight bias for other teams' decisions in a competitive setting. The interdependence of the teams' performances produced heightened relevance, which appears to have triggered self-serving mechanisms. This, in turn, prompted participants to show hindsight bias when other teams' outcomes were unfavorable but not when they were favorable. Unlike in past work—and as we expected for settings in which individuals want their own team, but not another's, to perform well—the patterns of hindsight bias for other-evaluation and for self-evaluation participants were opposites.

Finally, these findings were obtained using a conservative within-subject hindsight measure. Attesting to the strength of self-serving mechanisms, participants' recall of their predictions was influenced by outcome feedback in the pattern we anticipated.

The findings for the participants' interest in the task of making postdictions were not as consistent as we expected. The results prompt the question of why the interest ratings were significantly different, as we anticipated for the favorable but not the unfavorable outcome participants, and why the open-ended responses were significantly different, as we expected for unfavorable but not favorable outcomes. The answer may lie in the nature of positive and negative feedback for self-evaluation participants on personally relevant tasks. Research findings suggest that individuals strive to obtain a positive self-view, and hence are optimistic that they or their team will perform well (Taylor & Brown, 1988). When feedback is favorable, individuals may positively evaluate the tasks related to their performance but may not have many comments because the outcome matches their expectations.

In contrast, unfavorable feedback is unanticipated. Individuals are prompted to reconcile the discrepancy between what was expected and what actually occurred (Mandler, 1982). This may account for the higher number of negative comments from the unfavorable outcome participants in the self-evaluation rather than the other-evaluation condition. It is not clear why the former, relative to the latter, participants did not downgrade their rating of the task. However, it is possible that their required and continued participation in the game for their class assignment prevented them from expressing their discontent through a direct-ratings measure. In short, perhaps because of prior expectations and the anticipation of future performances, favorable and unfavorable outcome participants reacted differently to the interest measures.

Implications of Hindsight Bias in Team Decision-Making Settings

The findings help to explain why team members who receive unfavorable outcome feedback, such as the WPPSS officials, do not show hindsight bias. Alternatively, when outcomes are favorable, there are many implications when team members show the bias. Research suggests that hindsight distortion is linked to exaggerated confidence (e.g., Bodenhausen, 1990; Bukszar & Connolly, 1988) and to reduced predictive accuracy (Hoch

& Loewenstein, 1989). Team members should beware of the hubris that can develop when favorable decision outcomes seem inevitable. One example of this is provided by Long-Term Capital Management, a group of prominent economists and stockbrokers who, some analysts would claim, became too self-assured that both, past and future financial triumphs were inevitable (Glassman, 1998). Confident because of their past success, the group continued investing and borrowing heavily even when they were warned that collapsing economies around the world made their actions extremely risky. As a result, during the stock market turmoil of 1998 the company lost 90% of its investors' money. To prevent mistakes fueled by hindsight bias, teams would benefit from occasional audits conducted by an external party that does not have a personal stake in—and hence would not fall prey to self-serving mechanisms from—the favorable outcomes in question. An auditor who is aware of the tendency to take credit for success could attempt to keep teams grounded in reality.

Another idea is that team members could attempt to self-monitor. Although some researchers found that participants continued to show hindsight distortion even after being warned of its existence and asked to avoid it (Fischhoff, 1977; Pohl & Hell, 1996), other findings indicate that participants can indeed eliminate the bias if they are informed of personally relevant consequences to showing it. For example, Louie (1999) found that participants who received favorable decision outcomes showed the bias, but not when they were warned that it reduces predictive accuracy. Perhaps in the same manner, successful team members can be given a self-relevant incentive not to show the bias or can be warned of its future personal consequences.

Perhaps a more direct approach to reducing hindsight distortion is to make decreasing the bias a team objective. Stahlberg, Eller, Maass, and Frey (1995), although they did not study group decision making, investigated how individuals separately or in groups showed hindsight bias upon learning the outcomes to scientific studies or the answers to complex questions. The researchers found that individuals and groups show the same extent of hindsight bias with a between-subjects design and that groups show less bias when using the more conservative within-subject design. Hence, team members can formalize the desire to reduce or to stifle hindsight bias by collectively making predictions, which would decrease the magnitude of the bias (Stahlberg et al., 1995) and serve as a reality check that can be referred to when necessary. This process can be used for both an individual's own, as well as for another's, team decisions.

Hindsight bias for favorable outcomes can be dangerous not only to team members but also to those who want to be like them. The Long-Term Capital Management team included two Nobel laureates in economics and a former Federal Reserve Board vice chairman. With such pedigrees on the team, many of those who entrusted their funds were confident that success would continue and were therefore less concerned than usual with knowing the specifics of the company's dealings (O'Brien & Holson, 1998). Also, bank investment managers who admired the company partners and who carried out transactions for them sought to imitate their strategy by making similar dealings for their own clients. Hence, those who aspire to be like a successful team should be careful, as they can be influenced by the team's biased perspective, as well as develop their own hindsight-based rationales. Should outcomes become highly unfavorable, the aspiring individuals can dissociate from the team and, like the WPPSS investors, become former allies turned legal foes.

When feedback is unfavorable, teams should be aware that even if they do not see the outcome as foreseeable, others, especially opponents, might. This perspective could be important in situations such as the WPPSS legal battle, in which team members must convince a judge that they did not have previous knowledge of potentially unfavorable outcomes. This point is also illustrated by the lawsuits faced by blood donation centers that collected and distributed blood in the early 1980s. During that time, thousands of individuals contracted HIV from contaminated blood-related products. Years later, some of those individuals or their families filed lawsuits, alleging that the centers did not do all they could to screen tainted blood (King, 1989). The donation centers responded by noting that the cause of AIDS was unknown until 1984 and that there was no antibody test available until 1985. This tragic example illustrates how important it can be to understand perceptions in hindsight; a crucial consideration in the cases was determining whether the donation centers should have known to be more careful with the blood products and should have warned blood recipients of the risk. An understanding of what causes hindsight effects could help teams in similar situations discern how their previous actions are perceived by others. (In the late 1980s, donation centers had won 57% of the cases against them; King, 1989.)

Although we hope that this work provides insight into hindsight bias for team decisions, it would be worthwhile to pursue research outside of a classroom setting to see whether the same pattern of hindsight bias emerges. In addition, this study is limited in that it measured hindsight bias for decisions at a competitive task that was new to the participants. Although research (e.g., Arkes, Wortmann, Saville, & Harkness, 1981) has suggested that even experienced professionals show hindsight bias, future research can explore the relationship between expertise and hindsight bias in personally relevant team settings. More generally, this study brings up the possibility that individual differences may play a role in hindsight bias. The Long-Term Capital Management example and the findings obtained in this work from experienced and bright MBA students suggest that achievement-oriented individuals (who have obtained past successes) may be more susceptible to hind-sight effects. This possibility can be examined in future studies.

Finally, it is interesting to note that the founder of Long-Term Capital Management tried to warn his colleagues that market conditions were changing to their detriment. Yet his colleagues remained confident until the failure became too large for them to fix (Henriques, 1998). This suggests that team members might reinforce hindsight effects by reassuring each other of continued success. Researchers can investigate conditions under which people who show hindsight bias for favorable outcomes are more prone to overconfidence for team than for individual decisions. In sum, research can test the applicability of, as well as build on, this work in a variety of team decision-making settings.

References

Arkes, H. R., Wortmann, R. L., Saville, P. D., & Harkness, A. R. (1981). Hindsight bias among physicians weighing the likelihood of diagnoses. *Journal of Applied Psychology, 66,* 252–254.

Baden, J. A. (1995, April 12). WHOOPS: An expensive, valuable history lesson. *Seattle Times,* p. B5.

Bodenhausen, G. V. (1990). Second-guessing the jury: Stereotypic and hindsight biases in perceptions of court cases. *Journal of Applied Social Psychology, 20,* 1112–1121.

Bradley, G. W. (1978). Self-serving biases in the attribution process: A reexamination of the fact or fiction question. *Journal of Personality and Social Psychology, 36,* 56–71.

Bukszar, E., & Connolly, T. (1988). Hindsight bias and strategic choice: Some problems in learning from experience. *Academy of Management Journal, 31,* 628–641.

Campbell, J. D., & Tesser, A. (1983). Motivational interpretations of hindsight bias: An individual difference analysis. *Journal of Personality, 51,* 605–620.

Christensen-Szalanski, J. J. J., & Willham, C. F. (1991). The hindsight bias: A meta-analysis. *Organizational Behavior and Human Decision Processes, 48,* 147–168.

Connolly, T., & Bukszar, E. W. (1990). Hindsight bias: Self-flattery or cognitive error? *Journal of Behavioral Decision Making, 3,* 205–211.

Curren, M. T., Folkes, V. S., & Steckel, J. H. (1992). Explanations for successful and unsuccessful marketing decisions: The decision maker's perspective. *Journal of Marketing, 56,* 18–31.

Fischhoff, B. (1975). Hindsight ≠ foresight: The effect of outcome knowledge on judgment under uncertainty. *Journal of Experimental Psychology: Human Perception and Performance, 1,* 288–299.

Fischhoff, B. (1977). Perceived informativeness of facts. *Journal of Experimental Psychology Human Perception and Performance, 3,* 349–358.

Fischhoff, B., & Beyth, R. (1975). 'I knew it would happen'—Remembered probabilities of once-future things. *Organizational Behavior and Human Performance, 13,* 1–16.

Glassman, J. K. (1998, September 27). A simple strategy beats the 'experts.' *The Washington Post,* p. H01.

Haslam, N., & Jayasinghe, N. (1995). Negative affect and hindsight bias. *Journal of Behavioral Decision Making, 8,* 127–135.

Hawkins, S. A., & Hastie, R. (1990). Hindsight: Biased judgments of past events after the outcomes are known. *Psychological Bulletin, 107,* 311–327.

Henriques, D. B. (1998, September 27). Fault lines of risk appear as market hero stumbles. *New York Times,* p. 1.

Hoch, S. J., & Loewenstein, G. F. (1989). Outcome feedback: Hindsight *and* information. *Journal of Experimental Psychology: Learning, Memory, and Cognition, 15,* 605–619.

King, W. (1989, June 14). AIDS, blood and liability. *Seattle Times,* p. Al.

Kinnear, T. C., & Klammer, S. K. (1987). Management perspectives on MARKSTRAT: The GE experience and beyond. *Journal of Business Research, 15,* 491–502.

Larreche, J. C., & Gatignon, H. (1990). *MARKSTRAT2.* Redwood City, CA: Scientific Press.

Leary, Mark R. (1981). The distorted nature of hindsight. *Journal of Social Psychology, 115,* 25–29.

Louie, T. A. (1999). Decision makers' hindsight bias after receiving favorable and unfavorable feedback. *Journal of Applied Psychology, 84,* 29–41.

Mandler, G. (1982). The structure of value: Accounting for taste. In M. S. Clark & S. T. Fiske (Eds.), *Affect and cognition; The 17th Annual Carnegie Symposium* (pp. 3–36). Hillsdale, NJ: Erlbaum.

Mark, M. M., & Mellor, S. (1991). Effect of self-relevance of an event on hindsight bias: The foreseeability of a layoff. *Journal of Applied Psychology, 76,* 569–577.

Mirels, H. L. (1980). The avowal of responsibility for good and bad outcomes: The effects of generalized self-serving biases. *Personality and Social Psychology Bulletin, 6,* 299–306.

O'Brien, T. L., & Holson, L. M. (1998, October 23). A hedge fund's stars didn't tell and savvy financiers didn't ask. *New York Times,* p. 1.

Ofir, C., & Mazursky, D. (1997). Does a surprising outcome reinforce or reverse the hindsight bias? *Organizational Behavior and Human Decision Processes, 69,* 51–57.

Peter, J. P., Churchill, G. A., Jr., & Brown, T. J. (1993). Caution in the use of difference scores in consumer research. *Journal of Consumer Research, 19,* 655–662.

Pohl, R. F., & Hell, W. (1996). No reduction in hindsight bias after complete information and repeated testing. *Organizational Behavior and Human Decision Processes, 67,* 49–58.

Schkade, D. A., & Kilbourne, L. M. (1991). Expectation–outcome consistency and hindsight bias. *Organizational Behavior and Human Decision Processes, 49,* 105–123.

Schlenker, B. R., & Miller, R. S. (1977). Egocentrism in teams: Self-serving biases or logical information processing? *Journal of Personality and Social Psychology, 35,* 755–764.

Stahlberg, D., Eller, F., Maass, A., & Fray, D. (1995). We knew it all along: Hindsight bias in teams. *Organizational Behavior and Human Decision Processes, 63,* 46–58.

Taylor, S. E., & Brown, J. D. (1988). Illusion and well-being: A social psychological perspective on mental health. *Psychological Bulletin, 103,* 193–210.

Taylor, S. E., & Koivumaki, J. H. (1976). The perception of self and others: Acquaintanceship, affect, and actor–observer differences. *Journal of Personality and Social Psychology, 33,* 403–408.

Wood, G. (1978). The knew-it-all-along effect. *Journal of Experimental Psychology: Human Perception and Performance, 4,* 345–353.

Wortman, C. B., Costanzo, P. R., & Witt, T. R. (1973). Effect of anticipated performance on the attributions of causality to self and others. *Journal of Personality and Social Psychology, 27,* 372–381.

Introduction: Critical Thinking Questions _____

? Describe the "knew-it-all-along effect", and how it relates to the opening scenario described by the authors (the Washington Public Power Supply System).

? Explain the between-subjects hindsight design and the within-subjects hindsight design. Which is the stronger test of hindsight bias and why?

? How does the existence of a self-serving bias in attribution lead to the prediction that the hindsight bias may operate for favorable outcomes, but not for unfavorable ones?

? For unfavorable group decisions it can be predicted that hindsight bias would be low or high. Explain the reasons for each prediction.

? Describe how attributions differ with the relationship of the person making the attributions to the person being observed. How might these differences in attribution affect the hindsight bias?

? The researchers asked participants to give an evaluation of the postdiction task. What was the purpose of this additional measure?

Method: Critical Thinking Questions _____

? Describe what you would have been asked to do, had you been a participant in the experiment.

? Name the independent variables in the experiment, and their levels. Describe how each of these variables was operationalized. For each variable, state whether it was manipulated in a between-subjects or within-subjects fashion. How many conditions were there in the experiment?

? What was (were) the dependent variable(s) in the experiment?

? What aspects of the methodology were implemented to deal with possible confounds?

Results/Discussion: Critical Thinking Questions _____

? Describe the pattern of results obtained in the prediction/postdiction task. Was a hindsight bias observed? If so, under what conditions?

? Describe the pattern of results obtained from participants' reaction to the postdiction task. Did the results indicate self-serving bias as the locus of the hindsight effects? Explain.

? The authors state that "…team members should beware of the hubris that can develop when favorable decision outcomes seem inevitable." Describe what they mean by this, and explain their example. How might such costly hindsight effects be avoided?

? The authors assert that "when feedback is unfavorable, teams should be aware that even if they do not see the outcome as forseeable, others, especially opponents, might." Why would keeping this fact in mind be important?

? Describe the avenues for future research suggested by the authors.

? After reading this study, you may feel there are probably other issues or questions that would be worthwhile or intriguing to address. Pose one of these questions (other than those suggested by the authors) that could be investigated empirically.

Elaborative Memory Strategies of Professional Actors

Helga Noice

Abstract

Analysis of expert performance in various domains has revealed not only that experts posses a high degree of knowledge, but that this knowledge is very efficiently organized. But increased understanding of expertise has shed little light on what specific strategy is best suited for a particular task. This study investigated the strategies employed by professional actors in the course of learning theatrical scripts. Seven actors were asked to describe the procedure they use in preparing and learning a role. These protocols were then analysed for commonalities among subjects. The most important finding was that there was unanimous agreement among actors that they do not memorize the lines in a rote-type fashion. Instead they read the script many times, trying to infer the motivation behind each utterance. All of the actors stressed the importance of identifying the underlying meaning and of explaining why the character said those exact words. Apparently this type of 'active' understanding leads to verbatim retention of the text and makes word-for-word or line-for-line memorizing unnecessary.

Conceptual Issues and Theoretical Questions

- What are the processes that underlie the transition from novice to expert in professional actors?
- What specific strategies do professional actors employ to learn their parts?
- Can an analysis of the learning processes of professional actors be generalized to develop training techniques for novices?

De-Jargonizing

verbal protocols: self-reports of problem-solvers as they "think out loud" during some task

epiphenomenal: describes a simple by-product that is not indicative of the underlying process of interest

Noice, H. (1990). Elaborative memory strategies of professional actors. *Applied Cognitive Psychology, 6,* 417–427.
Copyright © 1990 by John Wiley & Sons, Ltd. Reproduced by permission of John Wiley & Sons Limited.

In recent years there has been a great deal of inquiry by cognitive psychologists into the nature of expertise. One long-range goal of this type of inquiry is the design of instructional materials that would facilitate the process of transition from novice to expert. Among the many areas of expertise studied have been the solving of physics problems, the reading of electronic diagrams, the performance of expert mental calculations and the mastery of such games as Go and Chess (e.g. Charness, 1979; Chase and Simon, 1973; Chi, Feltovich, and Glaser, 1981; Egan and Schwartz, 1979; Reitman, 1976; Reitman and Rueter, 1980; Staszewski, 1988). It is surprising that very little investigation has been done on how professional actors learn their roles. Yet this constitutes one of the most complex examples of expert memory: the acquisition of over 2 hours of verbal material in a 2–3-week rehearsal period and the ability to retrieve it in real time without hesitation or obvious groping for words.

Is it possible that an understanding of professional actors' strategies could result in the design of instructional materials that would facilitate learning in similar tasks frequently faced by students, such as memorizing passages from Shakespeare, making speeches and preparing class or conference presentations? A complex programme of research would be necessary to accomplish that goal, and this paper focuses on the first step in such a programme: the collection and analysis of protocols in which actors describe the nature of their memory strategies.

A search of the literature reveals only two studies concerning professional acting, a field in which the participants must memorize incredibly large bodies of complex material. One study (Oliver and Ericsson, 1986) investigated the accessibility and speed of retrieval of various parts of a role *after* the role had been thoroughly learned and was being professionally performed in repertory. Although this study did not address the question of learning strategy, it presented fascinating evidence on the direct accessibility of specific lines from any part of the play with minimal (one- or two-word) probes.

Indeed, there appears to be only one study, that has looked at actors' ability to learn text (Intons-Peterson and Smyth, 1987). The design of this experiment did not permit the investigation of what these experts actually do in their work. That is, instead of theatrical scripts, the subjects were given short prose passages which they had to rehearse out loud, word for word as they went along. So although the study investigated such factors as frequency of rehearsal of individual words, organization of material, and the structure, length and complexity of the passage, the strategies actors use when working on a role were not investigated. Therefore, the goal of this research was the identification of the learning strategies that are actually used by professional actors.

Method

To investigate the nature of an actor's knowledge base, **verbal protocols** of professional actors were collected and interpreted. The use of protocols as a means of examining cognitive processes has been explored by Ericsson and Simon (1984). They discussed techniques for using verbal reports as data in order to study complex mental processes, such as solving a problem or comprehending a prose passage. Their demonstration that a verbalization is as much a result of cognitive activity as other recordable behaviour led to the acceptance of 'verbal protocols as data', and opened up a wide area of research in expert-novice differences.

The study reported here analysed the verbal protocols of professional actors of various ages, styles, background and training. Before listing those points on which there seemed to be general agreement, it needs to be pointed out that these verbal reports were not generated while the subjects were engaged in the task of learning a role, rather they represented retrospective reports. That is, actors retrieved from memory information about the strategies they use when memorizing a role. But as Ericsson and Simon (1984) point out, 'information retrievable from LTM when requested by instruction should also be available to the subject when found useful in other situations. In these cases it seems unlikely that the stored information would be **epiphenomenal** in relation to the processes going on when it was stored.'

In their opinion, verbal reports can be very useful in identifying the type of information subjects are attending to while performing a particular task. Furthermore, since the nature of information requested in these protocols was procedural rather than introspective, there should be no reason to doubt its accuracy. A further objective of this study was to identify the underlying processing skill that characterizes the performances of these experts.

Subjects

Nine experts participated in the study. All of them were professional actors, seven of whom worked in the New York area and two in the Florida area. Each was unknown to the others. All of them had been active in professional theatre for a minimum of 5 years.

Collection of Protocols

The subjects were recruited individually, and as each agreed to the project, he or she was mailed a blank cassette tape. The first two subjects received identical instruction asking them to describe the procedures they used in preparing and learning roles. Both actors gave a detailed breakdown of their approach to analysis, preparation and rehearsal. While a great deal could be inferred from their protocols about their memorization processes, they gave very few specifics in this regard and therefore were excluded from the final analysis. Because of this, instructions were reworded and the remaining seven subjects were asked to describe the memorization process they used in the course of learning a role. In order to avoid demand characteristics, no other instructions were given (see appendix). All subjects returned the completed tapes, which were then transcribed.

Protocol Analysis

Protocols were examined for commonalities among subjects. Table 1 lists the basic approaches that actors claimed they used when learning a role. The most important finding was that there was unanimous agreement among actors that they did not simply sit down and memorize the words in a script. In fact, not a single actor reported starting with rote

TABLE 1   *Factors Involved in the Memorization of Theatrical Roles*

Task	Number of actors mentioning this item
A: Statements indicating no intent to memorize until other procedures have been accomplished	
1. Read play many times before any memorizing	7
2. Learn lines generally after blocking	7
3. Used a procedure not based on rote repetition	7
4. Pick-up lines while rehearsing with other actors	4
5. Paraphrase first, learn exact words later	3
6. Divide a role into sections and learn those	2
B: Statements concerned with motivations, intentions or interactions of characters	
1. Consider character's growth or progress in play	7
2. Associate motivation with blocking	7
3. Study character's ideas before learning lines	7
4. Think about relations with other characters	5
5. Analyse character's motivations	3
C: Statements regarding technical aspects of role learning	
1. Use of friend or tape recorder for cueing	3
2. Reproducing lines exactly as written	3
3. Writing out long speeches	2
4. Picturing the way the page looks	2
5. Learning progression of events in play	2

memorization. All seven actors stressed the importance of identifying the meaning of each line before committing it to memory. While this consensus existed with respect to such concepts as taking the character's perspective or ascribing intentions, individual differences appeared regarding the mechanics of studying a role. For example, only three out of seven used a friend or tape-recorder for auditory cueing.

Highlights from Protocols

All seven actors stated that before committing any words to memory, they read the script many, many times. They also claimed that they first try to extract the meaning of the text before they aim for word-for-word-accuracy. That is, they try to understand and retain the ideas expressed in the play before trying to memorize the words in which these ideas were expressed. As Subject 7 put it,

> I pretty much learn the ideas first, before I really care about the exact words ...after all that's what we're doing here, exchanging ideas...we're imitating life after all. That seems to be the way it works in life, you know. Somebody throws an idea at you and you throw an idea back at them.

As a matter of fact, many stated explicitly that they make an effort not to learn any of the words prior to rehearsal. Subject 3 explains,

> Now one of the things I don't want to do as an actor is memorize the lines out loud in a certain rote fashion, so that I say them the same way every time. It would be faster—it is faster to just memorize all the words rotely out loud. But that—you don't want to do that.

Subject 4 concurs:

> What I don't do: I don't memorize right away. And, in fact, if I have a problem, it's in keeping myself from memorizing too soon. Most of the time I memorize by magic—and that is I don't really memorize. There is no effort involved. There seems to be no process involved: it just happens. One day early on, I know the lines.

In general the actors said they read the script the first time to extract the story line, but on second reading they tried to discover the personality of the character they were portraying. This is a very active problem-solving process and seems to involve a number of steps which consist of obtaining answers to questions such as, What does my character want? How does my character think and feel? Why does my character act in certain ways? Or as Subject 7 puts it 'trying to find out the whys'.

This attempt to obtain detailed information about why the character acts in certain ways bears similarities to aspects of plan recognition. In both cases, actions are observed from which the underlying plan is to be inferred. According to Subject 7,

> We do things in reverse in the theater. We get the script which is…at the end of the thought process: we have the lines there. Normally in life, you have an impulse and then a thought which you put into words. Well, I have the words, I get the words *first* in this finished script. And so I have to go back and find out what the thought was, to have you say those words. And more importantly. what was the impulse that created the thought that created the words, and usually it could be an emotional kind of thing. What is the reason for that thought? That's the way I have always thought of it.

Or as Subject 9 points out,

> I have to figure out what my character wants. I have to figure out how she goes about getting what she wants. Now, of course, a lot of times the character doesn't get what she wants but you have to play the [psychological] action; an action to get what you want. Every character, in every play, I think, is trying to find something. So you have to put those in doable verb terms… 'I want to make him apologize'.

This emphasis on psychological action was apparent in the other protocols as well. A number of subjects stated that they didn't try to remember the words but the actions or the thoughts that produced the actions. That way, a line is not said in a vacuum but in response to something: a causal relationship is established. Subject 6 put it this way:

> I memorize not the words I'm saying but the thought process that's going on in the scene. I hear somebody asking me something or requesting something of me and logically I say the following thing.... It's me responding to something someone has asked of me or is saying to me.

Subject 9 agrees that he tries to remember the reason for saying a particular line and that often this line is said in direct response to a question. He explains 'The line for me needs to grow out of what the other person is doing'.

It appears what this subject memorizes is what it is the other person said that caused him to say those particular words. Discovering the intentions that prompted an action seems to be an integral part of a professional actor's approach to studying a role. All seven actors expressed the thought that, before learning any of the lines, they tried to discern the character's intentions. (The two actors who were excluded from the formal analysis put all of their emphasis on intentions without even addressing memorization.) Although actors used different terms, such as goals or actions or motivations or 'figuring out the whys', all of them reported that they analysed a play from the standpoint of what the character is hoping to accomplish. According to Subject 1, he never learns a line verbatim until he has decided on the character's intention. Or as Subject 9 put it, 'After I figure out for myself pretty much what the character wants and how she thinks she can get it, you step into rehearsal.'

Dividing a play or a scene by objectives seems to give it structure. According to Subject 3, each objective functions as a chunk. As he puts it, 'a role is a whole thing. It's a person who starts at one place, goes to X events and ends up in another place. You do learn it by segments... and then the memorization is easier.'

Not surprisingly, all actors were concerned about being able to create an emotional reality on stage. In their view that is much harder than memorizing the words. Many of them explicitly stated that these emotions are memorized as well because, according to Subject 7,

> Something has to be going on underneath before you say the line in most cases. The lead female over here is doing a monologue which is making me angry. So that is something that has to be memorized too, isn't it'? I have to remember...yes, making me angry—and it's a page and a half before I even say anything. So, anyway...that's part of the play too, isn't it?

Thus it appears that actors encode the script in multiple ways. All of the actors made a point of emphasizing that they never learn their lines until they've learned the blocking (the movements and physical 'business' on stage) and that this helps them to retrieve the appropriate lines.

> It does help to know where you're going when you're learning your lines. If I remembered, ok, I get up here, I go to the chair, I set down my glass, the lines come with it (Subject 2).

Or in the words of Subject 3,

> The movement is a lot for the memorization.... If the blocking is good, then emotionally the words are right. So that when you move in a certain kind of way, it becomes natural to say those kinds of words.

This sentiment is also expressed by Subject 4, who stressed that he never memorizes any lines prior to having learned the blocking. He thinks that,

> You've got to have these two tracks going simultaneously, this is what I say and this is when and where I move. If they're somehow joined together and they get put in at the same time, one feeds the other, and you move and say the line.

Although many of the actors specifically mentioned that they did try to learn the lines exactly as the playwright had written them, none of them expressed any difficulty with accomplishing that task. Most of their effort seems to be focused on making that character they're portraying real and believable. Subject 4 expresses it as follows:

> This has been an interesting process for me, this memorizing a part—because it isn't words. The actor creates all that stuff that's underneath the words, and the words are just the topping, the words are the froth on top of the beer. The actor has to create the mug, and the hops and the beer and the fermentation and all of that; and when that happens, the foam just gets there—by some natural 'blump'. It's just there. It just happens.

An Example of Role Preparation

While all the actors stressed analysing before memorizing, none of them gave a step-by-step example of how this analysis was applied to a particular role. Therefore, one additional actor was recruited who was asked to both outline his method of analysis and to supply an example of the preparation with a specific role he had played. The actor's verbal protocol is shown in the form of diagrams in Figures 1 and 2.

As can be seen from Figure 1, the actor apparently organized the text in a hierarchical fashion: the top node is occupied by the superobjective, or the main goal that the actor believes the character would be pursuing for most of his life. The next level contains the main objective the character is pursuing during the time period covered in the play, and the level just below consists of each major objective the character tries to achieve each time he appears upon the scene.

The actor stated that each major objective is composed of a great many individual smaller action patterns, called beats. He defined beats as the smallest unit of goal-directed action: A character does something to attain an immediate goal; that is, he commits an action and someone else reacts to it which in turn evokes another action, and so forth until the character succeeds or fails to reach the immediate goal. This resolution leads to his attempt to reach the goal of the next beat, etc. These beats occupy the lowest level.

An example of how the actor reported to have 'scored' the role of Victor Velasco in Neil Simon's play 'Barefoot in the Park' is shown in Figure 2. Each of the slots has been instantiated with events of the text.

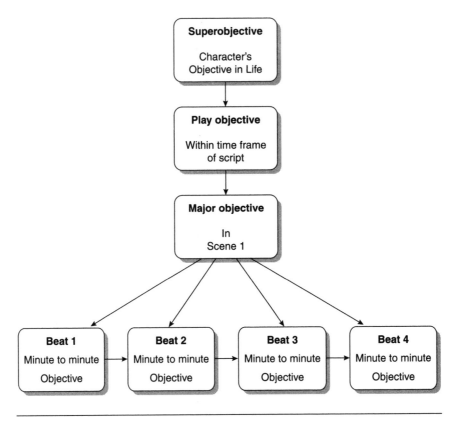

FIGURE 1   *Preparation of a scene from a contemporary play*

Thus it appears that the actor's strategy in learning a role consists of recognizing the assigned character's overall plan and also recognizing that a scene consists of a series of subgoals (beats 1 through 4) each of which must be accomplished in turn before the overall plan can succeed.

To summarize, this additional protocol in which an actor was directed to verbalize his analytical approach to a specific role pointed to a close relationship between acting technique and plan theory. It revealed that an actor apparently approaches a playscript as a plan-recognition task. He attempts to infer the character's motivations by supplying explanations for his actions.

Discussion

From the above it can be seen that actors do not consider themselves expert memorizers as such; rather they are expert re-creators of reality. Thus verbatim retention appears to be a byproduct of the strategy the actor uses to create the sense of reality in each ongoing mo-

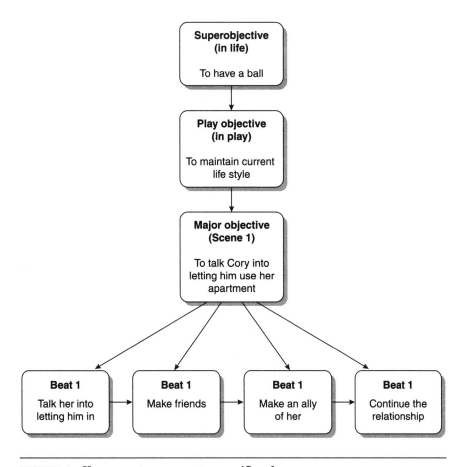

FIGURE 2 *How one actor represents a specific role*

ment. The actor determines what the character would be thinking when using those particular words and this in-depth understanding of the underlying thought allows the actor to do his real job of making the performance 'new' each night.

As was shown by the statements of the actors themselves, the script events are embellished in a colourful interactive manner for a very specific reason. In order to learn and perform the role the actor first must attempt to find reasons why his character says each line and performs each action. To do this, the actors engage in some form of 'plan recognition'; that is they try to figure out an explanation for the behaviour of the character every step of the way. And it is this explanation that allows them to infer the goal that is being pursued and the intention behind each utterance and action of the character. Therefore, when it is said that an actor 'creates' a character, it is literally true. The author supplies the words but the actor ferrets out the meaning.

It is an intriguing finding that a strategy not directed towards memorization nevertheless results in verbatim retention. It has been shown that elaboration leads to improved recall (e.g. Craig and Tulving, 1975). In addition, it has been shown that elaborations that are precise enough to reduce the arbitrariness between concepts can result in the verbatim retention of simple sentences (Stein and Bransford, 1979). However, what appears to be new here is that a strategy based on embellishing the text rather than memorizing it nevertheless leads to word-for-word retention of lengthy complex material. It has recently been shown that in many instances material that is supposedly reproduced verbatim (such as ballads) may in fact be subject to frequent paraphrasing (Hunter, 1985; Wallace and Rubin, 1988). However, actors' memory for roles is extremely accurate (Oliver and Ericsson, 1986). A possible explanation would be that actors repeatedly read the script to ascertain how the character's plan is furthered by those exact words; as a result the words become indexed to the plan. When the actor retrieves the plan, the exact words that are indexed to the plan are also retrieved even though they were never intentionally memorized. This would explain such typical actor comments as, 'the words just seem to be there' and 'I memorize by magic'.

This analysis of professional actors' protocols represents simply the first step towards determining the complex mental processes involved in the learning of a complete role. It remains to be discovered what differences there are between the thought processes of actors and novices when confronted with the task of learning the same theatrical script. Would novices put as strong an emphasis on emotion as actors who claim to memorize the emotion along with the meaning of the words? Whether emotionality is one of the prime factors responsible for the ease with which actors retrieve their role is an issue that still needs to be addressed.

References

Charness, N. (1979). Components of skill in bridge. *Canadian Journal of Psychology, 33,* 1–50.

Chase, W. G. and Simon, H. A. (1973). Perception in chess. *Cognitive Psychology, 4,* 55–81.

Chi, M. T. H., Feltovich, P. J. and Glaser, R. (1981). Categorization and representation of physics problems by experts and novices. *Cognitive Science, 5,* 121–152.

Craig, F. I. M. and Tulving, E. (1975). Depth of processing and the retention of words in episodic memory. *Journal of Experimental Psychology: General, 104,* 268–294.

Egan, D. E. and Schwartz, B. J. (1979). Chunking in recall of symbolic drawings, *Memory and Cognition, 7,* 149–158.

Ericsson, K. A. and Simon, H. A. (1984). *Protocol Analysis.* Cambridge, MA: MIT Press.

Hunter, I. M. L. (1985). Lengthy verbatim recall: the role of the text. In A. Ellis (ed.), *Progress in the Psychology of Language,* vol. l, (pp. 207–237). Hillsdale, NJ: Erlbaum.

Intons-Peterson, M. J. and Smyth, M. M. (1987). The anatomy of repertory memory. *Journal of Experimental Psychology: Learning, Memory, and Cognition, 13,* 490–500.

Oliver, W. L. and Ericsson, K. A. (1986). Repertory actors' memory for their parts. In *Proceedings of the Eighth Annual Conference of the Cognitive Science Society, Amherst, M. A.* (pp. 399–406). Hillsdale, NJ: Erlbaum.

Reitman, J. (1976). Skilled perception in Go: Deducing memory structures from inter-response times. *Cognitive Psychology, 8,* 336–356.

Reitman. J. and Rueter, H. H. (1980). Organization revealed by recall errors and confirmed by pauses. *Cognitive Psychology, 12,* 554–581.

Staszewski. J. J. (1988). Skilled memory and expert mental calculation. In Chi, M. T. H., Glaser, R. and Farr, M. F. (eds), *The Nature of Expertise* (pp. 71–128). Hillsdale, NJ: Erlbaum.

Stein, B. S. and Bransford, J. D. (1979). Constraints on effective elaboration: Effects of precision and subject generation. *Journal of Verbal Learning and Verbal Behavior,* **18,** 769–777.

Wallace, W. T. and Rubin, D. C. (1988). 'The Wreck of the Old 97': A real event remembered in song. In U. Neisser and E. Winograd (eds), *Remembering Reconsidered ecological and traditional approaches to the study of memory* (pp. 283–310). Cambridge: Cambridge University Press.

Appendix

The following instructions were sent to the two original subjects.

Instructions

We're interested in the mental processes underlying the learning of a complete role by professional actors. Please describe (on the tape) how you go about preparing a role in a play from the time you first read the script through the rehearsal period and up to the performance.

Your help is much appreciated.

The following revised instructions were sent to the seven remaining subjects.

Instructions

We're interested in the memory processes underlying the learning of a complete role by professional actors. Please describe (on the tape) how you go about preparing a role in a play from the time you first read the script through the rehearsal period and up to the performance.

Please note we're not interested in the analysis of the characterization but the process by which you commit the role to memory.

Your help is much appreciated.

Introduction: Critical Thinking Questions

? What are the potential benefits of systematically analyzing the manner in which professional actors learn their lines?

? What previous work has been done in analyzing expertise, and more specifically, in analyzing the expertise of professional actors?

Method: Critical Thinking Questions

? The protocols collected in this study were retrospective. What does this mean?

? Who were the participants in the study, and what were they required to do?

Results/Discussion: Critical Thinking Questions _____

? What were the most important similarities noted in the protocols of the actor participants?

? Describe the different approaches used by the actors to learn the script. Cite relevant evidence from the protocols.

? Consider Figure 1 and explain the step-by-step approach taken by the actor to learn the script and how this approach explains the author's statement that "actors do not consider themselves expert memorizers as such; rather they are expert re-creators of reality."

? Describe the author's explanation for why actors have verbatim recall of a script.

? In considering the memory strategies employed by actors, can you find any lessons that might apply to your studying?

? After reading this study, you may feel there are other issues or questions that should be addressed or would be interesting to address. Provide one of these questions/hypotheses (other than those suggested by the authors) that could be investigated empirically.

The Effects of Positive and Negative Mood on Divergent-Thinking Performance

Suzanne K. Vosburg

Abstract

*Previous work has shown that positive mood may facilitate creative problem solving. However, studies have also shown positive mood may be detrimental to creative thinking under conditions favoring an optimizing strategy for solution. It is argued herein that the opposite effect is observed under conditions promoting loose processing and **satisficing** problem-solving strategies. The effects of positive and negative mood on divergent-thinking performance were examined in a quasi-experimental design. The sample comprised 188 arts and psychology students. Mood was measured with an adjective checklist prior to task performance. Real-life divergent-thinking tasks scored for fluency were used as the dependent variables. Results showed natural positive mood to facilitate significantly task performance and negative mood to inhibit it. There was no effect of arousal. The results suggest that persons in elevated moods may prefer satisficing strategies, which would lead to a higher number of proposed solutions. Persons in a negative mood may choose optimizing strategies and be more concerned with the quality of their ideas, which is detrimental to performance on this kind of task.*

Conceptual Issues and Theoretical Questions

- Do the facilitatory effects of positive mood on problem solving extend to the domain of creative problems?
- Do positive and negative moods lead to the selection of different types of problem-solving strategies?
- How does the selection of problem-solving strategies induced by a given mood impact the progress of problem solving in different domains?

Vosburg, S. K. (1998). The effects of positive and negative mood on divergent-thinking performance. *Creativity Research Journal, 11,* 165–172. Copyright © 1998 by Lawrence Erlbaum Associates. Reproduced by permission of the publisher.

De-Jargonizing

insight problem: problems in which the solution seems to occur suddenly

categorization tasks: tasks requiring participants to produce associates to some concept

remote associates: a test used to assess creativity; requires that participants think of a word that can be associated with each of three (ostensibly unrelated) words

cognitive flexibility: willingness or ability to think creatively

loosening: thinking flexibly or divergently

tightening: thinking narrowly or convergently

divergent-thinking task: task that requires participants to produce as many solutions as possible

quasi-experimental: refers to an experimental design in which different groups are compared, but the variable of interest is not manipulated by experimenter (e.g., in the present study, participant mood was not manipulated; it was measured, and scores were used to determine whether participants were in a positive or negative mood state)

satisficing: searching until one arrives at a solution (but not necessarily the optimal solution)

heuristic strategy: rule-of-thumb approach to solving a problem

loose processing: see loosening above

stop rules: self-defined criteria that would lead one to quit working on a problem

A preponderance of the empirical literatures on mood and creative problem solving emphasizes the facilitating effect of positive mood. Most of these studies employ three types of tasks: **insight problems, categorization tasks,** and **remote associates.** Because divergent-thinking tasks represent an important element of creative problem-solving and because they have not been addressed as frequently, they were targeted in this study.

Isen, Daubman, and Nowicki (1987) found that positive mood had a facilitative effect on creative problem solving (i.e., Duncker's, 1945, candle task and Mednick's, 1962, Remote Associates Test) by facilitating the process of finding relatedness in diverse stimuli. Greene and Noice (1988) replicated the results for the insight task in a study with adolescents as participants. In a categorization task, adolescents in the positive condition generated more words and a greater number of atypical words with respect to a given category than did adolescents in other experimental conditions.

A series of related studies examined the influence of affect on categorization. Isen and Daubman (1984) demonstrated that induced positive mood led to more inclusive and broader categorization. Isen, Johnson, Mertz, and Robinson (1985) showed participants in whom positive mood had been induced produced more unusual first-word associates to presented neutral words. Both studies specifically related these findings to creative problem solving and suggested that positive mood may promote **cognitive flexibility.** Murray, Sujan, Hirt, and Sujan (1990) tested this hypothesis more directly and found positive mood participants were able to see relations between concepts. They were also superior in distinguishing the differences between concepts. Murray et al. bridged their findings to creative problem solving by arguing that participants in a positive mood are better able both to differentiate between and to integrate unusual and diverse information. Closely related to this suggestion was Fiedler's (1988), calling attention both to **loosening** and to **tightening** processes in the context of mood. He used the terms *loosening* and *tightening* to characterize the psychological function of cognitive processes under positive and negative mood, respectively (p. 102). In his view, loosening processes are most likely to accompany positive mood and tightening processes are most likely to accompany negative mood.

Other studies have demonstrated that the relation between positive mood and creative problem solving is anything but straightforward. In two studies, Abele (1992a) showed induced positive mood led to more ideas, which were generated via flexible processing, on a standard **divergent-thinking task** than negative and neutral conditions. She further reported a Mood × Instrumental Task Interest interaction. Negative mood facilitated task performance contingent upon task interest.

Jaušovec (1989) explored the influence of affect on the use of analogical problem solving. Participants were presented with base information—a problem that was considered to present an analogous solution to the criterion problem-solving task. After mood induction, participants were asked to solve the criterion task. His findings showed positive mood facilitated analogical transfer on the roof problem (Gordon, 1961) but not on the radiation task (Duncker, 1945), an insight problem much like the one Isen et al. (1987) used. Jausovec suggested that the degree of task structure is an important mediator of mood effects. This challenged the view that positive mood consistently facilitates creative problem solving.

Kaufmann and Vosburg (1997) employing both **quasi-experimental** and experimental approaches found that positive mood can significantly inhibit creative problem solving, which they operationalized as performance on insight problems similar to those used by Isen et al. (1987) and Jaušovec (1989). As criterion tasks Maier's (1970) hatrack and two-string problems were used. Two tasks from a standard intelligence test battery (Mønnesland, 1985) served as control tasks. In their first study, mood was measured at arrival prior to task performance. Here positive mood was associated with poor performance on the two insight problems. In the second experiment, Kaufmann and Vosburg replicated this finding with experimentally induced mood, and again positive mood seemed to inhibit task performance and negative mood enhanced it. Participants for whom negative mood had been induced had a higher solution frequency, lower latency rates, and superior performance on the insight tasks than all other groups. Participants experiencing negative mood performed the best, followed by neutral, then control participants, and finally positive mood participants. The insight tasks were presented in paper-and-pencil format, and participants did not receive external feedback on their solution attempts.

Kaufmann and Vosburg (1997) suggested that optimizing and **satisficing** strategies (Robbins, 1993; Simon, 1976) may be important moderators of the influence on positive and negative mood on creative problem solving. When satisficing, decision makers will construct a simplified version of the problem being solved. In doing so, they will identify a subjective criterion of task fulfillment from their subjective level of aspiration. The problem is then solved by accepting the first solution that meets or satisfies the subjective criterion. Optimizing maximizes the outcome of problem solving by searching for the best possible solutions. Ideally, when making a decision, the decision maker will identify and explore all decision criteria and then develop and explore alternatives before selecting the best one.

An example of a strict optimizing requirement is the typical insight problem where only one ideal solution exists, according to the strict solution requirements. The mood literature suggests the properties of processing under positive mood include being guided by a general **heuristic strategy** (Abele, 1992b; Schwartz & Bless, 1991), loose processing (Fiedler, 1988), and simplified processing (Clore, Schwarz, & Conway, 1994; Isen, Means, Patrick, & Nowicki, 1982), all of which are in contrast to processes under negative mood, and all of which are in line with the idea of processing with a satisficing strategy. Positive mood could be detrimental to creative problem solving under such optimization requirements because optimizing requires systematic processing of all alternatives. Conversely, if negative mood promotes optimizing behavior, then task performance would be maximized under such strict solution requirements.

This can explain the discrepancy between the findings of Kaufmann and Vosburg (1997) and those of Isen et al. (1987). In Isen et al.'s tasks, participants manipulated physical objects. Kaufmann and Vosburg used paper-and-pencil measures. Solution feedback from physical objects can show the solution attempt is not adequate and at the same time instigate further search. Participants in a positive mood may be more optimistic and less vulnerable to failure, so the search for an adequate solution continues until the solution is found. In the tasks used by Kaufmann and Vosburg, no outside feedback was given, so participants could stop prematurely before reaching an adequate solution. They suggested that when participants are left to set their own subjective solution criteria, positive mood may induce a satisficing strategy, and participants who set lower criteria for solution are prone to accept lower quality solutions without searching further for better ones.

The proposition of positive mood tending to lower and negative mood to raise criteria for acceptable solution is consistent with findings recorded by Martin, Ward, Achee, and Wyer (1993). They explored effects of mood on the **stop rules** participants employed by checking how long a person performed a task when instructed to stop when no longer enjoying a task versus stopping when enough information was obtained. In a set of two experiments, Martin et al. determined that an interaction existed among induced mood, stop rules, and how long participants stayed on task. When instructed to stop when they had enough information, positive mood participants stopped sooner than those in negative moods, and negative mood participants stopped sooner than those in positive moods when instructed to stop when they no longer enjoyed the task. In an extension, Martin et al. instructed a control group to stop when they felt like it. The results from this group were similar to those in the fast experiment: Those who indicated they were in a positive mood stopped sooner than those who indicated a negative mood. In the terminology of Kaufmann and Vosburg (1997), participants in a positive mood may be said to have used a satisficing criteria for task performance.

An example of a task with the strict satisficing requirement is the typical divergent-thinking problem where participants are encouraged to list as many ideas as they can think of and not to think about the quality of their responses. Negative mood participants may tend to be cautious and concerned with the quality of their responses, which could hamper their task performance. It follows, then, that divergent thinking would be maximized under positive mood and inhibited under negative mood. Thus, a reversal in mood effects occurs when comparing tasks requiring the generation of many ideas with insight problems, which require the selection of the singular correct solution. This reversal was the focus of this investigation.

Method

Participants

One hundred and ninety students from the University of Bergen and the National College of Arts and Design in Bergen, Norway, age 19 to 50 (*Mdn* = 22), took part in this study. Two participants scored 1.5 standard deviations above the group on the dependent variables and were diagnosed as outliers and removed from the analysis, rendering the total sample size of 188.

The university participants were 82 general psychology students (19 men, 63 women), 77 organizational psychology students (21 men, 56 women), and 29 art students (all women).

Instruments

Mood Assessments. The Russell (1979) Adjective Check List was specifically designed to assess positive and negative mood as well as general level of activation. The list consists of 58 items, including items relating to other personality dimensions (e.g., dominance and submissiveness). Two of the items were not used due to difficulties of translation from English to Norwegian. The unrelated items were used as distractors. Participants were instructed to check the items that most accurately described their current mood. Items were presented in randomized order. The score was a sum of the items grouped as positive terms, negative terms, and general-arousal terms following Russell's classification scheme. More is said about this in the results section.

Measures of Creative Problem Solving. Divergent-thinking tasks have an extremely low satisficing criterion because the idea is produce as many ideas as quickly as possible without critical evaluation. There are two types of tasks: problem finding and problem solving. In problem finding, participants are presented with a problematic vignette and asked to list all the problems they can find within a set time; the same procedure is used in problem-solving tasks, but here participants are asked to list all the solutions they can think of for a presented problem.

Four real-life divergent-thinking tasks were adapted from Mraz and Runco (1994): Two problem-solving and two problem-finding tasks (also see Okuda, Runco, & Berger, 1991). One of the problem-solving tasks is as follows:

> Your friend Rolf sits next to you in the classroom. Rolf likes to talk to you and often interrupts you when you are taking notes. Sometimes he distracts you so that you are missing important parts of lecture. What are you going to do? How are you going to solve this problem?

An example of the problem-finding tasks is:

> Write down problems you consider important to your studies. You can mention problems related to the university-site, professors, politics, other students or whatever you can think of.

Divergent-thinking tasks are typically scored for "ideational fluency," the number of responses; "ideational originality," the number of relatively unusual responses; and "ideational flexibility," the number of response categories (Hocevar, 1980; Hocevar & Michael, 1979; Runco, 1991). With the focus of this study on the effects of mood on problem solving, and on satisficing and optimizing strategies, the divergent-thinking tasks were scored only for fluency. It was, desirable that participants accept all their answers, thus maximizing the satisficing condition.

Considerable evidence indicates that the scores in the different task parameters are highly correlated. Hocevar (1979a, 1979b; Hocevar & Michael, 1979; Zarnegar, Hocevar, & Michael, 1988) suggested both flexibility and originality are a function of fluency rather than separate dimensions, and in a survey of available evidence, Kogan (as cited in Baer, 1993) found fluency scores so highly correlated that the sole use of the more easily scorable fluency index would be justified. The fluency criterion (i.e., simply the number of ideas produced) was chosen to maximize idea generation under the lowest possible level of satisficing.

The contrast tasks used in the earlier research were not included here because Kaufmann and Vosburg (1997) found no effect of mood on either analogies or number series tasks in both quasi-experimental and experimental settings.

Procedure

The divergent-thinking tasks were administered in groups as part of a larger experiment. Many tasks and questionnaires were presented that served to conceal the purpose of the experiment. Participants were asked to complete the Russell Adjective Check List, but were instructed to wait to begin the problem-solving tasks together. Participants could use 5 min on each problem-solving task: They began each task at the same time and did not return to previous tasks after completion of each task. They were timed by the experimenter. After completion of all questionnaires, participants were thanked for their participation and were given an extra lecture on a topic of interest as a reward for their participation.

Results

Scoring for the positive mood, negative mood, and arousal was based on dummy weights for each term, with 1 indicating a term was chosen and 0 indicating it was not. The independent variables were created by a multistep procedure. Each conceptually defined scale was factor analyzed, and Screen tests (Cattell, 1966) showed that for each separate scale, one factor accounted for all the systematic variation.

One factor accounted for 43% of the variance for the positive mood scale, 33% of the negative mood scale, and 49% for the arousal scale. For each scale, index scores based on principle component factor scores were used as the independent variables in the further analyses. Factor loadings for the items representing the three different mood indexes ranged from .434 to .791 on the positive scale, .252 to .802 on the negative scale, and .54 to .72 on the arousal scale. Positive terms used were *satisfied, pleased, happy, joyful* and *content.* Negative terms used were *unhappy, depressed, discontented, sad* and *blue.* Arousal tends were *wide awake, activated alert, full of pep,* and *clutched up.*

The proportion of variance accounted for on the negative mood scale and the ensuing factor loadings on the negative mood index were small. Negative mood seems to exist in two ways: one is sad or one is discontent/dissatisfied. For this reason, obtaining strong and unidimensional factor loadings is difficult. The asymmetrical qualities of positive and negative moods, as well as the complexity of negative moods, have been discussed in the mood literature (Brown & Taylor, 1986; Isen, 1984; Peeters & Czapinski, 1990; Taylor, 1991; Worth & Mackie, 1987). Also, very few participants checked negative terms on this scale, and this resulted in highly skewed variance. This was taken into account in the ensuing analyses.

The product moment correlations between independent and dependent variables are shown in Table 1. The mean for the total divergent-thinking task score was 23.10 with a standard deviation of 7.99. For problem finding, $M = 12.13, SD = 5.58$; for problem solving, $M = 10.77, SD = 3.51$. The four divergent-thinking tasks are highly correlated: Cronbach's (1951) alpha was .77. For this reason they were added together to create the dependent variables of problem solving and problem finding. The problem-solving and problem-finding scores were then added together to create a total divergent-thinking task score.

As was the case in earlier work with insight problems (Kaufmann & Vosburg, 1997), no relation existed between arousal and divergent-thinking task scores.

As seen in Table 1, positive mood had a significantly positive relation to task performance: $r = .241, F(1,186) = 1150, p = .0009$. Negative mood had a significantly negative relation: $r = -.191, F(1,186) = 7.07, p = .0085$. Arousal was not significantly related to task performance. There was a preponderance of women in the sample, but a comparison between the correlations in Table 1 with those with gender partialled out revealed no differences (i.e., gender was not strongly related to task performance). After partialling, mood effects were still positive and significant, $r = .242, F(1, 186) = 11.505, p = .0008$, for positive mood and negative and significant for negative mood, $r = .185, F(1, 186) = 6.578, p = .011$.

TABLE 1 *Product Moment Correlations of Independent and Dependent Variables*

Variables	Negative	Arousal	Total divergent	Problem Finding	Problem Solving
Positive	−.37***	.37***	.24***	.20***	.23**
Negative	—	−.16*	−.20**	−.14*	−.21**
Arousal		—	.10	.06	.13
Total Divergent			—	.93***	.80***
Problem Finding				—	.52***

*$p \leq .05$. **$p \leq .01$. ***$p \leq .001$.

However, for subsequent analyses, gender remained partialled out of the total divergent-thinking task score to prevent the possibility of confounding.

Figure 1 depicts the relation between positive mood, negative mood, and divergent thinking by showing the regression lines between the respective mood factor scores and the combined divergent-thinking task performance score. Positive mood had a positive relation to divergent thinking and negative mood had a negative relation to divergent thinking.

As seen in Table 1, positive and negative mood were significantly negatively correlated, $r = -.369$, $F(1,186) = 29.343$, $p = .0001$. When negative mood was partialled out, the relation between positive mood and divergent thinking was still significant, $r = .187$, $F(1, 185) = 6.694$, $p = .01$. Negative mood and divergent thinking was no longer significant, $r = .104$, $F(1, 185) = 2.009$, $p = .1581$. This could mean there was no independent effect of negative mood, and that negative mood had a negative effect simply as a by-product of the intensity of positive mood or a measurement error due to covariance.

An inspection of the data led to the observation the correlation of $r = -.37$ between positive and negative terms could have been due to those who checked many positive terms and a few negative terms at the same time. To avoid such confounding, two independent, nonoverlapping comparison groups were created. The first—high positive—consisted of the group with high positive scores (i.e., three or more positive terms were checked) with no negative terms checked. The second group—high negative—comprised the group checking negative mood items and no checks on positive mood terms. A two-tailed t test was performed between the contrast variable (high positive/high negative) and the total divergent score to check the differences between the means.

The mean difference between the two groups was 5.12, $t(80) = -2.81$, $p = .0063$. The effect size was computed by dividing the mean difference by the pooled standard deviation

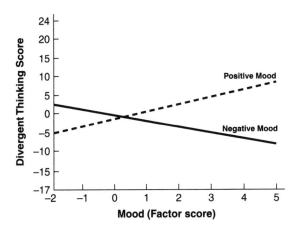

FIGURE 1   *The regression lines for negative mood and positive mood factor scores against total divergent-thinking task performance scores (with gender partialled out).*

of divergent-thinking scores, rendering Cohen's d of .61, a medium size effect (Cohen, 1988). Taken in the context of the current limitations in reliability in independent and dependent variables, it is a fair estimate that these effects would be stronger if a more reliable mood measurement was used.

Nearly 80% of the participants did not circle any negative terms. To counter this effect, a subset of the data was created, excluding all participants who were nonreactive; that is, participants who did not check either a positive or a negative term. Arousal was excluded because no significant effects were attained from this variable.

Principal component analyses were carried out with positive and negative mood terms. The number of terms had to be reduced to four on each scale to preserve factor scores higher than .30. Then regression analyses between the principal components and the total divergent-thinking score were carried out. For both positive and negative components, regressions with total divergent-thinking were equal in size but opposite in direction: $r = .239$, $F(1, 150) = 9.123$, $p = .003$ for positive, and $r = -.216$, $F(1, 150) = 7.323$, $p = .008$ for negative. When this control for nonreactivity was carried out, positive and negative mood contributed equal amounts of experimental variance in opposite directions as predicted by the satisficing/optimizing theoretical model presented earlier.

Discussion

Studies of mood effects on creative problem solving have shown seemingly contradictory results. Many have demonstrated a facilitating effect of positive mood on creative problem solving, but others have demonstrated effects in the opposite direction. This investigation suggested a potential solution to the mixed results by testing the idea of creative problem solving taking place under optimizing and satisficing task requirements.

In terms of the satisficing/optimizing model, negative mood should facilitate task performance under strict optimizing requirements and positive mood should inhibit it. Positive mood should facilitate task performance under satisficing requirements, and negative mood should inhibit it.

Insight problems exemplify problem solving under optimizing conditions because strict solution requirements exist and there is only one acceptable solution. Ideational fluency is at the other extreme on the continuum: Solution requirements are loose; ordinarily, instructions for ideational fluency are to generate ideas without any regard for quality. This takes place in a nonevaluative situation. At most, evaluation takes place after the solutions have been generated. In this experiment, mood at arrival was used as the predictor variable, and ideational fluency taken out of divergent-thinking tasks was the criterion variable. Positive mood was found to have a significantly positive effect on problem solving (i.e., increased fluency), whereas negative mood had a significantly negative effect on problem solving (i.e., decreased ideational fluency). In terms of the satisficing/optimizing theory, task performance under satisficing requirements was facilitated by positive mood and inhibited by negative mood.

Although the findings in this study confirm the proposed theory, a number of limitations that derive from the quasi-experimental nature of the design should be mentioned. First, an experimental replication involving a mood induction with the same tasks would definitely strengthen the validity of the findings. Second, although our research has shown the satisficing/optimizing theory may have some validity, supporting evidence is thus far scarce, and moreover, has limited comparability: Different tasks have been used, as well as different measures and types of mood (natural versus induced). To test the model exhaustively, both divergent-thinking and insight tasks need to be included in the same study. Optimizing and satisficing criteria could be systematically varied within the same kind of task. For instance, instructions given for insight problems would be to provide as many solutions as the person can think of versus provide the one best solution; and the instructions for divergent-thinking tasks would be to give only top quality ideas versus all of the ideas the individual can think of. An analysis of this type would allow for a better test of the satisficing/optimizing model and a better account of mood effects with the hope to separate the effects of different moods on different types of creative problem-solving tasks.

Two sets of problems arise when measuring negative mood. The first is methodological. In this study, participants in an everyday life situation did not seem to check many negative terms on this particular adjective check list, which actually may not be that surprising. In a university setting, without a particular challenge such as exam preparations, only a few students may be in a bad mood. And if they are, the checklists may be too crude to measure mild variations of negative mood because they allow only checking particular items. If no items are checked, no information about a particular mood state is available, leaving many participants without measurements. A solution to this problem would be to use scales that will allow for a measured response only on reactive terms, where no response is not an option and item intensity is measured (Watson, Clark, & Tellegen, 1988). This will provide more reliable measurements that will contribute to a more valid analysis. To increase the negative mood variance range, the mood scales could be administered right before students were to take an exam, or a group of students could be preselected on the basis of their depression scores (e.g., as measured by personality questionnaires and asked to take part in the same procedure). This might provide more negative mood variance within the quasi-experimental design and possibly render a more robust negative mood effect.

The second problem with measuring negative mood is of a qualitative nature and is intertwined with the methodological problems. The data show that negative mood could be manifested in two ways: One is sad or one is discontent/dissatisfied. That is, negative mood does not have the same unidimensional quality as does positive mood. In this sense, an asymmetry exists between the two: Positive mood is relatively straightforward and unidimensional, whereas negative mood may be multidimensional and more complex (Brown & Taylor, 1986; Isen, 1984; Peeters & Czapinski, 1990; Taylor, 1991; Worth & Mackie, 1987). This asymmetry is a fundamental problem in the mood literature. It implies that measurements must take this quality of negative mood into account and that the comparison of positive to negative mood may not be meaningful in the way it is normally treated in these studies because they cannot be compared as equal entities or opposites (see Watson & Tellegen, 1985).

Studies focused on negative mood are necessary to sort out this set of problems. Clarifying the basic nature of negative mood and developing reliable measures are necessary steps to take in order to continue the elucidation of the relation between mood and creative performance.

References

Abele, A. (1992a). Positive and negative mood influences on creativity: Evidence for asymmetrical effects. *Polish Psychological Bulletin, 23,* 203–221.

Abele, A. (1992b). Positive versus negative mood influences on problem solving: A review. *Polish Psychological Bulletin, 23,* 187–202.

Baer, J. (1993). *Creativity and divergent thinking: A task specific approach.* Hillsdale, NJ: Lawrence Erlbaum Associates, Inc.

Brown, J. D., & Taylor, S. E. (1986). Affect and the processing of personal information: Evidence for mood-activated self schema. *Journal of Experimental Social Psychology, 22,* 436–452.

Cattell, R. B. (1966). *Handbook of multivariate experimental psychology.* Chicago, IL: Rand McNally.

Clore, G. L., Schwarz, N., & Conway, M. (1994). Affective causes and consequences of social information processing. In R. S. Wyer & T. K. Srull (Eds.), *Handbook of social cognition. Vol. 1. Basic processes* (2nd ed., pp. 323–417). Hillsdale, NJ: Lawrence Erlbaum Associates, Inc.

Cohen, J. (1988). *Statistical power analysis for the behavioral sciences* (2nd ed.). Hillsdale, NJ: Lawrence Erlbaum Associates, Inc.

Cronbach, L. J. (1951). Coefficient alpha and the internal structure of tests. *Psychmetrika, 16,* 297–334.

Duncker, K. (1945). On problem solving. *Psychological Monographs, 58*(5, Whole No. 270).

Fiedler, K. (1988). Emotional mood, cognitive style, and behavior regulation. In K. Fiedler & J. Forgas (Eds.), *Affect cognition and social behavior* (pp. 100–119). Toronto, Canada: Hogrefe.

Gordon, W. J. J. (1961). *Synectics: The development of creative capacity.* New York: Harper.

Greene, T. R., & Noice, H. (1988). Influence of positive affect upon creative thinking and problem solving in children. *Psychological Reports, 63,* 895–898.

Hocevar, D. (1979a). Ideational fluency as a confounding factor in the measurement of originality. *Journal of Educational Psychology, 71,* 191–196.

Hocevar, D. (1979b). The unidimensional nature of creative thinking in fifth grade children. *Child Study Journal, 9,* 273–278.

Hocevar, D. (1980). Intelligence, divergent thinking, and creativity. *Intelligence, 4,* 25–40.

Hocevar, D., & Michael, W. B. (1979). The effects of scoring formulas on the discriminant validity of tests of divergent thinking. *Educational and Psychological Measurement, 39,* 917–921.

Isen, A. M. (1984). Toward understanding the role of affect in cognition. In R. Wyer & T. Srull (Eds.), *Handbook of social cognition* (pp. 179–236). Hillsdale, NJ: Lawrence Erlbaum Associates, Inc.

Isen, A. M., & Daubman, K. A. (1984). The influence of affect on categorization. *Journal of Personality and Social Psychology, 47,* 1206–1217.

Isen, A. M., Daubman, K., & Nowicki, G. (1987). Positive affect facilitates creative problem solving. *Journal of Personality and Social Psychology, 52,* 1122–1131.

Isen, A. M., Johnson, M. M. S., Mertz, E., & Robinson, G. F. (1985). The influence of positive affect on the unusualness of word associations. *Journal of Personality and Social Psychology, 48,* 1413–1426.

Isen, A. M., Means, B., Patrick, R., & Nowicki, G. (1982). Some factors influence decision-making strategy and risk taking. In M. S. Clark & S. T. Fiske (Eds.), *Affect and cognition: The 17th Annual Carnegie Symposium on Cognition* (pp. 243–261). Hillsdale, NJ: Lawrence Erlbaum Associates, Inc.

Jaušovec, N. (1989). Affect in analogical transfer. *Creativity Research Journal, 2,* 255–266.

Kaufmann, G., & Vosburg, S. K. (1997). Paradoxical effects of mood on creative problem solving. *Cognition and Emotion.*

Maier, N. R. F. (1970). *Problem solving and creativity in individuals and groups.* Belmont, CA: Brooks/Cole.

Martin, L. L., Ward, D. W., Achee, J. W., & Wyer, R. S. (1993). Mood as input: People have to interpret the motivational implications of their moods. *Journal of Personality and Social Psychology, 64,* 317–326.

Mednick, S. A. (1962). The associative basis of the creative process. *Psychological Review, 69,* 220–232.

Monnesland, K. (1985). *Intelligensprover for voksne* [Intelligence tests for those older than age 14]. Oslo, Norway: Tano.

Mraz, W., & Runco, M. A. (1994). Suicide ideation and creative problem solving. *Suicide and Life Threatening Behavior, 24,* 38–47.

Murray, N., Sujan, H., Hirt, E. R., & Sujan, M. (1990). The influence of mood on categorization: A cognitive flexibility interpretation. *Journal of Personality and Social Psychology, 59,* 411–425.

Okuda, S. M., Runco, M. A., & Berger, D. E. (1991). Creativity and the finding and solving of real-world problems. *Journal of Psychoeducational Assessment 9,* 45–53.

Peeters, G., & Czapinski, J. (1990). Positive-negative asymmetry in evaluations: The distinction between affective and informational negativity effects. In W. Stoebe & M. Hewstone (Eds.), *European review of social psychology* (Vol. 1, pp. 33–60). New York: Wiley.

Robbins, S. P. (1993). *Organizational behavior.* Englewood Cliffs, NJ: Prentice Hall.

Runco, M. A. (1991). *Divergent thinking.* Norwood, NJ: Ablex.

Russell, J. A. (1979). Affective space is bipolar. *Journal of Personality and Social Psychology, 37,* 345–356.

Schwartz, N. & Bless, H. (1991). Happy and mindless, but sad and smart? The impact of affective states on analytic reasoning. In J. P. Forges (Ed.), *Emotion and social judgments* (pp. 55–71). New York: Pergamon.

Simon, H. A. (1976). *Administrative behavior: A study of decision-making processes in administrative organization* (3rd ed.). New York: Free Press.

Taylor, S. E. (1991). Asymmetrical effects of positive and negative events: The mobilization-minimization hypothesis. *Psychological Bulletin, 110,* 67–85.

Watson, D., Clark, L. A., & Tellegen, A. (1988). Development and validation of brief measures of positive and negative affect: The PANAS scales. *Journal of Personality and Social Psychology, 54,* 1063–1070.

Watson, D., & Tellegen, A. (1985). Toward a consensual structure of mood. *Psychological Bulletin, 98,* 219–235.

Worth, L. T., & Mackie, D. M. (1987). Cognitive mediation of positive affect in permission. *Social Cognition, 5,* 76–94.

Zarnegar, Z., Hocevar, D., & Michael, W. B. (1988). Components of original thinking in gifted children. *Educational and Psychological Measurement, 48,* 5–16.

Introduction: Critical Thinking Questions

? The results of several studies are presented as evidence for a facilitatory effect of positive mood on creative problem solving. Briefly describe this evidence.

? Some evidence suggests that positive mood may inhibit creative problem solving. Briefly describe this evidence.

? According to the author, people in a positive mood tend to use a satisficing strategy to solve problems while people in a negative mood tend to use an optimization strategy. She also asserts that creative problem solving is enhanced by an optimization strategy. Explain how this proposed interaction between mood and strategy may explain facilitatory effects of positive mood on creative problem solving in some situations, and inhibitory effects in others.

? The author predicts an interaction between the type of creative problem (i.e., a divergent-thinking problem in which many solutions are to be generated vs. an insight problem) and mood (positive versus negative). Describe this predicted interaction and explain why it was predicted (a good answer will make connections to strategy use in the different moods).

Method: Critical Thinking Questions _____

? Describe the basic difference between a problem-finding task and a problem-solving task. How is performance on these tasks typically scored?

? Describe what you would have been asked to do, had you been a participant in the experiment.

? Name the independent variables in the experiment, and their levels. Describe how each of these variables was operationalized. For each variable, state whether it was manipulated in a between-subjects or within-subjects fashion. How many conditions were there in the experiment?

? What was (were) the dependent variable(s) in the experiment?

? What aspects of the methodology were implemented to deal with possible confounds?

Results/Discussion: Critical Thinking Questions _____

? Describe the relationship between mood and divergent-thinking performance indicated in Figure 1.

? What are some potential problems with the quasi-experimental design of the study (especially with regard to mood) that may limit the conclusions?

? The author cites two separate problems with the assessment of negative moods, one methodological and one conceptual. Describe each of these problems.

? After reading this study, you may feel there are other issues or questions that would be worthwhile or intriguing to address. Pose one of these questions (other than those suggested by the authors) that could be investigated empirically.

Index